2nd edition

Pacific Mexico:
Baja, Sea of Cortez & all mainland Mexico from Puerto Vallarta to the Guatemala border

"The Rains Guide"

Smooth Seas to You!

Jim

Pat Rains

ISBN 9780963847058
© Point Loma Publishing 2006
P.O. Box 60190
San Diego, California, USA

This book and its text, charts, illustrations and photos are to be used for planning and reference purposes only. They are specifically not to be used for navigation. Some of this book's charts are taken from the latest DMA, NIMA, SM and NOAA charts, and some of the previously charted shorelines have been corrected to agree with high-resolution satellite imagery. For the sake of clarity, the authors have deleted some soundings and added new shoreline data such as breakwaters, marinas, fuel docks, shoals and rocks. Other charts in this book were created from the authors' own sketch charts compiled from their onsite GPS triangulations and depth soundings, topographic maps and aerial photos.

The text has been carefully prepared, based upon personal inspections, official publications and other data deemed reliable, with the objective of making the boating visitor's voyage more enjoyable. Every reasonable effort has been made to achieve up-to-date accuracy, but the infinite complexities of personal observation and a constantly changing world render total accuracy impossible.

Thus all sailing, navigation, anchoring and docking information in this book must be checked against the skipper's own eyes, ears, navigation equipment and latest charts and publications. Every skipper is alone responsible for the safety of his or her crew and vessel, and he or she must plot the safe course.

The authors and the publisher must therefore both specifically disclaim any and all personal liability for loss or risk, to persons or property or both, which might occur either directly or indirectly from any person's use or interpretation of any information contained in this book. No publication can substitute for good sea sense.

Library of Congress Control Number: 2005908620

© **Point Loma Publishing 2006**
San Diego, California, USA
www.MexicoBoating.com
Printed in Mexico

Why take your boat to Mexico?

Last fall, more than 27,500 *yates* (recreational boats) entered Mexican waters. They explored the pristine solitude of remote anchorages. They roamed between tropical gunk-hole and fancy resort ports – much easier thanks to Mexico's new streamlined port clearance rules. They enjoyed sportfishing, snorkel and scuba diving, birding, shelling, learning Spanish and exploring ashore.

The kinds of boats vary from 45' long-range cruising yachts, 65' sportfishers and 150' motoryachts to 24' pocket sailors. Yacht cruising Mexico is a popular dream, but it comes true for thousands of adventurous boaters each year – whether they stay a few months and come home – or leave the boat in a marina for a few years while they fly back and forth. Many yatistas cruise Pacific Mexico en route to Costa Rica and the Panama Canal.

How to use this book?

From a dream-book at home to the chart table in Mexico.

If you're still at the dreaming stage, *Mexico Boating Guide* ignites your imagination – but also fills in the blanks on your itinerary with a justified sense of realism. If you're preparing for a cruise through Mexican waters, the Preparation and Paperwork chapters – and their check-lists – are written for you.

Already underway? Keep this practical guidebook on your chart table to use daily, hourly – that's what boaters tell us about previous editions.

Route planning, coastwise directions are given between ports. Each destination chapter tells what's there of interest to boaters, what are the safe approaches and known hazards, where can you anchor safely or find a marina slip. In each location, it details where to find fuel, provisions, boat yards, repairs, port officials, emergency & medical resources, etc. We include interesting shore explorations near marinas and a bit of local history and culture.

Mexico Boating Guide includes and clearly labels a few marginal anchorages, because if conditions are ideal for you, they might provide just the temporary stop you need. In some very popular stops on the gringo trail, we've moved rather quickly, because no mysteries exist there. We've skipped some spots reported by other veteran boaters as useful under a narrow range of conditions but that we thought were unfit or unsafe for various reasons. We've included a few spots reported by other veteran boaters as useful but that we haven't tested overnight, or at least not in all condition.

Point Loma Publishing welcomes reader feedback on any anchorage or port, whether we've included or skipped it.

Who are the authors?

The authors, Capt. Patricia Miller Rains & Capt. John E. Rains, are both veteran Mexico cruisers on their own various *yates*, and have been delivering yachts – both sail and power – throughout Mexican waters on a professional basis for more than 25 years. John retired in 2005, Pat continues to run Point Loma Publishing, and they now cruise with friends just for fun.

The Rainses' nautical guidebooks grew out of requests from yacht insurance companies to list all the safe stops in Mexico and Central America, and to detail the safe approaches, shore services, etc. The Rainses valuable experience and painstaking research yielded hundreds of useful anchorages, interesting ports and strategic passages. Nautical research is an on-going activity in their normal lives. Along the way, they share news with fellow mariners who are also out there doing it.

They didn't just take a voyage and then write a book about it.

The Rainses have written hundreds of news and feature articles for national publications such as *SEA, Cruising World, The Log Newspapers* and others. Their previous books are: *Mexico Boating Guide*, 1st edition, and *Boating Guide to Mexico: West Coast Edition*; and *Cruising Ports: Florida to California via Panama*, in 6th edition; and *MexWX: Mexico Weather for Boaters*

Mexico Boating Guide

2nd edition

Pacific Mexico:
Baja, Sea of Cortez & all mainland Mexico from Puerto Vallarta to the Guatemala border

"The Rains Guide"

Mexico Boating Guide
2nd edition

Gracias!

The authors and publisher express thanks to Avocet Communication in Point Loma for getting this book ready for the printers in Queretaro. We thank Sra. Tere Grossman of the Mexican Marina Owners Association for helping get the streamlined port-clearance rules passed; she champions nautical tourism. Thanks to Neil Shroyer of Marina de La Paz for his aerial photos. Thanks to our patient advertisers and to 10,000 adventurous yatistas for making this book possible. And thanks to 50 busy Port Captains and Naval officers and to 1,000 nameless panga fishermen for sharing with us their intimate local knowledge and love of the sea.

Thanks for helping us help others!

A portion of the retail price you paid for Mexico Boating Guide, 2nd edition, has been donated by Point Loma Publishing to two worthy non-profit organizations in Pacific Mexico. Please visit these projects in Sonora and Baja California.

1.) **Women's Empowerment International** (WE) in San Diego, in partnership with **Grameen de la Frontera** (GDLF), makes micro-credit self-employment loans to 2,000 of the poorest women (dirt floors,

public wells, zero collateral) in Huatabampo village near Puerto Yavaros, Sonora. By raising bees and goats, they now sell honey and cheese. By growing fruit trees, they make jams to sell in the *mercados*. With a few tools and spare parts, they repair bicycles for families who have no cars. With a used sewing machine, they make and sell clothing. WE and GDLF help these entrepreneurs create solid business plans, work in small groups from home and repay their loans on schedule. Repayment rates have been 98% - better than most traditional banks. Contact www.Womenempowerment.org or in San Diego call (858) 486-6466. Or visit **www. grameendelafrontera.org**

2.) **Los Niños del Capitán** (The Captain's Kids) in Cabo San Lucas is a pre-school, day-care center and health clinic for 120 children of poor working mothers, women who have no traditional family network to care for youngsters. Thanks to loving *abuela* (grandma) Herminia Losada and dozens of volunteers, Monday through Saturday these kids get three meals daily, medical & dental care, help with homework, and are not left to run wild in the streets of this non-traditional port city. This supervision program has kept a lot of kids away from gangs and drugs. Call to visit the school and clinic in the residential north side of Cabo San Lucas; 011-52 (624) 173-3807. The address is Manzana 89, Lote 5, Colonia Mesa Colorado, Cabo San Lucas, BCS. To donate online through International Community Foundation in San Diego, visit www.ICF.org and type in Los Ninos del Capitan, or call in the US (858) 677-2913.

Donations to both these groups are tax deductible. Thank you.

We're generally outfitting a boat for at least one year in Mexico, then we'll look at Provisioning it with food and consumables. Most yatistas perform both tasks simultaneously over a period of weeks or months. (Personal preparations are next.)

Outfitting the Boat

Basic Boat: We think any boat (power or sail) voyaging through Mexico should (a.) be a proven sea-worthy design from the keel up, (b.) be in A-1 mechanical condition, (c.) have reliable propulsion, and (d.) be large enough for its crew to make 300-mile offshore passages (high-seas conditions) with complete safety and reasonable comfort.

Outfitting: Bring repair manuals and sufficient filters and spare parts for any systems unique to yachts, such as a watermaker, heads, bow thruster or stabilizers. Parts and repairs for mechanical systems normally found on commercial vessels (common diesel mains and generators, pumps, hoses, refrigeration) will be readily available in larger ports, such as La Paz, Guaymas, Puerto Vallarta, Manzanillo, Acapulco and Salina Cruz. Mexico refines oil, so lube oil is readily available in these ports in 5-gallon buckets. Thanks to the ubiquitous "panga," outboard parts are readily available in almost every coastal town.

Bridge: For Mexican waters, you should have: a recently adjusted compass and error card, a reliable depth sounder (min. 100-fathom), a good radar (min. 15-mile) and an installed GPS, and all spare parts to keep them running; installed VHF and at least 1 hand-held VHF, ham-capable SSB radio, (WX-fax optional); updated nav charts for overall planning, coastal cruising and harbor charts; rolling plotter or parallel rules, dividers with lead in 1 end for radar plotting; lots of #2 pencils and sharpener; hand bearing compass with light; Navigation Log Book, at least 1 pair of 7 x 50 binoculars (stabilized or night vision optional); barometer; anemometer, 2 flag halyards; Q-flag, Mexican flag, US flag; original valid vessel document

Email Underway

HF email is the most cost-effective long-distance communication method for boating in Mexico. It requires only an onboard lap-top computer linked to an SCS modem, linked to your SSB radio. You reach special shore stations (world wide) at vast distances; they link you to internet email, so you send and receive emails on board. The modem also serves as a WX-fax demodulator, so you can receive the broadcasted WX-fax charts and satellite photos without having a separate system.

If you're a ham-radio operator with a general class license or higher, you may use this system cost free for non-business communication. For more information go to www.winlink.org and look at the useful links page. Non-hams use commercial organizations that charge a monthly fee plus per character. Sailmail is very popular.

or registration, 12 clear copies of vessel document or registration; 12 clear copies of each passport and validated Tourist Card and Temporary Import Permit after you get them; Spanish-English dictionary; "Rules of the Road;" "Sailing Directions;" Reed's "Nautical Almanac;" "Light List;" "MexWX: Mexico Weather for Boaters;" " Mariners' Guide to Single Sideband."

Deck: storm anchor, standard overnight anchors and stern hook; all chain setup, plus chain to rode setup with chafe gear; a good inflatable dinghy with hard bottom, athwartship seat, hard transom and reliable non-wimpy outboard motor, oars and spare gas can; marine grade padlock and cable for

Excellent awnings for cruising the tropics.

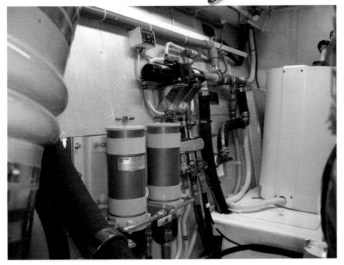

Dual Racor filter system.

outboard & gas can; dinghy anchor & rode; (dinghy wheels optional); (dinghy davits or crane optional); dinghy patch kit; canvas pontoon covers; spare diesel jugs and water jugs; 3 large heavy duty round fenders (not tubular); (fender board optional); extra long heavy duty dock lines & spring lines, all with chafe gear; flashlights with spare bulbs & batteries; omni-directional high-powered spot light; sturdy 10' to 12' wooden or polypro boat hook; 50' non-toxic water hose; 25' diesel hose; sun awning for cockpit & deck); marine grade padlock and cable for permanent deck gear; foldable dolly or dock cart; swim ladder;

boarding plank; snorkel gear (mask, snorkel, fins) for bottom cleaning; exterior cleaning supplies; (optional bikes or roller scooters for land transport).

Engine Room: repair manual, rebuild kit and spare parts for each engine on board; plumbed dual Racor filter system for changing filters without shutting down; filters x 4 for fuel, oil and water; bilge & water pumps & extra impellors & float switches; battery charger system; 1 spare injector, set of belts & gaskets; spare fuel line & flare tool; spare starter and fuel pump; generator shut-down solenoid & brushes; spare prop & puller; come-along; distilled water & hydrometer, refrigeration freon charge kit; shaft packing material; hydraulic fluid; steering diaphragms or seals; long jumper cables; soldering gun & flux solder; autopilot relays & connectors; spares x 4 for running lights bulbs; paper for WX-fax; PL-259 connectors, RG-58U cabling & SWR bridge; fuses x 4 for all electronics; oil-absorbent pads; trouble light & long cord; Simple Green® bilge cleaner; a complete set of hand tools tailored for your machinery.

Safety Equipment: all the required items to pass US Coast Guard inspection, including bell and pollution placards; certified 6-man SOLAS offshore life raft with extra water & food packed inside; first-aid medical bag that can go into the ditch kit; buoyant ditch kit (abandon ship) duffle bag to hold hand-held VHF & GPS & 406 Mhz EPIRB, plus spare batteries for each; PFDs with strobes for twice as many crew, children & pets; extra flares for flare gun; at least 3 ABC fire extinguishers and/or installed system; collision kit: bungs, underwater epoxy, fiberglass matt and resin hot batch supplies; MOB system; swim steps; VHF loud hailer; safety mesh for forward lifelines; dive gear (scuba tank, regulator and BC vest) for emergency underwater repairs; kelp cutters on the prop shafts, especially for Baja; employable jack lines and clip-in safety harnesses for at least 2 crew; spare standing rigging (1 x longest run wire) and swedge tool & fittings; spare running rigging (halyard, sheave, blocks, shackles and lines); duct tape (keep in cool spot);

Ship keeping: oil-absorbent pads for

engine areas; watermaker, or large capacity water tanks with access ports for cleaning; reliable refrigeration system; reliable stove & oven; (propane tanks optional); (deck barbecue optional); (optional trash compacter); hatch wind scoop; 2 – 4 small interior fans or air conditioning; fine mesh port and hatch screens; non-spring mattresses; fine-gauge 100% cotton sheets or sheet pockets; spray anti-mildew solution (white vinegar or Lysol™); thermal insulating window covers; Raid™ roach spray for grocery cartons; unbreakable covered serving bowls for beach pot-lucks; tension-bar keepers for inside upright refrigerator; lanyard flashlights for each crew and guest; interior cleaning supplies.

Haul-outs:
Mexican bottom paints are very effective (types no longer sold in the US), skilled labor is generally cheaper, but anything imported is taxed. Emergency haul-outs get top priority in commercial ports like Topolobampo, Manzanillo, Lazaro Cardenas and Salina Cruz.

Haul-out yards for yachts: Ensenada, Cabo San Lucas, La Paz, Puerto Peñasco, San Carlos, Guaymas, Mazatlán, Puerto Vallarta, Acapulco.

Provisioning

NOTE: Mad Cow Disease and Asian Bird Flu precautions have banned raw US meats (beef, pork, chicken, turkey, eggs) from entering Mexico aboard boats and RVs.Cooked meats have always been fine. Many southbound yatistas are provisioning their meats in Cabo or La Paz.

Some restrictions were lifted as we go to press, but the situation is fluid. Keep your grocery receipts showing the meats' state of purchase; this may prevent Mexico's Agriculture officials from confiscating and incinerating all the meats in your freezer at your first Port of Entry.

Don't sink your waterline. Mexico is not the end of the world. But do stock up on your favorite items that may be hard to find in coastal Mexico – such as specialized paper products: holding-tank friendly TP, small-sheet paper towels, good paper napkins, heavy paper plates & the newer feminine-hygiene products.

    zip-locking plastic bags
    microwave storage containers
    air-tight storage containers

    hypo-allergenic laundry detergent
    hypo-allergenic bath soap
    cleaner: teak, stainless, fiberglass
    albacore packed in water
    canned chicken and turkey
    brown rice, wild rice
    soy flour or fine gravy flour
    kalamata olive tapenade
    ketchup with low sugar content
    peanut butter with low sugar & salt
    canned whole tomatoes
    sun-dried tomato puree
    herbal & rice vinegar
    cranberry or fancy mustards
    cranberries & whole turkey
    dry yogurt culture
    sour dough bread mix
    bread machine mixes
    sugar-free drink mixes
    seedless jams

Re-provision in Mexico

All big ports have super mercados that are air-conditioned, well lighted and stock a wide array of canned foods and dry staples (many familiar brand names). All mid-sized ports have fruterias (produce markets) and abarrotes (grocery stores). At cruiser hangouts like La Paz and Barra Navidad, farmers bring truckloads of fruits, veggies, cheese, eggs and bakery goods right to the anchorages and marinas on a regular schedule – they even take orders!

Plan a major restock at Cabo San Lucas, La Paz, Mazatlán, Puerto Vallarta, Manzanillo and Acapulco. Some reliable chain supermercados are: Aramburo's, CostCo, Comercial Mexicana (CoMex), CityClub, Sam's Club, WalMart, CCC, Blanca y Negra, El Rey, El Dorado. In rural areas, the only store may be a Conasupo, a government subsidized cooperative that specializes in basics (rice, beans, maize, flour, lard,

Mexico's supermercados (left) are air conditioned, well stocked and a fun cultural experience. Municipal Markets (below) are great for fruits, veggies, eggs, honey, homemade jams and cheeses, and fresh tortillas.

candles).

Many supermercados have a "carniceria" or meat shop where they routinely cut and package to your order – hard to find in the US and Canada. Marigolds are fed to chickens, making their flesh juicy and producing golden-yoked eggs. Larger grocery stores contain separate delicatessens for sandwich meats, cheeses and salads.

In Baja, the "panaderia" sells the local recipe for bread ("bolillos", pronounced "boh-LEE-ohz." On the mainland it's "barras". Also pan dulces (sweet buns, cookies, tarts). Mexican breads are baked fresh daily, without preservatives, so they mold quickly. Spritz outer crust with a solution of apple cider vinegar and water (6:1) to discourage mold. The "cervezaria" sells cases of beer, and the "deposito" recycles glass bottles.

Kid baggers who cart your purchases out to the taxi or way down to the dock should be tipped 10 to 25 pesos. If you box your goodies, take along a can of roach spray to thoroughly dose the cardboard if possible before putting your groceries inside, or at

least before bringing the cartons into your dingy or on deck. Never leave cardboard boxes on deck for an hour – roaches will find a way down.

Street food: Eventually, you'll get food poisoning if you routinely eat uninspected food prepared by people who have no way to wash their hands or utensils. It happens in some restaurants, so street food is highly suspect – unless you personally know that vendor is sanitary.

Mercado Municipal: Each town has a traditional farmers' market, individual stalls under one roof, often less clean and less well lighted than grocery stores. Municipal markets generally have slightly lower prices on fresh produce and eggs, but we don't buy their unrefrigerated meats or cheeses. Think of the municipal market as cultural entertainment, then as a good place for vegetables, fruits and flowers. Wheat flour tortillas are a recent "norteño" thing, while corn tortillas are still more common as you move S; tortillas are always fresher at the local "tortillaria."

Fresh farm eggs (unwashed, unchilled) keep 10 to 14 days without refrigeration, as long as you don't wash or chill them. But brush off possible chicken do and feather dander before bringing into the galley, then keep them separate from other open foods. In rural towns, we re-use our own Styrofoam or papier maché egg crates, because eggs there may still be sold by the kilo in a plastic bag or in a wobbly flat of 20.

Fresh egg test: Set each egg in a 4" to 6" deep basin of water; if it floats, 86 it. Obviously, you can't "float test" in the ocean or you'd lose the good eggs.

Wash all fruits and veggies if you're going to eat the skin. Use detergent or bleach water, or buy special produce sterilizer solution from health food stores. Learn 12 cabbage salad recipes. If you must buy lettuce, buy only the wrapped ice burg heads marked "certified hygienic" – meaning no manure was used to grow it – thus avoiding one of the most common sources of amoebic dysentery.

Water: Bottled drinking water (purified) is sold

in gallons and cases in all major grocery stores – especially important in Cabo San Lucas and Acapulco after heavy rains when municipal water sources may become contaminated.

Save watermaker filters and membranes by making water only in deep open ocean, not near a tide line and never during a red tide. We highly recommend the UV treatment.

Water Treatment

Treat any questionable dock water with chlorine bleach, because the chlorine found in household bleach is a relatively safe form. **Use one quarter cup of chorine bleach per 100 gallons of water.** If water is seriously tainted, you could double this dosage. (Note: too much chlorine will corrode water heater elements, impellers and pipe joints.) Don't add chlorine bleach all at once; dribble it in incrementally while you're taking on water, then leave your deck fills wide open for a few hours to vacate dangerous chlorine fumes. Add a bottle of white wine to the tank to remove lingering chlorine smell – or at least to improve the flavor after treatment.

Returning? Before you return to the US from Mexico, check www.aphis.usda.gov for the latest list of banned items.

Preparing the people

Preparing yourself, your crew members and those back home is almost as important as prepping the boat.

Personal fitness: To be as safe and happy during your Mexican boating adventure, you and your crew should: (a.) be in good health, (b.) know most of "Rules of the Road," (c.) be proficient at coastal navigation (plus radar fixes, GPS waypoints, set & drift), (d.) be comfortable with basic maintenance & repair of your engines & gear, (e.) and be able to gather and understand critical WX data for your present and upcoming areas (using your SSB, WX-fax, ham radio, etc.). You certainly must (f.) be willing to appreciate the differences in other cultures, and you should probably also (g.) love to swim or fish or explore ashore.

We highly recommend yatistas take up a hobby that's absorbing and boat friendly – but not boat work! A hobby will smooth the normal psychological transition into "cruising speed." When fully adjusted, you're said to have a temporary case of "cruise-

heimers." Don't worry; just like a tan, it fades after you return from Mexico.

Spanish: You should speak enough Spanish to keep out of trouble: Can you ask for (and understand) directions and weather reports over VHF? Stand boarding and inspection at sea? Clear official papers in port? Order diesel and lube oil from a Pemex station (pesos por litro)? Reprovision weekly (pesos por kilo)? Explain medical problems to a doctor or nurse? The farther S or more remote you go, the less English is spoken. Without conversational Spanish, you're missing the better half of visiting Mexico. Veteran cruisers who enjoyed Mexico say their meager Spanish opened the doors.

Skill Classes: Take USCG Auxiliary or US Power Squadron classes in coastal navigation and diesel mechanics. Yacht clubs and Gordon West Radio School offer ham radio classes for FCC licenses. Community colleges offer classes in SSB communications, marine meteorology, Spanish, scuba diving, underwater photography, oceanography, macramé, water colors, pen & ink and boat friendly hobbies.

Sea trials: Practice anchoring in unfamiliar coves. Practice Med-mooring to a high concrete pier, hand steering downwind, and navigating by radar & depth sounder alone as in fog or blinding rain. Practice launching your dinghy and landing on a sandy beach. If you plan to tow your dinghy (not recommended), practice it. Practice cooking and eating underway..

Design and practice your own safety drills: (1.) MOB (man overboard) including retrieving the unconscious captain, (2.) fighting a fire in the engine area, (3.) broadcasting a May Day in Spanish & English, and (4.) abandoning ship into the life raft.

Keep the home fires burning

Even free spirits need to keep the gears of their world spinning smoothly. In fact, the more smoothly your financial and familial affairs continue to operate back home, the more free you'll be in Mexico.

Email is the easiest and most popular way to keep in touch. Set up an email account either at Winlink.org for hams, at Sailmail.org for SSB users, or at Yahoo.com to access from internet cafes that are common throughout Mexico. Ham radio phone patches are a great way to keep in touch on personal matters, but you need an SSB link to talk business.

Yatistas usually plan to fly home at least once a year for business and family needs.

Power of Attorney: To free yourself from daily worry about details back home, you might designate a very capable, responsible and trusted person to act in your behalf with your limited "power of attorney." This is not a simple favor any relative could perform, so choose wisely and pay for this multi-faceted service. You might ask him/her specifically to: (a.) receive, open and respond to your mail, business and personal; (b.) field your phone calls, business and personal; (c.) forward important messages and items to you at designated ports along your route; (d.) access your bank accounts solely to deposit your income and pay your bills; or (e.) even to make minor business or personal decisions for you.

Anticipate situations and make a list of all the tasks this person may need to perform, then ask your favorite attorney to help you draw up a simple Power of Attorney. Give your designee all the phone and account numbers and bank materials he/she might need. Make a list of friends you wish to stay in contact with, who may be coming to visit you in Mexico. We think forwarding a package of mail to you in care of a marina address (even if you're not there yet) is much more secure than addressing it to you "lista de correo" at town post offices.

Social liaison may be another duty. Give Joe your original itinerary, and once you're traveling, phone Joe at regular intervals so that at least one person will always know (a.) your present whereabouts, (b.) your probable next port, and (c.) sometimes two alternate routes in case you change plans due to weather, breakdown or serendipity.

Having a social liaison makes it much easier and less confusing when friends or family try to link up with you – off in the wild blue yonder, in places they can't pronounce or find in the Atlas Britannica, places their travel agents don't believe exist. And if you should ever "go missing," this link will prevent a needless Search & Rescue Operation along Route A when you're simply following Route B. And if you really do need help, it will narrow the search area. Ham radio nets are very helpful in this area.

Mail forwarding: If you don't have a designated Power of Attorney, you may want to forward all your home and office mail (or that screened by your Power of Attorney) to one of these reliable stateside services. They'll hold and package it up for you. After a phone call or a designated date, they send it all to you at your next designated port. Have your mail forwarder use DHL, Estafeta or FedEx international express delivery service to get your mail to you, not the general Mexican mail service, which has no Aduana clearance service and may take "forever" – literally. Al reverso, you can express a package of mail to your forwarding service, through Customs, and your service will stamp and mail it all for you.

Plan Ahead

Banking & money: Visa or Visa/MC credit cards are most widely accepted in Mexico and Central America. But do notify your credit card company and bank in writing that you're going to be traveling in Mexico and estimate how many months. Many cards require a new pin # for foreign use. Banks in larger ports have ATMs from which you can withdraw cash using your credit card. In others, you stand in line to get cash from your credit account.

Before you depart, set up secure online banking and automatic payment of your monthly bills. From Mexico, you can manage and transfer money between accounts through the internet.

All marinas take plastic, as do many

Free spirits out here doing it started with a solid plan.

Almost half the cruising boats we meet in Mexico have kids aboard. Many resorts have programs that yatista kids can join.

fuel docks and larger restaurants in resort areas. For all the rest, there's cash. Take about half your cash kitty in bills. Of that amount, take as many $20s bills as possible (perfect condition, no tears or missing corners), because only banks and large grocery stores make change for $100 bills. Find a safe hiding place onboard, and keep bills in zip plastic bags. Take the other half in travelers' checks; plan to cash them at banks using your passport and tourist card for ID.

As we go to press, the exchange rate posted in all banks is 11.3 Mexican pesos to each US dollar – if you're buying pesos. Do your dollar banking early in the day, because banks won't accept US dollars after 1200 noon Mexico City time; tomorrow's exchange rate may be different. Spend all your pesos before returning, because you lose on the reverse exchange.

Most yatistas find that average daily expenses are 10% to 15% less in Mexico than in the US, if they eat and socialize onboard 90% of the time. Most marinas have US rates. Naturally, resort hotel meals and drinks are way more costly than fresh seafood tacos in remote beach palapas. So how much money you'll need depends on your lifestyle.

Clothing: Pacific Baja California Norte can be cold and damp, but south of Cabo, La Paz or Mazatlán you won't need sweat clothes in winter. Instead of heavy-duty foul-weather wear, take a simple windbreaker and breathable rain jacket.

Casual 100% cottons work best, plus a few wrinkle-resistant blends. Shorts and T-shirts make up 90% of clothing for both men and women, plus lots of swim suits as the seats wear out fast. Pack two "town outfits" for visiting the Port Captain and fancy dinners ashore. John likes drawstring pants and light cotton guayabera shirts – which are making a trendy comeback. Pat favors broom-stick skirts (stowable) with an open blouse over a halter top.

Good restaurants may refuse men without shirts - except in the many sand-floored palapa cantinas near yacht anchorages. Nudity is not tolerated even in resort areas. Test drive flip-flops or sandals with wide straps; sand makes some straps chafe your tootsies. But do wear shoes ashore to avoid cuts, infections and parasites.

Land transport: Folding bicycles with wide tires are best for Mexico's dirt, gravel and sand roads. Big boats carry small scooters for long-term cruising. Skateboards don't work on broken concrete streets.

Taxi cabs are inexpensive (except in resorts) and used by everyone. We use them for port clearance, provisioning and sight-seeing. A good taxista can recommend mechanics, shops, wait for you (meter running), load and unload your bags, and deserves a tip. In rural areas, agree on the taxi price before you get in, but in big cities the rates are posted on the windows.

Medical: No shots are currently required for Mexico. But a tetanus shot and flu shot for Mexico are usually a good idea.

To prevent sea-sickness, we pack OTC Dramimine®; Pat's preventive method is a quarter of a Dramamine tablet with a cup of strong coffee. The prescription patch Sturgeron® is sold in Mexico. To prevent bites from mosquitoes, bees and no-see-ems, we like Crocodile® herbal insect repellant.

Ask your doctor for a legibly written prescription for each drug you take, make copies and take them along. Navy boarding officers can demand to see the paper prescription for each medicine bottle. Even rural farmacias are well stocked with the generic form of common prescriptions.

Worldwide, the turistas is a common temporary complaint from drinking municipal water your body isn't familiar with, so if you're normally susceptible, treat all water going into your boat's tanks, avoid ice cubes, then pack your favorite OTC remedies. In case of food poisoning, remember that it's better out than in.

Guests & Pets

Guests: Their names must appear on your Crew List if you leave port with them. This requires a full domestic port clearance, not the streamlined version. Show long-term guests how to stop the boat and use the radios to call for help. Unfamiliar food and water may distess new arrivals. Urge guests to use their own Spanish ashore. The best guests are open to experiencing what's different, not just like at home.

Pets: From your home veterinarian, get an International Health Certificate (USDA form 77-043 or a state form) that shows all required shots as current for 12 months and your pet's good state of health. You'll need it to get Fido back into the US; without it, he will be quarantined for weeks at the border. If Fido's health certificate expires in Mexico, take him and the old certificate to a Mexican vet for an exam and new International Health Certificate. We adopted a Mexican mutt and brought her home with a health certificate. (Parrots require a lengthy quarantine before reentering the US.)

We highly recommend monthly Frontline® or Advantage® flea protection for dogs and cats, because even beaches have fleas, also the monthly tablet against Heartworm. Broken glass is fairly common on streets and beaches. Screw worm infects dogs through tiny cuts and scrapes, so inspect Fido often, especially his foot pads. We seldom see a yatista dog that doesn't have its own PFD and life harness. In marinas, rig a cling-to loop or ladder. Every country requires some official port paperwork from the skippers of visiting vessels. Mexico recently streamlined all port-clearance procedures for recreational boaters.

Eco-Boating in Mexico

Point Loma Publishing encourages yatistas to explore Mexico's environmental and archeological treasures. Use your dinghy, binoculars and durable digital camera. Pack your hiking shoes and bird book. (Mexico has 50 species of hummingbirds!) Or book private tours with local guides. You'll see that all levels of comfort are available. We recommend Planeta.com for details and links to local naturalist and archeo-guides and savvy travel tips. Here are a few to start you off.

Baja California

El Vizcaíno Desert Biosphere Reserve contains the world-famous Laguna San Ignacio whale spawning region. Anchor at Abreojos; park guides take you in their pangas into the lagoon. Gray whales arrive around New Years, depart in March.

Based at Cabo San Lucas, the ASUPMATOMA group protects sea-turtle nests (Leatherback, Pacific Black, Olive Ridley, Hawksbill, Loggerhead) and releases hatchlings throughout the Sea of Cortez and Pacific Baja – children and parents can participate.

Cabo Pulmo National Underwater Park on East Cape is the only living coral reef system on the western shore of North America. Pulmo Reef is wonderful snorkel and scuba diving, but anchor outside the park or arrive by road from Cabo or La Paz.

Hike to see prehistoric Pericue *campestre* (cave paintings) in the Sierra Giganta near Puerto Escondido and Mulege. Cultural trails include the Misiones de Baja California chain of 17th Century Jesuit missions, the 1st is at Loreto.

Sea of Cortez

Islas del Golfo de California Protected Area encompasses 900 islands and islets from Cerralvo to the Enchanted Isles. The Islands of the Gulf park is a UNESCO World Heritage Site sustaining living examples of more than 39% of the world's species of marine mammals.

In the Midriff Islands, tiny Isla Raza protects the world's largest flock of the beautiful Hermann's gulls.

Sonora

El Pinacate & Gran Desierto Altar Biosphere Reserve encompass the whole N end of the Sea of Cortez and around Puerto Peñasco, Sonora.

The indigenous Seri people around Kino Bay and Isla Tiburon have revived their annual Sea Turtle Ceremony and allowed the first visitors in spring 2005; ask in Kino Bay.

The new Guaíma underwater & desert park is 20 miles north of San Carlos. Yatistas can anchor off the park shoreline or enter by land.

Sinaloa

Copper Canyon (Barrancas del Cobre) nature preserve stretches from Los Mochis through six canyon systems in the Sierra Tarahumara range to the state capital of Chihuahua; train tour, hiking, camping. Travel from San Carlos-Guaymas, Topolobampo or Mazatlán.

Nayarit

Isla Isabela National Park on this tiny island is the world's largest frigate sanctuary and a popular yatista anchorage. Help college students observe head-high nests, fuzzy nestlings and graceful adult frigates – also called *tijereta* (scissor-tails) and Man of War birds.

Michoacan

Billions of delicate monarch butterflies migrate from Canada to five mountain peaks in central Michoacan. Yatistas can travel from Puerto Vallarta or Manzanillo to the El Rosario Monarch Sanctuary near Ocampo and Angangueo, where vast colonies of *monarcas* cloak the oyamel pine trees from December through March, but the peak is early February.

Oaxaca

From Ixtapa-Zihuatanejo, it's a quick trip to Monte Alban, the 2,500-year old Zapotec ruins – some of Mexico's most exquisite archeological digs, still being uncovered.

Chiapas

Dozens of ancient Mayan and Aztec ruins around Palenque, Bonampak and Piedras Negras are easily visited from marinas in Acapulco and Huatulco. El Triunfo Biosphere Reserve and Volcan Tacaná are both near Puerto Madero on the southern border with Guatemala.

Paperwork for Mexico

International Entrance: At your first Port of Entry, you'll make your International Entrance (Entrada Internaciónal) and clear into Mexico. Ensenada and Cabo San Lucas have new CIS (Centro Integral de Servicios) offices where a representative from all the required port authorities (Migración, Capitanía, Aduana, API, SEMARNAT) are waiting to square you away, plus a bank kiosk where you pay several small fees at once by credit card. Instructions are posted; they speak English.

When done, keep all stamped documents and receipts until you leave Mexico.

TIP: We urge yatistas to take advantage of this improvement, especially at Ensenada. If you want to wait to enter at Cabo San Lucas, you cannot stop at Puerto San Carlos in Mag Bay. And if you are boarded or have trouble down the Baja coast, you are technically in violation of the law.

To enter Mexico at any Port of Entry other than Ensenada or Cabo San Lucas, you must visit Migracion, Capitania, Aduana and API (if it's an API port) separately, often spread across town. Between each office, you dash to a bank to stand in line to pay a small fee, dash back to get a stamp, then on to the next port official elsewhere. That method of International Arrival can take all day – two days if you don't start early.

Domestic Port Clearance: After you're cleared into Mexico, each controlled port (meaning it has a Port Captain) that you enter requires you to notify the Port Captain of your arrival and departure. To comply, you notify either (a.) the marina in that port (call on VHF, sign their log book or fill out their form) or, if there's no marina, (b.) the Port Captain by VHF or in person. This is the streamlined version.

However, if someone on your Crew List wants to leave your crew, you must make up a new Crew List and do a complete domestic port clearance with that person's passport before he or she departs. It's considered a potential crime to arrive in port with someone on your Crew List missing. If you wish to add someone to your Crew List, same procedure: visit the Port Captain, Migracion, Aduana and API to get your new Crew List signed and stamped.

Mexican Navy patrols can inspect your despachos in port and at sea. It's quite awkward if the people on board don't match your Crew List.

International Exit: At your last Port of Entry before you depart Mexico, take your Crew List and Entrada Internaciónal papers to the Port Captain, and you'll get a Zarpe or International Exit paper to cover you while crossing borders. You'll be asked for it by US Customs, US Coast Guard or your next country's Navy or Port of Entry officials.

Documents Checklist

Stow all ship's documents in a water-tight safe or

secure place onboard. Make 12 copies of everything, but don't laminate anything. Carry documents ashore in a zip plastic bag.

Have on board before entering Mexico:

1.) Vessel Document or Registration
2.) Passports
3.) Proof of Insurance & Endorsements
4.) Crew List (See below)
5.) Fishing Papers (if fish hook onboard)

Receive during International Entrance:

6.) Mexico Tourist Cards
7.) Temporary Import Permit or TIP

Optional documents:

8.) Serial Numbers List (highly recommended)
9.) Captain's Letter (optional)
10.) Minor Child Permission Letter (optional)

1.) USCG Vessel Document or state Registration: Have one or the other for (a.) your yacht, and (b.) your dinghy, and (c.) any other motorized craft such as jet boat or land scooter. If your document or registration says "commercial," the streamlined rules don't apply to you; hire a ship's agent in each port to clear your papers.

2.) Passports: Everyone aboard needs one. Keep at least 2 color photocopies of at least the 2 data pages stowed in a separate location onboard. If your passport expires before you return or if the back pages are nearly filled, turn it in and get a new one before entering Mexico. Getting a new passport takes 90 days, valid for 10 years.

3.) Proof of insurance liability and the endorsement for Mexico coverage area and period is required (a.) by Mexican marina and (b.) by Port Captains if you leave your boat in Mexico and fly out.

4.) Crew List or Lista de Tripulantes: See form below.

5.) Fishing Papers: If your boat, dinghy or life raft contain a fish hook, you're required to purchase from SEMARNAT (a.) fishing Permits for the boat and dinghy, plus (b.) individual fishing Licenses for each person aboard. No hook? No fishing papers.

If you're clearing into Mexico (International Entrance) at Ensenada or Cabo San Lucas, you can wait to get them there, but you won't be in compliance in the meantime. Not all Ports of Entry have a SEMARNAT (formerly Pesca) office. To be safe, get them at SEMARNAT in the US before departure. The 1-page "Application" for Boat Permits and Individual Licenses is free at 100 chandlers and tackle shops in Southern California and Arizona. To obtain the Application or a list of places where it's available, write, call or go in person to:

SEMARNAT
2550 Fifth Avenue, Suite 101
San Diego, CA 92103-6622
Phone (619) 233-4324
Fax (619) 233-0344

Fishing fees change each January 1 and June 1. Call to find out your exact fees, and get a cashier's check in the exact amount made out to SEMARNAT. (Two banks are across the street.) Submit the completed Application, a copy of your valid document or registration and the cashier's check for payment, and get your papers in a few minutes. Or, if you want them to mail your documents, include a business-size SASE.

6.) Tourist Cards or Transmigrantes are issued by Migración (Immigration) at your first Port of Entry, requires your passport number. Yatistas should ask for the full 180-day validation. Make a copy of your validated Tourist Card and carry it with you. Keep the original with your passport for port clearance and boardings.

7.) Request your Temporary Import Permit from the Aduana's office (Customs) in your Port of Entry. The TIP is valid for 10 years, permits you to leave your boat legally in Mexico while you fly out, also to import parts for your boat duty free.

8.) In some situations, Aduanas request the **serial numbers** of all your engines, outboard, dinghy, generators, installed and hand-held radios, GPS and other electronics. Before departure, engrave you boat name or your own ID number on any item not already numbered. This discourages theft and helps recover stolen property. Make a list and give

your insurance company a copy.

9.) Captain's Letter: When a captain clears a boat into Mexico without the registered owner onboard, the captain must present a NOTORIZED letter in Spanish from the boat's legal owner stating specifically that the owner gives permission to the named captain to take the named boat into Mexico over specific dates. (See our sample below.) The Port Captain and Aduana want to see and stamp the original letter, and each may keep a copy on file, so make extras. The purpose is to discourage boat thieves from hiding out in Mexican waters.

If the boat's owner is a corporation, the letter must be on corporate letterhead stationery, and a list of the corporate officers must accompany the letter. This could occur even if the captain is also an owner, if the boat is documented to a corporation.

10.) If a **minor child** (under 16) travels without both parents, the present named parent must present to the Port Captain, Migración and Aduana at the Port of Entry a NOTORIZED letter in Spanish from the other named parent stating that he/she gives specific permission for the present parent to take the named minor into Mexico for a specific time period. A death certificate would fulfill this requirement, but divorce certainly does not, because the purpose is to discourage kidnapping for ransom and child-custody disputes. Make copies, as boarding officers and port officials may keep at least one.

Port Clearance Lexicon

Aduana: A department of Treasury equal to US Customs; they issue the TIP (Temporary Import Permit) that permits you to leave your boat in Mexico and to import boat parts duty free.

API: Administración Portuaria Integral or Administration of Integrated Ports; in some municipal ports API charges a daily fee for anchoring and mooring based on boat length. They'll let you know when you arrive in that port.

Capitán de Puerto: The Port Captain is the highest nautical authority in his jurisdiction; his word is law. His office is the Capitanía. In big ports, the Port Captain has a staff of dozens, and yacht paperwork is handled by his designee. In small ports, the Port Captain may also handle Migración and Aduana duties.

Despachos: General word for port paperwork.

Entrada, Salida: Entrance, Exit. After notifying a marina or Port Captain of your exit, you get 48 hours to leave. If you get delayed, simply notify them again.

Marina despachos service: All marinas are authorized to record the streamlined domestic port entrances and exits of recreational boaters and report it to the Port Captain. Some marinas can also help you handle your full domestic port clearance if you make crew changes or import parts. Ask the marina.

Migración: Immigration, they issue Tourist Cards. You are an immigrant visiting Mexico for pleasure for at least 180 days.

Ports of Entry: Ensenada, Cabo San Lucas, La Paz, Guaymas, Topolobampo, Mazatlán, Puerto Vallarta, Manzanillo, Lazaro Cardenas, Acapulco, Huatulco, Salina Cruz, Puerto Chiapas (formerly Puerto Madero). If you're southbound after Mexico, we suggest clearing out at Huatulco.

Ship's Agents: Recreational boaters (yatistas) aren't required to hire a ship's agent in tourist ports. But if you have a problem in Cabo San Lucas or Lázaro Cárdenas, we recommend you hire a good one known to have yacht experience. If you don't know whom to hire, ask the Port Captain about an agencia maritima.

Zarpe: Specifically the International Exit paper you receive when you clear out of Mexico for your next country, even the US.

Crew List

The following Crew List form is copyrighted property of Point Loma Publishing and the Rains family. We allow the purchaser of this book to make one copy in order to clear his/her own boat into Mexico. All other use is unauthorized.

Fill in the blanks in this order: Boat captain's name. Boat Name. Home port. Doc or Reg #. Gross tons. Net tons. Farthest destination in Pacific Mexico. Crew name. Nationality. Position onboard. Age. Passport #. Total # of people onboard. Month. Day. Year. Boat captain's signature.

Make one copy, fill in the blanks and take 12 copies of that to your Port of Entry officials. You'll receive one validated version; keep it safe. Make 20 copies for for boardings or changes at domestic ports.

WARNING: Anyone copying this form to sell or share, and anyone using a boot-legged copy, is guilty of stealing and violating our legal copyrights in the US, Mexico and North America. They shall also incur very ugly sea karma.

Estimado Capitán de Puerto,

Presente_____, Capitan de yate de placer "_____"

numero de _____ de la matricula de _____ del porte de _____

tonelados brutas y de _____ netas de arqueo, siendo la tripulación de este yate

procedente del puerto de _____ como sigue:

Nombre	*Nacionalidad*	*Cargo Abordo*	*Edad*	*# de Pasaporte*

Comprende este Rol los asientos de _____ personas y es de mi satisfación, como Capitán que soy, manifestar que me obligo al exacto de todo cuanto disponen las Leyes y Reglamentos actualmente en vigor.

Fecha_____de

El Capitán _____

Estimado Capitán de Puerto,

Presente _**boat captain's name**_ , Capitan de yate de placer " _**boat name**_ "

numero de _**Reg or doc #**_ de la matricula de _**home port**_ del porte de _**gross tons**_

tonelados brutas y de _**net tons**_ netas de arqueo, siendo la tripulación de este yate

procedente del puerto de _**last port before entering Mexico**_ como sigue:

Nombre	*Nacionalidad*	*Cargo Abordo*	*Edad*	*# de Pasaporte*
name	*nationality*	*position aboard*	*age*	*passport #*
		total #		

Comprende este Rol los asientos de _**people**_ personas y es de mi satisfacción, como Capitán que soy, manifestar que me obligo al exacto de todo cuanto disponen las Leyes y Reglamentos actualmente en vigor.

Fecha _**mm/dd**_ de _**yyyyy**_

El Capitán _**boat captain's signature**_

MARITIME INSTITUTE
INCORPORATED

Captain's License

**6 Pack
100 TON
RADAR
NAVIGATION
GPS & Celestial**

or **for the best boating handling courses available!**

The Assurance You Deserve:

Our Captain's license course instills *lasting* knowledge. You, your Captain, or crew will receive the best training available, anywhere. For those not yet qualified to receive a license, the same course covers basic to advance boat handling in a way which is valuable to all.

For Cruisers: Why Take Our Captain's Course?
- You will have the skills which make you, your family, and crew, safer at sea.
- Supplement your cruising funds by accepting paying charter assignments.
- You will be better equipped to handle or assist should there be an emergency.

For World-Class Yachts

International Yachtmasters Training is *the* standard for measuring excellence. We are proud to offer a series of courses, tailored to the requirements of large power or sailing yachts.

International Yachtmaster Training®

**CALL TOLL FREE:
888-262-8020**
www.MaritimeInstitute.com

20

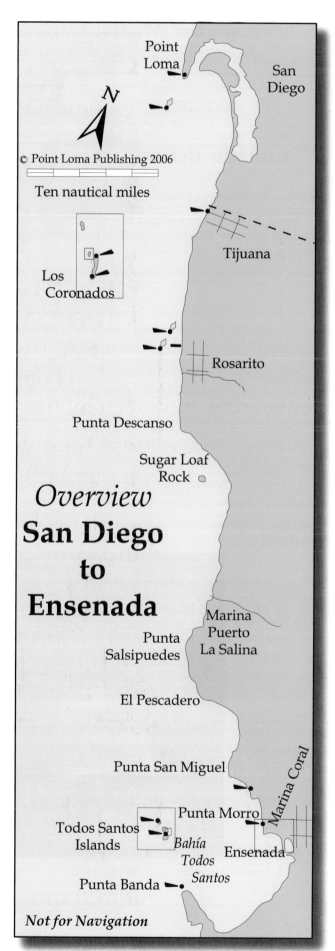

1
Coronados to Ensenada

Overview
San Diego to Ensenada

Not for Navigation

COASTWISE: US border to Ensenada

The border city of Tijuana has no port or anchorage. We don't recommend sightseeing close to the small border monument or Tijuana's bull ring – due to possible immigration smugglers in small boats and Border Patrol activity near the fence. Instead, pick a safe course midway between shore and the Coronado Islands, or outside of them.

Coronado Islands

The four small Coronado Islands (Crown Islands) lie only five miles off shore and 15 miles south of Point Loma, making them well visited for fishing (yellowtail, halibut, barracuda, giant sea bass, white sea bass) and diving. You can anchor as long as you like, but the Coronados are a national wildlife refuge, so stepping ashore is prohibited.

If too many farewell parties keep you from stashing last-minute items, slip out to the Coronados for a "separation zone" from shore life.

In 1542, Juan Rodriguez Cabrillo described these as *islas desiertas* (desert islands), and in 1602 Vizcaíno's priest named them Los Cuatro Coronados (the four crowns) to honor four martyrs. But fishermen who later saw floating coffins, ghostly faces and shrouded bodies amid the ancient rocks dubbed them Old Stone Face, The Sarcophagi, Dead Man's Island, and Corpus Cristi.

Goats left here by early explorers flourished until the 1950s when the last Coronado goat died of dehydration. Sea otters frolicked here until 1890 but were killed off by hunters. Many species of sea birds nest here, especially on North Island, which has no rattlesnakes. The Coronados are the primary home of the *Xantus Murrelet*, a small black and white sea bird numbering fewer than 10,000 in the region. Elephant seals bask on eastern ledges.

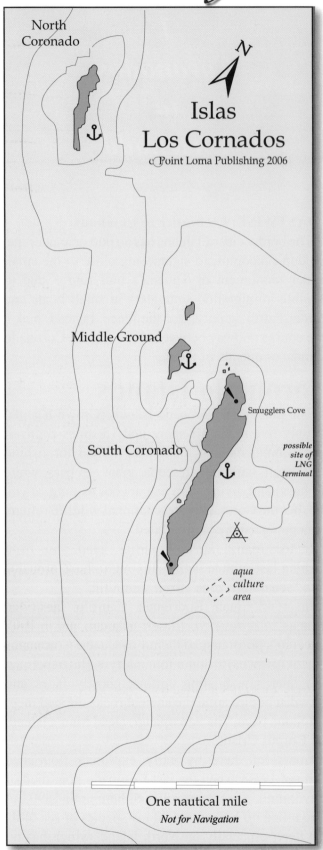

North Coronado

Islas Los Cornados

© Point Loma Publishing 2006

Middle Ground

Smugglers Cove

South Coronado

possible site of LNG terminal

aqua culture area

One nautical mile

Not for Navigation

Coronado del Medio:
The east side of Middle Coronado makes a mediocre day anchorage called Moonlight Cove, but it gets too much wave action for comfort overnight. Anchor at 32°25.05'N, 117°15.52'W. The smallest islet, Middle Ground Rock, is just north of Coronado del Medio.

Coronado del Sur:
South Coronado is the largest island, running two miles north to south, and has a nav light on each end.

Puerto Cueva (Cave Port), the small bay on the NE side of Coronado del Sur, is not an anchorage during prevailing NW weather, because it has no protection. And it completely closes out in NE or east weather. However, in calm conditions Puerto Cueva can be an interesting dinghy expedition. A nav light and Navy detachment top the cove's east wall. Inside you may see only the stone foundation of a famous 1930s casino hotel, hence the nickname Casino Cove. During the US Prohibition, it was called Smugglers' Cove; on foggy nights (common here) and before radar, these waters swarmed with so many booze smugglers that collisions were common. If gambling is allowed in Mexico, someone may build a new casino here – but it would need a big jetty. Meanwhile, the islands are a refuge for wildlife.

South Coronado's only anchorage is a mediocre roadstead with west-wind shelter. Look for the vertical scrape or ravine midway along the island's east side, and anchor about 100 yards off shore in 36' to 48' of water. Our GPS approach waypoint to this anchorage is 32°24.35'N, 117°14.46'W.

Coronado del Norte:
Farthest NW, this island doesn't have a good anchorage, but two locations on its east side are popular for scuba diving and underwater photography.

South Coronado anchorage off the ravine.

Navy base on hills above South Coronado's Smuggler's Cove has patrol boats checking papers.

Fishing the Coronados: Schools of yellowtail frequent these islands, and other prize catches include white sea bass, blue-fin tuna, calico bass, halibut, barracuda and bonito. Radical underwater topography and kelp ridges make this the most prolific region north of Mag Bay and Cabo San Lucas. Close to San Diego, live bait is usually worth the effort (or *vale la pena*) even on cruising boats.

Diving North Coronado: Lobster Shack is just a place name about midway down the east side. It's mostly a 45° boulder slope. The Arch, visible above water and extending 15' below, is just north of a 100' vertical wall with colorful Garibaldi, gorgonians, nudibranchs, stars, fans and sponges.

COASTWISE continued

From the east side of the Coronados, you can point-hop into Bahía Todos Santos (All Saints) by staying about 2.5 miles off each of the major headlands. Along shore, the Transpeninsular Highway 1 and its many conspicuous road cuts are visible on the steep, brush-covered coastal hills. (This highway will be visible on and off until you're south of San Quintín.)

Rosarito Beach has several landmarks: high-rise hotels and lights, an 1,800' mini-cruise ship dock (not for yatistas) and planned breakwater, and the tapered smokestacks at the Pemex refinery. It's fun to check out Rosarito Beach, but if you're coasting within three miles of the refinery, look out for at least two giant mooring buoys used by oil tankers.

NOTE: If the LNG terminal is built at South Coronado, expect dredges and work boats during construction here too. At least one more LNG terminal is planned somewhere along Pacific Baja by 2009, but with so much environmental protest about the Coronado LNG terminal, the oil companies aren't yet revealing additional locations.

Punta Descanso is the north end of open Descanso

Marina Puerto La Salina 30 miles N of Ensenada.

Sugar Loaf Rock

Bay, and in that north corner Sugar Loaf Rock (Pilon de Azucar) looks like a white ship anchored on the 20-fathom line.

Marina Puerto La Salina lies about nine miles south of Sugar Loaf Rock, inside the more southerly of two sandy beaches backed by low lagoons, so it's an "innie" type marina basin. The entrance jetties (32°03.45'N by 116°52.76'W) lie a couple miles north of the curving Punta Salsipuedes. The entrance channel is dredged to 12', nine feet inside. Marina Puerto La Salina is detailed with Ensenada's other marinas below.

South of Salsipuedes, the coast runs ESE, marked by Punta San Miguel, the lesser Punta El Sauzal, the lighted Punta El Morro (The Moor) and then Ensenada's municipal harbor. The small private commercial harbor of El Sauzal has a breakwater on the east flank of low Punta El Sauzal, but it's not open for yatistas.

Marina Coral, on the east flank of lighted Punta El Morro, has a larger lighted breakwater and welcomes yatistas. Our GPS approach waypoint just outside the breakwater opening is 31°51.5'N by 116°39.7'W.

Marina Coral is part of a resort hotel 2.75 miles N of Ensenada.

Give a mile-wide berth to El Morro and the kelp beds NW of it, entering the marina breakwaters from the SE for a better view of the baffled entrance. Marina Coral is detailed below.

Come into Bahía Todos Santos by rounding Punta San Miguel about two miles off, thus avoiding an 18' deep rock pile (about 3.5 miles SW of Punta San Miguel) and thick kelp beds around it. The white scar-face of an old quarry marks what's left of the headland on the NW edge of Ensenada's municipal harbor breakwater, but its .75 mile-long riprap breakwater (lighted) is open only to the south. However, avoid the sandy shoals off Estero Beach, four miles SE of the harbor entrance.

Ensenada

Ensenada (pop. 177,000) is the 1st port south of the US-Mexico border – and only 65 nautical miles SE of Point Loma Light, eight miles NE of Punta Banda, 100 miles NW of San Quintín.

Ensenada harbor is a pleasant mix of tourism, sportfishing and boat yards. The annual Newport to Ensenada Race is the world's largest international

yacht race, bringing about 1,500 sailboats here each spring. The sportfishing docks are always busy, because even California boats come down here for the fishing. Spring break brings college crowds to the waterfront, and Ensenada hosts a fabulous culinary and wine festival, a Baja mountain bike race and an off-road car race. Ensenada's weather mirrors San Diego's but a big foggier.

Many California residents spend at least 12 months fishing and cruising Ensenada after purchasing their new vessels outside the US – earning an exemption from state sales and use tax, at least temporarily. Ensenada makes an excellent mini-vacation site for West Coast boaters, often in preparation for more extensive cruising along Mexico's 3,300-mile Pacific coastline.

Because Ensenada is so convenient, thousands of ocean-going yacht owners (*yatistas*) and long-range fishing expeditions make it their Port of Entry into Mexican waters, performing the official International Arrival or *Entrada Internaciónal*. North-bounders heading to California can get their exit papers or Zarpe here and officially clear out of Mexico.

Lay of the Land

The city and port of Ensenada are nestled into the WNW corner of the large and fairly open Bahía de Todos Santos. The municipal harbor itself measures a mile north-south, and is formed by two riprap breakwaters opening south.

Buoys mark the main channel (18' depth), lined by moorings and anchorage. Cruise ships may dock on the big mole surrounding Cruiseport Village Marina, on the east side of the harbor just south of the river mouth. A nice pedestrian walkway (*paseo*) runs north-south. North of the river you'll see a huge flag on a Navy base, then Baja Naval Marina and several sportfishing docks. The harbor's north wall has two shipyards (Astilleros Rodriguez, and INC recently purchased by Baja Naval) with large cranes.

The landmark quarry scar is N of Ensenada harbor, which has moorings and marinas.

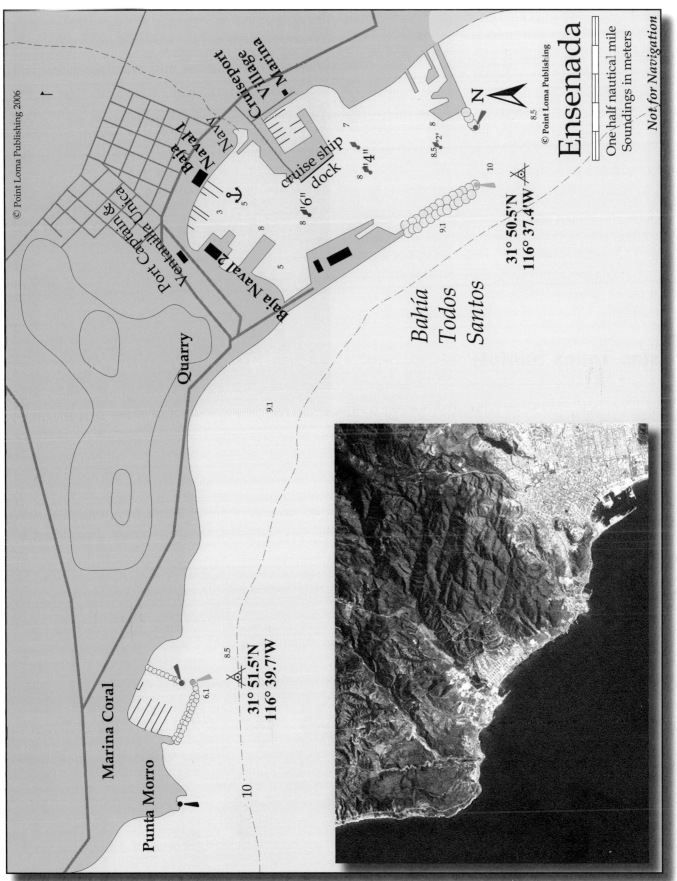

Port Captain & Ventanilla Única

Baja Naval 1

Navy

Cruiseport Village Marina

cruise ship dock

Baja Naval 2

Quarry

Marina Coral

Punta Morro

8.5

6.1

**31° 51.5'N
116° 39.7'W**

10

Bahía Todos Santos

9.1

**31° 50.5'N
116° 37.4'W**

10

9.1

8.5

8.5,2"

8

8.5

8

8 "4"

8 "6"

7

3

5

5

8

5

N

Ensenada

One half nautical mile
Soundings in meters

Not for Navigation

*High-resolution satellite image corrects old chart
errors. This image shows from Punta Salsipuedes to
Ensenada harbor.*

One block north of the NE corner of the harbor, the red brick Centro Integrales de Servicios (CIS) building handles international arrivals and departures. See port clearance in Local Services below.

Ensenada's colorful downtown is the first two streets (named Costero-Cárdenas and Matéos) east of the waterfront street known throughout Mexico as a *malecon*. Downtown has great restaurants, touristy shopping, nightclubs and hotels.

Anchor & Berth

Yachts can anchor inside Ensenada harbor, staying off to either side of the main ship channel marked by buoys. The bottom (14' to 28') is soft mud, not great holding. If you leave your boat uninhabited overnight, hire a guard from one of the marinas to keep an eye on it and don't leave expensive temptation out on deck.

Islas Todos Santos: These two small

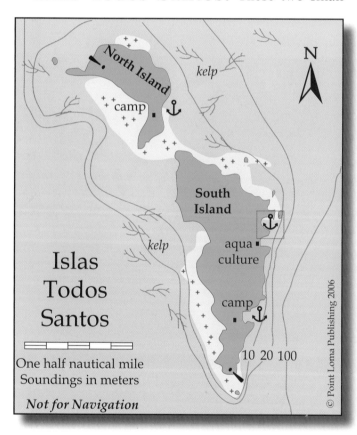

the cove prevent you from snuggling in as close as you might like. However, if you can take a stern line ashore, you'll find two eye bolts imbedded in a dark reddish rock pinnacle just N of the head of the cove.

If you can't squeeze in, try anchoring just outside this cove in 45' to 50' of water. This anchorage is

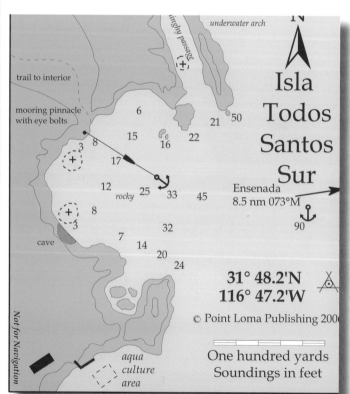

islands lie 10 miles SW of Ensenada, their south end only 3.5 miles NW of the seaward tip of the Punta Banda peninsula.

The higher south island has four narrow coves on its east side and in the 2nd cove from the top two cooperating boats can anchor bow and stern in about 36' of water. Two submerged rocks in the head of

Isla Todos Santos anchorage has room for 2 or 3 small boats.

safe only in NW or west weather, not in anything nearing east. If the wind swings around or a Santa Ana is predicted, get out of here immediately.

A small, grassy footpath leads up behind the stern-tie pinnacle. Yes, you can go ashore here, following the paths between cactus gardens and guano deposits. Don't hassle nesting seabirds. The night lights of Ensenada are visible from Islas Todos Santos. Immediately to the south of the anchorage is an aquaculture operation with an offshore float and a building ashore. A sign on the cliffs says what it is (in Spanish), but not "Keep out."

The smaller north island is flat except for the tower of Todos Santos Light. Scuba divers poke around on the north side, but it offers no significant anchorage. Pangas transit the pass between the islands, but we haven't tried that, because this pass is also a world-famous surfing spot. Opal eye, sheep heads and bass are the prominent catches in the kelp along the north shelf.

Estero Beach: Multihulls, trailer boats and kayakers can explore inside this huge estuary (*estero*) five miles south of Ensenada, full of reeds for good bird-watching and fly fishing. Five launch ramps in this area bring crowds on weekends, but the entrance has shoals.

Punta Banda: Along the south side of the Punta Banda peninsula, we've seen small boats anchoring in tiny Bahía Papalote (also called Bufadero Cove) where the famous blow-hole squirts, and also in Bahía Escondida, the next cove SE which is slightly wider. We haven't had the nerve to test these yet.

Moorings: Renting a mooring from an Ensenada marina or sportfishing dock at least gives you somewhere to land your dinghy, even if they charge a couple extra bucks per night for this service.

If you spot an empty mooring, circle it and wait for that mooring operator to come out in his skiff. Sometimes, skiffs from several moorings operators will vie for your business. Inspect the connections well, and specify if you want the mooring fee to include either (a) landing your dinghy at their secured dock, or (b) them shuttling you to and from shore a certain number of times. Do tip your guard and shuttle driver, and don't leave your dinghy at any dock without a written agreement.

Marina Puerto La Salina, 35 miles south of the border, has twin baffled and lighted entrance jetties at 32°03.40'N by 116°53.34'W. This marina and residential development opened in 2005 with power and water slips for 25 yachts to 55' LOA drawing no more than 6' of water at the smaller slips, plus a launch ramp. A quarter mile south is a hotel with cantina, a small grocer and laundry.

The marina plans 500 full-service floating slips

Aqua-culture pens may fill the coves S of the main anchorage.

Departing Cruiseport Marina's breakwater into Ensenada harbor.

with a few 120' side ties, a fuel dock, dry storage yard and yacht club with restaurant. Highway 1 runs along the east end of the basin; homes are in construction just south. Until this marina is complete or has full-time staff, hail "any yacht inside" for channel depths before entering. If you're new to Mexico boating, you'll see that *puerto* is a marketing term, not necessarily a port. FMI: www.baja-web.com/la-salina

Marina Coral: Located 2.75 miles NW of Ensenada's harbor entrance, Marina Coral (pronounced *coh-RAHL*) has 500 full-service slips to 150' and a 135' fuel dock in the NE corner of the enclosed basin just east of El Morro Light. Our GPS approach waypoint for entering Marina Coral's south-opening breakwater is 31°51'N, 116°40'W.

The marina can help you document your boating activities for the IRS, and marina guests can use the hotel gym, pools, restaurants and shuttle van into town. Trailer boaters have a 2-lane concrete launch ramp and good parking. Slip reservations are required,

and this marina is usually 99% full. Call Dockmaster Fito, toll free from US (866) 302-0066. Everyone who answers speaks English.

Cruiseport Village Marina is on the east side of Ensenada's municipal harbor, inside the big cruise ship mole. The opening faces south, but your view at first might be obscured by cruise ships. The marina has 210 full-service floating slips to 60' LOA, depth of 8.5', very helpful staff and new shore facilities (laundry, showers) all inside a secured gate. Restaurants and shopping are within two blocks. Plans call for a fuel dock on the east wall; (646) 173-4157 or www.ecpumarina.com

Baja Naval (pronounced *nah-VAHL*) is just north of the big flag, and its marina docks protrude from the east seawall inside Ensenada harbor, above Baja Naval's boatyard. The marina has 50 full-service slips (including wireless internet access) to 110' LOA off two gated docks west of the harbor paseo. This marina is often full, so they may find you a mooring and charge a minimal fee to let you land your dinghy on their secure docks. The boatyard's concrete Travelift piers serve as fuel piers; you order the quantity of diesel you need, and it's delivered by truck. Baja Naval's marina and office staffers are very helpful and speak English. FMI: www.bajanaval.com or (646) 174-0020.

Bandito's Docks are orange and white sportfishing docks next to Baja Naval, but there is sometimes a slip (not full service) or moorings to rent. To ask what's available, call "Bandito" on VHF-06.

Juanito's Sportfishing: Juanito's blue and white docks are north of Bandito's and below the pink shopping center. Juanito's runs dive and fishing charters and harbor excursions, but they occasionally have moorings or slips with 110-volt (30-amp) dock power for visiting yachts. Hail "Juanito's Boats" on VHF-18a. Owner Luis Juan Cardona speaks perfect English and can arrange

Cruiseport Village Marina is inside a cruise-ship mole in Ensenada harbor.

Baja Naval's boat yard overlooks its marina.

for fuel delivery, laundry service and standard provisioning. FMI: juancard@telnor.net or (646) 174-0953.

Sergio's Sportfishing Marina in the NE corner (close to port offices) has 24 full-service guest slips to 85' LOA, 15' depth. Guest slips are near active sportfishing docks with boats and passengers that depart at 0700 daily, but Sergio's has 24-hour security and offers boat maintenance. They may also have a few moorings to rent. Ashore are showers, phones and a snack bar. Sergio's has daily or monthly rates and is a block off downtown. FMI: www.sergios-sportfishing.com

Local Services

Ensenada is a Port of Entry, probably the easiest place for yatistas to arrive and depart Mexico. Before you go ashore for dinner and drinks, gather up all your ship's papers, passports and crew members. Walk or take a taxi to the CIS (Centro Integrales de Servicios) building (red brick) across the street from the NE corner of the harbor, on the main street into town. It's next door to the Capitanía or Port Captain's office.

Here you'll find representatives of the Port Captain, Aduana and Migración waiting to get you cleared in. There may be reps from Agriculture or the Navy, if required. There's a copy machine for your documents and bank kiosk to pay your fees by credit card. Hours are 0800 to 1700, M – F except holidays. Called a *ventanilla unica*, this integrated service is a tremendous improvement from recent years.

We suggest purchasing the TIP (Temporary Import Permit) now. You'll need it before you can leave your boat

in a marina or municipal harbor, and before you can ship anything (boat parts, charts, meds) into Mexico. When a yacht race is set to finish at Ensenada, the Port Captain issues special clearance and berthing instructions for registered participants.

If you're departing Ensenada within about 48 hours, clear in and out of the port at one time. If you're staying at a marina, your dockmaster may need to give you a receipt to speed your departure.

VHF 09, 12 and 14 are restricted to Ensenada' port ops, so yatistas should not use them for calling or for the morning VHF net. The Port Captain posts daily weather-fax charts in the front hallway of the Capitania, and during stormy weather he updates them as often as three times a day. Cruisers can always call "Capitán de Puerto" on VHF 16 to ask

Ensenada's CIS building lets yatistas clear into Mexico in 1 easy visit.

for the latest local weather summary in Spanish.

Ship's Agent: The owners of recreational boats aren't required to hire a ship's agent, but if you think you might have problems with your papers or crew, it's best to have an agent represent you before the waters are muddied. The Gil Ojeda Agency is the one we've used over the years, and they speak English. Agencia Ojeda is (646) 178-3615 or agojeda@telnor. nct

Fuel: Marina Coral has a floating fuel dock with pumps at the NE end of their enclosed darsena north of Ensenada harbor. Ensenada harbor itself has no public fuel dock, but you may arrange to take fuel

The fuel dock inside Marina Coral's darsena N of Ensenada is very handy.

through any of the marinas (Baja Naval is easiest) or at the INC Shipyard. Small quantities are brought dockside in 55-gallon drums by hand truck. Large quantities will be brought down by tank truck. Check Updates on www.MexicoBoating.com

Haul-out yards: Baja Naval's 75-ton Travelift (22' beam) and enclosed boatyard specializes in yachts. Baja Naval's fenced yard and big white shed are usually crammed with US or Canadian yachts, both power and sail, even an occasional racing hull. You can do some of the work yourself, but we've heard good reports on their workers' quality.

Recently purchased by Baja Naval, the big Industrial Naval de California (INC) shipyard has a 2,500-ton synchrolift dock, 80-ton Travelift and cranes on the north end of the harbor. Large yachts should keep this in mind as one of the few yards for emergency haul-out. INC is (646) 178-1901.

Provisioning: The big Comercial Méxicana and Gigante supermarkets on the highway south of town are your best bet for staples and meats. The fish market stalls lining the harbor offer the freshest thing this side of catching it yourself.

However, to get your Mexican galley cooking, buy braided strands of fresh garlic bulbs, delicious home-cured olives in all colors, and local honey at farmers' market stalls alongside Highway 1 on the south edge of Ensenada. Several craft shops downtown sell tortilla presses (two sizes) and garlic and lime squeezers – mandatory utensils in your tropical-cruising galley.

If you're northbound to the US, find a deserving local family to accept whatever fresh food items would otherwise be confiscated at your US Agricultural inspection: uncooked fresh meats, raw eggs, oranges, limes, avocados and mangoes.

Internet: CompuNet is downtown on Mateos; MaxiComm is on the corner of Mateos and Miramar.

Transportation: All over Mexico, taxis are far cheaper than in the US, so they're the practical way to run errands around town. Agree on the fare for where you're going before you climb in and close the door. If your cab picks up other passengers en route, they're supposed to split the fare. However, if they try to stick the gringo with the full fare, make them pay by giving you a quickie Spanish lesson in the taxi. It's fun and everyone wins.

Ensenada has two bus lines that go north to Tijuana, south La Paz and Cabo San Lucas, east to Hermosillo in Sonora. Most buses have a toilet and air conditioning, and some have videos. In Baja, fares average around $2 per hour of travel.

Ensenada's small airport is on Highway 1 south toward Estero Beach. An irregular flight loops to Cedros Island, Turtle Bay and back. Tijuana's international airport Rodriguez Field is about 65 miles north.

Eateries: Several times a year, the whole town turns out for 7-day international seafood festivals, then a Paella Fair, then wine festivals. Fine restaurants offer their special dishes, and the public samples them along with judges from around the world. Lots of *cerveza*, *vino* and free *botanas* or hors devours.

A few of our favorites eateries are Mariscos

The dinghy passage at Isla Todos Santos .

Ensenada (great seafood, inexpensive) on Riveroll near Mateos, Las Cazuelas (authentic Mexican dishes, warm ambiance) just past where the Malecon turns east at the south end of the waterfront, El Rey Sol (incredibly good French cuisine) on Mateos north of the river, and the fresh fish-taco stands inside the modernized fish market. Katrina and Andrés Tinoco, owners of Restaurant La Vendimia at 85 Riveroll near Costero, welcome all boaters to their informal "yacht club" for cheap drinks, discounts on food and Thursday Happy Hour. Katrina is a bubbly Brit who helps visiting yatistas with translations and locating Ensenada resources. Katrinamex@hotmail.com

Spanish: Learn nautical Spanish privately or form a weekly class of five yatistas, as well as Mexican cooking: Baja California Language College on Riveroll at 13ᵗʰ Street near the bus station. US: (619) 758-9711; college@bajacal.com

Emergency: For emergency help afloat, hail "Capitanía" or "Armada de México" on VHF 16. With a good VHF antenna, you can reach the San Diego Marine Operator (VHF 28 & 86) and place a collect call into the US. Vessel assistance services charge extra for entering Mexican waters.

If you have a life-threatening emergency afloat, hail "US Coast Guard San Diego" via SSB or VHF; state your GPS position in Mexican waters, your nationality and your boat's homeport. This will cut diplomatic red tape and get help to you faster.

Ensenada has a 3-digit hotline on any land phone: for emergency medical help, dial 132. For police, dial 134. For fire-fighters, dial 136. Highway help, call the Green Angels tourist assistance service: (646) 176-4675. Ensenada's main hospital is (646) 172-4500.

Explore Ashore

Ensenada has many notable vineyards and wine tasting shops, some in town, others by tour bus: L.A. Cetto, Monte Xanic, Domecq, Santo Tomas, Adobe Guadalupe, Bodegas San Antonio, Cavas Valmar and Chateau Camou are just a few. Ninety percent of Mexico's table wines are produced in Ensenada's Valle Guadalupe and Valle de Santo Tomas, so stock up on good wine here. It's like gold in the Sea of Cortez and farther south throughout Latin America, because the few bottles you find may have spoiled in hot warehouses.

The venerable Estero Beach Resort Hotel south of town has a nice museum of pre-Columbian art and natural history worth a visit. The sandy estero next door is a good place to swim, kayak, bird watch and wind surf.

History & Culture

A few months before Cabrillo "discovered" San Diego Bay, he named the Todos Santos (All Saints) Islands and the Bahía de Todos Santos. The town that sprouted in the sheltered NE corner of that bay was called Ensenada de Todos Santos – later shortened to Ensenada. Today the two port cities on either side of the border share similar development histories and nautical cultures.

Much of Baja California Norte and Sur was settled by adventurers who arrived here by boat from the mainland or by horse-drawn wagon from San Diego – then spread south down the mission trails which were mostly interior.

Visit Ensenada's beautiful Museum of History and Culture in the former Riviera del Pacifico center on the malecon just south of the river: (646) 177-0594.

2
Santo Tomás
to
San Quintín

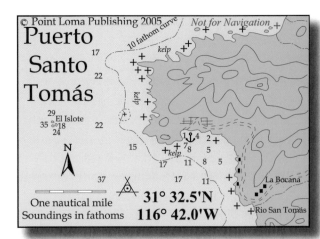

© Point Loma Publishing 2005   *Not for Navigation*

Puerto Santo Tomás

10 fathom curve

kelp

17

22

kelp

29 El Islote
35 °○18
24
22

15

N

17   11

37   17   11

One nautical mile
Soundings in fathoms

**31° 32.5'N
116° 42.0'W**

La Bocana

Rio San Tomás

COASTWISE: Ensenada to San Quintín

Isla Todos Santos: From Ensenada, you can make your southbound departure midway between Punta Banda and Islas Todos Santos. Stay 0.75 of a mile off the NW tip and Punta Banda Light, and half a mile off the SE tip of the S island. The racon on the N island doesn't always work. Or go N of both islands, but we don't recommend passing between them.

Rocas Soledad (Solitary) is a composite pinnacle about a mile W of the rocks at the base of craggy Punta Santo Tomás. We usually go outside this pinnacle, but if you must pass between them, favor Rocas Soledad, because it has deep water close on all sides.

Puerto Santo Tomás

Puerto Santo Tomás is a marginal rest stop, a picturesque sea-urchin diving village on the S side of the point. The tiny anchorage SE of the point is surgey, open to SW swell – and sometimes clogged by kelp. But in settled weather we've anchored here in around 20' at 31°33.16'N, 116°40.69'W. This should be just outside the panga's mooring area. Stone steps lead up to the village, which has a lunch cantina. Not every puerto is a port.

The panga fleet has a beaching shingle, a seasonal floating barge and lobster pots around the cove. Try to avoid commercial divers – they seldom show a "diver down" flag. A gravel road leads S from the cove, past some nice adobe homes and a beach campground at the river mouth before it turns inland for 35 miles to Highway 1. During Spanish colonial days, thousands of barrels of wine were loaded here from the Santo Tomás wine-producing valley 30 miles inland.

An indent on the N side of Punta

Puerto Santo Tomas anchorage.

Overall Ensenada to San Quintín

Islas Todos Santos

Ensenada

Punta Banda

Estero Punta Banda

Roca Soledad

Punta Santo Tomás

Punta San Jose

© Point Loma Publishing

Punta Cabras

Rio San Vicente

Laguna Salado

Twenty nautical miles

Cabo Colonet

Punta San Telmo

Punta San Jacinto

Punta Camalu

Rio Santo Domingo

Isla San Martín

Laguna Figueroa

Ben's Rock

Old Mill

Laguna San Quintín

Bahia San Quintín

Not for Navigation

Santo Tomás called Bahía Soledad is too exposed and surgey for anchoring. Ling cod have been taken around Rocas Soledad and S of the village, but we wouldn't suggest competing with the local divers for lobster.

COASTWISE continued

Punta San Jose Light is a small bluff 5 miles S of Puerto Santo Tomás, and on it you'll see a large processing plant for the local sea urchins and a seasonal offloading quay for pangas. In NW weather, you may find small shelter just SE of this point, but it's often clogged with thick kelp.

Fishing: At 20 to 25 miles SE of Santo Tomás, from shore almost out to the 100-fathom line, you'll find a major mixed-bag fishing ground: barracuda, halibut, ling cod, giant sea bass, yellow tail, whitefish, white sea bass and various rock fish. One theory is that they're nourished by the agri-fertilizers flowing out of the San Vicente River. Two roadsteads are N of the river, where there's a beach camp, and about 5 miles N of that, off Punta Cabras Light.

Between Santo Tomás and Colonet, coasting down the 100-fathom line or about 2 to 5 miles off the beach keeps you out of the kelp and off lying rocks.

Cabo Colonet

Cabo Colonet (Punta Colonet) lies 41 miles SE of Santo Tomás, about 65 miles SE of Ensenada. These sheer cliffs and flat plateaus are an easily distinguishable landmark – visually and on radar. Binoculars reveal 300' to 400' vertical palisades rising from talus, sliced off to a flat mesa top, forming this prominent headland. Cabo Colonet Light tower stands on the tip.

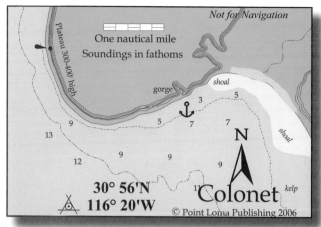

Radar paints a giant nose in profile, facing W: the nose's 10-mile bridge angles SW straight from the sandy lagoon at Arroyo Salado, ending at the semicircular W tip of Cabo Colonet.

Bahía Colonet is SE of Cabo Colonet, formed by the "nostril" area of the nose curving back ENE. In prevailing NW winds, the best anchorage is about 1.6 miles E of the tip, just beyond the obvious notch in the middle of the cliffs, in 25' to 30' of water. Our GPS waypoint for the anchorage area is 30°57.64'N by 116°17.63'W.

TIP: Don't anchor directly below the notch, because our nose analogy holds true. When a normal breeze up on the mesa gets amplified and funneled down the notch, it sneezes!

Plans call for a major cargo terminal to be built here. The anchorage may one day be filled with ships and piers, and the table top of Cabo Colonet will be a parking lot for containers.

Cabo Colonet: Cliffs and plateau (left) are a good landmark. The notch (above) near the prevailing wind anchorage sometimes sneezes - a blast of wind. This area is slated for commercial development.

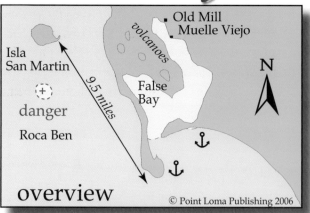

Isla San Martín

9.5 miles

danger

Roca Ben

volcanoes

Old Mill
Muelle Viejo

False Bay

N

overview

© Point Loma Publishing 2006

COASTWISE continued

From Colonet, it's a straight 30-mile shot to Isla San Martín. Stay 1.5 miles off the bluff point of San Telmo to avoid a rocky shoal, and stay 2 miles off

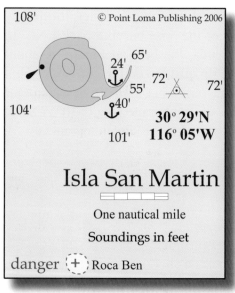

108'

© Point Loma Publishing 2006

24'   65'

55'   72'   72'

40'

104'

101'   30° 29'N
116° 05'W

Isla San Martin

One nautical mile

Soundings in feet

danger Roca Ben

Punta San Jacinto (It's pronounced *ha-SEEN-toe*), the next low sandy point.

Lights on Highway 1 may be seen at night. Campers sometimes clam in the shoals between Punta Camalu and Laguna Mormona, either side of the mouth of Arroyo Santo Domingo, where trailer boats sometimes launch over the sand. A new fish processing plant has sprouted on the beach opposite Isla San Martín.

In clear weather, you may sight Calamajue Peak atop San Pedro Martír (almost 10,000' elevation) only 37 miles E of this stretch. This highest point in Baja gets snow in winter.

Isla San Martín & Ben's Rock

Isla San Martín & Ben's Rock should be thought of as one entity, if only as a memory trick so you won't forget the location of dangerous Ben's Rock.

Isla San Martín (pronounced mar-TEEN) is a small round island, a volcano cone about a mile in diameter, shaped like a Chinese coolie hat with two 500' peaks. Isla San Martín lies 30 miles SSE of Cabo Colonet, 9.5 miles NW of Cabo San Quintín, and 2 miles W of the 4 larger volcano peaks on shore.

Hassler's Cove is a natural lava breakwater curving NE from the island's SE corner, providing shelter inside from W and S wind and from light NW weather. Our GPS 30°28.83'N by 116°06.20'W is inside the cove.

Anchor in 20' to 30' off the tiny village, or farther out in 40', but there's less protection near the gap. The village has no services, and seasonal aquaculture buoys may block all or part of this cove.

NOTE: Keep Isla San Martín in mind, because anchorages with southerly protection are very rare along Pacific Baja.

South Martín: In moderate NE weather, we've anchored outside along the S shore of the island, in 40' of water over sand and rock that's not especially good holding. In a blow, this gets wrap-around swell. A small lagoon SW of Hassler's Cove supports aquaculture buoys and nets, but kayaks and some dinghies can ford the rock-blocked entrance at high tide. Ashore are lava tubes and a seal colony.

Ben's Rock rises sharply from 150' and has claimed at least 9 lives. Waves break over this submerged pinnacle every day but only sporadically.

Hassler's Cove anchorage on the E side of Isla San Martin is withn view of San Quintín's volcano cones (left).

When one does break, it's huge and deadly. One 100' fishing vessel was instantly flipped with fatal results. Even in calm weather, giant breaking waves can rise anywhere within a 1-mile radius. Ben's Rock lies 2.5 miles due S of Isla San Martín and about 7 miles NW of the outer edge of the Cabo San Quintín. Avoid transiting this area.

San Quintín

Cabo San Quintín (pronounced keen-TEEN) lies about 110 miles SE of Ensenada, 38 miles N of the dangerous Sacramento Reef, about 135 miles NW of the N end of Cedros Island, and about 180 miles NW of Turtle Bay. Bahía San Quintín provides two excellent overnight anchorages in prevailing NW weather.

Lay of the Land

San Quintín refers to 3 local features.

Cabo San Quintín is the S seaward end of a prominent 10-mile-long volcano-studded peninsula pointing S. The 4 small volcano cones (757' to 876') are distinctive landmarks forming the W side of the 10-mile-long estuary. Monte Mazo cone stands about 160' high on Cabo San Quintín. Punta Entrada is its E tip.

Bahía San Quintín is a 5-mile-wide, crescent-shaped bay in the normal lee SE of Cabo San Quintín. It' open to the S. See Anchorage below.

Estero San Quintín E of the peninsula and N of Punta Azufre peninsula is a large, shallow, mostly tidal estuary. Sandy shoals and lines of breakers foul the .75-mile wide entrance to San Quintín's estuary. Silt frequently changes the bottom contours. Dinghies, shallow draft boats, trailerable craft and kayaks may be able to enter the estuary – but only with the aid of a local panguero to guide them safely between the ever-shifting shoals.

Anchorage

Outside the estuary, ocean-going cruisers can usually find excellent overnight anchorage and shelter from NW winds. But fuel, water or provisions are not readily available from this anchorage.

Our GPS approach waypoint half a mile S of Cabo San Quintín is 30°21'N by 116°00'W. From here, we round the black reefs at least half a mile off.

2 Santo Tomás to San Quintín

Punta Entrada: We've found two places to anchor. First is in the lee E and SE of reef-strewn Punta Entrada, which is the E edge of Cabo San Quintín. Anchor S of the breakers, in 18' to 25' of water; the holding is good in sand and shell. From here, you can most casily watch how the pangueros navigate their way through the breakers.

Playa Santa Maria: This level, crescent-shaped beach wraps the NE sides of Bahía San Quintín, and behind the beach berm you may see

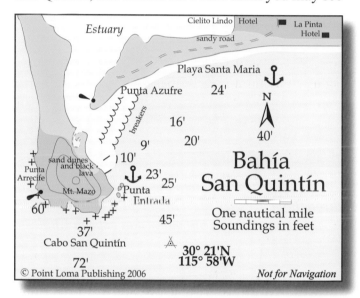

two hotels with campgrounds. You can anchor off Santa Maria Beach, outside the surf line, in 24' to 27' over a regular sand and shell bottom. The hard sand beach is used for launching smaller trailer boats.

Dinghies with wheels can be dragged 100 yards across the nearly level beach, where two hotels are hiking distance: family Cielito Lindo, chain La Pinta. Ask permission to use the restaurant and bar, and if they're not too busy you may be able to buy a hot shower.

Local Services

If you do successfully negotiate a safe path through the breakers and shoals to enter the estuary – with a guide or not – remember to take careful bearings while going in, because it won't look the same when you're trying to find your way out.

Inside the estuary, pangas haul out on the N side of Punta Azufre (Sulfur Point), the sandy peninsula that separates the estuary from Bahía San Quintín. From there an unmarked 10-mile channel winds N, skirting the E flanks of the volcanoes, missing the Old Pier (Muelle Viejo), and then NW to end at a wide launch ramp next to the Old Mill (Molino Viejo) restaurant and campground.

Several fishing guides who live here can draw you a map of how to get through the breakers in your dinghy, but it's accurate for only a few days or weeks – depending on the weather. One month the deepest pass is next to Punta Azufre, the next it's along the other side.

The town of San Quintín and Highway 1 are another 5 miles inland, via washboard gravel roads through farmlands. The nearest Pemex station and grocery store are in town.

Panga fishermen (pangueros) are a common sight throughout Mexico. Most are helpful and courteous to visiting yatistas, but many don't speak English.

Fuel: Don't count on marine services here. But you may use VHF 16 to hail a guide or hire a panguero to shuttle emergency fuel in your jerry jugs: Here are a few we've heard of: Chino, El Tiburon, Gene, Pedro's Pangas. With phones are El Capitan Sportfishing (616) 713-3087, Ernesto's Hotel (616) 756-9522, Hotel Cielito Lindo and the Old Mill.

The nearest Pemex station (diesel & gas), grocery stores and public phones are in San Quintín, 5 miles from the Old Mill via washboard gravel roads through farmlands. San Quintín's bus station is on Highway 1, about a mile N of where the Old Mill road intersects it.

Bus: The nearest station is in Lázaro Cárdenas 5 miles N of San Quintín on Highway 1. Don't leave a boat unattended anchored at Bahía San Quintín. Hotel La Pinta has guides, horse riding and a sandy air strip: (616) 165-9008.

About 5 miles E of Estero San Quintín, Highway 1 runs N-S through the busy farming town of San Quintín.

Emergency help or taxi may be called from the two hotels with radio phones: Cielito Lindo (US tel: 619-593-2252), and the Old Mill (US tel: 619-428-

2779) or local: (616) 176-3376. A clinic is NE of the town.

History & Culture

English settlers in 1882 grew wheat in the fertile valley, and built a grist mill and pier in the estuary linked by a railway to their fields. Draught wiped it out in 1900. You can still see weathered wooden crosses in what's called English Cemetery overlooking the estuary, and a sunken steam engine remains somewhere near Punta Azufre where its barge went down.

San Quintín residents voted not to let Fonatur build a resort and marina here.

Experienced divers comb the deeper volcanic formations fringing the volcanoes, and along the rocks skirting Cabo San Quintín and Punta Arrecife Light (Reef Point) on its W tip. (Johnston Seamount 5 miles WSW of Cabo San Quintín is said to offer good visibility, pinnacles and a reef.)

Birders enjoy the marsh between the two larger volcanoes and N of the Old Mill. You may find 1.5-inch butter clams in the shoal False Bay NW of Punta Azufre, but don't trespass into the commercial oyster farm. Clams are also found outside the estuary, along the W beach called the Medano. But hope is that some of the abalone farms will repopulate this area.

Estero San Quintin is popular with trailer boaters (and dinghy sailors) for sheltered fishing – halibut, croaker, perch and bass. Fishing outside the estuary is mainly for red snapper, yellowtail, barracuda, grouper, giant sea bass, ling cod and rock fish, and sometimes yellowfin and dorado. Surf fishing can be good on S beaches.

Departure: Be aware of two navigational hazards when departing the San Quintín area: Sacramento Reef if you're southbound, and Ben's Rock if you're northbound.

ROUTE PLANNING:
Crossing Bahía Vizcaíno

S-bound from San Quintín to Cedros Island, you'll encounter tiny Isla San Geronimo, Punta Baja and the dangerous Sacramento Reef – all described below. After studying your weather forecast, you must decide how to cross Bahía Vizcaíno, the largest bight on the N half of Pacific Baja.

Vizcaíno's hilly N shore angles NW to SE and contains several marginal anchorages – from Fondeadero San Carlos down to Santa Rosalillíta, all described below. They may provide rest stops, but none is reliable overnight in a strong NW blow, because wind and swell wrap around the points. We call them the Small Hopes of Vizcaíno.

Vizcaíno's low S shore is called the Malarrimo Coast. In Spanish, *mal* means bad, and *arrimo* refers to anything that has been stowed or supported. Beachcombing yields parts of shipwrecks, flotsam and jetsam. Malarrimo has only 30' of water 6 miles out. Shallow private channels are for salt barges towed between Cedros Village, Scammon's Lagoon and Guerrero Negro.

So for both N- and S-bounders, power and sail, we recommend avoiding the S end of Vizcaíno Bay between Morro Santo Domingo and Punta Eugenia.

Direct vs. Angled: Yatistas can (a) take the more direct route, the open-water passage between the outside of Sacramento Reef and the N end of Cedros Island, possibly with a San Benito Islands stop, or (b) angle SE to stay closer to Bahía Vizcaíno's curving N shore, then eventually angle SW or W across Vizcaíno Bay to Cedros

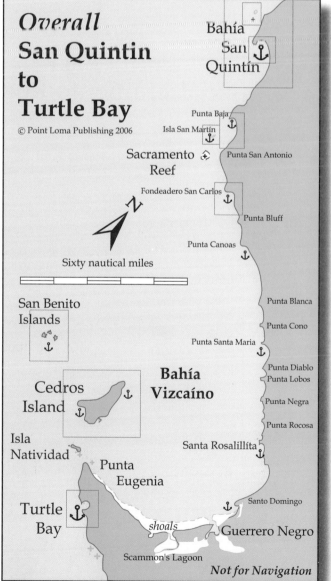

Island, to avoid the shoal Malarrimo Coast and its lee shores.

Direct: In winter when we're trying to get S and warm, we normally shoot straight from outside Sacramento Reef (inside passage is often kelp clogged) toward Cedros Island, about 130 miles SSE of San Quintín. From our waypoint outside Sacramento Reef, it's 95 miles across Vizcaíno Bay to the N end of Cedros Island. In moderate WX, we may stop at the San Benito Islands to dive and spend the night en route to Turtle Bay.

Because the N shore of Vizcaíno Bay drops away E, you're actually going off shore and should expect somewhat stronger wind and larger seas. Trim the autopilot for following seas. Larger cruising sailboats love this route, because they find consistent winds without losing any easting. Sportfishers usually get lucky around the deeper water seamounts, and some head out to Isla Guadalupe.

Angled: First-time S-bounders usually like the idea of staying closer to shore, within sight of the Small Hopes of Vizcaíno. That's fine, but consider in advance what the wind

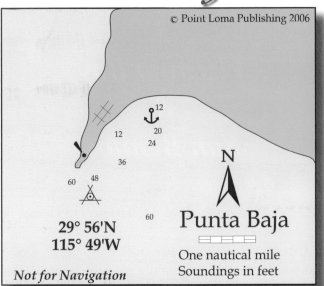

12
20
24
12
36
60 48
60

**29° 56'N
115° 49'W**

N

Punta Baja

One nautical mile
Soundings in feet

Not for Navigation

Punta Baja

Bahía el Rosario (Rosary Bay) is a wide crescent between Punta Baja and Punta San Antonio, 13 miles SSE. If kelp isn't clogging this whole bay, a sheltered anchorage tucked up in the N end of the bay holds 20 boats – more during a long NW blow. In S wind, Rosary Bay is a surf zone, not an anchorage.

Upon N approach, give the tip of Punta Baja a half-mile berth for rocks and kelp. From S, Punta Baja looks detached. When entering the bay, avoid the 15' deep shelf of breakers that starts a quarter mile off the beach.

In the shelter of 300' Lomas el Carrizo, we've

angle will be when you eventually must angle across to avoid Guerrero Negro and the Malarrimo zone.

N-bound can be rough bashing into NW winds and seas, so we angle E to NE from the N end of Cedros in varying degrees, skirting 2 to 5 miles off the N shore of Vizcaíno Bay to gain some meager protection. After reaching the N side of Vizcaíno, we generally continue NW while skirting a few miles off – sometimes clawing as best we can, sometimes in blessed calm behind a visible wind line.

Your exact N-bound course and landfall will depend on the angle and strength of the wind and seas that your boat can handle safely, and how much comfort you're willing to sacrifice to make your northing.

COASTWISE: Quintín direct to Cedros.

From the anchorage E of Cabo San Quintin, it's 27 miles SSE to Punta Baja Light. In between, Highway 1 is visible about half the way S, but at the point where it bends E to the town of El Rosario the coast changes from low dunes to steep eroded cliffs. The surf outside of the low S-pointing peninsula of Punta Baja draws surfers, and the beach inside is popular with RVers.

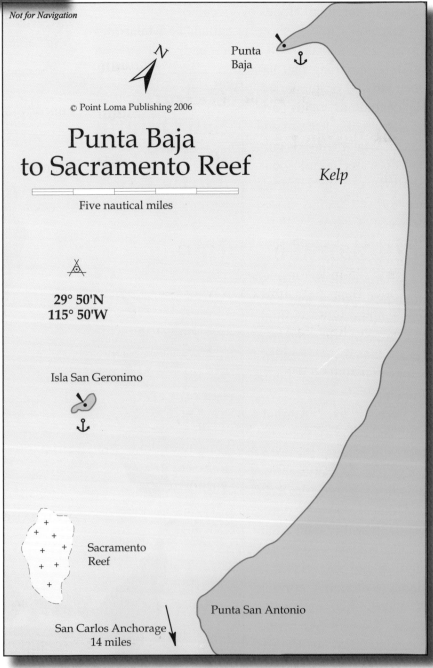

Not for Navigation

Punta Baja

Kelp

© Point Loma Publishing 2006

Punta Baja
to Sacramento Reef

Five nautical miles

**29° 50'N
115° 50'W**

Isla San Geronimo

Sacramento Reef

Punta San Antonio

San Carlos Anchorage
14 miles

*Punta Baja Light and the village inside
are visible from outside.*

anchored at about 29°57.28'N by 115°48.09'W over a regular sandy bottom. This is a quarter mile off shore and in 15' of water. Must move in this close to get out of the swell. Shore break inhibits landing, and the NW corner village has a steep beach ramp, no services. Nearest fuel is 8 miles, El Rosario on Highway 1. A few campers huddle on N bay, and a gravel road winds S to Punta San Antonio. Fishing is for yellowtail and kelp bass.

Departing S, avoid the reef, shallows and breakers W of Punta San Antonio.

Cabrillo slept here. It's froth with kelp flies by day, but on a quiet night, you can hear breakers on Sacramento Reef.

Sacramento Reef

Our GPS waypoint 2 miles W of Sacramento Reef is 29°44.0'N, 115°50.0'W.

If you're transiting this region, we recommend plotting a course that keeps you 2 to 5 miles outside this dangerous steep-to rock pile, because current can be strong and the inside passage is often clogged with impenetrable kelp paddies.

Sacramento Reef measures 2.5 miles wide (including a detached 18' spot), 2 miles long, and runs NW to SE. The N edge lies 2 miles S of the S tip of Isla San Geronimo; its NE corner is 2 miles W of Cabo San Antonio; its S edge is 3.25 miles WSW of Cabo San Antonio, and its W edge is about 4.5 miles W of San Antonio.

Local fishermen find wahoo, giant sea bass and shark around the reef. Sport divers explore its flanks. After making sure kelp doesn't clog the pass, we have run the 50' deep waters E of the reef several times now, staying a mile W of Punta San Antonio. When kelp dampens the waves crashing on the reef, it's harder to see.

Sacramento Reef is a killer. In 1872, the 270' side-wheel passenger steamship *Sacramento* hit this reef and was torn to shreds – with great loss of life. For decades, rumors persisted that tons of gold and jewel treasures were yet to be recovered.

Isla San Geronimo village.

Isla San Geronimo

This .75-mile long island lies 8.75 miles SSE of Punta Baja, 5.25 miles WNW of San Antonio Point, and 2 miles N of the N edge of the infamous Sacramento Reef. San Geronimo Light (11 miles) is the closest warning to Sacramento Reef. The island has a fish camp on the E beach. It's pronounced *hay-RON-ee-moh.*

If you must stop here, avoid the rocks a quarter mile off the island's SW side. The only spot we found to anchor is a sheltered but open roadstead off the rocky beach and shacks on the island's SE side. In light NW wind, we've anchored here in 25' to 30' of water, and our GPS read 29°47.32'N by 115°47.36'W.

San Benito Islands

On the 95-mile direct route across Bahía Vizcaíno, we pass Ranger Bank and the Islas San Benitos.

San Benito Islands from N.

Mexico Boating Guide

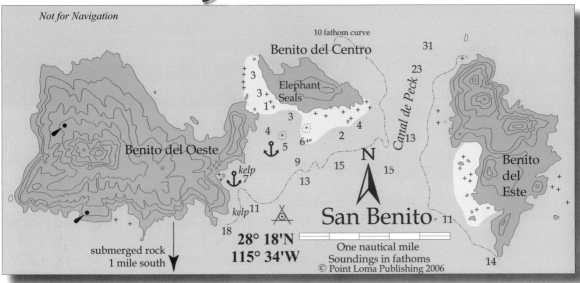

Not for Navigation

10 fathom curve

Benito del Centro

31

23

Canal de Peck

Elephant Seals

Benito del Oeste

Benito del Este

kelp

N

San Benito

28° 18'N
115° 34'W

One nautical mile
Soundings in fathoms
© Point Loma Publishing 2006

submerged rock
1 mile south

anchored a 115' schooner (bow & stern, in 30' of water over good holding sand) in the slightly larger cove S of the low spot you can almost see across. A path through the kelp is normally kept open by local pangueros. This anchorage is right in front of the village, which has a few shacks, a church, school and generator.

Scuba and snorkel divers find purple corals, caves, kelp forests and scads of tropical reef fish along the SE side of W Benito and around Rocas Pinaculos (Pinnacle Rocks) just less than a mile W of the SW corner of this island. The best fishing (yellowtail, opal eye, bass and sheep head) is reported around the pinnacles and off the N and S sides of W Benito.

Benito del Centro is the smallest of this
group, about 0.8 of a mile E-W and 0.3 N-S, around 82' high. The path between them is run by local pangas, but not by us. In flat weather, a roomier anchoring area is about 500 yards S of the SW side of Central Benito, between 2 small off-lying rocks, in about 24' over sand.

Elephant seals and sea lions haul out on the edges of this small island, and though they're fun to watch, they're noisy at night. For best viewing, anchor at 28°18.46'N by 115°34.20'W.

Benito del Este (E Benito) has 4 peaks to
421' running N-S. It has off-lying rocks N and SW of

Ranger Bank is a 400' seamount 10 - 15 miles N of the Benito Islands where marlin and yellow fin tuna are caught in fall and early winter warm water, and even sailboats get lucky with dorado by tossing a boat line over the side.

Islas San Benitos are also called the San Benitos. This group of 3 rocky islands and numerous reefs and rocks lies about 77 miles S of Fondeadero San Carlos, 18 miles WSW of the N end of Cedros Island, and 55 miles NW of Turtle Bay.

Our GPS approach waypoint (28°18'N, 115°34'W)

From the anchorage at W Benito, wildlife cavorts around this rock S of the Central Benito island. Peaks of E Benito are seen in background and in photo at bottom.

brings you in from the S side of the island group toward the main anchorage.

Benito del Oeste (W Benito) is the largest
in size (1.75 miles E-W, 1.5 miles N-S) and height (661'), and it carries a racon B (*dah di-di-dit*) facing S, and the group's only 2 lights: a 30-mile light on the NW side and a 9-mile light on the SW side.

The main anchorage in the Benito Islands is on W Benito's SE side. In moderate NW winds we've

40

the island, and more elephant seals and sea lions on the shingled shore. Divers frequent the rocks on the NW face, but it has no anchorages. The pass between Benito Centro and E Benito is called Peck Channel.

NOTE: Cedros Island and Turtle Bay are the next chapter.

ROUTE PLANNING: Angle
Punta San Antonio to Rosalillita

Some relief from heavy NW wind may be gained by traveling 1.5 (pay attention) to 5 miles off the NE shore of Vizcaíno Bay. But in a strong NW blow, the Small Hopes of Vizcaíno get too much surf, surge and

Sea lion rookery at San Benito Islands.

swell to provide safe overnight anchorage for boats larger than a trailerable craft or panga. Exceptions may be Fondeadero San Carlos, Bahía Playa Maria and Santa Rosalillíta.

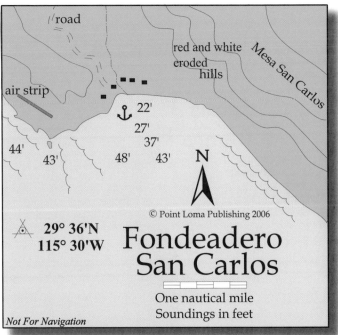

Fondeadero San Carlos is a 3-mile wide bight in the lee E of Punta San Carlos (100' hills) which lies 14 miles SE of Punta San Antonio, 53 miles SSE of San Quintin, 75 miles N of the Benito Islands, 78 miles NNW of the N end of Cedros Island.

In calm to light NW winds, this anchorage can be comfortable, and logistically it's the most useful of the Small Hopes. N-bound coastal cruisers overnight here to pass Sacramento Reef in daylight hours. It's a good goal when you're pointing up from Cedros on the direct route. But if the WX is good and you don't need to stop here, don't bother.

In heavy NW winds, swell can wrap around the

Fondeadero San Carlos

Fondeadero means anchorage; that's what Mexican charts call this, and the name helps yatistas distinguish it from other San Carloses.

Anchorage at Fondeadero San Carlos can be a comfortable reward for N-bound yatistas after crossing Vizcaino Bay, but it's not a reliable destination.

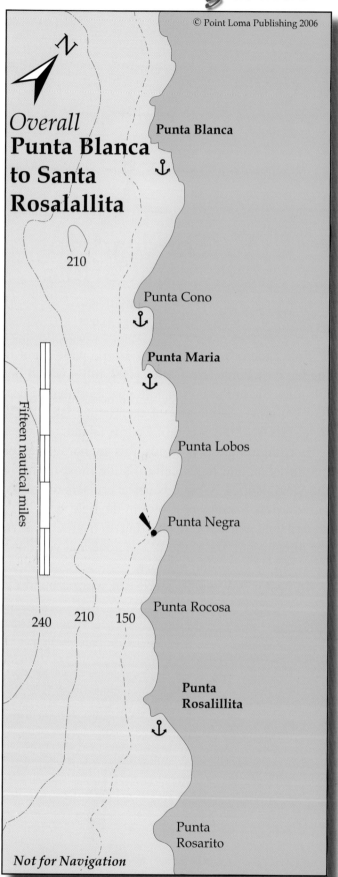

© Point Loma Publishing 2006

Overall
**Punta Blanca
to Santa
Rosalallita**

Punta Blanca

⚓

210

Punta Cono

⚓

Punta Maria

⚓

Fifteen nautical miles

Punta Lobos

Punta Negra

Punta Rocosa

240   210   150

**Punta
Rosalillita**

⚓

Punta
Rosarito

Not for Navigation

point and make the anchorage rolly to marginal. But if it's really bad out there, hunker down in the N corner of Fondeadero San Carlos and stand an overnight anchor watch. We've been blown out of here more than twice.

On approach from any direction, high plateaus mark the E side of Fondeadero San Carlos, and Cerro el Canasto (2,300') rises about 6 miles inland to the ENE of the anchorage. These 2 mountains are their most dramatic along Vizcaíno's N coast.

Our GPS approach waypoint a mile S of the point's off-lying rocks is 29°36'N by 115°30'W. About half a mile of breakers may line the W side of this lower mesa E of the anchorage, and that NE shore is backed by 1,650' Mesa San Carlos with its distinctive eroded red and white flanks.

Give the point a mile berth and avoid lobster pots on the 40' line. We've anchored (22' to 30') off the village in the NW corner of the bay, which spreads from the largest arroyo of this indent. Windsurfers camp on the point, pangas haul out below the village, and fishermen find white sea bass around a small seamount 5 miles W of the point.

COASTWISE continued

As you move SE down this scalloped coastline, its many steep hills are eroded by steep arroyos. About 7 miles S of Fondeadero San Carlos, Arroyo Canasto forms a small vertically striped point that we think has no anchoring merit.

Puerto Santa Catarina at the broad arroyo 6 miles further SE is a ghost port, not an anchorage, not even a good roadstead. But from the 1800s till the 1950s, marble quarried 50 miles inland was offloaded here, as was copper and iron ore. Neat history as you cruise on by.

Punta Canoas

At 20 miles SE of Fondeadero San Carlos this flat-topped plateau point resembles Punta Colnett, but this plateau lacks the talus fringe and there's a nasty rock about a half mile off its S tip. The indent bay E of the point is smaller and less sheltered than San Carlos. A gravel road 40 miles from Cataviña on Highway 1 dead-ends here. Our stand-off waypoint about 2.5 miles S of Punta Canoas is 29°23'N by 115°12.5'W.

Pangas may dart through the breakers outside Puerto Canoas 4 miles SE of Punta Canoas, but it's

Baha bash, slamming to windward across Vizcaíno Bay.

another non port, non anchorage for yatistas. As we coast SE toward Punta Blanca (32 miles SE of Canoas), the coastal shelf gets narrower and the hills retreat inland a few miles.

Roca Acme at about 29°17'N, 114°52'W is a tiny islet about 18.5 miles SE of Canoas and about a quarter mile off shore. Also called Piedra San Jose, a nav light ashore is slightly N of the rock. Some boaters report ducking in E of the rock to take advantage of calm water caused by kelp beds surrounding the rock and reef, but we haven't tried to anchor here.

From Roca Acme to Bahía Blanca, a dirt road flanks the hilly coastline. The 100-fathom curve is half a mile off shore at Punta Corbin (29°13 by 114°50'W) – bringing deep-sea fishing closer to shore.

Playa Pintada is a 2-mile beach arroyo about 10 miles SE of Roca Acme, and Punta Howard is the S end of the beach. The 2 prongs of Punta Blanca are about 4 miles SE of Punta Howard.

Punta Blanca: Our GPS approach waypoint is 20°04'N by 114°45.5'W. Punta Blanca is about 50 miles SE of Fondeadero San Carlos, 15 miles NW of Bahía Playa Maria. Punta Blanca is dark, rocky and not monumental.

Bahía Blanca under its lee is a 2-mile wide bay with fishing village tucked up into the NW corner. Light cliffs flank the E side of the main bay, 2 smaller points SE of the village straddle an arroyo, and the farthest point has a nav light tower.

Swell wraps Punta Blanca to the village beach and panga landing, but in rare calm conditions, yatistas have anchored along the bay's E flank in 25' to 35' off the S half of

the light cliffs. We've haven't had conditions calm enough to anchor here overnight – but you might get lucky.

Punta Cono (Cone) is a distinctive cone-shaped hill and low point 10 miles SE of Punta Blanca. The half-mile wide False Cove under its lee looks pretty good, and there's a village at the head of the cove, fringed in pretty beach cut by an arroyo. But again too much wave refraction invades for safe anchoring in prevailing NW conditions. Besides, a better possibility is next door.

Bahía Playa Maria

Only 5 miles SE of Punta Cono, multi-headed

Spectacularly rugged geology surrounds the N shores of Vizcaino Bay and elsewhere along Baja's Pacific coast..

Punta Maria has a road running out to its tip, which radar shows to point due S. Under its lee is Bahía Playa Maria, one of our Small Hopes.

Bahía Playa Maria (28°55.5'N, 114°33'W) lies 65 miles SE of San Carlos Anchorage, 50 miles NE of the N end of Cedros Island, 10 miles NW of Punta Negra Light and 33 miles NW of Santa Rosalillíta. We call this Playa Maria to help differentiate if from the commodious Bahía Santa Maria near Mag Bay and from other Marias in Baja.

Fishing shacks dot the first 2 beaches, but the village of San Jose de las Palomas (Doves) is a mile inland; neither have services but an improved road runs 60 miles S past Santa Rosalillíta and on to Highway 1.

The primary anchorage (18' to 28' over sand) is tucked up into the first indent, off the first sand dunes and W side of the village. The 100-fathom curve is about 3 miles off along this stretch.

Punta el Cordon (aka Punta Diablo) is a small but distinct point at the SE end of Bahía Playa Maria, about 3.75 miles SE of Punta Maria and around 2.5 miles NW of Punta Lobos.

Punta el Cordón or Diablo has a band of 60' high sand dunes draped across its midriff to a quarter mile N of its dark and lumpy S-pointing tip. In rare calm weather, a small cove E of Punta Diablo may suffice as a one-boat anchorage in 15' to 20' of water. E of the cove is an airstrip, the village of El Cordón and the seasonal Arroyo el Cordón.

COASTWISE continued

Punta Lobos, 5.5 miles SE of Punta Maria, is flat-topped and larger than Punta el Cordon. The wide bay under its lee normally has too much refractive wave action for anyone but surfers. However, in rare flat conditions some boats anchor in about 25' out in the middle.

Arroyo de Los Ojitos (Little Eyes) flanks the beach SE of Punta Lobos. The 100-fathom curve is still a good mile off shore, but it closes with shore as you approach the next point.

Punta Negra Light (28°49'N by 114°24'W) is about 10 miles SE of Playa Maria and 12.5 miles NW of Santa Rosalillíta. But Punta Negra Light is not particularly black, and it's mostly visible from the S because it stands on a smaller point about a quarter mile SE of the larger Punta Negra headland.

Adjacent to the E side of Punta Negra, El Marrón village nestles into the small bay, and the hilly foot of Sierra San Andrés shields the bay from the NW. But for ocean-going *yates*, too much swell reaches all the way in, except perhaps in those rare extended periods of flat conditions.

Punta Rocosa (Rocky) is a wide headland 7 miles NW of Santa Rosalillíta. The S end of the point shows mixed dark and light features, and the bulk of it is another leg sloping down from the 650' Sierra San Andrés inland.

In the lee E of the next small but broad point SE, the fishing village of Puerto San Andrés has a road but no services. Pangas pull up on a sheltered beach in the E corner of the bay. SE of San Andrés, the mountains retreat about 5 miles inland.

Isla Elide (40' high) is a tiny islet visible at the S end of this bay. Its E side is connected to the NW edge of Punta Santa Rosalillíta by a sandbar, so stay outside the islet. Above the bar are some metal sheds on the island's E side.

Reefs line much of Vizcaíno Bay's N shoreline.

Santa Rosalillíta

Bahía Santa Rosalillíta is a 4-mile wide bay E of the low-slung, double-headed point of the same name. This bay lies about 300 miles downhill from San Diego, 88 miles SE of Fondeadero San Carlos, 23 miles SE of Bahía Playa Maria and 58 miles ENE of the N end of Cedros Island.

Bahía Santa Rosalillíta (pronounced *roz-ah-lee-YEE-tah*) is the last of the Small Hopes of Vizcaíno, but may become the first place boats touch water after being trucked across the Baja Peninsula from LA Bay in the northern Sea of Cortez – if the Land Bridge project reaches fruition.

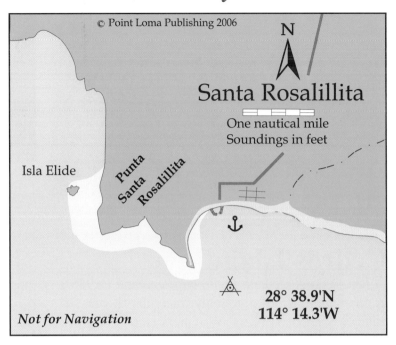

A small breakwater enclosed *darsena* (yacht basin) was built, but the plan calls for floating docks, a fuel pier and Travelift or marine ways to launch and retrieve ocean-going yachts, plus dry storage, a paved road in from Highway 1 and local services. Until there's fuel here, this is pretty far off course for N- and S-bound yatistas.

Our GPS position on the seaward end of the E breakwater is 28°39.89'N by 114°14.36'W. In fall of 2005, depth in the center of the darsena is about 15'; but sandbanks growing near the entrance show that a dredge is needed to keep it from sanding up. Check for Updates on www.MexicoBoating.com about this facility.

In calm WX, anchorage is possible in several spots around the bay. If a floating dinghy dock is built inside the darsena, the easiest spot to anchor will be just outside and W of the darsena in about 26' over sand and graveling, or from the darsena W for a few hundred yards. But out near the point is shoal.

Meanwhile, you can anchor off the village E of the darsena, in 20' to 26' of water. But it has no diesel, gas or potable water to sell to visiting yatistas, and their meager groceries are trucked from Guerrero Negro. Part of the road to Highway 1 has been paved. As we go to press, the nearest Pemex station is 28 miles inland.

Breakwater and village at Santa Rosalillíta have little to offer yatistas, but Fonatur has big plans for the Pacific terminus of a Land Bridge to transport boats across Baja.

4
Cedros Island
&
Turtle Bay

Fog or strong NW wind often keep yatistas hunkered down at the N end of Cedros.

Cedros Island

Isla Cedros (Cedars) is the largest island (3,988') in this region, and it is roughly triangular: it runs 20 miles N-S, about 3 miles E-W at the N end, to 10 miles E-W across the thicker S end. Isla Cedros Light (36 miles) stands low on the NE point, but in clear weather 2 peaks on the N half (2,742' and 3,488') are visible to S-bound boaters for 60 miles. May and June are the foggiest months.

The N end of Isla Cedros (pronounced "SAYD-rohz") lies about 135 miles SSE of Cabo San Quintín, 101 miles S of Punta Baja; the SE end of the island is 12 miles NW of Punta Eugenia, 29 miles NW of Turtle Bay. Although Cedros Island is not a destination, it's an important stepping stone.

In prevailing NW weather, the E side of Cedros Island provides 20 miles of welcome shelter and 3 roadstead anchorages. Deep water close in means you can anchor only on the narrow shelf close to the gravel beaches along this whole E side.

The W side of Cedros Island is normally less hospitable close in, but we have traversed it many times in calm weather when moving between the San Benitos Islands and Turtle Bay.

Cedros Island Yacht Club

N-bound boaters awaiting good weather to cross Vizcaíno Bay tend to accumulate at the anchorages on the NE end of the island, humorously dubbed the "Cedros Island Yacht Club." The captain of the 1st boat in becomes Commodore, the 2nd boat is Vice Commodore, and titles are handed down as boats head out.

SE of the lighthouse on the N end of the island are 2 small indentations, but the 2nd one down, about a mile S of the fishing village, usually provides better protection from NW wind and swell than does the anchorage right below the village.

*La Palmita (above) is usually green but may not have palms.
But the island terrain looks barren from off shore (left).*

We've anchored many times at about 28°20.21'N by 115°11.66'W in about 45' of water along the narrow shelf. This is usually dubbed the yacht club, but overflow spreads N and everyone is in VHF range.

Two deep arroyos with inviting beaches along the E side may provide anchorage off a slightly wider shelf, but W and NW gusts can intensify as they funnel down the arroyos, making these spots uncomfortable.

La Palmita

Manila galleons took on water from the spring that now fills the concrete cistern about a mile N of the E bulge of the island, and we've anchored here too. The Cedros water boat fills its tanks with the giant hose next to the cistern, thus supplying the only water to the seasonal fishing shacks on the N end of the island. Yatistas should not go near or tamper with this water system.

You can anchor on the very narrow 60' shelf at about 28° 09.88'N, 115° 09.32'W. The fan palms for which this canyon was named had died, then new ones sprouted.

Cedros Village

On the SE side of the island is the only real town, but the port authorities have asked that recreational boaters stop here only in emergencies. Turtle Bay nearby is a better choice.

Cedros Village is a Port of Entry for ocean-going freighters serving the towns industries: grinding fish into fertilizer and bagging it (the smell is overpowering), bagging sea salt (those 2 blindingly white piles S of the village, visible for miles) which is shipped over from Guerrero Negro's evaporation ponds, and loading those bags onto coastal freighters and barges.

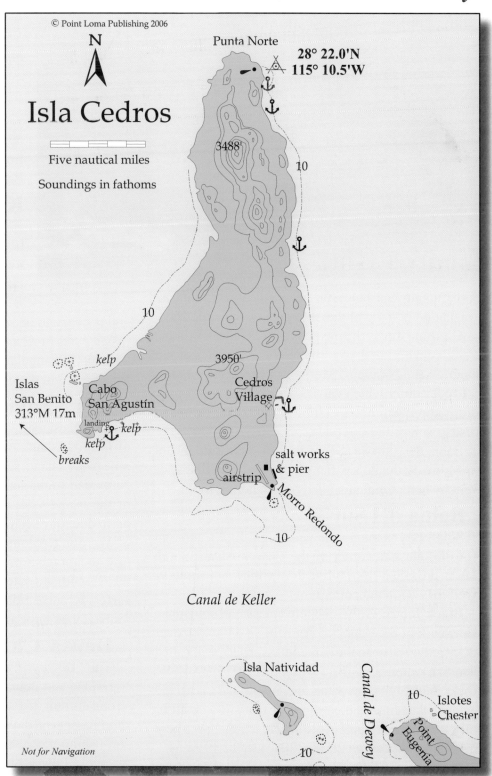

© Point Loma Publishing 2006

N

Isla Cedros

Five nautical miles

Soundings in fathoms

Punta Norte

28° 22.0'N
115° 10.5'W

3488'

10

10

3950'

Cedros Village

Islas San Benito 313°M 17m

Cabo San Agustín

kelp

landing

kelp

kelp

breaks

salt works & pier

airstrip

Morro Redondo

10

Canal de Keller

Isla Natividad

Canal de Dewey

10   Islotes Chester

Point Eugenia

10

Not for Navigation

If you must visit Cedros Village, hail "Capitania de Puerto Cedros" on VHF 16 and request permission. Anchor in 35' to 40' of water, 75 yards outside the N or S sides of the breakwater. Red and green lights mark its opening to the SE. Our GPS position in the entrance is 28°05.64'N, 115°10.99'W.

Inside the harbor, panga moorings are to port; don't leave your dinghy blocking the 500' commercial dock, seawall or high pier in the N end of the basin. The

Cedros Village brekwaters open SE, and docks are industrial quality.

Port Captain can help you get medical attention, air evacuation or a jug of diesel to get you to Turtle Bay.

Chaparritas is the next cove S of Cedros Village; it's filled with salt docks. Blazingly white piles of salt stand on the N side of Morro Redondo, the island's bold SE corner which carries Morro Redondo Light. Don't approach this operation by sea. Cedros Island airstrip is S of the salt piles.

Bahía del Sudeste (SE) is the 1.5-mile wide indent on Morro Redondo's S flanks. The last few times we went by here, freighters filled the anchoring room.

Bahía del Sur

South Bay is the 5-mile wide bight E of Cabo San Agustín, the SW corner of the Cedros Island. South Bay is protected from NE to NW winds, but some W swell may wrap the point.

Black Tooth: We've anchored in a small spot in the wide lee E of the Cabo San Agustín, in 45' to 50' over rocky gravel close to the dark tooth-shaped peak called Pico San Antonio, at about 28°04.65'N, 115°20.41'W. Rocks flank both sides of this anchorage, and a seasonal fishing village is visible ashore. If that's too small or rolly, try off the NE part of the beach; we anchored here in 45' at GPS position 28°05.27'N, 115°17.19'W.

If you round Cabo San Agustín or the next point N of it, give them both a 2-mile berth due to off-lying reefs, especially when coming down from the San Benitos toward Turtle Bay.

Keller Channel

The Keller Channel runs E-W between Cedros and Isla Natividad, 8 miles wide at that narrowest point. Depths change quickly from 280' to 28' so currents are strong and erratic, and it's easy to be set off course here. Fog is common in May and June, and Cedros' commercial traffic runs 24 hours. Triangulate on Morro Redondo Light, Punta Eugenia Light and Isla Natividad Light.

Isla Natividad

Isla Natividad (Nativity Island) lies 8 miles S of Cedros Island, 4 miles W of Punta Eugenia. This mile-wide island runs 4.5 miles NW to SE, and Isla Natividad Light house (30-mile light) is on the N side of the island's SE bulge. Give the SE side a 2-mile berth due to off-lying Lawry Shoal.

We don't recommend it, but if you must use the tiny anchorage S of Roca Plana and off the village on the SE end, it's safer to approach from due S. Gnarly surfers wrangle rides out to Natividad, and advanced scuba divers have at least 5 wrecks to explore.

Dewey Channel

The Dewey Channel runs N-S between Isla Natividad and Punta Eugenia, and this 4-mile slot has strong current, fog and traffic. We suggest running this short passage in daylight hours only, due to lobster pots and fishing nets. Favor the E side of Dewey Channel (to avoid Lawry Shoal) and pass a mile W of Punta Eugenia Light.

Black Tooth is landmark for anchorage at Cedros Island's Bahía del Sur.

Punta Eugenia (pronounced "ee-yoo-HAYN-yah") is the SW tip of Vizcaíno Bay and the extreme W end of the shallow Malarrimo Coast. A marginal anchorage is reported on the narrow shelf in the bight E of Rompiente Point's reef. From here, Turtle Bay is only 15 miles SE.

Turtle Bay

Turtle Bay is an important staging stop for rest and diesel, because it lies about halfway along the Pacific coast of the Baja California Peninsula. It's also the best all-weather bay between Ensenada (275 miles NW) and Magdalena Bay (240 miles SE). Cabo San Lucas is 400 miles SE.

The town of Turtle Bay has fewer than 1,000 people, mostly fishermen; it's been shrinking since the cannery closed in 1998. Isolated on the end of a huge peninsula, it's 135 miles of unpaved road to Highway 1. Ambiance? Turtle Bay has been called coyote ugly, but it's a relief to arrive.

Lay of the Land

Our GPS approach waypoint outside the entrance to Turtle Bay is 27°39.00'N, 114°54.00'W. From the S, don't mistake Thurloe Head (SE of the entrance) for Isla Natividad and attempt to pass E of Thurloe Head. Boats have beached after spying Turtle Bay's lights over the sand bar E of Thurloe.

Punta Sargazo Light (Kelp Point) on the N side of the entrance is a low point that rises to 871' Monte San Bartolome, for whom this port was originally named. As you enter the bay, favor the N side but keep half a mile off, due to rocks and kelp.

Avoid the 1-mile reef that runs NW from Cabo Tortolo,

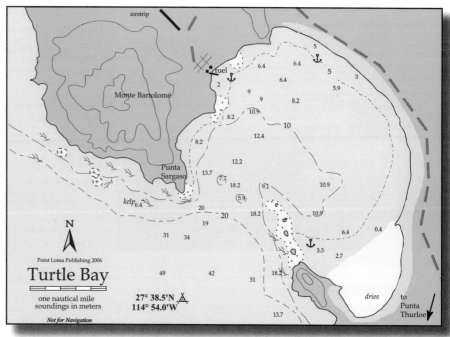

Turtle Bay's fuel pier is ancient, too high for safely fueling yates. We hope it will be replaced soon.

the peninsula enclosing the S side of the bay. From the light on Roca Ataud (Coffin Rock), the reef runs another half mile NW. Stay half a mile off the cliffs and 2nd point as you aim for the town tucked into the NW corner of this 9-square-mile bay.

Anchorages

Pier side: In prevailing NW weather, most boaters anchor in the N end of the bay, off the town beaches in 25' to 36' over good holding sand and mud. Land a dink on the beach or tie off to the metal stairs on the E side of the pier. Don't anchor too close to the pier; boats may have to take fuel there.

S side: In calm weather or a S breeze, we've anchored in the SE corner of the bay by setting the hook a quarter mile E of the lighted reef off Cabo Tortolo (Turtle Dove) in 12' to 36' over sand and shell, staying about half of a mile off the shallow beach.

A dirt road connects these few homes to the road inland and also back to town. In recent years, we've been unable to find clams here, but there's been talk of an aquaculture operation in the tidal wash behind this anchorage.

E side: Several times we've been here in a Santa Ana-like blow – ferocious wind from the E. We've found excellent shelter and holding along the NE corner of Turtle Bay, in 36' over good sand and mud. Of course, we got plastered with ochre dust from the foothills, but it was the safest place to be in such conditions. Everyone anchored off the village dragged.

You may see boats anchored just inside Punta Sargazo, but it's deep, poor holding and we've seen them drag onto the rocky shore.

Thurloe Head: Outside S of the entrance, this small cove NE of Thurloe headland has decent shelter from moderate N and NW wind, and the E side of the black reef extending off the S end of Thurloe provides good snorkeling. Anchor in 20' to 30' on sand.

The tiny meter on the fuel pump is at the end of the pier, facing out, difficult to read. Be sure it's set to 000.

Local Services

Turtle Bay is not a Port of Entry. Cedros Village has the nearest Port Captain, but the Navy battalion stationed here enforces the law.

Fuel Pier: Until Guadalupe Castillo's rickety old cannery pier is replaced, yatistas take diesel by Med-mooring off either side of its 15' high seaward end, depending on wind direction. Med-mooring (Mediterranean-style mooring) is very common throughout Mexico and Central America, so mastering the technique is important. However, this is the most awkward fuel pier in this guidebook.)

If it's windy, we hail the fuel dock on VHF 16 to get someone standing by to take our stern lines. If no one shows up, set an agile crew member off on the rickety steps. We use crossed stern lines, adding spring lines if the wind's on the beam.

Ask for the best cash price, and make sure the tiny meter is set to zero before the pump starts, or you'll pay for the last guy's diesel too. Be ready to convert gallons to liters, dollars to pesos. You pay in cash (dollars or pesos) and stuff your wad of bills into a can on a string that the fuel folks toss down and haul back up. If you want a receipt, write it yourself and have them sign it.

Fuel Panga: Anchored boats sometimes can take diesel and gasoline from stainless steel tanks delivered by various entrepreneurial pangueros. This fuel has been clean, the service fast and easy. But at press time, the fuel panga operation was temporarily shut down.

Gasoline is available at the Pemex station a mile N in the village. Some taxis will not haul you back with jerry jugs full of fuel; others will run this errand for you for a service fee.

Chandler: Turtle Bay has basic panga gear like light chain, 3-strand and outboard oil. It has more auto parts stores than groceries, due to unpaved streets and torturous roads.

High-tech payment method: Boat owner stuffs a wad of $100 bills into a can on a string.

La Purisma is one of Turtle Bay's larger stores, also has some marine items.

Provisions: Turtle Bay has 5 tiny grocery stores with a meager selection of staples and produce. Some canned goods are sold from front rooms of private homes. Local eggs, honey, avocados, oranges, tortillas and bolíllos (Baja buns) are abundant, but all else is trucked 400 miles without refrigeration.

Transportation: Not all taxis will carry gas from the Pemex station. The bus station is N of the big antennas. Buses leave daily for Vizcaíno (135 miles of dirt road), where you can catch a bigger bus N or S.

Several cantinas behind the beach berm are popular stops for yatistas and pangueros alike.

hill is also yatista friendly and sometimes has showers (sometimes hot) for about $2.

Emergency: Emergency help afloat comes from Navy battalions in Turtle Bay and Cedros Village. In Turtle, the Navy patrol may inspect papers, and some of the younger sailors try bashfully to practice their English with visiting yatistas. The Navy comandante once helped us settle a dispute with a local mechanic – in our favor.

Dr. Salvador Sanchez Santiago speaks English and his wife is a nurse. Their office and pharmacy (Farmacia Del Pueblo) is on the street running W from the gate of the old cannery. Turtle Bay has 2 small medical clinics and an ambulance. Med-evac planes have landed at Turtle Bay's paved air strip.

Telephone & Internet: The Internet Café is moving, so ask. Some cell phones work at Cedros Village and Turtle Bay, but gaps surround both. Turtle Bay has several local and international telephone offices, one at Farmacia Del Pueblo, another at the SCT office a block W of there.

Eats: Check out Maria's beach cantina W of the pier. The air-conditioned Veracruz Café atop the central

Internet shops are available even in remote places like Turtle Bay, BCN, but don't expect high-speed connections.

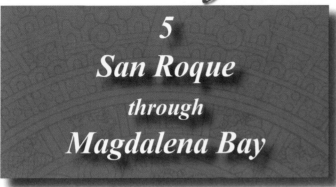

5
San Roque
through
Magdalena Bay

ROUTE PLANNING:
Turtle Bay to Magdalena Bay

From Turtle Bay to Magdalena Bay, the straight-line distance is 235 miles SE, and the first 90 miles down to Abreojos are within 20 miles of the coast. From there on, the shoreline cuts farther E, forming the second huge bight in Baja's Pacific profile.

The weather S of Turtle Bay is usually benign, but a strong NW wind can rise after noon. Close to shore the current sets you E, so pay attention. In the N section some swell wells up from deep water close to shore, but in the bight or S section, the bottom is very regular well off shore.

For passage-makers, we recommend coasting or point hopping as far as Abreojos (staying 6 miles off this point), then jumping offshore and heading directly to Cabo San Lázaro, the prominent headland you must round before approaching the entrance to Magdalena Bay. En route you'll catch dinner over Uncle Sam Banks.

The 7 places where anchorage is possible are San Roque, Asunción, Hipólito, Abreojos, Punta Pequeña and Santa Maria. However, if W or NW winds kick up big following seas, consider running 10 miles off the coast until you're S of Punta San Juanico, then tacking over for Cabo San Lázaro; that should keep the big seas more safely on your quarter.

N-bounders will lay as high a course as is comfortable. In moderate NW wind, the anchorages at Punta Pequeña and Asunción usually have better shelter than the other small bays. In a strong Norther, stay put in Mag Bay or Turtle Bay.

In mild southerly weather, tiny Isla San Roque is a possibility. In strong southerly conditions, stay put in Mag Bay or Turtle Bay.

COASTWISE: Turtle Bay to Mag Bay

The 2 fishing villages between Turtle Bay and Morro Hermosa have panga beaches but no real anchorages. Within 13 miles SW of Morro Hermosa, 3 seamounts are good spots for grouper, giant sea bass, yellowtail and yellow fin tuna. At 15 miles SW, a steep drop off brings summer tuna up from 4,000 to the shelf.

This underwater ridge runs SE to Uncle Sam Bank, an 800-square mile collection of seamounts, canyons and ridges about 60 miles S of Abreojos, which offers spectacular fishing – almost on the rhumb line between Turtle Bay and Punta San Lazaro.

But coasting SE from Turtle Bay, the landmarks are Morro Hermosa 8 miles SE of Thurloe Head, a lowering of the land, then a rise again at Punta San Pablo about 35 miles SE of Turtle Bay.

Bahía San Roque

Punta San Roque 4 miles SE of Punta San Pablo is a hilly point. Bahía San Roque E of this point has a village at the head of the bay, where the E beach begins. Anchorage can be taken off the village in 22' to 30' over sand. However, avoid the 10' shoal in the middle of the bay.

Isla San Roque Light stands on this tiny guano-covered island 3 miles SE of

The map within the text shows:

Turtle Bay

Bahía Vizcaíno

Punta San Roque

Bahía Punta Asunción

Punta San Hipolito

Punta Abreojos

Laguna San Ignacio

© Point Loma Publishing 2006

Overall
Turtle Bay
to
Mag Bay

Fifty nautical miles

Punta San Juanico

Punta Pequena

Baja California Sur

Thetis Bank

Boca de Soledad

Cabo San Lazaro

Santa Maria Cove

Puerto San Carlos

Bahía Magdalena

Not for Navigation

Asunción: Anchoring off the point is farther from the village, pier, dink landing and N anchorage.

Punta San Roque, submerged rocks lie off the E and W ends of the island, and a detached reef is usually visible less than a mile E of the island.

The small indent on the E side of Isla San Roque's low N point provides only marginal shelter from NW wind, because the island is too low and small. And the approach must be from the W, due to hazards off the island's E side.

But keep this anchorage in mind for when a storm way out in the Pacific brings SW swell to this coast.

Bahía Asunción

Bahía Asunción next door has an easier approach, a roomier anchorage with generally better shelter in prevailing conditions, and the village has some services for visiting yatistas. Bahía Asunción (pronounced "ah-soon-see-OHN") lies 50 miles SE of Turtle Bay, 50 miles NW of Punta, and 180 miles NW of Cabo San Lázaro – a logical rest stop for gunk-holers.

At 5 miles SE of Isla San Roque is the larger Isla Asunción (barren, unlighted, better radar target). It lies half a mile off Punta Asunción, which is a lower yellow sandstone point. Avoid the foul ground off the NW side and N tip of Asunción Island. Our GPS approach waypoint 2 miles SE of the island is 27°05'N, 118°16'W.

Anchorages

Village: The best shelter is off the village, which tucks onto the NE flanks of the point, below the whitish sand dune. Anywhere off the little cannery pier, you can anchor at 18' over sand. A dinghy landing is just NE of the village pier, right in the middle of town, and the beach below the village is a good place for dinghy wheels. We usually prefer to snuggle at far into this village cove as possible; our GPS at anchor is 27°08.26'N, 114°17.47'W.

A helpful former cruiser who lives ashore suggests on VHF that yatistas anchor farther SE of the pier where the pangas moor. That has good shelter from a small reef if there's any S swell, but it may be rolly in prevailing WX, it's a half-mile walk to town and shore break is worse there.

Island: Pangueros run in and out of the village and E beach all day. For more privacy, we've also anchored off Isla Asunción. In prevailing NW wind, you can anchor close E and NE of the island in 30' of water

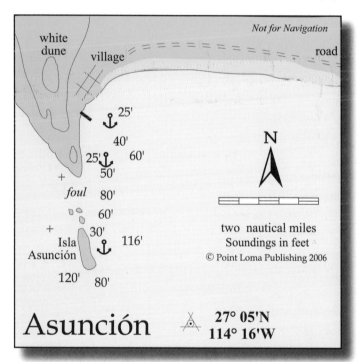

over good holding mud and sand. Note the concrete buildings and stairway.

Local Services

"Serena" on VHF 16 is the call sign of Sherry, a former Canadian cruiser who lives here with husband Juan and daughter Serena. "Serena" enjoys arranging rides for Pemex gasoline (no diesel) in jerry jugs, locating a mechanic or helping with your grocery run.

A 50-mile gravel road NE join another gravel road that runs between Turtle Bay and Highway 1 at Vizcaino. The locals are proud fishermen, and the local catch is bass, halibut and yellowtail.

Bahía San Hipólito

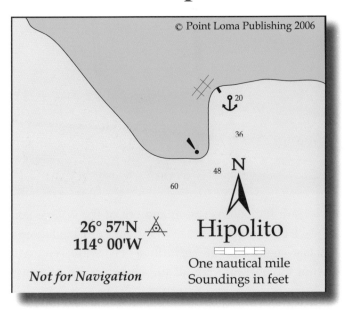

© Point Loma Publishing 2006

20

36

48 **N**

60

26° 57'N
114° 00'W

Hipolito

One nautical mile
Soundings in feet

Not for Navigation

Bahía San Hipólito is about 65 miles SE of Turtle Bay, 20 miles SE of Asunción and about 30 miles NW of the village of Abreojos. San Hipólito has no services for yatistas, but its anchorage is generally useful in prevailing winds.

The curve of Bahía Asunción is 15 miles point to point, and its SE point Punta Prieta, where there's a tiny village but no anchorage. Punta Prieta is the NW lump of the larger rounded Punta San Hipólito, which has a light tower at 26°58'N by 114°00'W. Table Mountain rises behind the larger point and San Hipólito Bay.

Black reefs with shipwreck debris extend E and W off the S end of this rounded point, so give the whole point a 1-mile berth. The village is tucked up along the NE side of the point, and its tumbled-rock beach is usually free of surf but no bueno for dinghy wheels.

The best anchorage in prevailing wind is off the village. We've anchored here in 24' of water about a mile off the village; our GPS position was 26°58.60' by 113°58.10'W.

The anchorage off downtown San Hipólito is good in NW wind.

Local fishermen have been friendly. The gravel road runs N to join a better road to Abreojos and out to Highway 1.

COASTWISE continued

By radar picture and by chart, Bahía San Hipólito looks a lot like Bahía Asunción; both ear-shaped, about 18 miles long, higher land rises behind the S end of both bays, and both their S points are not pointed.

If you're approaching this region directly from Punta San Lazaro, use our GPS positions above to confirm where you're making landfall.

La Bocana, 18 miles SE of Punta San Hipólito, is the tidal outflow of a 6-mile long, quarter-mile wide estuary, Estero La Bocana. But we recommend yatistas avoid this area due to a dangerous broken reef chain extending 3 miles S of Punta La Bocana. Pangas flit in and out, but not ocean-going yachts. In settled weather, this might make an interesting dinghy expedition from the anchorages at Abreojos.

Abreojos Light is near the village anchorage.

Punta Abreojos

Pronounced "ah-bray-OH-hoz," this word is the command to "open your eyes" – a valid warning about the 8 hazards found within the 10-fathom curve around Punta Abreojos (30 miles SE of Hipólito, 100 miles SE of Turtle Bay). Still, it offers 2 good overnight anchorages, excellent wind surfing and, if you're planning to visit whales in San Ignacio Lagoon, Abreojos is the nearest anchorage outside the regulated lagoon.

Locals who have been trained as park guides speak English. During the winter whale-spawning season, the fishermen are prohibited from setting their nets in Bahía Ballena, which extends 10 miles NE of Punta Abreojos, because it covers the shoaly entrance to the vast Laguna San Ignacio. This whole area, especially the Laguna San Ignacio, is a federal biosphere reserve for gray whales. The only winter industry in Abreojos is whale-watching tours.

Approaches

The mesa begins rising 2.5 miles N of the low point, and an abandoned lighthouse is a good landmark on this S edge of the mesa. Breakers line the shoaly W side of the point, closing off La Bocana Estuary.

Both anchorages are on the E side of Punta Abreojos and Punta Abreojos Light (26°42'N, 113°34'W), either off the large village or 2 miles farther NE off a less populated indent called Campo En Medio.

However, on approach we suggest staying outside the 30-fathom curve, swinging wide of the western hazards: the reef outside La Bocana Lagoon, Roca Ballena and La Rechinadora (both SW of the point), and Bajos Wright (S of the point). Then approaching the point and village from the SE. Keep track of the current setting toward the beaches in this region. If your draft is nearly 13', be aware also of Bajo Knepper (E of the point).

Anchorages

Village: We usually anchor a quarter mile E of the village church in 30' over sand, at our GPS position 26°42.65'N by 113°34.06'W. You can land on the panga beach NE of the church, but be aware of reefs in front of the old packing plant and by the church.

Abreojos village has about 500 houses, a Pemex station, grocery stores, Navy battalion, airstrip, renovated fish packing plant, camp grounds, small hotels, churches, schools and the region's main medical clinic.

Campo En Medio: To move to Campo En Medio's anchorage, skirt the NE shore a quarter to half mile off, going around the rocky, squarish point with a large tower assembly and the areas 3rd nav light, staying in 30' of water. A straight road runs down from the picturesque old lighthouse on the mesa, ending in the little settlement at Campo En Medio. A palapa-roofed RV shelter and new homes are good landmarks.

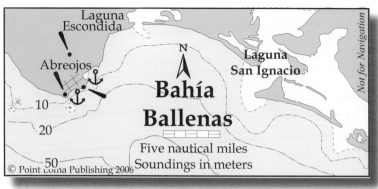

We anchor off this beach in 30' over sand and shell, at our GPS position 26°43.99'N, 113°32.63'W.

Laguna San Ignacio

San Ignacio Lagoon Biosphere Reserve is a regulated preserve (also the smaller Estero el Coyote

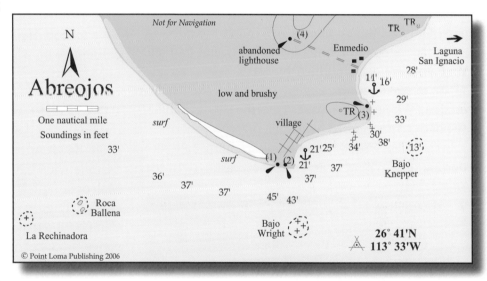

or Escondida closer to Abreojos), so you cannot take your own vessel or dinghy inside; we recommend anchoring off Abreojos and booking one of the half dozen licensed naturalists guides in their covered pangas, inflatables or kayaks. Don't anchor just outside either entrance to Laguna San Ignacio, or you'll be

Near Laguna San Ignacio, this Campo En Medio anchorage has new homes & RV palapa.

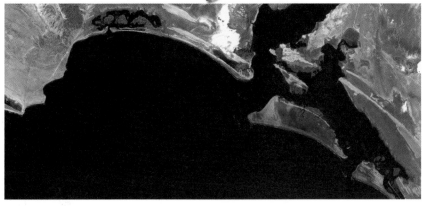

Satellite image shows Punta Abreojos and entrance to San Ignacio Lagoon, where whale-watching is the best in Baja.

altering the passage of the very whales we all come here to observe and protect.

The best time to visit Laguna San Ignacio is December 15 through February, but we've had good luck as late as May. The N end of Laguna San Ignacio is connected to Highway 1 by gravel road, and 3 villages there also operate licensed whale-watching tours. Only a limited number of visitors are allowed inside the lagoon at a time, including N end tourists. After your guide is notified by VHF, you enter the lagoon in small groups, explore and watch the whales for about 4 hours, then leave. Thus the shy leviathans are not overly disturbed by human presence.

In the deeper S half of the lagoon, adult whales are courting and mating or training the yearlings. In the shallower N half, mothers give birth and suckle their newborn calves. Look for spouts, spy-hopping, fluke flapping, and eye-balling the turistas. You might get lucky enough to pet a wild whale. This is a remarkable experience for youngsters and oldsters alike. Take your video and still camera, long lenses, binoculars, lunch and water.

Caution: The waters around Abreojos are ground zero for pods of whales entering and leaving the lagoon from all directions, so keep your eyes peeled. We often have to stop dead in the water or alter course to avoid colliding with whales around here and off the entrance to Mag Bay.

COASTWISE continued

From the Abreojos area, stay about 5 miles off shore down to Punta Pequeña. Bahía Ballenas is the 14-mile wide bay between Punta Abreojos and Punta Malcomb on Isla Arena, the larger of 2 barrier islands outside Laguna San Ignacio. About 6 miles NE of Campo En Medio is Rene's RV Camp and the shoaly panga entrance to Estero el Coyote. Isla Pitahaya is the second barrier island to the whale preserve, and its SE tip is about 26 miles ESE of Punta Abreojos.

Estero el Datil is a small estuary opening 10 miles ESE of Isla Pitahaya, and green mangroves N of and behind its Barra San Juan barrier peninsula may be visible from off shore. Mesa Azufreta gradually closes with the coast.

Punta Santo Domingo 12 miles NW of Punta Pequeña is a conspicuous rise of dark lava cliffs with flat top. It makes a good radar target, but we haven't tried to sound the little indents near the main point. As the shore lowers again, 2 small arroyos break the beach NW of Punta Pequeña.

Windsurfers flock to Punta Abreojos during winter Northers.

Punta Pequeña

Punta Pequeña (pronounced "pay-KAYN-yah") lies only 12 miles SE of Punta Santo Domingo, 66 miles SE of Abreojos, 166 miles SE of Turtle Bay, and 90 miles N of Cabo San Lázaro. Bahía San Juanico (same name as a popular anchorage in the Sea of Cortez) is the sheltered bay just E of Punta Pequeña Light – not the next bay 15 miles farther SE at Punta San Juanico, which has no anchorage.

We use Punta Pequeña's Bahía San Juanico anchorage mostly when we're N-bound in NW wind, because it's generally where we intercept land when laying a reasonable course up from Cabo San Lázaro. This is the best windy-weather overnight anchorage between Turtle and Mag.

Low, sandy and broad, Punta Pequeña has breakers along its SW side and a nav light (26°14.'2'N by 112°29.3'W) on its SE bulge. Stay a mile off this point and don't cut NW until you're past the tan sand dunes and black lava shelf that detaches at high tide.

Then you can anchor off the town in 15' to 20' over sand and broken shell, about a third of a mile NE of the lava shelf and a third of a mile SE of the white cemetery monuments. They stand on a 50' volcanic ridge NE of the town. We've anchored at GPS position 26°15.23'N by 112°28.21'W, and the dinghy and panga landing is below the old cannery buildings, where there's a path up through the ridge.

Or you could anchor in deeper water S of the long beach NE of the town; another foot path leads up.

The village of Bahía San Juanico is pleasant and has a medical clinic, airstrip, plaza and power plant, but only emergency gas and meager provisions. The nearest city is Villa Insurgentes, 80 miles SE on mostly gravel roads along the W side of Baja's Sierra de la Giganta Mountains.

COASTWISE continued

From Punta Pequeña, the coastline curves 15 miles S to little Punta San Juanico, which has no real bay or anchorage, just a fish camp called La Bocana and small estuary. From here S, the Giganta mountains part with the coast, the shore is low and sandy all the way around to Cabo San Lazaro, and the bottom is a 100' curve is about 4 miles off shore.

Thetis Bank rises to 118' and 36' about 18 miles NW of Cabo San Lázaro. It's where to go for marlin,

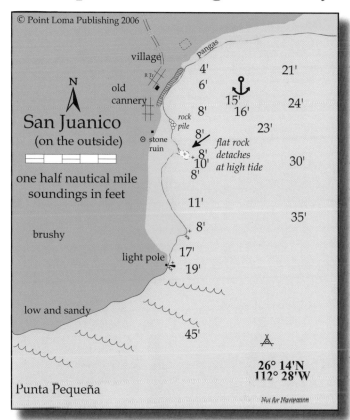

© Point Loma Publishing 2006

San Juanico
(on the outside)

one half nautical mile
soundings in feet

village
pangas
old cannery
R Tr
rock pile
stone ruin
flat rock detaches at high tide
brushy
light pole
low and sandy

4' 21'
6'
15' 24'
8' 16'
23'
8'
8' 30'
10'
8'
11' 35'
8'
17'
19'
45'

26° 14'N
112° 28'W

Punta Pequeña

Not for Navigation

dorado, wahoo, yellowtail, yellow fin and giant sea bass. We've seldom failed to snag breakfast, lunch or dinner here.

Similar to the Malarrimo Coast but not so extreme, here you'll find breakers 2 miles off the low, almost invisible coast.

Small openings of Estero de Soledad are almost invisible features in the 80 miles between Punta San Juanico and Cabo San Lazaro. At 25 and 33 miles S of Punta San Juanico, there's Boca las Animas and Boca de Santo Domingo, both shoal and obscured in breakers.

Boca de Soledad

Boca de Soledad, cloaked in breakers, is another shallow entrance to Estero de Soledad, a long and narrow estuary that meanders behind the beach berm for 30 miles SW toward Cabo San Lázaro and ends

Fishing is always worthwhile around Thetis Bank.

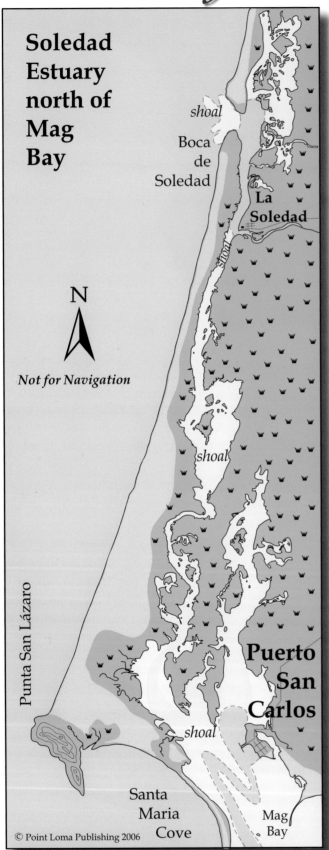

Soledad Estuary north of Mag Bay

shoal

Boca de Soledad

La Soledad

N

Not for Navigation

shoal

Punta San Lázaro

shoal

Puerto San Carlos

shoal

Santa Maria Cove

Mag Bay

© Point Loma Publishing 2006

NW of Puerto San Carlos in Mag Bay.

Our GPS stand-off waypoint 1.5 miles W of Boca de Soledad is 25°16.56'N, 112°10.07'W.

This mouth is of possible interest only to shallow-draft skippers who first hire a local guide to lead them through the dangerous shoals and breakers – if any entrance exists on that day. The fishing village of La Soledad is inside the estuary a few miles S of the boca, where you may see a crane working. Hail a guide on VHF-16 while you're standing well off the breakers. Beaches on either side are littered with shipwreck debris.

The estuary passage is not a short cut around Cabo San Lazaro. It's slow going, and shallow spots change after each heavy rain. We made a map of Estero de Soledad from satellite imagery, but soundings change too frequently for charting.

If you're hoping to explore Estero de Soledad by shallow-draft yacht, dinghy or kayak, it's much safer to start from inside Mag Bay. It starts N of the first leg of the channel to Puerto San Carlos and meanders through mangroves and brushy islands. Plan a full-day round-trip exploration of both legs of the estuary and take mosquito repellant.

In an emergency, if you have to ride out a hurricane in Estero de Soledad, don't attempt the boca, because it will be spouting. Instead, approach the estuary from Puerto San Carlos and enter the eastern leg, which affords more protection.

COASTWISE continued

Isla Magdalena: S of Boca de Soledad is Isla Magdalena, a 50-mile long barrier island that twists and turns, sometimes steep and mountainous, sometimes low and narrow, that encloses the N end of Magdalena Bay.

Punta San Lázaro (pronounced "LAH-sah-roh") is the significant turning headland, marking the end of Pacific Baja's S bight and the start of the Mag Bay region. Cabo San Lázaro (1,275' high) and its nav light on the NW tip (24°47.7'N, 112°18.5'W) are welcome sights 125 miles SE of Turtle Bay, especially amid all this shallow water and low land. Due to current and wind, we give this large cape a 4-mile berth.

Bahía Santa Maria

Bahía Santa Maria is formed by Magdalena Island's largest twist and low spot. This excellent deep-water bay is entered between rugged Punta Hughes (4 miles SE of Cabo San Lázaro) and Cabo Corso (7 miles SE of Punta Hughes). For an easy in, easy out rest stop, we normally prefer Santa Maria to Mag Bay. There's

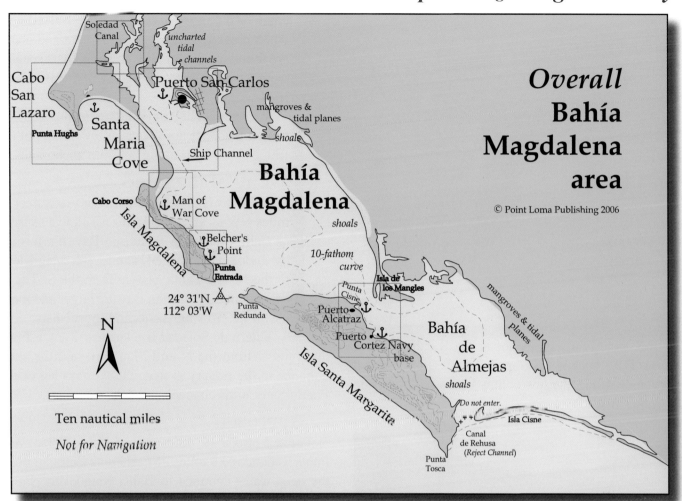

Overall **Bahía Magdalena area**

© Point Loma Publishing 2006

Cabo San Lazaro

Punta Hughs

Soledad Canal

uncharted tidal channels

Puerto San Carlos

mangroves & tidal planes

shoals

Santa Maria Cove

Ship Channel

Bahía Magdalena

Cabo Corso

Man of War Cove

Belcher's Point

Punta Entrada

Isla Magdalena

shoals

10-fathom curve

Isla de los Mangles

mangroves & tidal planes

24° 31'N
112° 03'W

Punta Redunda

Punta Cisne

Puerto Alcatraz

Puerto Cortez Navy base

Bahía de Almejas

shoals

Isla Santa Margarita

Do not enter.

Isla Cisne

Canal de Rehusa (Reject Channel)

Punta Tosca

N

Ten nautical miles

Not for Navigation

room for a navy to safely swing here, but give Punta Hughes a half mile berth when entering.

In prevailing NW weather, the best yacht anchorage is in the NW corner off the fishing village and lagoon entrance. We've anchored in 21' at GPS position 24°46.27'N, 112°15.52'W. Gusts may bridge the low spot, but this is good-holding sand.

If you want to land through the shore break, aim for the W side of the lagoon entrance. From there a trail runs W of mangroves to the outside NE beach and ends at Cabo San Lázaro lighthouse. The E rim of Santa Maria is so low you can see right into Mag Bay and watch ships maneuver the inside channel to Puerto San Carlos.

Tales from Punta San Lazaro

Punta San Lázaro has a shallow but regular sandy bottom and a strong E-setting current that can sweep the unwary into the shallows NE of the point.

In 1870, the massive side-wheeler "Golden City" was en route to San Francisco when she smashed up on the beach with all hands and crew – and an enviable treasure in golden bars. It's said that lifeboats were launched by Captain Comstock, but during the scramble for limited seats, fighting broke out. One James Murphy and several passengers were reportedly killed – by sabers.

Once the survivors were safely ashore on Isla Magdalena, they began imagining the pangs of death by starvation in a savage land. So when an unfortunate dairy cow strolled over the dunes from a nearby village, it was immediately seized, butchered and consumed – along with several casks of salvaged brandy. Captain Comstock did save most of his passengers and all his golden cargo, but pounding surf broke "Golden City" in half.

Today, a few of the hundido's weathered keel bones are still visible in the shallow water SW of Boca de Soledad, and the nearby beach yields bits of corroded silverware and crockery shards. If you beach-comb here, keep an eye out for James Murphy and his ghostly cohorts who can never disembark in San Francisco.

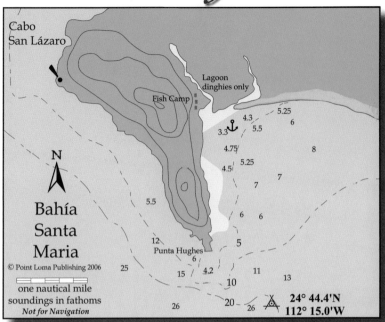

In S wind, yatistas anchor in the S end of Santa Maria Bay, tucked as far E as possible behind Howland's Bluff, the low yellow banks on the E side of Cabo Corso.

Santa Maria Bay's low spot sometimes gets gusty but this area is a reliable ancorage in NW wind.

You can anchor at about 24°40.5'N, 112°09.3'W in 15' to 20' of water. We've watched trucks unload fishing pangas here, on the 2.25-mile road over to an airstrip, Navy outpost and village of Puerto Magdalena in Man of War Cove, all inside Mag Bay.

Magdalena Bay

Bahía Magdalena (pronounced "mahg-dah-LAY-nah") is affectionately known to yatistas as Mag Bay. It lies about 245 miles SE of Turtle Bay and 160 miles NW of Cabo San Lucas, so it's logistically the primary rest stop in the S half of Pacifica Baja.

Puerto San Carlos in the N end is a port of entry, so if S-bound boats haven't already cleared into Mexico at Ensenada, they'll have to do so before being allowed to fuel here. Fuel and services are available at the commercial port at the end of a tricky channel, so we don't think of this as an easy in, easy out fuel stop.

Mag Bay is an excellent fishing destination; we

count on dorado and wahoo for lunch and dinner when passing by, and snook, halibut and clams are found inside. Smaller cruising boats spend a week or more gunk-holing around inside Mag Bay.

We once spent 9 days hiding inside Mag Bay from a whopper hurricane, safely riding out the fringe bands by moving between anchorages.

Lay of the Land

Mag Bay is a huge enclosed body of water (25 miles NW to SE, 13 miles E-W) almost as large as California's San Francisco Bay. It's formed by 2 elongated barrier islands, Isla Magdalena to the N, Isla Santa Margarita to the S. The N end and middle of Mag Bay are larger and more useful for cruising yachts and sportfishers.

Estero de Soledad is a shallow 2-leg estuary that runs N from the N end Mag Bay, and the safer entrance to the estuary is from the western leg of the Puerto San Carlos channel.

Approach

Punta Entrada (9 miles SE of Cabo Corso) and Punta Redonda (3.5 miles ESE of Punta Entrada) mark the deep-water entrance to Bahía Magdalena. Punta Redonda Light (24°31'N, 112°00.7'W) has a racon, not always working. Roca Vela pinnacle close to Punta Entrada looks like a sailboat. Avoid rocks off Punta Redonda.

Our GPS approach waypoint to the entrance of Mag Bay is 24°31.5'N, 112°03.5'W. In this 2.5-mile wide entrance, the long-shore current mixes with tidal flow from the huge bay, and it builds larger seas; we aim for the middle and push in quickly. Every year, some unwary yatista gets sucked onto Punta Entrada, so please steer clear.

Caution: Do not attempt to enter Almejas Bay through what may at first look like an entrance on the SE end of Isla Margarita. That wide opening is Canal Rehusa (Refusal Channel), a rocky white-water rapids foul with fishnets.

Anchorages

Punta Entrada: Just inside the N end of Mag Bay and within a quarter mile NW of Punta Entrada (24°32'N, 112°04'W), this small indent has pretty good shelter and room for one boat to anchor in about 30' of water off the seasonal fishing shacks and landmark shrine. In a strong NW blow, wind can funnel down the draw between hills. Current and swell can affect this toe hold, but it's a handy place to roost before an early morning departure N or S.

Belcher's Point

This low sandy half-mile triangular point lies 3 miles N of Punta Entrada. It's the easiest in and out, enjoys good shelter of 1,250' Mt. Isabel and you can anchor on whichever side suits your shelter needs. Concrete pilings and a pillbox are remnants of a phosphorus loading dock, but they still make good radar targets.

Off the S side of Belcher's Point, we often anchor in 15' to 20' of water at GPS position 24°35.12'N, 112°04.29'W. This is just outside the sandy and regular 12' shelf, which is not as wide as DMA charts show. It gets a bit of roll if the weather outside is nasty. On the N side of the point, anchor in about 30' over good sand and shell. Landing the dink is easy, and deserted Belchers' Point is the best place to run a dog.

Belcher's once housed a whaling station named after Edward Belcher, the British commander who first sounded Mag Bay, but it's uninhabited today.

Man of War Cove

Belcher's Point has remnants of several businesses, here with red longastina casings washing ashore.

Man of War Cove and its village of Puerto Magdalena are 8 miles NW of Punta Entrada. Spanish charts call it Caleta del Acorazado (Battleship Cove).

We anchor in 25' to 30' of water at 24°38.09'N, 112°80.13'W off the Man of War Light tower in the center of the village. But in a strong NW blow, wind can cross the barrier island from the S end of Santa Maria, and this isn't the best holding.

Puerto Magdalena's desalination plant supplies potable water for the region's many remote fishing villages, so the 60' long pier is always busy. The few trucks you see here were ferried to this island from Puerto San Carlos on a home-made barges. The older one flipped with someone's pickup aboard. Several new barges shuttle between here and the real port.

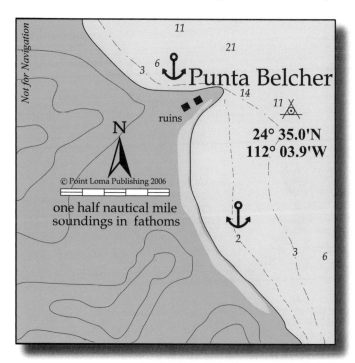

We discourage yatistas from clamming here, because the locals' resources are very limited and municipal sanitation is zilch.

Punta Delgado: If you're anchored off Puerto Magdalena and N wind over the berm from Bahía Santa Maria makes you drag, consider crossing the bay and tucking up in 15' to 20' of water off the N beach, just SW of the Punta Delgado knob.

This is the widest part of the barrier beach and it's not a lee shore. Unless you must be near the village, it's cleaner and quieter here. Shallower water is found off the airstrip and tiny Howland's Lagoon.

Mag Bay begins to shoal up NE of Punta Delgado, and the channel starts about 1.5 miles W of here.

Puerto San Carlos Channel

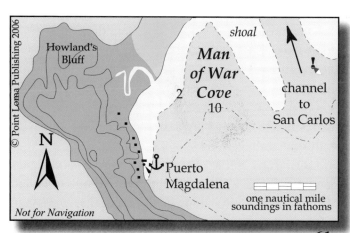

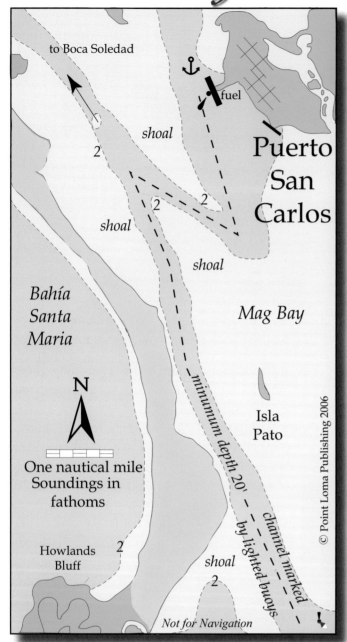

The narrow, 8.75-mile, N-shaped channel (12' depth) to Puerto San Carlos' commercial pier and anchorage starts at a lighted buoy 10 miles NNW of Punta Entrada (or 3 miles NE of Man of War Cove), close alongside Punta Delgado (Narrow Point).

Tune your radar and depth sounder, and get a good handle on the 3 legs before entering, because there's often a lot of current, and the buoys marking the channel are sometimes paired, or not, sometimes numbered out of sequence, or missing. The 1' shoals alongside the channel are easier to see at low tide with high sun.

Leg 1 runs NNW along the mangroves and sandy berm for about 4.75 nm. From here, if you continued NW you'd be approaching the S end of the W passage

(about 5' depth) through Estero de Soledad.

Leg 2 angles back SE for about 2 miles. This is the narrowest part. Before Buoy 4, you may see pangas using a shortcut channel that angles N, but it's even shallower, narrower, curved and unmarked – except perhaps by the latest mishap.

Using radar, when you're 2 miles SSE of the W tip of the warehouse sheds, turn again NNW for Leg 3 to the pier.

Puerto San Carlos

The port's piers were recently extended and shore facilities beautified for cruise ship passengers who someday will disembark shuttles for sportfishing.

N and W of the renovated piers, the large anchorage basin is backed by mud shoals, mangroves and only a few rusting hulks, because it's recently been cleared of hazards. N of the anchorage, Canal de Banderitas is the dead-end E leg of Estero de Soledad, and its side lobes can provide a hurricane crash spot.

Local Services

Puerto San Carlos is a Port of Entry, so you can clear into Mexico here – but it's not nearly as easy as Ensenada or Cabo. If S-bound yatistas come in for fuel but haven't done their international arrival in Ensenada, they'll have to do it here before fueling.

Migración and Aduana are on the pier, and they may ask to see your papers before letting you through the gate to town. They may hail a taxi for you. The Capitanía is 1.5 miles NW of the pier. If you can't get a taxi (the streets are not paved), walk NE for half a mile along the S side of the commercial facilities, then NE on Chamela past Rosalia and Campeche. Turn right on Acapulco and go 2 blocks. The Capitanía is S of the church on the plaza. Then head back to the pier for Migración and Aduana.

Fuel: Ask the Port Captain to help you make arrangements to take fuel, usually from a tank truck that comes to the pier. Be sure to tell them what size deck fills you have and how fast you can take fuel. They're used to commercial vessels.

Once the pier boss knows how much fuel you're taking, he'll direct you to the right spot on whichever pier you'll take it from. Use your largest fenders and longest dock lines, and if you're lying alongside camels you may need a gangplank.

Be prepared for very fast fuel flow unless you

convinced them otherwise.

Shrimpers normally raft alongside each other at a dock, and crew members clamber over the inner boats to pass the fuel hose and schlep their catch ashore. If you value your topsides, decks and privacy, we suggest that you do not let a rusty shrimper or commercial fisherman tie up along side you unless the Port Captain requires it.

If you need only a few jerry jugs of diesel or gas, at the S end of Calle Chamela is a Pemex gas station.

"Mar de Arena" is a gringo on VHF 16; you can hire him as a guide for navigating the port channel or Estero de Soledad channel, for fishing, diving and birding, or he may ferry fuel to your anchored boat.

Supplies: E of the port facilities, the dusty town on a low sandy peninsula has 2 basic chandlers or hardware stores, a grocery store, Pemex station, airstrip, 2 medical clinics, an oceanographic research station that doubles as a fishing resort, and bus service to 40 miles to Ciudad Constitución. RVs and trailer boaters camp and launch over the sand at the SE tip of the peninsula.

Eats: Hotel Alcatraz has a good restaurant and bar in their jungle patio, also a long distance phone. Go to the N end of Chamela, turn right for a short block, left for a short block, then right onto San Jose del Cabo. At the far end of this block is the brightly painted Hotel Alcatraz; don't judge by the exterior.

Puerto Alcatraz

Leaving the N end of Mag Bay and looking S, the first anchorage for yatistas is at Puerto Alcatraz on Isla Santa Margarita.

In the middle part of Mag Bay, Puerto Alcatraz lies 10.7 miles ESE of Punta Redonda, at the S end of the 1.25-mile wide Gaviota Channel between large shoals.

From the middle of the entrance to Mag Bay, come to 087°T for about 8.7 miles, lining up on the range markers on Isla Mangla. If the buoy is gone, look SE for your next ranges. Find the arrow outlined by white rocks on the hillside just S of Puerto Cortez; get the 2 white structures lined up below the arrow for a heading

of about 154°T.

Punta Cisne (Swan) is the low, sandy, hook-shaped peninsula jutting W into the channel. SW of Punta Cisne you can anchor off the village, S of the stubby pier that juts S from the industrial buildings. There's 30' of water at our GPS position 24°30.48'N, 111°50.31'W, and it's sheltered by a 1,683' island peak.

Fragrance from the new fish processing plant on

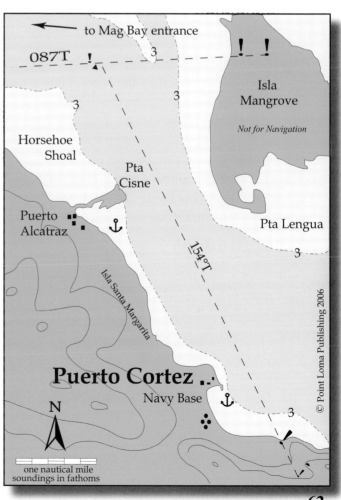

Puerto San Carlos marine research station and sportfishing resort has coconut palms and Tahitian huts.

sandbar closing off the very S end of Almejas Bay. A narrow panga channel breaches the W end of Isla Cresiente.

Playa Independence: Outside Mag Bay, on the E side of mountainous Punta Tosca, a precarious anchorage may be found about a mile NE of Punta Tosca Light, on a narrow shelf below the ravine and rocky beach called Playa Independence. This is tenable only in very calm conditions.

Punta Cisne occasionally reaches this anchorage. Another new fish factory is visible on Punta Lengua (Tongue) across the channel.

Puerto Cortez

Puerto Cortez is a better anchorage 3 miles SE of Puerto Alcatraz, and it's also a better hurricane hole. We've tried 'em all.

Visitors can anchor S of the longer Navy pier in 26' to 30' near our GPS position 24°28.42'N by 111°48.98W'.

Yatistas are welcome to anchor here, but don't go ashore without being invited by the Navy. They'll call on VHF-16 and may come out to check papers. They have helped us and other yatistas solve emergency mechanical problems, and we compared charts with the most courteous El Comandante while riding out the edge of a hurricane here. Outside the Navy gate, the village is pleasant but has no services.

From Mag Bay's solitude to Cabo's hum is only a 155-mile voyage - but a whole different world.

Bahía Almejas

S of Puerto Cortez is Bahía Almejas (Clams Bay) is so shoal around all edges that it's sometimes 3 quarters dry. A navigable 4-mile patch that opens 2 miles E of Puerto Cortez has depths of 50' or more. It's not protected from wind or current, but it's a great lunch stop for clamming, birding, kayaking, shelling, fishing, etc.

3 10' deep coves E of Isla Mangla are good for skiff fishing, kayaking and dinghy exploration. Trailer boating fish camps are at Estero Salina, Puerto Viejo, Puerto Chale and Puerto Datil. All are dry at low tide, and the later 2 have views across to Isla Cresiente, the

ROUTE PLANNING Mag to Cabo San Lucas

Top off with fuel and water, because no anchorages or services are available to ocean-going yachts in the 155 miles between Punta Tosca and Cabo San Lucas. Marine weather S of Mag Bay generally grows warmer, dryer and less windy. Going either direction, we usually run within 5 miles of shore. Distant storms in the mid Pacific bring big swell here.

S-bound, the hills rise to Sierra de la Laguna and on a clear night passage you may see the loom of La Paz and then Cabo over the mountains. You pass miles of open roadstead and a few beaches where pangas drag ashore, but no significant off-lying dangers and no shelter for anchoring. In dire emergency, the town of Todos Santos is the first or last sight of Highway 1; Todos Santos Light is 23°26.9'N, 110°14.6'W.

Cabo Falso suffers from "cape effect" – strong current and higher wind. We try to schedule this turn for late night to early morning, anytime but mid afternoon when local wind peaks.

COASTWISE Mag Bay to Los Cabos

The low spot on Isla Santa Margarita is often mistaken for another entrance, especially viewed from SW. In 1920, a US submarine grounded and sank reportedly 9.75 miles NW of Punta Tosca.

Punta Tosca (524') the bladelike S tip of Isla Santa Margarita deserves a 1-mile berth. Many ships wreck here, mistaking Canal Rehusa as an entrance to Mag Bay. (See previous section.)

The Magdalena Escarpment runs NW to SE paralleling the Baja coastline about 45 miles off shore, and numerous seamounts and deep fingers create world-class fishing grounds year round. Roca Pinaculo seamount is 8 miles SSW of Punta Tosca, and around this 132' deep pinnacle are marlin, yellowtail, giant sea bass and yellowfin tuna. Three Spot is a 20'-deep rise 20 miles SE of Punta Tosca, also rewarding.

Lusitania Banks (23°37'N, 111°42'W) and Finger Banks (23°18'N, 110°35'W) are lucky spots offshore on the way down from Mag Bay. Rooster fish are taken off the beaches. This escarpment eventually narrows at the Golden Gate Banks and St. Jaime Banks W of Cabo Falso. We often see migrating grays and other whales year round on this huge shelf.

Isla Cresiente beach runs SE, regular and almost unbroken for 150 miles to Cabo San Lucas, providing safe coastal cruising 2 to 10 miles off. Sage and cactus cover the sandy foothills. Punta Conejo Light marks a small arroyo, and Punta Marquez Light marks a half-mile rocky projection.

Todos Santos Light (23°26.9'N, 110°14.6'W) is 40 miles NNW of Cabo Falso. Todos Santos shows a palm oasis N of town, but only steep panga beaches. Cerro Picacho (4,300') and lesser Cerro Aguja (needle) of the Sierra de la Laguna range are visible 15 miles E of Punta Lobos.

Cabo Falso Light (22°52.7'N, 109°57.6'W) is a bit E of the abandoned lighthouse on Cabo Falso, appropriately named, so don't turn yet. Go 4 miles E, passing a low beach with hotels on the cliffs and shoreline. Land's End is rocky and the photogenic "arches" let you peek into the bay before rounding them half a mile off. Avoid swimmers, scuba divers and kayakers as you enter the bay.

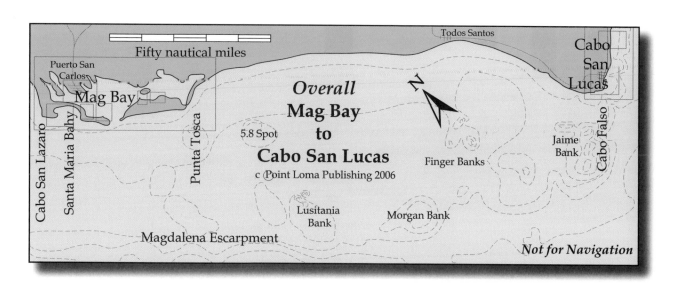

Overall Mag Bay to Cabo San Lucas
c Point Loma Publishing 2006

Not for Navigation

Mexico Boating Guide

6
Los Cabos

Los Cabos

Cabo San Lucas, affectionately known as "Cabo," lies 720 miles SE of San Diego, 155 miles SE of Magdalena Bay, and 150 miles S of La Paz around the East Cape. More than 25,000 recreational boaters visit this tropical paradise each year, and for those of us who arrive from the N by private yacht, Cabo's warmth and welcoming ambiance are our first real rewards for the months of preparation and rugged coastal voyaging required to get here.

As you enter Bahía San Lucas (St. Luke Bay), you may be greeted by whales spouting, bill fish leaping and the exotic fragrance of flowers and sage, roasting tortillas and wood-fired ovens – a welcome to weary sea farers for more than a century. Of course, 20-deck cruise ships and a fleet of glass-bottom pangas packed with lily-white tourists will greet you as well.

"But I thought we were going to Los Cabos," cried a young crewmember. The marketing term "Los Cabos" refers collectively to the towns of Cabo San Lucas and San Jose del Cabo, the next town E. San Jose del Cabo, or San Jose to locals, SJC for brevity, has the international airport and a new marina basin; the Highway 13 corridor linking the 2 cabos is stuffed so full of resort hotels and golf courses that nobody under 30 can tell you where Cabo ends and San Jose begins.

Cabo San Lucas

Cabo has marinas, moorings, anchorage, fuel, chandlers, groceries, haul-out yard, repair service, ground transportation and more than 100 restaurants and bars. While coasting down Baja California, we boaters have had virtually no place to spend money. The opposite is true in Cabo. The Baja Ha Ha has traditionally ended here, but due to Cabo's high prices and slip shortage, many cruising boats opt to push on

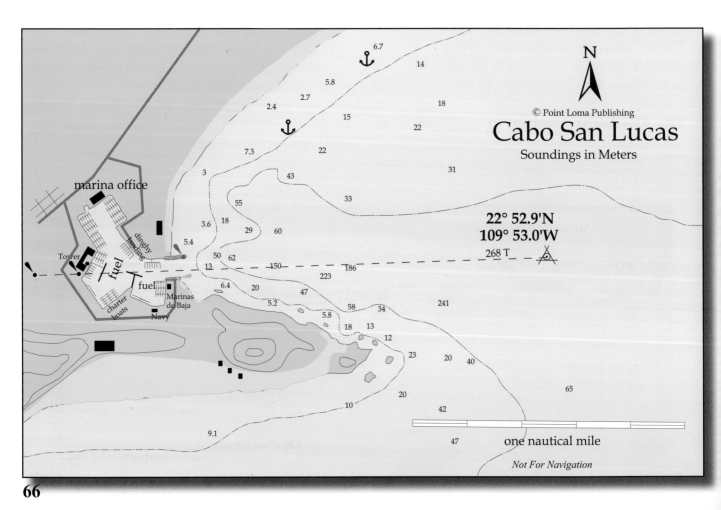

© Point Loma Publishing

Cabo San Lucas
Soundings in Meters

22° 52.9'N
109° 53.0'W
268 T

one nautical mile

Not For Navigation

The famous Arches at Land's End are cracked and being cemented in place.

toward La Paz, Mazatlán or Puerto Vallarta where their cruising kitties last longer.

San Jose del Cabo is tranquil and traditional, a bit of old Spain at its center, but fast expanding into the tourism overflow from Cabo. The new marina harbor in SJC will relieve the slip shortage and give sportfishing boats another base of operations a bit closer to Gordo Banks. Many sportfishing charter boats work "the Cape" year round, but summer brings on bill-fishing tournaments. World cruising motoryachts consider Los Cabos a must do, but more are venturing up the Sea of Cortez these days.

We've been stopping here for fuel since 1978, and the old-dude boaters hanging out here then told us that Cabo was already ruined by developers. Yet it seldom fails to enchant first-timers.

Lay of the Land

Cabo San Lucas has a natural bay, Bahía San Lucas, plus a man-made harbor. San Jose del Cabo has a man-made harbor 15 miles E of Cabo San Lucas.

Cabo: Bahía San Lucas is 2.25 miles wide and has very deep water in the center ringed by a narrow sandy anchoring ledge. The bay's NW corner has good shelter from winter's prevailing NW weather, so it's filled with rental moorings for about 120 yachts large and small. The free anchorage covers the 15' to 40' shelf along the N and E end of the bay. Shore boats ferry yatistas between moorings and inner harbor.

Bahía San Lucas is wide open to the S and E. Although 80% of summer brings flat seas, wind and swells from tropical storms come right into the anchorage.

Cabo's man-made yacht harbor or darsena is divided into 3 sections; as you enter from sea they are the outer harbor, the middle basin and the N end. Enter the darsena's outer harbor between lighted jetties. To port is the first marina which may reopen its fuel dock, then Navy base; to starboard is the primary dinghy

landing and shore-boat dock.

A huge, striped and T-shaped commercial mole divides the outer harbor from the middle basin. The mole was built to lessen surge, but it sure cramps maneuvering room for larger boats. Pangas and excursion boats line its sides, and trinket stalls fill the top. Cruise-ship shore boats unload passengers on this mole as well.

The middle basin has more panga docks, a large fuel dock and Med-mooring slots for big boat of the second marina you come to.

The N end is smaller, packed with residential slips of the second marina. At the N end of the fairway is a launch ramp and the Travelift platform for the boat yard a few hundred feet away.

The saddle in the Pedregal hills W of the inner harbor was opened by a hurricane, but the peaks still protect the darsena from W wind. Runoff from heavy rain drains into the darsena's N end. The landscaped paseo or pedestrian walkway surrounds the darsena, and the malecon is the Boulevard Marina, the street running along the harbor. You don't have to wander far past the paseo and malecon to find lots of action.

Cabo's inner harbor looking out.

Mexico Boating Guide

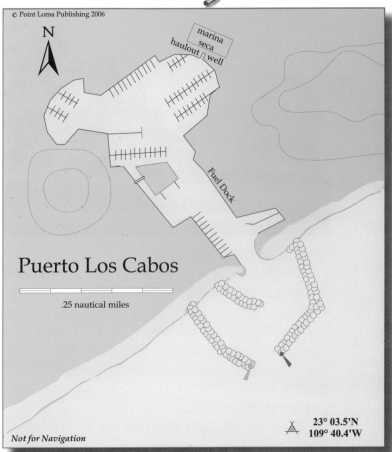

© Point Loma Publishing 2006

N

Puerto Los Cabos

.25 nautical miles

Not for Navigation

23° 03.5'N
109° 40.4'W

San Jose del Cabo

Just past Punta Palmilla, the new harbor of The Marina at Puerto Los Cabos is the only feature of significant interest to ocean-going yachts at San Jose. While coasting E about 14 miles from Cabo, you'll see the highway hotel corridor turn inland at San Jose, because it can't bridge Estero San Jose.

The entrance to the new marina harbor (an innie-type) lies immediately E of Estero San Jose at 23°03.5'N, 109°40.4'W. The 3-jetty entrance is approached from S and baffled; when past the second

rip-rap jetty on port, you turn NW to enter.

The marina basin is surrounded by Puerto Los Cabos resort, which sprung up in the tiny fishing village of La Playita. San Jose del Cabo Light on the hill E of the marina.

San Jose's historic core is about 10 blocks square, bounded by 4 streets: Highway 13 along the W side of town, Zaragosa and Doblado across the N, shady divided Mijares along the E side, then Canseco across the S. Narrow streets (some re-cobbled), stone fountains and Spanish architecture fills the N two-thirds of the town's center. Most of the historic buildings are in the NE corner. Between Canseco and the beach is golf course and condos.

From the marina, go E on Benito Juarez (only linking to town), turn N on Mijares, and 2 to 3 blocks up you'll find Doblado and Zaragosa, the plaza with a band stand, cathedral and several street cafes.

Anchorages

Bahía San Lucas anchoring space is not roomy. E of the moorings, you can anchor on the narrow shelf in 25' to 45' of clear water over sand. We suggest bow and stern, and you must set

San Jose Light is on the hill NE of the new marina at Puerto Los Cabos.

an anchor light. Avoid the arroyo in rainy weather, as run off turns to flash flood in a heartbeat.

Shore break increases toward the E end of the bay, and the water taxi gets down there less frequently. But closer to town, hotels, palapa cafes and swim zones line the beaches, and jet boats can be noisy. The sand bottom of Bahía San Lucas is constantly slipping into the deep center of the bay.

Between Cabo and San Jose, only a couple small day anchorages are available for ocean-going yachts.

Satellite image shows Bahía San Lucas (lower left) to to Punta Palmilla and San Jose del Cabo.

Kids making bait at the fuel dock.

it to relieve the chronic slip shortage. Unlike most resort developments, Puerto Los Cabos actually built their marina before hotels went in; the marina opened in early 2006.

The Marina at Puerto Los Cabos is at San Jose del Cabo. It lies inside its own 2-lobed yacht harbor a mile SE of the quaint downtown. This marina has 535 full-service slips to 150' and end ties to 300.' This marina also produces its own water, and slips have internet & satellite TV hookups.

The 500' fuel dock is to starboard in the middle of the 2 basins, megayachts to port in the first basin, and all others slips are tucked around the irregularly shaped basins. Covered and open dry-storage yards with Travelift, a chandlery, grocery, shuttle bus and a ferry service to Cabo and La Paz are planned; check www.MexicoBoating.com for updates.

The Marina at Puerto Los Cabos lies 15 miles E of Bahía San Lucas. Our GPS approach waypoint just outside their lighted 3-jetty entrance is 23°03.5'N, 109°40.4'W. Reservation required. Call (624) 105-6028 or www.puertoloscabos.com

Local Services

Cabo San Lucas is a Port of Entry, and it has a ventanilla unica clearance service next door to the Capitanía, on Matamoras just past 16th of September (about 4 blocks N the malecon). Patrols from the port captain's office and Navy occasionally check papers of boats entering and leaving the inner harbor. WX info is available from the Port Captain on VHF.

Fuel: The bigger fuel dock inside Cabo harbor is at Marina Cabo San Lucas, the long dock with white building almost due W as you enter the middle basin (traffic can be nuts). It has fast pumps, centrifuged fuel, convenience store for bulk lube oil, gallons of water. (624) 143-1252.

If the fuel dock reopens immediately to port as you enter Cabo's inner harbor, it will be easier in and out. The entrance suffers wakes and storm waves. This fuel dock has belonged to several folks, recently to Marinas de Baja. Check for updates on www.MexicoBoating.com

The Marina at Puerto Los Cabos in SJC has a 500' fuel dock on the starboard side of their main fairway through the Puerto Los Cabos harbor. This is 15 miles E of Cabo San Lucas. Go NNE through the 3-jetty entrance, then turn NW into the main fairway. The fuel dock is just past the charter-loading corner. If you pass the island (port), you've gone too far. Call (624) 105-6028 or www.puertoloscabos.com

Haul-out: The Marina at Puerto Los Cabos has a haul-out yard with 75-ton Travelift in the N end of their yacht basin in SJC. The large fenced repair yard is adjacent to the dry storage sheds; (624) 105-6028.

Cabo Yacht Services has a 70-ton Travelift next to the launch ramp at the N end of Cabo San Lucas harbor.

The large fenced repair & dry storage yard is half a block NE of the ramp. CYS performs warranty work and can service boats in slips. (624) 143-3020.

Ship's Agent: We highly recommend the services of the Barreda family (Victor, Pati and Victor Jr.) at the Sea Preme Agency on VHF 88a. Office is at their Sea Preme Chandlery, foot of the Pedregal. They help yatistas clear parts through Aduana, make crew changes, get permits to visit the Socorros, iron wrinkles, etc. Call (624) 143-0007, or fax 143-0002.

Provisions: Cabo's new CityClub, CostCo and Soriana's make Cabo a moderately priced place to provision. For a little of everything, Arámburo's market is within walking distance of Cabo harbor and has a panaderia and farmacia next door. Cabo and San Jose are

Victor Barreda of Sea Preme Agency is the boaters' friend in Los Cabos.

You may have heard the rumors...

A world class marina for world class sportfishing...

2000 acres in a master-planned beach community...

Jack Nicklaus and Greg Norman golf courses...

Puerto Los Cabos

The Marina at Puerto Los Cabos...
the rumors are becoming reality.

www.puertoloscabos.com
or contact us at marinainfo@puertoloscabos.com

GRUPO
QUESTRO
www.questro.com.mx

The Corridor of hotels links Cabo San Lucas and San Jose del Cabo.

Marinas & Berthing

Call "Cabo Moorings" on VHF-68 to be guided to a vacant mooring in Bahía San Lucas. Don't just grab one; it might belong to someone out fishing.

Marinas de Baja is the first marina to port as you enter Cabo's inner harbor. It has 120 full-service slips to 143' and end ties to 300'. Reservation required; (624) 143-6523 or www.marinadebaja.com. Their fuel dock immediately to port as you enter the inner harbor may reopen.

Marina Cabo San Lucas docks fill half the middle basin and all the N end with 380 full-service slips to 180' plus Med fingers for 400.' Marina Cabo San Lucas has its own watermaker plumbed to all slips. Long-term slip leasing is very popular for sportfishing charter boats. Yatistas hoping to spend 2 weeks at the start of cruising season may have to switch slips. Reservation required. (624) 143-1251 or www.cabomarina.com.mx. Marina Cabo San Lucas also owns the big fuel dock in the 2nd basin.

Marina at Puerto Los Cabos: This is the newest and largest marina in the neighborhood, so we expect

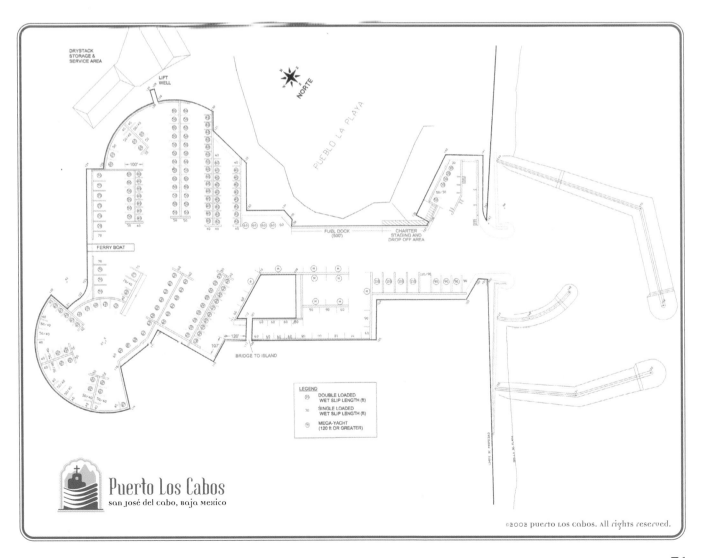

Marinas de Baja is just inside Cabo's inner harbor.

good for meats and staples, a few gourmet shops.

San Jose has a Comercial Mexicana and other good groceries. San Jose's huge mercado municipal has the best fruit & veggie stalls (some organic) early on weekdays; between Coronado and Green 3 blocks E of the highway.

Chandlers: Coast Chandlery near the office of Marina Cabo San Lucas has a good inventory of basics, and they order weekly from the US. Sea Preme Chandlery has all the basics, foot of the Pedregal.

Tanks: Propane refills at Gas de La Paz, road toward San Jose. Both dive shops on the Cabo harbor seawall fill tanks, rent gear and have scuba guides for El Aguila, the sand falls, Chileno Reef, Los Frailes and Cabo Pulmo Reef. (See East Cape section.)

VHF net: Cabo's informal net is usually VHF 22 at 0800 hours daily, and the volunteer net control usually has an agenda something like: emergency traffic, welcome boats new in port, farewell to departers, weather from earlier ham nets, local tides, news, and who's looking for whom. Selling is forbidden by Mexican radio rules, but trading is permitted.

Trans Com: Los Cabos International Airport (SJC) is 5 miles N of San Jose del Cabo; toll road entrance is faster. Car rentals are easy at SJC airport (Pemex stations are on both sides of the highway S of the airport) and many hotel lobbies. Buy debit cards in the markets to work the pay phones. Rental bikes &

scooters are more practical in town than cars.

Emergency: Cabo's Port Captain is (624) 143-4771, and SJC's Port Captain is 142-0722. Cabo Medical Center 143-0774, and English-speaking Dr. Alejandro Avalos on VHF-22. Medica Los Cabos in San Jose is 142-2770. In San Jose Dr. C. Gonzalez speaks English; 142-0056, and dentist Rosa Elena Pena speaks English; 142-6192. SkyMed International air ambulance is (624) 143-1212.

Santa Maria Cove is a 1-boat spot W of Punta Cabeza de Ballena and the Twin Dolphin Hotel, providing marginal protection from the NW wind and none from swell. Santa Maria Cove lies at about 22°55.65'N, 109°48.85 W. Drop bow and stern hooks over sand as far in between the rocky sides as you feel comfortable.

Chileno Bay 4 miles W of Punta Palmilla is a small anchorage for NW weather, located W of Chileno Reef and E of the red-roofed Hotel Cabo San Lucas. Anchor in 35' to 46' at about 22°57.00'N, 109°48.16'W. Great day stop for diving Chileno Reef, but not for overnight except in glass conditions.

Punta Palmilla: Marginal anchorage may be taken

Lighthouse tower is at Marina Cabo San Lucas.

Pedistrian walkways and gringo cantinas surround the marina basins.

W of Hotel Palmilla in NW weather in 25' to 38' of water (23°01.00'N, 109°42.74'W) over sand and some rocks on the point. Moorings are for hotel boats. The landing is for embarking hotel guests, so get permission first. The N end of this small anchorage has silted in. From here you'll be able to see the lighted jetties of the Marina at Puerto Los Cabos.

Explore Ashore

El Triunfo: Former silver-mining town with Eiffel chimneys on E side of Sierras on Highway 13 (Cortez side) toward La Paz. EA train track runs down to Muertos Cove. The photo above shows the classical facade of lovely home restored as a museum of music, but El Triunfo hasn't yet been discoverd like Todos Santos has.

Todos Santos: Hip artist colony around a palm oasis, 200-year old brick buildings from sugar-mill era, blooming with vegan eateries, health retreats, Spanish & yoga classes. Todos Santos is about 20 miles N of Cabo on Highway 1 (Pacific side) toward La Paz.

Biosphere Reserve Sierra de la Laguna: Need a break from blue over blue, a chance to stretch your legs? High up between the peaks Cerro Picacho la Laguna, Cerros Candeleros and Cerros Chuparosas you can visit hidden lakes, waterfalls and flower-strewn meadows. Guides take you in 4-wheel drives to a rustic rancho. Proceed either on 4 hiking trails through aspen, pines, palms, cacti; or on horse back with pack mules to higher campsites. Spring is best. Todos Santos Eco Adventures (612) 145-0780.

History & Culture

San Jose del Cabo's patron St. Joseph is celebrated around March 19 with traditional cuisine fairs, ranchero music, street dancing, children's carnival rides, horse races, fishing events, religious parades; around mid March.

Cabo San Lucas was a watering port for European merchant ships for centuries, thanks to aquifers in the Sierras.

San Jose del Cabo's plaza church.

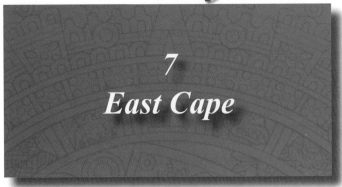

7
East Cape

Where is East Cape?

East Cape or "the Cape" is the bulging SE tip of the Baja California peninsula, mostly below the Tropic of Cancer. Fishing is the main draw, plus some diving. We chart only 2 reliable anchorages in prevailing conditions – Frailes and Muertos – but we note many marginal spots that may be useful.

The Gordo Banks and sandy shelves rise from deep water, so marlin, yellow tail and yellowfin tuna are the major catches. Dozens of small sportfishing hotels dot the mostly undeveloped shoreline, accessed by land from the old road between San Jose and La Paz. Some of these Mom 'n Pop resorts have portable boarding docks, private airstrips and campgrounds, but so far no permanent docks have survived a summer.

Las Arenas has a pargo & cabrilla classic in March,

fly-fishing events in May, spear-fishing meet in June, and rooster-fishing school in July. Hotel Buena Vista has catch and release charity tournaments June – October.

Cabo Pulmo Reef is the only living hard-coral reef system on the W side of North America, and it's well worth a visit. In warm turquoise waters of Cabo Pulmo National Marine Park, you'll see docile whale sharks and hammerheads, a colorful array of tropical reef fish, flaming flora and deep ocean species. The wreck dive on "Colima" is nearby. This is what underwater cameras are made for.

ROUTE PLANNING: Los Cabo to La Paz

If you plan to cross the Sea of Cortez to Mazatlán on the mainland, jumping off from Las Frailes makes the shortest offshore passage, about 160 miles. If you're crossing down toward Puerto Vallarta or Manzanillo, you may as well depart from Cabo or San Jose – lessening the "cape effect."

Rounding East Cape: From Cabo Falso to Isla Cerralvo, Pacific wind, waves and current mix with those flowing out of the Sea of Cortez. Even as you enter the S end of the Sea of Cortez, you may feel weather farther N.

If you're coasting from Los Cabos around East Cape and up to La Paz (about 150 miles), the most reliable and comfortable overnight anchorages in prevailing N winds are at Los Frailes and Muertos, before the long stretch up the Cerralvo Channel (often upwind.) An anchorage at Punta El Coyote is serviceable in light NW wind, but don't plan too far in advance to overnight here.

COASTWISE: Los Cabos to La Paz

Punta Palmilla: It's 10 miles E from Cabeza Ballena (Whale Head) Light on the E side of Bahía San Lucas to hilly Punta Palmilla, then 4 miles NE to the jetty entrance to SJC's new yacht harbor for the Marina at Puerto Los Cabos. San Jose Canyon drops off only a mile W of the harbor opening, jogging SE below the Gordo Banks, then SW.

Coasting NE, 4 miles up from SJC, semicircular Iman (Magnetic) Bank begins spreading to 5 miles offshore NE of Punta Gorda, then narrowing at Tule Light. We run this coast at least 2 miles off to avoid seasonal shoals off the arroyos and a series of detached rocks.

Punta Gorda (23°05'N, 109°36'W) has a

© Point Loma Publishing 2006

Overall Cabo Pulmo to Cabo San Lucas

N

Ten nautical miles

© Point Loma Publishing 2005

Lower East Cape

Pulmo Shoals
Cabo Pulmo
Los Frailes
Pulmo Canyon
Frailes Canyon
Salado Canyon
Tule Light
Tule Canyon
Vinorama Canyon
Punta Gorda
Gorda Shoals
San Jose del Cabo
Inner Gorda
Outer Gorda
Gorda Banks
Punta Palmilla
San Jose Canyon
Cabo San Lucas
Santa Maria Canyon
San Lucas Canyon
Cabrillo Seamount

Not for Navigation

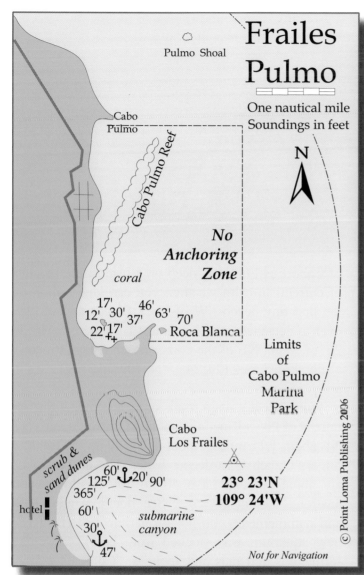

Frailes Pulmo

One nautical mile
Soundings in feet

N

Pulmo Shoal

Cabo Pulmo

Cabo Pulmo Reef

No Anchoring Zone

coral

17'
12' 30' 46'
37' 63' 70'
22' 17'
Roca Blanca

Limits of Cabo Pulmo Marina Park

Cabo Los Frailes

scrub & sand dunes

60' 20'
125' 90'
365'
hotel 60'
30'
47'

submarine canyon

23° 23'N
109° 24'W

© Point Loma Publishing 2006

Not for Navigation

landmark whitish flat-top hill, Cerro Santa Cruz (314') about half a mile W of the low point. The newly paved coastal access road is visible from E of SJC past Punta Gorda to about Tule Light. Until long stretches were ripped out by 2003 storms, it linked most East Cape beaches, so we hope it can be repaired.

Gordo Banks: The bottom contours of these offshore waters are well known to sportfishers. Banco Gorda Afuera (Outer Gorda Bank) is 7 miles SE of Punta Gorda, and Banco Gorda Adentro (Inner Gorda Bank) is 5 miles SE of Punta Gorda. Even the smallest sailboat fishing here with a boat line tossed

over the side is likely to snag dorado dinner.

Roca Salado: From Boca de Tule Light (about 23°15'N, 109°24'W) 8 miles N to Cabo Los Frailes, we stay at least 2 miles offshore to avoid a dangerous rock reported to lie 1.2 miles off, rising from 150' of water about 5 miles S of Cabo Los Frailes.

Similar to Ben's Rock, such obstacles near deep water can build dangerous breaking waves that rise only occasionally. For lack of an official name, we'll call it Roca Salado, because it appears to lie NE of Arroyo Salado and N of Salado Canyon underwater. We hope to chart it next time.

Los Frailes

Cabo Los Frailes (the Friars) is 38 miles NE of Puerto Los Cabos, 45 miles SSE of Muertos, 90 from La Paz. This significant (755') rocky headland is a good radar target jutting from East Cape's E tip. From S, the headland's profile of gray shale slabs looked to Spanish explorers like friars climbing the steep angle. The headland's blunt E side is lower and runs about a mile N, then it recedes W to a sandy beach.

Bahía Los Frailes (pronounced "FRY-layz") S of the point is extremely deep due to a canyon dropping off close to shore, forming sand falls.

Cabo Pulmo National Marine Park encompasses both sides of Cabo Los Frailes. Cabo Pulmo village is N of Frailes Point.

Anchorage

Coming in from 2 miles off shore in any direction, our GPS approach waypoint about 1.5 miles SE of the friars' point is 22°23'N, 109°24'W. Anchoring is not permitted N of the point where the coral reef might be damaged.

In strong N wind, we anchor in 20' on a narrow shelf about 40 yards off a stony beach almost out to the rocky tip. This has the best dinghy landing spot, at the E end of the beach where it meets the rocky headland.

We've also anchored in 30' off the S end of the sandy beach near the dive hotel. Although many casual beach hotels in Mexico welcome yatistas to their restaurants

Ocean-going yachts are no longer allowed to anchor off the N side of Los Frailes, because anchors and chains destroyed delicate coral formations. If you anchor in the no anchor zone, park rangers will come by to ask you to leave. Even when you anchor S of Los Frailes, please turn off your bilge pump and don't let sink, deck or laundry detergent go overboard – it kills living corals.

Los Frailes are climbing this slope, S side of the Cabo Los Frailes headland.

with prior permission, the one S of Cabo Los Frailes seems to be an exception.

Local Services

A road behind Frailes Beach runs 2 miles N to Cabo Pulmo village, which is devoted to sport diving tourists who come for Cabo Pulmo National Marine Park. Behind the berm and chaparral, we found 3 very active dive shops with compressors for filling tanks, guides certified for the park, full equipment rentals, film, sunscreen, snacks and hand-drawn diagrams of the reef layout (no 2 alike).

The village has 2 small 2-story hotels and 3 small restaurants with 4 or 5 tables each. A couple Marin-style homes dot the beach, and developers are carving up the hillside behind the village. Cabo Pulmo has been discovered.

Cabo Pulmo National Marine Park

From the N corner of Los Frailes headland for about 5 miles N to the lesser Cabo Pulmo is the No Anchoring zone of Cabo Pulmo National Marine Park, a PROFEPA protected entity created to protect Pulmo Reef – the only living hard-coral reef system in the Sea of Cortez and only one of 3 such reefs in North America. See our chart for the park boundaries.

To visit this beautiful snorkel and scuba park, hire one of the certified dive guides from Pulmo village N of the point where you can fill or rent tanks and rent fins & masks. Certified guides will take you in their pangas (no 2-strokes allowed) to the exact kind of diving you prefer.

If you don't use a 2-stroke outboard, dinghy to any of the beaches and wade in from there, but be very mindful of divers down. Roca Blanca (23°24.48'N, 109°24.81'W) a quarter mile off the NE tip

of Cabo Los Frailes is deep on all sides, but has lots of current. In calm weather, you can land a dink on the first tiny beach SW of Roca Blanca and snorkel over to detached coral heads just E of there, in 13' to 26' of water. NE of the corner beach (Playa Rincon), a submerged rock (23°24.35'N, 109°25.35W) rises in about 15' of water.

Pulmo Reef's main trunk starts less than a quarter mile N of Playa Rincon in about 25' of water and runs NE about 1.25 miles. About half way up the trunk, 8 fingers branch E to deeper water. The deepest parts are about 60' and have 40' to 100' visibility, and a strong current reverses. See docile whale shark and hammerheads, brilliant aquarium fish (La Paz's new aquarium was stocked from here), castle-like formations, red fans and sponges. "Colima," a 1929 shrimper that sank in 1980 in 45' of water about a mile N of Cabo Pulmo, is in the park but outside the no anchor zone.

COASTWISE continued

To depart the anchorage S of Los Frailes, head E

Cruisers stroll powder white sand on Frailes beach.

for 2.5 miles, then N for at least 4 miles before making any westing, thus avoiding divers and the dangerous detached Pulmo Shoal (6' depth), which lies about half a

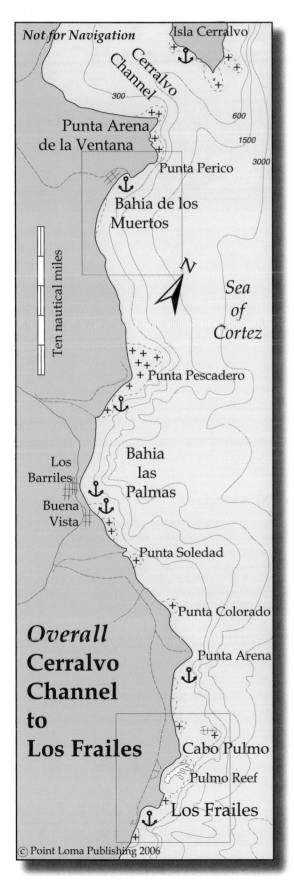

Not for Navigation

Isla Cerralvo

Cerralvo Channel

300

600

1500

3000

Punta Arena de la Ventana

Punta Perico

Bahia de los Muertos

N

Ten nautical miles

Sea of Cortez

+ Punta Pescadero

Los Barriles

Bahia las Palmas

Buena Vista

Punta Soledad

+ Punta Colorado

Punta Arena

Overall Cerralvo Channel to Los Frailes

Cabo Pulmo

Pulmo Reef

Los Frailes

mile NE of Cabo Pulmo. After Pulmo, the coast turns NW and a gravel road flanks the coast.

Punta Arena de la Rivera (23°33.35'N, 109°27.83'W) is the next point 10 miles NW, marked by Punta Arena Sur lighthouse. Give this low, wind scoured, breaker lined point a 2-mile berth due to rocks off the point. The indent S has very little wind shelter, and although the N side is shallow way out, it's at least a small hope in S wind.

Bahía las Palmas, a 19-mile bight up to Punta Pescadero, is shallow along shore in its S third, but deep canyons fill its middle near Buena Vista and its N third. Fishing resorts are visible at Punta Colorado, La Ribera and Punta Soledad.

La Ribera (emergency roadstead) has a Pemex station and good road to La Paz.

Buena Vista & Los Barriles (The Barrels) are adjacent towns 25 miles WNW of Frailes at the head of Bahía de Palmas. A fair-weather roadstead in 20' to 35' lies at about 23°39'N, 109°41'W just off Buena Vista (smaller, more southerly, behind the beach). In fair weather, hotel boats and a few yatistas anchor on a small shoal NE of Buena Vista, or 3 miles N off Los Barriles (Barrels). The towns almost connect; the visible highway heads inland N of Barriles and a lesser road coasts N to Punta Pescadero.

Punta Pescadero (9 miles N of Buena Vista) gets a 1.5-mile berth on all sides due to rocks, but local pangas know a path to the beach where they drive ashore. The fishing resort has an airstrip NW of the point, where the beach road ends.

Muertos is 13.3 miles NW of Punta Pescadero.

Muertos Cove

Muertos Cove is useful when waiting for better weather to head up into the Cerralvo Channel. It lies 47 miles NW of Los Frailes, 55 miles from La Paz harbor, 67 miles from Cabo San Lucas.

Ensenada de los Muertos is the cove in the N end of Bahía de los Muertos, so we call it Muertos Cove. Bahía de los Muertos is the 5-mile open indent SW of Punta Perico (pronounced "pay-REE-coh"), the 627' headland on the S end of the broad

Giggling Marlin Beach & Yacht Club is the first restaurant at Muertos, aka Bahía de los Suenos.

Punta Arena de la Ventana corner. Perico (parakeet) hill paints a hard radar image from all approaches.

Ashore in the sheltered head of Muertos Cove, the remnants of a stone wharf and warehouse are historic landmarks. The word muertos referred to the dead-man mooring system used in the early 1900s for barges that loaded ore from the silver mines at El Triunfo. Early guidebooks told of giant buried anchors (called "dead men" or muertos) SW of the wharf, and of ore carts from the mine train that were dumped in the bay.

We searched the sandy bottom with scuba gear, but it probably requires a metal detector if they're buried very deep. We once found a half-buried metal mooring ball (others rusting on shore) buoyed with a plastic bleach bottle, and a couple modern engine blocks used as moorings or dead men by locals.

Anchorage

Muertos Cove is a comfortable and reliable overnight anchorage that's sheltered in N weather by Cerro el Perico, and in W wind it's protected by El Palmar Peak (3,300'). But Muertos is wide open to the S and E. Our GPS approach waypoint half a mile outside the N end of the bay is 23°59'N, 109°49.3'W.

The favored spot in Muertos Cove is tucked up into the N end, just W of the reef on the tip of land, in 13' to 23' over good-holding sand and mud. But in fair weather you could anchor almost anywhere 400 yards off the beach running SE in 15' to 25' of water. 2 small reefs block the shore S end of the beach, unless you can anchor bow and stern between them in 17' to 20'.

Local Services

The Giggling Marlin Beach & Yacht Club has a pleasant cantina and restaurant welcoming yatistas on VHF 16. Dinks land on the beach out front. Someday a marina or moorings may be installed.

Developers didn't like or understand the name

Bahia Las Palmas has no shelter, only temporary docks for local sportfishing boats.

Muertos, so they dubbed it Bahía de los Sueños (Dreams). The expanding RV park behind the beach berm is the end of the 35-mile paved road from La Paz, so we expect this place to sprout a gas station soon. Locals say the airstrip E of the point may be refurbished, also the side road N to the lighthouse at Punta Arena de la Ventana. The town San Juan de los Planes 10 miles inland has groceries and a medical clinic.

A few elegant homes dot the cactus-covered hillsides along the S half of Bahía de los Muertos. One of these homeowners said a gringo boater wandered into his living room one day, asking to see a room.

COASTWISE continued

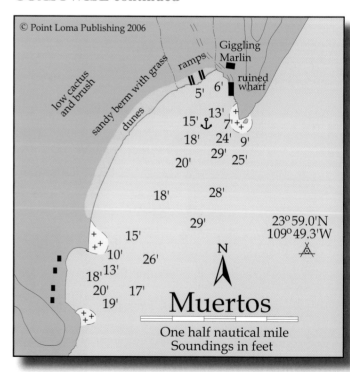

© Point Loma Publishing 2006

Giggling Marlin

ramps

ruined wharf

low cactus and brush

sandy berm with grass

dunes

5'   6'

13'

15' ⚓   7'

18'   24'   9'

29'   25'

20'

18'   28'

29'   23°59.0'N
                109°49.3'W

15'

10'

26'

18' 13'

20'   17'

19'

N

Muertos

One half nautical mile
Soundings in feet

Motoring past Punta Coyote, North of Isla Cerralvo.

In the reef-bound 5-mile corner between Muertos and the lighthouse at Punta Arena de la Ventana, pangas haul up on 2 tiny beaches wedged between the

cliffs and foaming rocks.

Punta Arena de la Ventana Light on the sandy headland marks the S end of the Cerralvo Channel at its narrowest point, 5 miles across to Isla Cerralvo. Round this shifting shoal point at least a mile off, and watch for a strong tidal current. Slower boats should plan to transit this channel on a slack or favorable tide.

We've anchored for a few hours 1.5 miles W of Ventana lighthouse, in very calm weather, at 24°05.6'N, 109°53.22'W, but it's better for light southerlies. A spectacular beach runs 8 miles W to Ventana village. Pods of whales are common passage mates in this gateway channel.

Cerralvo Island

This island is the southernmost in the Sea of Cortez, mountainous (2,518'), runs 16 miles NW to SE. Roca Montaña rock field guards its SE tip, and its similarly reef-bound SW corner carries Piedras Gordas Light (24°09.2'N, 109°50.8'W).

Marginal anchorage is reported about midway between these S points in 22' to 30' of water but with poor shelter from N wind.

Within 3 miles of Cerralvo's blustery E side, a steep drop-off paralleling the island brings marlin, dorado and tuna. Crossing to La Paz from the mainland, be aware of Arrecife de la Foca (Seal Reef), sometimes lighted, 4 miles N of Cerralvo's N tip.

Ray Cannon's 1966 classic adventure book "Sea of Cortez" says the S end of Isla Cerralvo is the ancient burial ground of native sea gypsies called Vagabundos del Mar. While alive, they roamed the Sea of Cortez in dugout canoes powered by triangular sails or paddles. Fishing and foraging, they lived in small family groups and avoided outside contact except to trade for fish hooks or water. When they died, their bodies were supposed to be brought here. Cannon said fewer than 300 Vagabundos were still alive then, yet

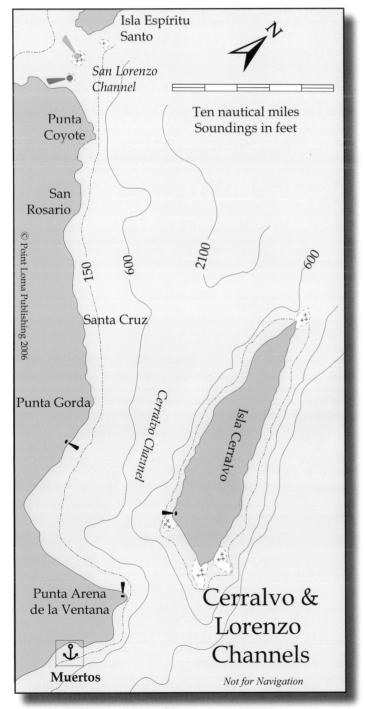

Isla Espíritu Santo

San Lorenzo Channel

Punta Coyote

San Rosario

© Point Loma Publishing 2006

N

Ten nautical miles
Soundings in feet

150

600

2100

600

Santa Cruz

Punta Gorda

Cerralvo Channel

Isla Cerralvo

Punta Arena de la Ventana

Cerralvo & Lorenzo Channels

Muertos

Not for Navigation

San Lorenzo Light looking S toward La Paz peninsula.

he found crosses, gravesites and lighted candles. We used to tell yatistas not to anchor here on Isla Cerralvo, but if you must go ashore, please consider this hallowed ground and don't tamper.

Punta Gorda (12 miles NW of Ventana) is the steep point opposite the island, and behind the point the Sierra la Palmillosa rises to 2,800.' We run the 17-mile coast from Gorda around Coyote about 2 miles off to avoid off-lying rocks.

Rancho Santa Cruz 5 miles NW of Gorda is a private club on an alluvial delta fronting a distinctive arroyo. Sail-ins are not welcomed, but it's good to know that in an emergency they have 2 breakwaters sheltering 2 roadstead, and the secondary road reaches La Paz.

Punta Coyote Light is actually on the N side of the headland, at Punta Piedra de Bulle. Marginal anchorage is found S of Punta Coyote in calm conditions. Round Coyote and Bulle points at least 1.5 miles off, then head for a point about a quarter mile N of Bajo Scout Light.

San Lorenzo Channel

was named for one of many shipwrecks here. This E-W pass between Punta Tecolote and Isla Espiritu Santo has shoals along both sides, and 2 lighted towers mark 2 rocky shoals in the deeper middle. Pass between the 2 lighted shoals, favoring Bajo Scout (or San Lorenzo Sur) at 24°22.1'N, 110°18.5'W on the S side of the channel, because it's better marked. San Lorenzo Reef Light on the N side of the channel marks San Lorenzo Reef (9') which spreads N of that N light. About 0.75 of a mile NE of Lorenzo light is dangerous Suwanee Rocks shoal (not always marked).

We pass about a quarter mile N of Bajo Scout, so we're 1.5 miles off Arranca Cabello Point (translates to "pull your hair out by the roots!") as we round it

and begin angling SW. The next large point 2.5 miles SW of Arranca Cabello is the entrance to Balandra Cove or Puerto Balandra (See next chapter.), and you can round it as close as .25 of a mile off.

If you're heading non-stop to La Paz harbor, stay a mile W of tall Nepomuceno Island, then round Punta Prieta (24°13'N, 110°18'W) half a mile off. Go ESE for about a quarter mile to enter Marina CostaBaja's new breakwaters. See next chapter.

Turn S into the lighted, buoyed La Paz Channel. At 2 miles S, the marina called Palmira Yacht Club (See next chapter.) has a breakwater entrance on the E side of the channel, and another 2 miles finds you at the main anchorage of La Paz harbor.

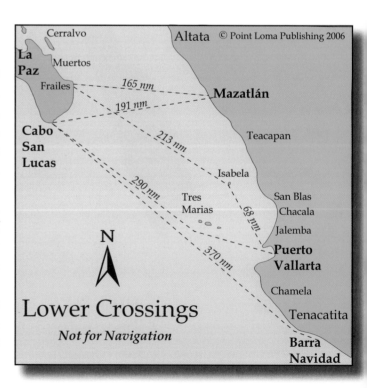

Lower Crossings
Not for Navigation

La Paz & Vicinity

La Paz (The Peace) lies about 150 sea miles from Los Cabos, 130 miles S of Loreto, 240 miles WNW of Mazatlán on the mainland. It's the capitol city (pop. 190,000) and largest harbor (2.5 miles long) in Baja California Sur (BCS).

More than 1,000 pleasure boats spend many months (years) home-ported in La Paz among its 4 marinas and large anchorages. It has several chandlers, fuel docks and haul-out yard for repairs and dry storage, excellent provisioning, an international airport, the Cruisers' Club, morning VHF and ham nets and a wide variety of good eateries.

From La Paz, yatistas enjoy 20 anchorages N of the harbor and at nearby Isla Espiritu Santos and Isla Partida.

Early fall brings sportfishing tournaments to La Paz and East Cape. The season's new fleet of cruisers arrives in November. December is a month-long cultural festival, much less commercial than in Cabo. Mardi Gras is in February, and March is the Festival of the Whale. Sea of Cortez Celebrations may resume in April. Cortez first visited La Paz on a May 13th, now celebrated with food, music, dancing, parades and other events.

The Corumuel wind is unique to La Paz. It's usually a gentle breeze that begins from the S around sunset and dies at sunrise or mid morning, relieving the heat and humidity. Occasionally, a Corumuel gets strong enough to disrupt navigation. See ***MexWX: Mexico Weather for Boaters*** by Capt. John E. Rains.

COASTWISE: La Paz Approach

We'll look at the anchoring coves now on our route into La Paz harbor. (See next chapter for Islas Espiritu Santos.) On your way S along the E side of Bahía de La Paz, Balandra Cove is the first anchoring opportunity. El Merito, Isla Lobos, Playa Pichilingue and Bahía Falso are small getaway spots.

If you like wreck diving, try the 300' hull of the ferry "Salvatierra," located at a 60' depth between Punta Coyote and Isla Espiritu Santo. This unprotected dive is subject to a 3-knot current.

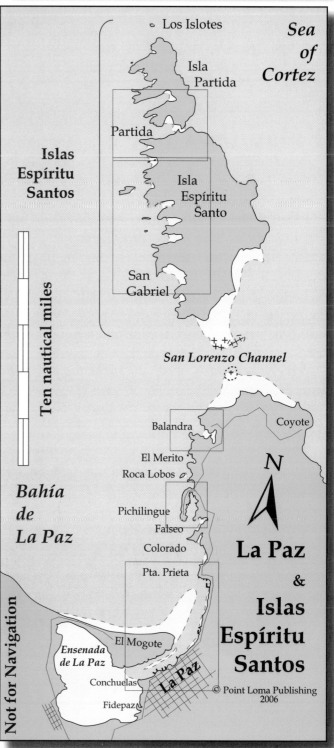

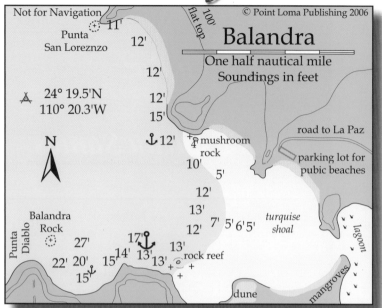

Not for Navigation
© Point Loma Publishing 2006

Punta San Loreznzo
11'
12'

Balandra
One half nautical mile
Soundings in feet

100' flat top

24° 19.5'N
110° 20.3'W

N

12'
12'
12'
15'

⚓12'

⚓12' mushroom rock
10'
5'
road to La Paz

parking lot for pubic beaches

12'
13'
12'   7' 5' 6' 5'

Balandra Rock

27'
17'⚓
22' 20' 15' 14' 13' 13' 13'
15'⚓   rock reef

turquise shoal

lagoon

Punta Diablo

dune

mangroves

Buoy marks Balandra Rock.

Balandra Cove

Balandra Cove (Puerto Balandra) lies between the W tip of Punta San Lázaro and Punta Diablo. Balandra is pretty and it may be logistically useful for entering and leaving the La Paz channel with favorable light or tide, but it's not an all weather anchorage.

Our GPS approach waypoint for entering Balandra Cove is 24°19.5'W, 102°20.3'W.

In deeper water outside the bright shoal line, we've found 12' - 11' anchoring spots along the N wall beach and just outside Mushroom Rock, and on the S wall in 20' - 13' outside the obvious reef.

NOTE: Off the S wall, a lighted buoy usually marks a detached pinnacle at our GPS position 24°19.146'N, 102°20.199'W. At lower low water, Balandra Rock is 5' awash.

The back half of Balandra Cove is a turquoise shoal shelf fringed in mangroves and powdery white beaches; it draws hundreds of weekend bathers. On week nights, we've anchored a trimaran bow and stern in the 5'- 7' deep tongue in the center of the outer edge of the shoal, but it's too close to the noisy parking lot on weekends.

Mushroom Rock was formed by erosion of the sandstone layer below the harder lava cap, but it's been toppled over and cemented back in place so many times that the town council had fiberglass replicas made for temporary replacement. You can't tell if it's real unless you tap on it. A second replica is a fountain in the town square.

El Merito Cove

About a mile SSW of Diablo Point lies flat-top Roca Lobos, which carries Roca Lobos Light. There's deep-water passage on both sides of Roca Lobos.

E of Roca Lobos, tiny El Merito Cove is the narrow 2-finger bay. El Merito Cove is sometimes called Caleta Lobos, but that's confused with the area E of Isla Lobos, so we'll stick with the original Spanish name El Merito – merit.

Aquaculture pens may temporarily occupy the middle of this intimate cove, but as long as you avoid them, you can anchor almost anywhere else in calm weather.

We've found 15' to 30' over sand off the S side of the S finger, 18' S of the tip of the middle peninsula, and 10' to 15' behind the little islet

Mushroom Rock at Balandra Cove is one of many in the Sea of Cortez.

Balandra Cove and the surrounding peninsula off San Lorenzo Channel.

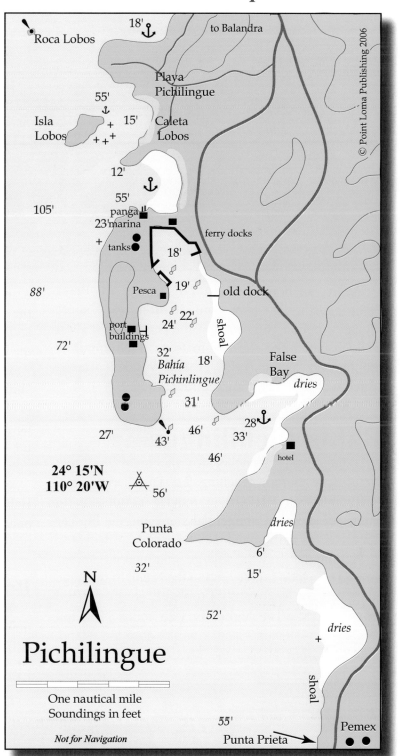

(not to be confused with lighted Roca Lobos). Multihulls can tuck closer toward the N beach shoal.

The first time we tried El Merito Cove, we anchored behind the detached islet at twilight. After dark we cooled off with a swim over the N beach shoal, enjoying the phosphorescent sparkles swirling around our bodies and the dazzling stars in the black velvet sky. Such is the fabric of cruising, eh?

Next morning we snorkeled the shoal again. To our horror, 8 baby sea snakes (poisonous) raced out of the reeds and poked repeatedly at the glass in our facemasks. Instinctively, we ripped off the masks. The snakes continued attacking masks, and we made all speed in the opposite direction.

This is about the N limit of sea snakes, which feed on fish eggs in reeds and mangroves. The prudent mariner would inquire on VHF before swimming unfamiliar coves.

Isla Lobos

Less than a mile S of El Merito Cove, the whitewashed Isla Lobos is a landmark for everything N of Pechilingue harbor and is often visible at the Espiritu Santos islands. A shoal saddle (22' to 6' depth) links the islands NE side to shore, and a rock pile lies off the E side, great for snorkeling.

The anchorage in standard NW to N breeze is SE and S of the island, where the rock pile adds some protection, but we approach the anchorage from S. Small boats anchor in 22' off the island's NE side shoal; or in calm weather, in 13' over sand toward the mainland beach in the broad indent.

Playa Pichilingue Cove

This pretty beach cove is N of the land bridge that forms Bahía Pichilingue harbor. Lots of traffic on Balandra road skirts its SE side, and on the land bridge of its S side you'll find Cantamar, a group of docks used by pangas and small commercial fishing boats, then a launch ramp and a dry storage yard. Boats using this marina must clear a finger shoal that points NE from their E docks.

Pichilingue Bay's entrance is to the south, top of photo. Playa Pichilingue is bottom right.

We've anchored in the NE corner of Playa Pichilingue in 18' over sand. It offers easy shore access, a public bathroom on the beach and a short walk to cafes and the bus to town. Pichilingue is pronounced "pee-chee-LING-way" – taken from a Dutch word for a particular pirate group.

Bahía Pichilingue

If you need to anchor for the night in Bahía Pichilingue before reaching La Paz harbor, call "Capitanía" on VHF-16 to request permission to enter and anchor. Commercial ships and the big car ferry use this harbor, and they have right of way.

Pichilingue Bay is a large commercial harbor formed by a land bridge linking the N end of the huge Isla San Juan Nepomuceno to shore, so it's entered only from S. The harbor is 1.25 miles N-S, but very narrow. A stone quarry works atop the island, and the harbor houses the Mexican Navy base, a commercial Pemex dock, a fish unloading wharf, long-term shrimper and tuna piers, some government docks, a parking lot for semi-trucks and their cargo trailers, and the Mazatlán ferry terminal.

Pichilingue Bay isn't a pleasant destination, due to wakes and noise from the highway to La Paz (6 miles S) skirting the E side of the bay, and it's noisiest here with truck traffic for the ferry and quarry.

The main N-S main ship channel through the center of this narrow bay is busy but well marked and lighted. Landing on the shore is prohibited by the Navy.

Hurricane hole: Pichilingue Bay is Baja's only "hurricane hole" S of Puerto Escondido, and its use is regulated by the La Paz Port Captain. Some years he prohibits any anchoring in this bay, reserving it for emergency use. Other years it's OK as long as you don't swing too close to the channel.

Our GPS waypoint outside the entrance to Bahía Pichilingue is 24°15'N, 110°20'W. A lighted buoy marks a shoal off the SE tip of Nepomuceno peninsula.

Bahía Falso

False Bay is a small mostly shallow cove immediately E of the entrance to Pichilingue Bay, still NE of Punta Colorado. Aquaculture floats may fill the shoal NE end, but you can anchor in 15'-20' in the middle of the cove.

Playa Tesoro (Treasure) is the E beach, where you can land near the highway, but don't leave a dinghy unattended. 2 shallow bights SE of Punta Colorado have beach cantinas, hotels, water slides and good dinghy exploring. During road construction, a treasure was unearthed here, hence its name.

Marina CostaBaja basin, top, and Punta Prieta, bottom left.

COASTWISE continued

At 2.5 miles SE of Punta Colorado is a large headland called Punta Prieta (24°13.2'N, 110°18.7'W). The W side of this high bluff has smoke stacks and tanks of a power generating station, an antenna farm and Punta Prieta Light.

As the land cuts E for half a mile, the old cement factory and its big pier are long gone, but Berkovich Boat Yard (See local services.) has a marine ways and smaller docks jutting S from shore, plus a few hundidos partly blocking the entrance to its new neighbor.

The well lighted breakwaters shelter the Marina CostaBaja yacht basin in the E corner of this sandy bight. The marina (See below.) is entered on its N side. About 50 yards S of Marina CostaBaja, you can't miss the first buoys marking the dredged channel into La Paz harbor.

La Paz Channel is well lighted and buoyed, 12' least depth, only about 200 yards wide in spots, and the old range markers are still visible. A serious shoal parallels the W side of the channel. About 1.75 miles down the channel is the riprap entrance jetty to Marina Palmira Yacht Club. See below.

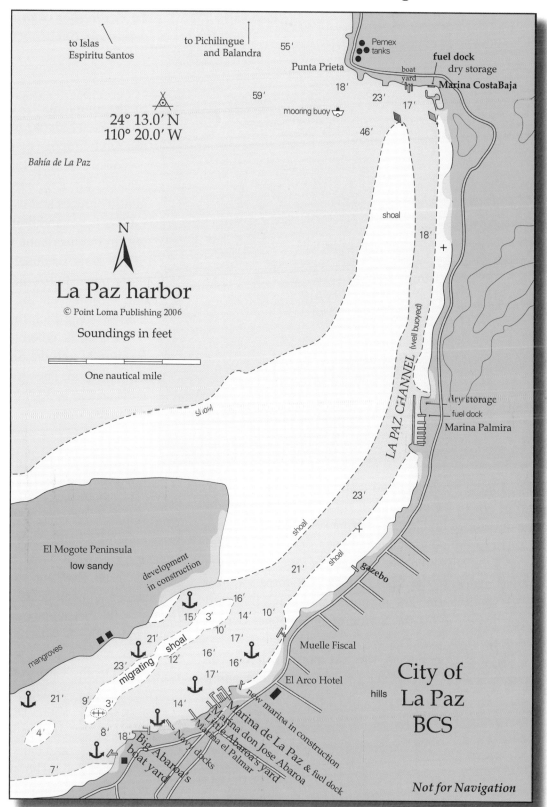

La Paz harbor
© Point Loma Publishing 2006
Soundings in feet
One nautical mile

24° 13.0' N
110° 20.0' W

Bahía de La Paz

Not for Navigation

La Paz Harbor
Lay of the Land

At the S end of the well lighted and buoyed La Paz Channel, the city's downtown waterfront runs along the SE shore of 12-mile wide Bahía La Paz, and it is somewhat sheltered from NW winds by low

La Paz harbor channel and El Mogote peninsula. Shoals in channel can change.

to the municipal sewage plant and the once abandoned Fidepaz marina basin. Fonatur plans to revive Fidepaz marina.

During most of the year, especially cruising season, La Paz enjoys balmy temperatures, gentle breezes and clear skies. By late summer, La Paz is hot and humid, and its latitude is well within the hurricane belt. The narrowest width of the Baja peninsula is W of La Paz, so the more powerful tropical storms can surmount it and reform over the hot waters of the Sea of Cortez. Keep Pichilingue in mind.

La Paz is where yatistas decide if they're heading N into the Sea of Cortez or crossing to the mainland. The crossing distance from La Paz to Mazatlán is 50 miles shorter than from Cabo to Puerto Vallarta.

Anchor & Berth

"The La Paz Waltz" is the dance anchored boats do when the 3-knot tidal current flows in or out, with eddies along the irregular bottom, while the wind opposes the current – or there's no wind. Boats kiss, hopefully gently, whenever their owners aren't looking. You need about twice as large a swinging circle as usual. Bow and stern is impossible.

Malecon anchorage is from S of Muelle Fiscal (leave a 500 meter maneuvering area on all 3 sides) and parallel the S side of the channel, past Marina de La Paz (See below.) to about the old Gran Baja high rise. Depths vary from 24' near the channel, to drying sand and mud shoals near shore. Don't swing into the channel. Anchor lights are required at night and balls by day.

The malecon anchorage is the largest and most popular, despite the fact that the La Paz Waltz is often more pronounced here. It provides

El Mogote Peninsula and a shoal that extends there miles NE of Mogote. The E tip of El Mogote might be developed and have a marina some day.

The prominent municipal pier or Muelle Fiscal marks the NE end of the main anchorage. Behind the noisy malecon, the first 2 blocks of stores climb a huge sandy berm. The harbor's marina and boatyard area lies close off the S side of the channel, which ends at Punta Conchuelas.

Beyond Conchuelas, the SW portion of La Paz harbor is shoal, except for a narrow channel leading

Malecon anchorage is popular despite La Paz Waltz.

Large breakwater shields 100-footers in Marina CostaBaja's outer darsena. Sailboats fill the inner darsena.

easy access to shore, and street lights illuminate the first row of boats at night – thus discouraging petty theft.

El Mogote anchorage is N of the channel, S of the low sandy El Mogote peninsula, in unmarked patches of 15'-22' of water between the migrating mud shoals. It's quieter here but farther to town. To avoid the shoals, cross the bay due N from the municipal pier (24°09.69' N, 110°19.19' W), then head for the distinctive white cross on the El Mogote shore (24°10.05'N, 110°19.58'W). We measured a 10' least depth. When closing with shore, swing to the SW to anchor safely behind the shoals. A larger landmark building on El Mogote has operated variously as a nightclub, hotel, ashram and health club, and been abandoned several times. A developer plans a marina off Mogote (an outie, not an innie this time), and its construction could impinge on this anchorage.

Marina CostaBaja

This new marina is closest to open sea, located 50 yards N of the start of the La Paz Channel, in the corner E of Punta Prieta. The marina entrance is just a hundred yards NW of the N end of the La Paz Channel, 4 miles N of downtown. Our GPS position in the entrance is 12°14'04"N, 110°18'21"W.

Some marina basins are "innies" meaning they're carved into the existing shoreline behind the beach berm. "Outies" are behind a protruding breakwater. Marina CostaBaja has both, and its location in the corner E of Punta Prieta headland should give it good shelter

from tropical storms.

Marina CostaBaja has 250 full-service slips to 200'and a fuel dock in 2 sequential basins. Their 400' long fuel dock is immediately to port opposite the breakwater entrance and below the marina office. Big boat slips are to starboard in the first basin, and all others are in the more sheltered second basin. Besides the usual amenities, each slip has Internet hookup and a pumpout. The channel connecting the 2 basins curves around a landscaped island, and the outer side of the high mole separating the second basin from Bahía de La Paz is lined with condos, palms and a beach.

The marina has a water taxi to downtown's Muelle Fiscal, also a shuttle van for marina guests. A dry storage yard with Travelift for boats to 50' is planned for 2006. Ashore are a laundry, dive shop, tackle shop, mini market, fitness center, pool, beach

Big-boat docks at Marina CostaBaja.

La Paz Channel runs alongside Marina Palmira.

cantinas, small shopping center and hotel. The US company BellPort Group opened this marina in 2004. (612) 121-6225 or www.MarinaCostabaja.com

Marina Palmira Yacht Club is 2 miles S of Marina CostaBaja, 2 miles N of Muelle Fiscal downtown. Palmira is an "outie," opens to the N. You enter its lighted riprap jetty only a few yards E of the La Paz Channel. Marina Palmira (pronounced "palm-EE-rah") Yacht Club 240 full-service slips to 120' LOA.

The fuel dock and pumpout is immediately to port as you enter the marina. Ashore are a laundry, small chandler, mini market, restaurants, pool, hotel and The Moorings yacht charter. When this marina was the closest to open sea, it was packed almost exclusively with sportfishing boats, but now cruising sailboats are enjoying it as well. Palmira's owners also own

Marinas de Baja in Cabo. (612) 125-3959.

Marina de La Paz, the original yachting facility in town, lies farther down the channel, about half a mile SW of the Muelle Fiscal, just off the S side of the curving channel. Marina de La Paz has 120 full-service slips for boats to about 70' and end ties to 200'. When rebuilding after Hurricane Marty, Marina de La Paz added a beefier pile and curtain type breakwater to shield it from wind across the harbor.

Located within walking distance of downtown, Marina de La Paz becomes home to each new season's cruising fleet. It's no longer exclusively filled with sailboats, as more power cruisers enjoy being near town.

Marina de La Paz's 200' fuel dock and pump out is easily accessible on an outside dock a few yards off the harbor channel. For large quantities during the peak of cruising season or sportfishing tournaments, request your fuel the day before. Used-oil collection is on the fuel pier. Ashore at the marina's gated compound are the Dock Café, internet access, a chandler, dive school, mechanical & electrical repairs, laundry, storage lockers and the Club Cruceros.

Day Use: If the marina is full or you prefer to anchor nearby, you can enjoy the security of the marina by signing up for temporary use of the dinghy dock, showers and parking. Marina de La Paz is a family run marina (Mac, Mary & son Neil Shroyer), very friendly and helpful. (612) 125-2121 or www.Marinadelapaz.com

Marina Don Jose is next door and SW of Marina de La Paz, just off to port from the main channel. Also known as "Big Abaroa's" in honor of its patron Don Jose Abaroa V., this smaller 18-slip marina was recently rebuilt.

Marina Don Jose's E slips are so close to Marina de La Paz that it's hard to tell where 1 ends and the other

Patio at Marina de La Paz has cafe overlooking harbor.

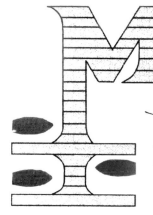

MARINA DE LA PAZ
S.A. DE C.V.

Mailing address	Street Address
Apartado Postal 290	Topete 3040 y Legaspi
23000 La Paz	C.P. 23060
Baja Calif Sur, Mexico	Tel. (612) 122-1646 and 125-2112
Email: marinalapaz@prodigy.net.mx	Fax: (612) 125-5900

- All new hardwood docks
- The same old helpful bilingual staff
- Protected by fixed breakwaters
- Water and electricity on docks
- Wireless internet
- Clean restrooms and showers
- Restaurant, Laundromat
- Chandlery, Mechanic services
- Centrally located in downtown La Paz

Reserve early to assure a space for the high season, November through May

begins. Their higher W dock is part of the busy boat yard (See local services). Marina Don Jose has secure parking and dock gates. From land, the marina entrance is at the foot of Calle Encinas. Marina Don Jose is owned by the Abaroa family. (612) 122-0848.

Future marinas? As we go to press, a developer on El Mogote plans an outie marina - mañana. Fonatur hopes to revive their abandoned Fidepaz project. It's in a nice basin but next to the sewage treatment plant at the end of a narrow channel to the shallow SE corner of Ensenada de La Paz. Check www.MexicoBoating.com for updates.

Local Services

La Paz is an API Port of Entry and many long-range cruising boats wait to make their international arrival till here. The API office is on Muelle Fiscal. The Capitanía is near Revolución and Guerrero. If you're expecting boat parts flown directly to La Paz, you'll want to show the Aduana your TIP to make arrangements to receive them. We've done this several times, and La Paz is 1 of the easier places to have parts flown down.

Fuel: The marinas CostaBaja, Marina de La Paz and Palmira each has a floating fuel dock with diesel and gas.

Haul out: La Paz has 4 good boat yards. Abaroa's Boat Yard (612-122-8915), also known as Big Abaroa's, has a 120-ton marine ways, covered sheds and does good work; they're at the foot of Encinas next to Marina Don Jose. Little Abaroa's Boat Yard and big work dock is about 5 blocks S of Big Abaroa's. Coast Marine (612-121-6738) haul-out, repair and dry storage is at Marina Palmira. Berkovich Boat Yard (612-121-6363) is next to Marina CostaBaja.

Chandlery: La Paz has many. Seamar Marine at Marina de La Paz has surprisingly wide array of goodies (612) 122-9696 and it's near Abaroa's yards. Coast Marine has its own hardware store at Palmira.

Provisions: Four main grocery stores are well stocked, full-service, air-conditioned; 10 small grocers; great mercado municipal. La Paz is Baja's best port for restocking galley larders.

Marina de La Paz slip layout with new breakwaters drawn in.

Local directories: Marina de La Paz and the Club Cruceros regularly update their listings of 100s of services – from all grocery stores & Spanish classes to the 10 closest scuba rentals and AA meetings, from English-speaking doctors & dentists to generator- and outboard-rebuild shops. Internet cafes, banks, travel agents & car rentals abound. Club Cruceros (clubhouse at Marina de La Paz) are boaters helping boaters & raising funds for La Paz charities; if Sea of Cortez Sailing Week is revived, Cruceros will have a hand in it: Cruceros@baja.com.mx

The La Paz morning net is on VHF-22 at 0800 M-Sat. They'll find the answers to all questions.

Ship's Agent: Dick Fifield is a friend to yatistas, can get your parts through Aduana, clear your papers and assist with glitches. Hail "Beach Comber" on VHF-16; or (612) 222-2291.

Club Cruceros

Club Cruceros de La Paz has office at Marina de La Paz.

Culture & History

Museo de Antropológia (Anthropological Museum) at Cinco de Mayo at Altamirano. Casa de Cultural is on Madero at Salvatierra. Both have new exhibits, classes for kids & adults, evening events - an excellent way for cruising kids to interface with local school children, in Spanish, with museum teachers and parents in attendance.

Mercado Municipal: For many West Coast boaters, La Paz is their first excursion into a Mercado Municipal or Central, a Mexico-style farmers' market – many stalls for individual vendors all under 1 giant roof that may take up a whole city block. Every pueblo in Latin America traditionally has at least one Mercado Central, allowing regional farmers to sell their crops wholesale to stores and directly to city dwellers. It's a good cultural experience.

When Hernán Cortez sailed into Bahía de La Paz in 1535, the Cochimé Indians were thriving around the oyster beds, and Cortez sailed on. The next European to arrive was Sebastian Vizcaino in 1596, and he stayed long enough to name the region La Paz (The Peace). Padre Kino led another expedition that left Chacala on the mainland N of Puerto Vallarta in 1683 and landed in La Paz on April 1st. They stayed less than 4 months and left when the Indians become hostile.

Misión La Paz was founded in 1720 by the Jesuits, and a settlement was begun in 1749, but both were abandoned and no ruins remained. Jose de Galvez established the 1st permanent town in 1811, and it became the state capital in 1830.

Bahía de La Paz was famous for pearling from 1616 until 1940, when the oyster beds were destroyed by a blight. Red tides are still common in these waters.

Dry storage yard is popular place to leave your boat on the hard while you fly home. The general term is "marina seca" or dry marina.

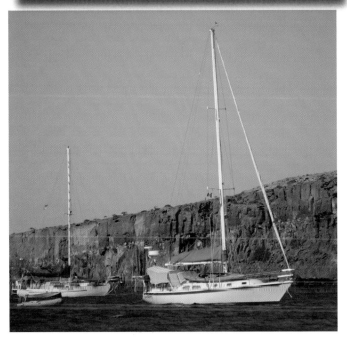

Islas Espíritu Santos

Explore Ashore

Mountain Mule Trip: For a 4- to 10-day excursion, visit the lakes and meadows up in the Sierra de la Laguna. Your group and a guide take a van from La Paz or Los Cabos up into the foothills, then a 4-wheel drive to La Reforma, Miraflores or one of several rustic ranchos still in operation high in the rugged mountains. Then you travel by horseback with a pack-mule carrying the gear to the pristine lakes and meadows tucked between Cerro Picacho (Peaked), Cerros Candeleros (Candlesticks) and Cerros Chuparosas (Hummingbirds).

Scout by Ferry: Mazatlán or Topolobampo (near Copper Canyon) are only a quick ferry ride away, much faster than bringing your own boat across the Sea of Cortez. To and from both locations, Baja Ferries operates the passenger-only ferry and a separate ferry for cars, boats on trailers, RVs, cargo trucks and passengers. We booked a 2-bunk air-conditioned cabina with private head for the 15-knot overnight voyage to Mazatlán; restaurant and cafeteria on board. Buy passenger ferry tickets at least a week in advance, even earlier for boats on trailers, both from Baja Ferries (800) 884-3107. They work with Native Trails tours in Texas for train excursions into the Copper Canyon.

Farmers visit all the marinas with truckloads of fresh fruits, veggies, eggs, homemade cheeses and tortillas. Place your order, and they'll bring it next week.

The islands are an easy day sail from La Paz.

Islas Espíritu Santos

Satellite imagery gives us the only accurate view of the spectacular geography of Isla Espíritu Santos and Isla Partida – referred to jointly as Islas Espíritu Santos. We're grateful to SEMARNAT and CONANP rangers and guides who aided our research and filled us in on all the tiny indents, anchorages and history of these islands – so we can share their local knowledge with our fellow yatistas.

N of the San Lorenzo Channel, the 2,000' high, 7.75-mile long island of Espíritu Santo (Holy Spirit) is joined at Partida Cove to the 3.5-mile long 1,099' high Isla Partida (Parted). The tiny Los Islotes lie half a mile N of Partida. Together they form a wonderful 12-mile yatista paradise within 20 miles of La Paz harbor.

We'll look at all 28 coves, anchorages and points of interest on both sides. On the W side, 8 coves have overnight anchoring potential for coastal cruising craft. All are open to W and SW wind, but some have a portion sheltered from S wind. All are delights for smaller boats, multihulls, dinghies, kayaks and divers.

Candelero,
Las Ballenas,
Raza Cove
Gallo, Gallina
& Empachado

© Point Loma Publishing
2006

to Partida

El Mezteño
to overlook
trail
15' ⚓
trail to well & falls
15' ⚓
Caleta el Candelero
12'
20' ⚓
Monument Rock

Manglecito
Calaveritas
highest peaks
Caleta Ballena
18' ⚓

Isla Ballena
⚓
22'
cave
Punta Ballena

Ensenada de la Raza
18'

Gallo
26' ⚓

24°26.85'N
110°24.43'W

Puerto Ballena

Gallo's Roost
20' ⚓

Ensenada el Gallo
20'   6'
10'

Ensenada la Gallina

Gallina

N

trail
18' ⚓
El Empachado

One nautical mile
Soundings in feet

Not for Navigation

We'll start SE and circumnavigate the islands:

Playa Ayla is the open bight at the island's very S end, between low sandy Punta Lupona and a small detached ledge off the larger Punta la Dispensa (Exemption). Multihulls swing over the N shoal and E side, but we found 19' off the W side at our GPS position 24°24.085'N, 110°20.309'W. The shallows SE of Punta Lupona extend about a mile to Suwanee Rock shoals.

Las Navajas (Razors) is the tiny beach immediately N of the rounded tip of Punta la Dispena and below a landmark eroded lava cone. The pinkish stone is volcanic ash called "estufa." In calm conditions you could anchor a dinghy in the rocks off the beach or swim S from La Dispensa.

La Dispensa Cove
immediately N of the Las Navajas is shoal at the back but has about 10' of water on a line between Punta la Dispensa and Punta Colorado, the next butte-like point N. The narrow draw NE of the beach is pretty and often green with cactus.

Bahia San Gabriel

Widest cove (but not largest anchorage) on the islands, the startlingly white beach at the head of San Gabriel Cove runs almost mile in a straight line NW to SE. Behind the berm, a seasonal lagoon meanders NE. A foot trail from the E end of the main beach crosses the island to Playa Bonanza. On each end of the main beach, 2 tiny side lobes have curved beaches, each with a snorkeling reef. Remnants of La Paz's historic pearl farms are preserved in the N lobe.

We've anchored here in 14' at 24°24.86'N, 110°21.02'W. Multihulls can cozy onto the vast turquoise shelf, but anchoring depths of 10' to 15' are out so far they lack sheltered from NW wind.

El Erizosa is a V-shaped indent between 2 ridges on the N flank of Punta Prieta, which itself points almost due S. Erizosa means Bristled Sea Urchin.

El Empachado (clogged) is the next indent N, and its campsites, trail, beach and snorkeling rocks are ideal for kayakers.

Ensenada la Gallina (hen) is the more S of 3 finger coves that cut almost a third of the way across the width of the island. Gallina Cove is N of Punta Gallina and SE of Isla Gallina. Gallina cove has no beach at its head, but it's good for multihulls,

Spectacular geology of the W side coves includes red sandstone sculpted into fantastic shapes.

Los Islotes

Islas Espíritu Santos
© Point Loma Publishing 2005

Los Muellecitos

El Embudo

Roca Embudo

Isla Partida

Sea of Cortez

Ensenada Grande

La Tijereta

La Cueva

El Cardonal

Partida Back Door

N

Five nautical miles

Isla Espíritu Santo

El Cardoncito & reef

Partida Cove

El Mezteño

Caleta el Candelero

Punta el Pailebote

Caleta Ballena

Salinita Cove

Laguna la Salinita

Isla Ballena

Ensenada de la Raza

Punta Lobos

Isla Gallo

Punta la Bonanza reef

Ensenada el Gallo

Isla Gallina

Ensenada la Gallina

Playa la Bonanza

El Empachado

Punta el Erizosa

Bahía San Gabriel

Punta Morritos

Caleta la Dispensa

Las Navajas

Suwanee Rock

Bahía de La Paz

Punta la Dispensa

Playa Ayla

Punta Lupona

San Lorenzo shoals

San Lorenzo Channel

93

Aerial shows Partida, Candelero and Isla Ballena.

kayaks and snorkelers – not an anchorage for cruising boats.

Isla Gallina is the tiniest of the 3 islands off the W side of Espirítu Santo, great for fishing and snorkeling.

Ensenada el Gallo (rooster) is next N

of Punta Gallina, S of Punta Gallo. Playa Gallo is a tiny white beach and campsite on the NE side of Punta Gallo.

Although Gallo Cove is mostly shoal, a 15' anchoring hole is found just S of the tip of Punta de la Raza, the next dividing finger of land N, where minimal protection from N wind is found.

Isla Gallo (just off Punta de la Raza) is larger and closer to shore than is Gallina, but there's passage depth on all sides. You can anchor in fairly deep water close off the higher S side of Isla Gallo, and pangueros placed an eye ashore.

Ensenada de la Raza is the N of the 3

finger coves and offers better anchorage, framed by Punta de la Raza to the S and Punta Ballena to the N. Good anchorage is found in 9' to 15' under the lee of Punta Ballena. Above the turquoise shoal head

of La Raza Cove, the highest ground of the island rises to the NE.

Isla Ballena (24°28.96'N, 110°23.92'W)

is the largest of the 3 islcts, distinctly tilted up on its S side. A nav light tower is visible on its SW tip, as are rock off its E side.

In N wind, we found ample protection in the large anchorage area off the SE side of the island in 23' to 28' over sand. In a Corumuel or S, you could anchor in deeper water off the NW tip.

Indents on the N and W sides of Isla Ballena have good snorkeling in calm conditions, and an old military vessel was recently sunk in 65' to attract more fish and for wreck diving. One of the underwater caves has a dry air-pocket cave inside the island – like Jonah in the whale's belly. In the deep rocks NE of Ballena Island, you might catch tasty cabrilla and winter yellowtail.

Caleta Ballena is the small squarish

cove directly opposite Isla Ballena. (Historically, this was called Puerto Ballena, according to the naturalist guides and local fishermen.) Caleta Ballena has major historic significance and a pretty beach called Playa Ballena where pangas deposit tourists. The straight valley behind it rises gently and almost crosses the island, where its E end is surrounded in 2,000' peaks.

The only place to anchor (marginal) in 15' to 18' of water is almost outside the 2 bladelike headlands, so you may be better off S of Isla Ballena.

Calaveritas & Manglecito are 2 tiny deepwater clefts immediately N of Caleta Ballena, and in the N one you'll find a small rock jetty for landing folks from a panga or dinghy, and a trail goes up the draw to a campsite.

Candelero Reef (left) offers great snorkeling for novice off the beach and for advanced around the Candlestick in deeper water.

Caleta el Candelero is easy

identified by a strikingly layered ridge on its high N wall and by its landmark candlestick rock out in the middle of the cove. A rock reef (primo snorkeling) running NE divides the cove's pretty beaches.

Behind the N beach a trail leads to a well, natural rock amphitheater, dry waterfalls, caves and hanging fig trees pollinated by a bee specie unique to these islands. Another trail over the central ridge connects to the S beach. Kayak groups camp overnight behind both beaches.

In a strong NW blow, we've anchor in 18' to 25' off the N wall where our GPS position was 24°30.451'N, 110°23.334'W. In calm conditions you can anchor S of here down to W of the candlestick. We found 26' in the middle of the S half of this cove, and a 13' spot of clear sand just N of the middle of the reef – which might be useful in a Corumuel.

El Mezteño is the slot between Candelero and Partida, useful for its very well sheltered dinghy beach. A trail leads to an overlook of Partida Cove.

Partida Cove

connects the islands. Its W opening forms a huge L-shaped cove with good shelter from all directions. A quarter-mile sandbar prevents boats from sailing through, but most dinghies can ford the meandering tidal channel at high tide. (We'll look at Partida Back Door anchorage on the E side below.) Panguero fishing shacks cover the tiny ledge on the port corner of the N lobe and part of the sandbar along with a few park campsites.

Red lava boulders dotted with green cordon circle the white beaches and turquoise shoals - spectacular.

8 La Paz & Islas Espiritu Santos

The only time Cruising World magazine had Partida Cove on their cover, it was Pat's photo. Partida's E end and NE lobe form a vast shelf (3' to 6' sand and shell) ideal for multis, but the rest is deeper.

Our favorite large spots in N to NW wind are (a.) S of the N lobe shoal and W of the fish-shack ledge, in anywhere from 9' to 36' of water (our GPS

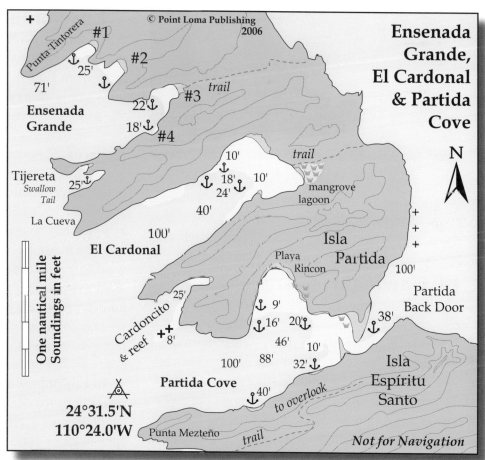

position 24°31.95'N, 110°22.91'W), or (b.) W of the shoaly sandbar, in 13' to 20' of water. We've also anchored in 2 spots off the S wall; in N wind about 32' W of the sandbar, and in E wind in about 40' of water farther W off a rock shingle.

On N approach or departure, avoid Cardoncito Reef, line of rocks running a quarter mile ESE off the tip between Partida and El Cardoncito. This is a popular scuba spot, so look for divers.

El Cardoncito (little cardon cactus) is a great dinghy excursion from adjacent anchorages in calm

Isla Ballena has caves.

Gorilla Rock is fun for kids to spot.

weather. Steep cliffs shelter the narrow slot (not an anchorage), so the pretty beach is an easy landing. A grove of trees shades some campsites, and a trail leads to an old well (not potable). This beach is a handy rest spot when diving Cardoncito Reef.

El Cardonal

El Cardonal (cardon grove) cuts deeper E-W across the island than does Partida Cove, and Cardonal (pronounced "kahr-doh-NAHL) is larger if you include its shallow-draft shelf – which consumes the NE third of the cove. All the rest of us can anchor almost anywhere in the middle third of the cove, E of the shelf in 10' to 36' over sand. We anchor in 25' at out GPS position 24°33'N, 110°23.3'W. This still has good N and S shelter.

The beautiful NE beach is in a bowl of hillside similar to Partida's N lobe, but behind the S beach is a seasonal lagoon with mangroves and trail over to the E side of the island. Some years, mosquitoes are pesky at sunset if the wind's gone.

Caleta Tijereta (swallow-tail frigate bird) is a small 2-headed or swallow-tail cove immediately S of Ensenada Grande. Pangueros pull up onto the tiny

N beach, and one cruising boater reported anchoring the S slot in calm conditions, bow and stern, in 25' over sand. It looks like a good dinghy excursion from Ensenada Grande.

Ensenada Grande

Ensenada Grande or Big Cove is 4 coves in one. 3 obvious anchoring coves fan across the NE end of this bay: #1 small, #2 medium and #3 large from E to W. All 3 are open to the SW.

When anchored in about 20' of water off #1 and #2, some swell can come around Punta Tintorero to the NW and you can see your neighbors. A picnic palapa on #2 beach is for day use only.

The largest cove #3 is farthest E, has more privacy, better swell shelter, and you can get further in to anchor in 15' to 38' over sand. The larger #3 beach is where day tour boats from La Paz bring tourists to hike the maintained trail to the island's E side. If you want to know if the N wind is still blowing, but don't want to up anchor and poke your nose out, you might hike across to Playa Mullecitos to see for yourself.

The smallest spot at Ensenada Grande is #4, a rectangular niche out of the S wall of #3, where one boat can swing in 20' over sand.

El Embudo (Funnel) on the NE end of Isla Partida is too tight for ocean-going yatistas and subject to N swell. But it's useful as a dinghy beach and snorkeling spot in calm conditions or a rest stop for kayaks or dinghies going out to Los Islotes.

Los Islotes

Los Islotes (Islets) lie about half a mile NNW of the N tip of Partida Island. 2 white-washed pinnacles rise 50' high from depths of at least 75' – so this is a good place to drift, rather than anchor, while watching the sea lion rookery on the N shelf and the thin reef that connects the islets. Seals cavort with divers, but you must avoid aggressive bulls in mating season. There's a spectacular grotto at 25' depth. Only in calm seas can you swim through the arch in the E island to visit both sides.

Los Islotes Light (24°35.85'N, 110°24.18'W) is on the larger, flat-top W islet. There's deep water all

Kayakers circumnavigate Isla Espiritu Santo, Isla Partida and out to Los Islotes.

Anchoring just outside the shoals.

around Los Islotes, so don't hesitate to cut between when rounding the N end of Isla Partida.

El Bajito (little shallow spot)
is a popular scuba site about half a mile SW of Los Islotes. The flat-top pinnacle has a least depth of about 20' down to about 90' at the sand and coral floor. Good fishing, too.

Marisla Seamount is about 8.25 miles ENE of Los Islotes. 3 peaks rise from 300' up to between 52' and 82' below the surface, drawing a wealth of beautiful sea creatures – giant manta rays, octopus, dorado. Underwater filmmakers come to Marisla to witness the annual courtship dance of the hammerhead shark – hundreds of them.

Los Muellecitos (Little Piers) is a protected beach where sea turtles lay eggs and hatchlings dash to the sea, located about a mile down the less sheltered E side of Isla Partida. We think the name refers to eroded fingers in the sheer cliffs above the beach. Nearby is a scuba dive site with a 75' wall lined with sea fans.

Partida Back Door is the E side of
Partida Cove, blocked by the sandbar. In fair or moderate NW weather, small boats can find marginal anchorage in about 20' over sand, off the corner where the hill to the NW meets the cobble beach.

La Salinita (Little Salt Pan) is 4
miles SE of Partida Back Door. La Salinita is the sheltered N corner of the long indent between the S side of Punta El Pailebote and the N side of Punta Lobos. Pailebote is the prominent (about 600') N-pointing headland. Boats anchor in 35' to 40' of water S of S slope of Pailebote and E of the cobble beach. Laguna La Salinita is the large lagoon behind the berm. We think Pailebote refers to a ship's boiler.

Bonanza Beach is a mile of blindingly white sand between Punta Lobos and Punta Bonanza. Punta Lobos (24°27.5'N, 110°17.6'W) overlooks a wide reef that spreads a half mile SE from the low point, so take care when approaching from NE. In fair weather, anchorage is possible anywhere off of the beach in 15' to 28' of water. In moderate NW wind, tuck S of the Punta Lobos point and W of its reef in 15' to 25' of water.

However, in a strong blow, the low land doesn't provide good shelter, especially below the draw leading N from the corner anchorage. Bonanza means good sailing weather, as in the friendly nautical salutation "Ir en bonanza!" S of Punta Bonanza has no anchorage.

Going ashore requires park permit.

9
San Jose Island
to
Puerto Escondido

The nicest cruising grounds in the Sea of Cortez are the 115 miles between La Paz and Puerto Escondido, including the Espiritu Santo Islands (previous chapter). This stretch gives you many anchorages, wild geology, fantastic sea life, uninhabited islands and a pleasant marine climate.

Don't forget to pay the SEMARNAT fee (about $2/person/day) in La Paz or Loreto, if you want to go ashore on any of the islands of the Sea of Cortez, because they're all regulated within the Islas del Golfo nature preserve.

Provision well in La Paz or Loreto, because no food, water, fuel or other services exist between. We discourage yatistas from taking water from the few wells or tanks that isolated villagers and Navy outposts must depend on. If you lightened your larder while exploring the Espiritu Santos or languishing at Puerto Escondido, restock before heading out.

If you developed a case of "cruise-heimers" while growing to the bottom in La Paz or Puerto Escondido, you may want to practice your seamanship skills and buff up your traveling gear before getting underway.

ROUTE PLANNING: La Paz to Puerto Escondido

Weather along this stretch is usually benign, but when a Norther begins, it may last for days. Pay attention to the ham and VHF net WX broadcasts.

Fortunately, anchorages are close enough for most boats to anchor up every night if the weather cooperates. After Balandra (See La Paz chapter.) and Islas Espíritu Santo and Partida (See previous chapter.), we'll look at Islas San Francisco and San Jose, mainland Mechudo, Evaristo, Nopolo, Timbabichi, El Gato, San Telmo, Santa Marta, Punta Marcial, Agua Verde, San Cosme and Rattlesnake Cove or Candeleros, plus the islands San Diego, Catalina, Monserrat, Candeleros and Danzante, plus a few marginal toe holds - before entering Puerto Escondido.

The San Jose Channel has a fast and reversing tidal current due to its radical bottom contours, and N wind tends to venturi here,

Map labels

Punta San Telmo

El Gato

Punta Botella

Timbabichi

Rocas Morenos

N

Five nautical miles
Soundings in feet

Punta Montalvo

Isla
Santa
Cruz

Isla Habana

Isla San Diego

Rancho
Dolores

© Point Loma Publishing 2006

Los
Burros

Isla
Las
Animas

3000'

Punta Alta

NW
Point

1200'

600'

Nopolo

Cazadero

600'

Isla
San Jose

**San
Evaristo**

Punta Salina
salt pond

Overall

**Isla San
Francisco
to
El Gato**

Islas
Cayos

Amortajada
Lagoon

Punta
Mechuda

Rocas
Focas

Isla Coyote

Isla
San Francisco

600'

Not for Navigation

Air and sea level, the Hook at Isla San Francisco is inviting.

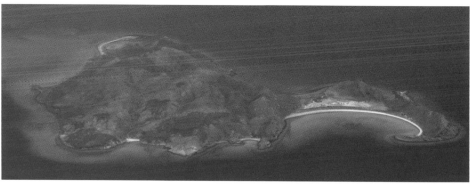

so try to time this passage with favorable conditions. We've never failed to see vast schools of dolphins feeding through here, often whales too.

Plan time to fish for cabrilla and grouper at rock piles and shelves on the islands' S and W sides, but spear fishing is not allowed at the protected islands or in Loreto National Marine Park. Summer bill-fishers will plan their route along the E side of all the islands atop the steep drop off.

COASTWISE: La Paz to Puerto Escondido

Half way around the 50-mile W shore of Bahía La Paz, the fertilizer pier at San Juan de la Costa (24°23.7'N, 110°41.4'W) has a deepwater T-head and open roadstead. Yatistas normally depart La Paz from Punta Prieta or Balandra Cove and head 14 miles N up the W side of the Espíritu Santos, to avoid shoals S of those islands and N of La Paz harbor.

Cabeza de Mechudo (Mechudo Head) on the mainland and Isla San Francisco 4 miles off shore frame the S entrance to San Jose Channel, the 1.75 miles wide passage W of Isla San Jose. The channel's abrupt bottom constriction increases the current and attracts dolphins and whales.

Mechudo Head (GPS 24°48.37'N, 110°39.40'W) is a modest point below landmark Cerro Mechudo (3,600'), 4 miles inland. In S breeze, anchorage is possible on the N side of the point. In NW wind, pangueros anchor in the sandy cove S of Punta Coyote, about 6 miles SW of Mechudo Head. A graded road behind both spots connects Evaristo to La Paz.

The San Jose Shelf rises abruptly from 4,200' to a relatively shallow bottom around the islands San Francisco, Coyote, Cayo, San Jose, Animas, San Diego and Santa Cruz. Expect 1- to 3-knot current. Cetacean and pelagic species abound.

Isla San Francisco

San Francisco Island lies 13 miles NNW of Los Islotes, about 2-mile width by radar, and from S blends with the dramatic geology of the much larger Isla San Jose, which lies a mile N.

The Hook: The anchorage for deep-draft boats is on the SE side, inside a picturesque half-mile wide semicircle cove called the hook, open to SW. It has a nav light tower on the point, lovely white beach and fairly good shelter from N wind. We've anchored in 15' to 25' over sand in the NW end at our GPS 24°49.3'N, 110°34'2'W. The middle has only about 32' depth. The SE end is 18' to shoal draft, and the NE window lets in some breeze.

At sunset, if there's no breeze to blow away the pesky "no-see-'ums" or "jejenes" (pronounced "hay-HAY-nayz") – stinging gnats so tiny they get through window screen – you might want to burn fibrous coconut husks in the BBQ as a pleasant-smelling non-toxic bug-repelling smudge, or slather on repellent. Folks allergic to bee stings sometimes react to multiple no-see-'ums stings.

2 small coves on the island's E side are good for dinghy trips to snorkel or for trailer boats. Pangas drag ashore on the island's NE end. Using your skiff to fish or snorkel (lots of current), you can explore Rocas de la Foca and other detached rock piles N of Isla San Francisco, but high sun defines the safe dinghy passages.

NOTE: Departing the Hook to go N to Isla San

Jose, we go at least 2.75 miles E before making any northing, to avoid 4 dangers: Sea Rocks, the reef E of Isla Coyote, an unmarked rock between them and another unmarked rock a few hundred yards NW of Isla Coyote. Approach Amortajada on Isla San Jose between Punta Ostiones and the S end of Isla Cayo.

Isla Coyote

This tiny round-topped islet (24°51.10'N, 110°34.7'W) is midway between Isla San Francisco and Isla San Jose. The family village crammed on Isla Coyote is one of the few year-round island settlements in the Sea of Cortez. Coyote's children attend school in Evaristo via panga – viva suburbia.

A reef perimeters the island and stretches W, prohibiting ocean-going yachts from anchoring off the village. A detached rock pile awash is reported a few hundred yards NW of Isla Coyote, outside the perimeter reef.

We've seen one local fishing boat anchor just S of the perimeter reef but haven't tried it ourselves. Kayaks and dinghies can follow pangueros through 2 narrow cuts in the perimeter reef.

Rocas de la Foca

Isla Coyote is best as a reference point for avoid hitting Rocas de la Foca (Seal Rocks) a quarter mile wide rock patch partly awash, partly submerged. They lie about 0.75 of a mile NW of the NW tip of Isla San Francisco, 0.75 of a mile W of Isla Coyote, and 0.75 of a mile SW of the SW tip of Isla San Jose.

Isla San Jose

Isla San Jose is a beautiful giant, stretching 16

miles NW to SE. The S tip is 42 miles NNW of La Paz harbor, and the N end is 55 miles SSE of Puerto Escondido. The Guayacura who once thrived on the flanks of the 2,077' peak are gone, but 6" scorpions still roam the foothills.

Amortajada Lagoon

Laguna Amortajada (Shrouded Lagoon) is the largest mangrove lagoon on an island in the Sea of Cortez. The roughly triangular lagoon is hidden behind long beaches on its N and S sides, and a shallow panga channel separates it from the island's SE slope. The lagoon's SW tip, Punta Ostiones (Oyster) was flattened by hurricanes, and the nav light has moved to Isla Cayo. Beware of uncharted rocks S of Isla Cayo.

Bahía Amortajada is a 3-mile wide corner N of the lagoon and W of the island's SW side. Elbow room in Shrouded Bay is limited by migrating sandbars; it's open to WNW wind, but waves from that direction are baffled by Isla Cayo, a half-mile white blade with a quarter mile submerged reef of its NE end. Shrouded Bay is good in southerlies and moderate N wind.

Enter close S of the S end of Isla Cayo (24°52.41'N, 110°36.19'W). In moderate N weather, we anchor in the NE corner in 15' to 18' over sand at our GPS position 24°52.9'N, 110°34.45'W, which is handy to the lagoon entrance but can be buggie at sunset. In calm or S weather, we've anchored at 24°52.05, 110°35.15' N of the neck to Punta Ostiones.

In a Norther, the S side of Laguna Amortajada at least offers wave shelter. Take great care as you move there. We sounded 20' to 40' of water along the S beach of Laguna Amortajada.

Punta Salinas: At 4 miles NW of Amortajada, this 3-domed hill and low triangular point poke a mile SW from the base of the island's SW slope, and salt evaporation ponds and a salt works are inside the triangle, which has a flood gate on its N side. A red cylindrical tower stands next to the new frame light tower.

In moderate N wind, we anchored in

*Amortajada Lagoon estuary
makes a good dink trip.*

Bahía San Evaristo has good shelter in N wind.

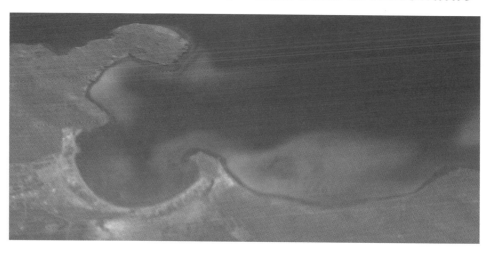

the S corner in 33' over sand and found good wave shelter at 24°54.86'N, 110°37.49'W. But in a Norther, the slopes funnel wind down onto this area. From Punta Salinas, you can see 1.75 miles across the San Jose Channel into Bahía San Evaristo.

Punta San Ysidro 2 miles NW pokes half a mile out from Isla San Jose, and the low point contains another small lagoon. We have not tried to anchor near this point (24°56.80'N, 110°39.33'W), but its sandy S side might be a lunch stop.

Bahía Cazadero (Hunting Place) about 2 miles SE of the island's NW tip is a mile-wide bite backed by foothills from the island's 1,500 high N ridgeline. Behind the bay's NW berm is a tiny marsh where waterfowl used to be hunted. Anchorage is possible in 20' to 25' off the berm with good shelter from NW wind; 25°01.13'N, 110°41.04'W.

NW Point on Isla San Jose is only about 2.5 miles across from Punta Nopolo, and the 800' bottom of the San Jose Channel brings lots of current, but fair anchorage in calm wind is found SE of the point at 25°01.72'N, 110°42.37'W.

Kelter's Coves on Isla San Jose's NW side looked too open and too small, but our GPS approach waypoint off the middle point is 25°01.37'N, 110°34.79'W.

Islas las Animas (26°6.4'N,

110°31.5'W) is a detached cluster of islets 6 miles NE of Punta Colorado Light on the NE corner of Isla San Jose. The Spirits have a nav light, no anchoring shelter – but they're where to go for winter barracuda, for summer marlin, dorado and tuna, and for tasty cabrilla in the rocks year round.

Bahía San Evaristo

Punta Arena: Less than 3 miles SE of Bahía San Evaristo, low, sandy Punta Arena (GPS 24°53.03'N, 110°41.08'W) offers a fair-weather toe-hold just S of the shoal and rocks off its point. This is W of Isla Cayo and Punta Salina across the channel.

San Evaristo (pop. approx. 200) is a fishing, salt mining and goat-herding village on the W side of San Jose Channel, 50 miles NNW of La Paz, 65 miles SE of Agua Verde. The 65-mile paved road from La Paz has brought a few new homes and a big round palapa.

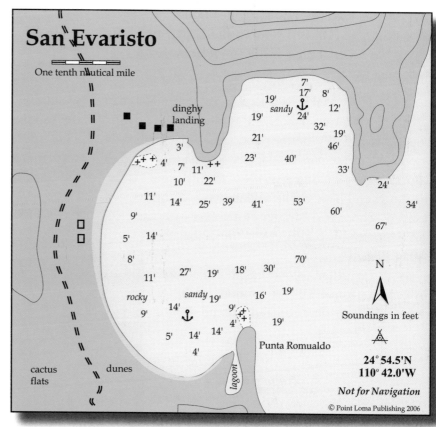

***Nosing into Evaristo's
North Cove.***

Bahía San Evaristo is a 2-lobe bay with excellent shelter from N and S weather thanks to the N headland Cerro San Isidro (490') and the lesser, under-lapping Punta Romualdo (24°54.5'N, 110°42.2'W) to the S, which has a light tower. You can enter fairly close to Punta Evaristo, but Romualdo has a reef tip.

North Cove

This is the large, cliff-lined rectangle framed by the S-pointing Punta Evaristo and the S flanks Cerro San Isidro. It's almost a quarter mile across, room for several boats. North Cove has good protection in all weather but S or SE. It's quiet and private, except for an occasional goat bleating on the steep hills.

We have anchored on the 15' to 20' deep turquoise shelf across the NW half of the cove at our GPS position 24°54.817'N, 110°42.17'W. In the E half of North Cove, we've anchored in the middle in 36' 40' of dark blue water.

Village Bay is a larger crescent-beach bay

SW of North Cove. The N end is close to the village, but it has a rocky bottom and less shelter when N wind bridges the gap W of Cerro San Isidro – though a good dinghy landing is just N of the little reef visible off the N-end beach. The village has a couple dozen houses, school and meager store. Just over the rise, salt evaporation ponds cover the N beach, called Playa Panteón.

In S weather, good anchorage and protection from swell are found in the S end of Village Bay, tucked behind Punta

***Goats with bells
visit the anchorage.***

Romualdo and its N-pointing reef. We anchored here in 14' and 19' over sand.

Playa Panteón (Cemetery Beach) is
a separate beach cove on the N side of Evaristo village, NW of Cerro San Isidro. This open bay (GPS approach waypoint 24°55.25'N, 110°42.59'W) is useful in very calm periods or S weather. Corumuel winds are seldom felt this far from La Paz, but summer storms could bring wind from the S. You can anchor 18' to 30' over sand. Salt evaporation ponds, a pile of white salt and a panga landing mark the shore.

Punta Nopolo (Punta Alta) is a peaked almost detached headland 7.5 miles NW of Bahía San Evaristo, 2.5 miles across from Isla San Jose's NW point. (Don't confuse this Nopolo with a Fonatur development N of Puerto Escondido.) 2 deep and marginal coves lie SW of Punta Nopolo (GPS 25°00.81'N, 110°45.41'W).

Nopolo: The better spot
is the larger and more S of the 2. We've anchored off the steep beach in 45' of water at our GPS position 24°59.85'N, 110°45.36'W. Smaller boats can get in closer. The green valley has a few houses, cemetery and black spires in the S hills.

Nopolo Alta: In light NW wind or settled weather, larger boats can anchor in 60' of water off the saddle immediately SW of the bigger headland. This spot is smaller and a bit NE of the Nopolo settlement. Expect lots of current at this N end of the San Jose Channel.

COASTWISE continued

***Nopolo is hard to find,
not usually worth it.***

Bahía Rincon: 5 miles NW of Punta Nopolo, Punta los Burros marks the NW edge of a small steep-sided Bahía Rincon (Inside Corner). The village of Los Burros is S of the NW point, and a panga settlement of Las Higueras (Fig Trees) clings to the SE end of the bay. A 20-mile mountain track links it to Highway 1.

We haven't tried to anchor in either end of Bahía Rincon, because it's open to prevailing NW wind and S-bound current flowing into San Jose Channel. But Bahía Rincon has long been reported to provide good S protection. In fair weather, it could give an underpowered vessel a place to await favorable tides in the San Jose Channel. Our GPS approach waypoint just N of Bahía Rincon is 25°02.31'N, 110°47.89'W.

Rincon Bay is the last reasonable road contact for 35 miles N, until Agua Verde, and that isn't much. From there, it's only 23 miles to Puerto Escondido. The Sierra de la Giganta (Giant) provides magical scenery.

The next 13 miles between Punta los Burros and Timbabichi, we stay at least 4 miles offshore to avoid 4 hazards: Isla Habana, Punta Montalvo reef, Rocas Moreno and Black Rock. A sloped plain fronts the mountains.

Los Dolores:
Midway between Punta Los Burros and Isla Habana (Havana), thriving Rancho los Dolores (Pains) is visible behind the beach. An open roadstead from here 8 miles N has 20' to 30' of water over sand. A trail from the ranch goes 1-.5 miles up to ruins of Misión los Dolores, then another 1.5 miles to link with the track behind Bahía Rincon. N of the irrigation ravine is 25°04.61'N, 110°51.14'W.

Isla Habana is flat-topped, stark white and makes a good landmark. Its E side is 25°07.76'N, 110°51.55'W, or about 2 miles off shore N of Rancho Dolores.

Isla San Diego is tiny, only a mile long, and lies 5 miles N of the sharp Punta Calabozo (Pruning Hook) on the N tip of Isla San Jose. Reefs jut 3 miles SE of Isla San Diego and 2 miles N of Calabozo. Marginal anchorage is found off Isla San Diego's NW side in 22' to 30' of water. For scuba divers, Isla San Diego's 2-tiered reef is a honeycomb of colorful caves and grottos.

Isla Santa Cruz (1,500' high, 4 miles NE to SW, barren) lies 4 miles N of Isla San Diego, 11 miles

E of Timbabichi. Water depths near 200' too close to shore prevent anchoring, but summer marlin are drawn to its SE proximity.

Montalvo & Moreno: We avoid the rocky shelf from Punta Montalvo up to Punta Rocas Moreno (Dark), but some boaters report anchoring S of Rocas Moreno and Punta Moreno in 20' to 30' over sand. Beware the submerged reef jutting a quarter mile SE

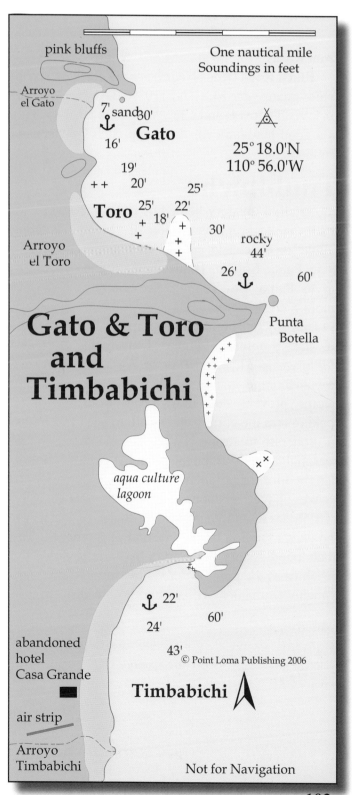

pink bluffs

One nautical mile
Soundings in feet

Arroyo el Gato

7' sand 30'

16'

Gato

25° 18.0'N
110° 56.0'W

19'

20'
++

25'

Toro 25' 22'
+ 18' +
+

30'

rocky
44'

Arroyo el Toro

26'

60'

Gato & Toro and Timbabichi

Punta Botella

aqua culture lagoon

22'
24'

60'

abandoned hotel
Casa Grande

43'
© Point Loma Publishing 2006

air strip

Timbabichi

Arroyo Timbabichi

Not for Navigation

from Rocas Moreno at 25°12.61'N, 110°54.88'W.

Black Rock (Roca Negra) is a big black rock with white guano (25°14.81'N, 110°55.34'W), a smaller rock visible just E and a few stragglers in close. This is a good landmark for the S approach to Ensenada Timbabichi.

Timbibichi

Satellite imagery helped us correct mistakes we made in the previous edition of "Mexico Boating Guide" on the coastal contour from Punta Timbabichi N to Punta Botella, Bahía El Gato and up to Punta San Telmo. (See satellite photo.)

Timbabichi bight immediately SE of the S-pointing Punta Timbabichi (GPS 25°16.31'N, 110°56.29'W) is a fair anchorage in fair weather. Shallow depths prevent deep-draft boats from tucking into the corner, and swell invades in moderate to strong NW to N wind. A seasonal lagoon behind the point has been dammed for irrigation; no entrance.

We have anchored at GPS 25°16.16'N, 110°56.53'W and nearby in 28' to 30' of water, off the panga landing on the NE end of the beach. The abandoned 2-story building a half a mile down the beach from the point is not visible from S approach. Rancho Timbabichi village and an old dirt air strip

Hotel Timbabichi, abandoned.

Timbibichi Point points S, shields an aqua-culture pond & village.

are nearby. Timbabichi is the Pericue name for a 5-mile arroyo behind the village.

Los Pargos: This small, reef lined indent is a mile N of Punta Timbabichi and just S of Punta Botella (see below). A rocky ledge fouls the N end, a reef fouls the S point, and we've never found good holding or shelter in the middle. However, the ledge and reef are good snorkeling for a dinghy jaunt around from Timbabichi or Gato y Toro.

Gato y Toro

Bahía Gato y Toro is picturesque. Dramatic pink-peach-oxblood red cliffs of sandstone form curvaceous bubbles, swirls and water ledges behind the white beaches, turquoise water and lava black reef. But in windy conditions, Bahía El Gato's marginal shelter is cramped for all but multis.

NOTE: El Gato technically refers only to the smaller N lobe, where the narrow El Gato Arroyo enters the bay. According to locals, that seasonal flow was named for puma that lived a mile up this canyon. The larger S lobe is El Toro, backed by a wider El Toro Arroyo. After Pat anchored her trimaran in El Gato and El Toro in 1979, she refused to disclose this location for fear it might suffer from discovery. By 1995, it was discovered, and common usage clumped El Gato with El Toro into Los Gatos. This never was a port, and maybe it's time to separate the puma from the bull.

What we call Bahía Gato y Toro is a 1-mile long, 2-lobe bay immediately N of Los Pargos, 2 miles N of Timbabichi and 11 W of Isla Santa Cruz. Bahía El Gato is framed on the S by the radar prominent Punta Botella (GPS 25°17.487'N, 110°56.00'W)

Picturesque cliffs shelter El Gato's N side.

Kayakers haul out on one of Gato y Toro's beaches.

and at the N by Cantil Colorado. Botella (Bottle) is a narrow point of gray-black rock. Cantil Colorado's S tip is low black and red, then grows into 4 large pink orange cliffs with flat faces reaching .75 of a mile N.

Our GPS approach waypoint about half a mile E of Bahía Gato Y Toro is 25°18'N, 110°56'W. A rosy hill behind the beach separates the canyons and the lobes: El Gato N; El Toro S.

El Gato lobe:

Gavilán or hole for oar locks.

In moderate NW weather, the N end of this smaller lobe has marginal shelter under the lee of pink Cantil Colorado, in 15' to 20' over sand. Multis can tuck into the NW corner. Beach landing is fine. You can snorkel the water ledge that circles the cliffs. A hill divides El Gato beach from that of El Toro, and off a rock pile jutting E off that hill we find 20' over sand.

El Toro lobe: A flat-top reef juts NNE from

where Punta Botella meets the beach; it's spectacular snorkeling, and scuba divers enjoy the 60' deep Punta Botella. But the reef reduces anchoring room, and this lobe is more open to N weather.

We've anchored just outside the reef in 26' to 30' over gravel, but it's open to N and NE wind and swell. In S wind, swell invades outside the reef. Multi's may squeeze behind the N end of the reef in 18' to 25' over sand and enjoy reasonable shelter from moderate N and S wind and swell.

COASTWISE continued

Punta San Telmo (Punta Prieta) lies 2 miles NW of Punta Botella and has black pillars off its N side and a bold detached rock. Our GPS just off the rock is 25°19.74'N, 110°57.15'W. In calm weather, anchorage is found S and N of the point in 15' of water over sand. In NW wind, the best shelter is off the shingle beach on the S side of the point.

Marcial Corner

Punta San Marcial ("mar-see-AHL") is a major headland 25 miles SE of Puerto Escondido, 3 miles E of Agua Verde, 80 miles NW of La Paz. If you don't want to stop here, avoid the dangerous reefs and offshore rocks by standing 2 miles off the lighted but dangerous San Marcial Rocks (25°29.8'N, 111°01.5'W).

That large flat-topped rock and encircling reef lie about 1.5 miles NE of the point. We sounded deep water in the middle of the passage between Marcial Reef and the point, but uncharted reefs fringe both sides, and there's lots of current, so why chance it.

For gunk-holing, the 5-mile span SW of Punta San Marcial has 3 coves with varying shelter in NW conditions. In a Norther, these are better than Agua Verde.

Punta Berrendo, Punta San Marcial and Marcial Reef (far right).

Satellite image shows relationship between Berrendo, Marcial and Agua Verde. Note volcano caldera in center of the peninsula.

Bahía Santa Marta:
The private Rancho Santa Marta is visible on the S end of the beach SW of Punta Gavilán. The best shelter is off the N end of the beach in 18' to 20' over sand. The nautical meaning of *gavilán* is a thole or oarlock, referring to round holes in the ridgeline of this majestic point.

The green arroyo behind Marta runs NW, and broad strata of pink and white rock near the top of the mountains run 2 miles behind this S cove and the next one N.

Bahía Berrendo,
the next cove N, is smaller and has no settlement nor much beach, but it may prove more useful as you can tuck into 20' to 24' close S of steep-sided Punta Berrendo (Brindled), which displays bands of light and dark rock. Kayaks explore the small sea cave on the point.

Bahía San Marcial:
Radar paints a good picture of this half-mile long cove, the N-most of these 3, but navigate with caution. The bay is SW of a sheltering hatchet-shaped wedge projecting SE from the massive headland. A dangerous submerged reef trails almost 2 miles SE from the hatchet, and the sheltered spots are behind the reef. So we approach and depart from S to stand clear of all dangers. In NW wind, the cliffy N end of Bahía San Marcial has decent shelter in 18' to 22' over sand. But in NE wind it's no bueno.

Agua Verde

Bahía Agua Verde (2.5 miles W of Punta San Marcial) is a popular 23-mile day trip SE of Puerto Escondido. It has coral sand, turquoise water, a tiny village and several anchoring choices, but it's not an all-weather anchorage. Agua verde means the color turquoise. The 25-mile road from Highway 1 is partly paved, so big RVs reach Agua Verde and 3 beaches N. Agua Verde's wells are not potable, but they have a new desalination plant and small tienda.

Our GPS approach waypoint is 25°32'N, 111°03.5'W, about a quarter mile E of the detached spire Roca Solitaria (115').This landmark spire has a "cuff" ledge on all sides, frequented by swimmers and seals, but you can pass close in +100' of water.

AVYC:
In moderate NW wind, we anchor in the NW corner off what's laughingly called Agua Verde Yacht Club beach. A dozen cruising boats tuck in SW of the little thumb of sand and rock off the S slope of Cerro San Pasquel. To enter this bight, give the thumb a wide berth, then anchor S of the prominent sandy isthmus in about 25' over sand and shell.

NOTE: We charted a dark-yellow

Agua Verde Yacht Club anchorage has a picture window view N.

*Aguaverdeño kids grow up
with one foot in the water.*

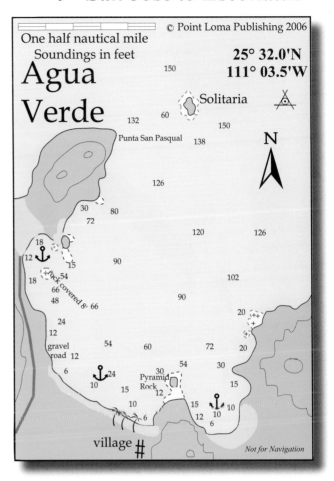

rock pinnacle covered by 8' of water at low tide at our GPS position 25°31.416'N, 111°04.391'W. Some boats hit it.

So many yatistas visit here that we've dubbed a cement building the Agua Verde Yacht Club for its good BBQ and rendezvous potential. The dirt road that rings the yacht club bight takes you over to the village.

SE Bight is a cove in the lee W of another

detached landmark, Roca Pirámide (Pyramid). We've anchored in 15' to 30' over sand and shell, depending on wind direction. This is good shelter in S wind.

Caves dot the hillside and beach. From the beach landing, you may walk to the village via a hidden rock ledge and an arch through the cliff S of Pyramid Rock. Note the tide, so you don't get your knickers wet on return (as Pat did).

Village Beach: In days of flat calms, you

can try anchoring well off Agua Verde's broader central beach lined with palms, where it's easier to dinghy ashore and visit the village. But a shale shelf makes it difficult to get close and the holding is lousy.

We've inspected El Pórtico, the cliffy bight a half mile W of Agua Verde's entrance, but haven't anchored there.

Gene Kira's delightful novel "King of the Moon" seems to us to have been written about Agua Verde and its humble, hopeful, brave pangueros. This would be a great place to read it.

COASTWISE continued

Punta San Cosme (our GPS 25° 34.64' N, 111° 08.97' W) or 5 miles NW of Agua Verde has a small reef jutting NE from the point. An abandoned hotel and round palapa are visible on the W side of the point, and a marina might be built in the half-mile long estuary SW of the point. A seasonal hot spring is behind the NW end of the beach. The road behind the estuary is paved 20 miles to Highway 1.

*Village Beach anchorage
is well off the beach.*

Not for Navigation

Islas Coronados

Punta Tierra Firma

Loreto

Sea of Cortez

Punta Cholla Rocks

Punta Tintorera

La Lancha

V-Neck Slot

Balandra Cove

salt pond

Nopolo

Isla Carmen

Bahia Salina

Punta Perico

Puerto Escondido

Marquer Cove

South Slot

© Point Loma Publishing 2006

N

Is. Danzante Primero

Candeleros Cove

Candeleros Rocks

Punta Candeleros

white rock

Rocas Galeras

Isla Monserrat

Overall Loreto to Agua Verde

Caleta San Cosme

Five nautical miles

Isla Santa Catalina

Bahía Agua Verde

Marcial Reef

Punta San Marcial

Bahía San Marcial

Rancho Santa Marta

Half a mile N of the point is a small Isla San Cosme, which has a marginal cove on its S side. A quarter mile E is tinier Isla San Damien, but beware the reef that links the islands. Fishing and diving are good and handy to Puerto Escondido.

Coasting NW from Agua Verde, we plot a course to a point 1.5 miles E of Punta Candeleros, thus avoiding Damien, Cosme and the tiny Rocas Blancas 4 miles SE of Punta Candeleros.

Los Candelcros look like 3 candle stubs, 2 of them close off Punta Candeleros and the third closer to the S tip of Isla Danzante. Fishing and diving are good, but the current is strong. We've passed safely in 86' of water between Punta Candeleros and the nearest of the 3 candle-stubs (Isla Pardo), but the standard passage is close along the N side of the NW candle.

Mano de Dios

About 8 miles S of Puerto Escondido and half a mile S of Punta Candeleros, Caleta Mano de Dios is a tiny niche named for the 70' tall hand-like formation of stone clearly visible on the E face of the white massif that forms the cove's E wall. Sheer cliffs seem to part to allow a boat to enter.

Our GPS approach waypoint just outside the entrance to Hand of God Cove is 25°42.6'N, 111°12.85'W.

Open to N wind, the slot has room for 1 or 2 yatistas to swing in 15' to 20' of clear water over sand. The beach has a 3-hut village and a few tent campers who brave a 10-mile dirt road to get here, so it's pretty quiet. You can snorkel though the gap and all around the Hand of God massif. Some call this Little Candeleros, but we like the local name.

Bahía Candeleros

This pretty-beach cove is 12 miles SE of Puerto Escondido, 4 miles S of Isla Danzante, on the N side of Punta Candeleros. Bahía Candeleros (GPS 25°43.80'N, 111°14.40'W) is a popular getaway in

Look for this Mano de Dios in stone outside Hand of God Cove.

Cliffs line the entrance to Mano de Dios Cove.

flat or S weather, and cruisers potluck on the beach. A spa hotel graces the hill in the middle of the small valley. However, locals call this Rattlesnake Cove, so don't venture too far inland. Enter down the middle to avoid a detached rock almost in the middle. Anchor in either end in 15' to 20' over sand. The fishing village of Liguii is half a mile N.

Gerry's Rock: Gerry Cunningham reported a dangerous rock detached about 2 miles S of Danzante's S tip; he said it's about 300' wide, covered by about 5' of water at his GPS position 25°46.18'N, 111°10.70'W.

Bahía Candeleros is a summer getaway from Puerto Escondido.

Isla Danzante Primero

Isla Danzante Primero (Prima Ballerina) lies about 2 miles ESE of Puerto Escondido. Isla Danzante Light is on the NE side of this 2.5 mile long uninhabited island. The rocky S tip is good for scuba diving. A small chunk off the N end is linked by a rocky channel. From Puerto Escondido, Danzante looks like a spiky-haired dragon swimming N, not a ballerina.

Honeymoon Cove on the NW is an intimate sandy cove, split into 3 lobes. The N lobe is smallest, ideal for multihulls that can snuggle into the 10' N end, which has the best beach. The middle lobe is larger, has a steeper bottom, so anchoring comfort is about 50' over sand.

Danzante Reef is off S end of the island.

The S lobe is more open to N swell but not bad in about 18' to 22' over sand, but avoid the rock off the S point.

The whole W side is a picturesque open roadstead. Look for a little Mushroom Rock about half way down. A blue park sign is south of Mushroom Rock.

Loreto National Marine Park

This park covers 500,000 acres of the Sea of Cortez, including the islands of Santa Catalina, Monserrate, Danzante, Carmen and Los Coronados. The park is 35 miles long and extends 20 miles off shore, encompassing some of the best fishing, diving and shore walks. The park is regulated to preserve its beauty and keep out commercial fishing. The park's HQ is in Puerto Escondido, and the naturalist guards and Navy patrols monitor VHF-16.

Relatively shallow water surrounds the 5 major islands around Puerto Escondido (Catalina, Monserrat, Danzante, Carmen, Coronados), unlike those of the San Jose Shelf, so open roadsteads and benign conditions are more common.

Catalina Island 14 miles NE of Punta San Marcial is remote. Isla Santa Catalina Light is on the S tip of the 1,500' tall island (13 mi N-W, 2 mi E-W). Santa Catalina Island has unique rattle-less rattlesnakes that shed their entire skin, so no rattle develops. Naturalist cruise ships ferry passengers

Honeymoon Cove on Danzante is closest getaway spot to Puerto Escondido.

ashore at the N tip, which has anchoring depths on both sides. Two S-facing coves on the island's SSW corner (GPS 25°30.7'N, 110°47.1'W) have marginal holding. Several small coves are reported off the scalloped S end. A reef off the N tip is good fishing in cruising season.

Isla Monserrat, smaller and lumpy, is 8 miles N of Marcial Point, 10 miles ESE of Punta Candeleros. Las Galeras are 2 boxy, flat islets 2 miles N of Monserrat. A reef fouls the passage between Monserrat and Las Galeras, and it extends about a mile N of the Galeras. *Galera* means rowing galley.

In S breeze or flat calm, you can anchor N of the long beach on Monserrat's NW corner (GPS 25°43.1'N, 111°03.6'W) in 18' to 25' over sand, which is handy for diving the Galeras reef. Small boats can try the 2 tiny coves along the NE side of Monserrate.

Puerto Escondido

Puerto Escondido (Hidden Port) is the vortex of cruising, sportfishing, sport diving and RV-ing in this region because of the large all-weather bay with ample room for anchoring and 119 rental moorings. And thanks to Hidden Port Yacht Club, sponsor of the annual Loreto Fest (10th anniversary 2006), and a floating fuel dock (stalled as we go to press), a launch ramp, day-sail island getaways and many services at boater-friendly Tripui RV park nearby.

From November through May, an average of 2,050 pleasure boats bask in the shelter of this 1-mile by .75-mile harbor, making it their home base for weeks at a time, some for months and a few for years. More than 150 trailer boats homeport at Tripui year round.

From June through October in recent years, more than 300 coastal cruising yachts (power and sail) were summering over in this region, staying close to Puerto Escondido's shelter as a hurricane hole, but spending most of their time visiting nearby islands.

Lay of the Land

Puerto Escondido is a large, nearly land-locked bay only a mile E of Baja's Highway 1, about 12 miles S of Loreto, 115 miles NW of La Paz, 105 miles SE of Santa Rosalia, and 130 miles due S of San Carlos, Sonora.

The majestic façade of Sierra La Giganta shoots to 908' just 3 miles behind Puerto Escondido, and the 350' Cerro La Enfermeria E of the bay blend with the background, effectively camouflaging the bay's entrance behind Punta Coyote.

The Spanish named it Hidden Port. Before radar and GPS, it was easy to miss Puerto Escondido's hidden entrance until sailboat masts showed above 2 low land bridges ("the Windows") along the NE perimeter of the large inner bay.

Our GPS approach waypoint half a mile E of Punta Coyote Light near the entrance is

One of 2 windows or low spots in.

25°48'4N, 111°17'N.

The next beach cove NW is the village of Juncalito (pronounced "Hoon-kah-LEE-toh"), shielded by little Isla Chuenque but open to N winds. A landmark crown-shaped peak in the mountainous skyline of Sierra La Giganta just W of Juncalito is visible for 10 miles in all directions.

The Waiting Room

This is an adjacent, quarter-mile wide bay that you pass through on entrance to Puerto Escondido. Deep-draft vessels waited here for high tide to enter the inner bay. A large anchorage lies along the sheltered NE side.

The W shore has a prominent stone building, a small metal pier in disrepair and a 250' long concrete T-head pier with black rubber fenders. We sounded 25' of water alongside this concrete pier. Yachts have used it to take fuel from a tank truck; see Local Services.

Channel: The lighted entrance channel in the NW corner of the Waiting Room. Is more a stubby bottleneck than a channel. It's 60' wide, with 9' at low water after summer silting, 10' during most cruising seasons. We hope it will be dredged to 12' soon.

The Ellipse

Puerto Escondido's natural W shore was altered by developers, never completed. The "ellipse" is an acre-wide semi-circular basin built to house a marina, now vacant, but anchoring is prohibited. We sounded 4' at the W edge of its high concrete seawall, 23' in the middle. The S end has a launch ramp, parking lot and a building that's had various uses.

Concrete piers W of the ramp are for a future Travelift. There's a spigot for potable water on the seawall (only 4' of water alongside) and a rickety ladder. Cruisers built a dinghy landing and tied it off to the ship-size bollards in the ellipse. The NW arm of the ellipse forms a lighted breakwater leading to the main bay.

Launch ramp in the Ellipse is popular spot.

© Point Loma Publishing 2006

Puerto Escondido
B.C.S.

N

one half nautical mile
soundings in feet
Not for Navigation

Windows

40' 46'
36'
20'
40' 36'
7' 26'
6' 48'
24'
36'
fuel 25'
4' 9' 60' 68' 24'
dinghy dock 70' 50'
70'

Cerro La Enfirmería

Waiting Room

25° 48.4'N
111° 18.1'W

Punta Coyote

shoal

Main Bay

The W and SW side of this large inner harbor has several silted up, dead-end channels lined in concrete seawalls and foot bridges, backed by a maze of gravel streets, curbs and defunct street lamps, once intended for residential development. It's too bad this pristine natural harbor was ever carved up for development, but it's even worse that the construction project has remained unfinished – a hazard and eyesore – for more than 2 decades. However, Puerto Escondido's

The Waiting Room anchorage is just outside the Puerto Escondido's main bay.

large main bay provides ample room for anchoring and mooring.

Anchor & Moor

The Waiting Room has good shelter for a couple dozen boats to swing in 15' to 20', and fair shelter for another dozen in 20' to 50' of water. Shelter is by Cerro La Enfermeria, which means Infirmary, but its nautical reference is the cockpit of a warship where the wounded received first aid. Mangroves line the SE side, fed by a spring.

About 119 single point moorings line the Windows in the main bay. You can anchor anywhere else in the inner bay in from 12' to 48' of water. We've seen more than 100 boats spread around here.

At press time, Fonatur (Singlar) charges a peso per foot per night (no discount by week or month) plus 10% tax for yatistas to anchor their own boats inside Puerto Escondido and the Waiting Room, the same fee for using a mooring. Look for Updates on www.MexicoBoating.com

Hurricane Hole: The Sierra La Giganta (3,674') provides Puerto Escondido's hurricane shelter, combined with the 350' hills on the N and E sides. When a hurricane comes ashore between 24°N and 26°N and bridges the narrow peninsula, its surface-wind strength is usually (not always)

lessened as it moves E over the gradually rising land. Then the plunging E side of the mountains seems to disrupt the wind flow for a few miles eastward, creating a small lee at Puerto Escondido. We've seen such storms reform over the warmer Sea of Cortez and bash the mainland.

TIPS: Unattended boats dragging into other boats - the classic "10-pin effect" - was the main cause for severe damage or total destruction of nearly 100 boats here in 2003. The Windows admit the strongest

sustained winds, and flash flooding enters the W shoreline.

Loreto National Marine Park covers 500,000 acres of the Sea of Cortez, including the islands of Santa Catalina, Monserrate, Danzante, Carmen and Los Coronados. It's 35 miles long and extends 20 miles off shore. Started in 1996 to preserve the underwater habitat, this unique park prohibits shrimping and commercial fishing of certain species. Some special rules apply. The HQ is in the stone building at Puerto Escondido, and the guards monitor VHF-16.

PE has only floating fuel dock in 100s of miles.

Mooring blocks are inspected by yatistas in Puerto Escondido.

Local Services

Puerto Escondido has its own harbormaster annex, so boaters call on VHF 16 to clear in and out. (Loreto has the Capitanía; see below.) SEMARNAT's office for Loreto National Marine Park is in the stone building, as is the API office (613) 133-0992. Marine patrols occasionally check boats at the islands for park permits.

Fuel & water: The aboveground diesel and gas tank is full, and the floating fuel dock is N of the ellipse just inside the larger bay. Water faucet is in the S end of the ellipse, but only 4' depth alongside until it gets dredged.

Hidden Port Yacht Club sponsor the annual Loreto Fest in late April or early May; organizes trash pickup, oil recycling, and helps needy local families. They may soon have a clubhouse with email & internet hookup. We're members. www. HiddenPortYachtClub.com

VHF 22 at 0800 is the morning VHF net in Puerto Escondido, providing the latest news on the coconut telegraph. Bloated taxi rates have spurred boaters to buy a junker car for getting to Loreto every few days, and when they move on, they trade it to others coming in.

Tripui RV Park a mile inland at Highway 1 rebuilt after a major fire. Boaters come for showers, coin laundry, groceries, restaurant, fax, dry storage and pool. Their campground is handy for your overflow guests.

Provisions: Farmers from Ciudad Constitución stop by the port regularly to sell fresh veggies, citrus, eggs and tortillas. They call on VHF as the pickup pulls in. Loreto has excellent grocery stores, pharmacies, eateries.

Marina? Fonatur (aka Singlar) has promised a full-service marina here for 20 years. Loreto Bay at Nopolo plans a small marina someday, and Marina San Cosme is in limbo.

Explore Ashore

From Puerto Escondido, we've hiked up what we dubbed "Steinbeck's Canyon," the narrow but deepest ravine in the Sierra la Giganta immediately W of the road into the port. The lower parts are shady and easy to climb. After heavy rains, we've slid down spillways, dipped in a 30' waterfall and splashed in bathtub size pools in the rocks. The upper parts may require a rope or boost up, but they go to plateau meadows where John Steinbeck reported healthy big-horn sheep. In fact, this is a great place to read "Log of the Sea of Cortez."

Loreto, BCS

Loreto is the largest town N of La Paz on the Baja side of the Sea of Cortez. Combined, Puerto Escondido and Loreto provide almost everything a yatista could wish for – except a real marina, and many are doing fine without. A strong boating community

Loreto's Capitanía governs Puerto Escondido.

Loreto's darsena is for pangas.

has developed, including HPYC volunteers and about 200 retired Americans living in Loreto.

Loreto (pop. 7,900) is 15 miles N of Puerto Escondido, 200 miles N of La Paz, and 85 miles S of Mulegé. Eco-tourism (sportfishing, kayak & diving tours, cruisers) panga fishing and agriculture are the main industries.

Loreto is a good service town for boaters based in Puerto Escondido, but it's easier and safer to get here by land. Loreto has a darsena for local pangas only inside 2 riprap breakwaters off the malecon. The nearby open roadstead in 25' to 50' is windswept most afternoons, but you can land your dinghy inside the darsena. We've found better anchorage a mile S on the leeward side of the river shoal.

Local Services

The Capitanía is a block E of the N end of Loreto's malecon (Calle de la Playa) and seawall, near the fishing pier and riprap darsena for pangas and skiffs.

Loreto has at least 2 Pemex stations, 2 banks, 4 grocery stores, several dive shops that fill tanks and rent gear, at least one kayak rental, many eateries favored by yatistas.

The international airport is S of town, reached by Calle Madero through the river bed or from Highway 1. Budget and Thrifty rent here. Bus lines go to Tijuana & La Paz daily and can drop you off at the Puerto Escondido turnoff, but no pickup there.

History & Culture

Misión Nuestra Senora de Loreto is the oldest mission in Baja California, founded in 1696 by Jesuit Fra. Salvatierra. In 1697 it became the state capital (moved to La Paz after Loreto was destroyed by a hurricane in 1829). The church operates a museum preserving more than 300 years of local history, on Paseo Hidalgo, the walking street just W of the plaza and post office.

Ann & Don O'Neil wrote Loreto, Baja California: First Mission and Capital of Spanish California, an excellent history that also has Puerto Escondido and Isla Carmen. It's a great read for here.

Loreto Fest is late April, early May, mostly at Puerto Escondido, but all the Loreto merchants participate. Loreto Foundation Day in late October has parades, dancing, traditional dishes and cultural events.

From Loreto, yatistas can take a tour bus to visit Misión San Francisco Javier, founded in 1699 at Biondo Springs, an oasis and citrus orchard up in Sierra La Giganta.

Isla Carmen to Santa Rosalia

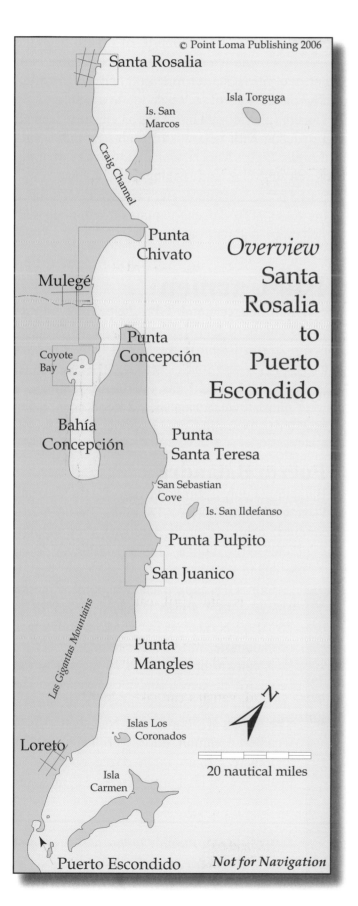

© Point Loma Publishing 2006

Santa Rosalia

Isla Torguga

Is. San Marcos

Craig Channel

Punta Chivato

Mulegé

Coyote Bay

Punta Concepción

Overview Santa Rosalia to Puerto Escondido

Bahía Concepción

Punta Santa Teresa

San Sebastian Cove

Is. San Ildefanso

Punta Pulpito

San Juanico

Las Gigantas Mountains

Punta Mangles

Islas Los Coronados

Loreto

Isla Carmen

N

20 nautical miles

Puerto Escondido

Not for Navigation

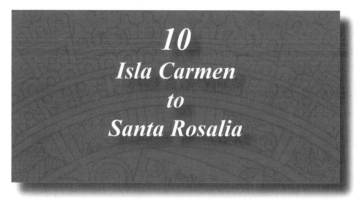
N of the Puerto Escondido and Carmen area to Santa Rosalia harbor, this approximately 110-mile stretch has interesting popular stops at Juncalito, Isla Carmen, Islas Los Coronados, Punta Mangles, Bahía San Juanico, San Sebastian, Bahía Concepción (the "sea within a sea"), Mulegé (fresh river), Punta Chivato and Isla San Marcos. It ends at tiny Marina Santa Rosalia inside the harbor breakwater.

Many folks find this leg even more enjoyable than the previous section between La Paz and Puerto Escondido.

ROUTE PLANNING: Carmen to Rosalia

For boaters planning to hop across the Sea of Cortez to the San Carlos-Guaymas area, Santa Rosalia makes a good departure point, because it's only 75 miles across. Santa Rosalia is the only convenient place for yatistas to fuel up in this region.

If you're coasting NW to Santa Rosalia, staying 2 miles off keeps you outside off-lying rocks, but 4 places require close attention: Los Coronados, Bahía Concepción, Isla Santa Inez and Isla San Marcos. If you're not visiting Bahía Concepción, you can head directly to Mulegé, then coast NW and N of Isla San Inez and her reefs.

After Santa Rosalia, the next opportunity for a short crossing is 110 miles farther up the Baja coast,

115

Danzante Island from N looks like a slumbering dragon; show the kids.

from San Francisquito to Kino Bay using the Midriff Islands as stepping stones, so the longest offshore hop between anchorages need be only about 35 miles. The next diesel dock N on the Baja side is at San Felipe.

COASTWISE: Escondido to Concepción

From Puerto Escondido to Loreto's darsena is 12 miles.

Bahía Chuenque: Just N of Puerto Escondido is Isla Chuenque, Bahía Chuenque (Bahía Juncalito) and the camper-fishing village of Juncalito. Chuenque Bay makes a good S-wind anchorage (GPS 25°50.00'N, 111°19.56'W) on the beach shelf in 20' to 35' over sand.

But enter Bahía Chuenque well NW of a detached rock off Isla Chuenque's N tip; a reef off its S end is good snorkeling. Divers enjoy the sunken twin-engine plane in about 22' of water off the islet's S side. "Sun Lover" is a yatista couple who retired in Juncalito and offer good advice on VHF 22.

Punta Nopolo Norte 5 miles N is a big rock on the beach, good radar target. Nopolo Estuary opens on the rock's S side. The Loreto Bay project is restoring the estuary and palm grove in exchange for getting to build homes and a marina just S the airport.

N of the airport control tower visible from off shore, a broad Rio las Parras arroyo divides the S suburbs of Loreto from the downtown and central parts. A shoal N of the arroyo juts a quarter mile out, and pangas often anchor on all sides of it. We do too in a pinch.

Loreto (previous chapter) has an elevated seawall and malecon with yellow streetlights on either side of Loreto Light. The N end of town has a riprap enclosed darsena and fishing pier. Cruise ships disgorge passengers here, and pangueros Med-moor to the rocks. The darsena contains a wide concrete launch ramp, and parking is nearby.

Isla Carmen

Satellite imagery and GPS helped us correct previous charts of Isla Carmen and its anchorages. This 6th largest island in the Sea of Cortez is 18.5 miles NE to SW and 8 miles across at the cross arms. This 1,400' high island has interesting geology, a historic ghost town, a salt lake, 2 good anchorages tucked under its arm pits and a couple weeks' worth of lunch stops.

Puerto Balandra

Balandra is only a 9-mile voyage for trailer boats and pangas from Loreto, 15 miles from Puerto Escondido, so this well sheltered cove is very popular. The entrance to Balandra is 2 miles S of Punta Cholla, the island's NW arm.

Our GPS approach waypoint for the entrance to Carmen's Puerto Balandra is 26°01.09'N, 111°10.18'W. Avoid both edges of the quarter-mile wide entrance.

A canyon brings 65' to 70' depths to the center of the cove, and an easy anchoring shelf rings all but the rocky NW corner. The cove's NE corner has best shelter in N weather common during cruising season, and there's room for a dozen cooperative boats. We've anchored here in 35' of water

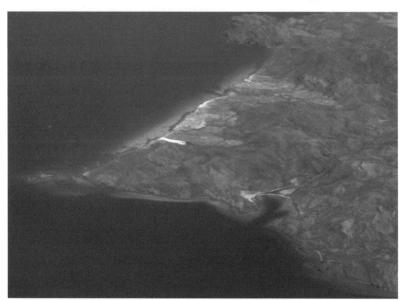

Isla Carmen's Punta Chollas with reef, and Puerto Balandra in lower right..

over sand. In S wind, the SE corner has 18' to 25' NE of the peak guarding the S side of the entrance.

A trail crosses Isla Carmen to the salt pond N of Bahía La Salina, but we haven't tried it. Salt barges used to park here.

Bahía Marquer

Marquer (pronounced "mar-KAYR") is a wide indent, not a bay, about 5 miles NW of the island's S tip. Our GPS approach waypoint outside Marquer is

25°52.33'N, 111°13.43'W.

It's good for a lunch stop or extended periods of calm weather. It's open to N and NW wind, but a small hook at the SW arm provides some shelter from S swell, in 18' to 22' over sand.

S End: The light on Punta Arena is across the 2-mile wide channel from 2 lights on the N end of Isla Danzante. Almost 2.5 miles SE of Punta Arena, the

Carmen's Puerto Balandra is within sight of Loreto.

S end of Carmen is Punta Baja, a broad, low sandy delta fringed in shoals a third of a mile out on all sides. Our GPS position off the S end of Carmen is 25°48.0'N, 111°12.2'W.

Punta Colorado Cove: This broad bulge 3.5 miles N of Punta Baja shelters a small anchorage in its lee during prevailing NW to NNE wind. Punta Colorado is the S-most point of the bulge, fringed in reefs, but this crescent bay with white beach is about a quarter mile SE of Punta Colorado. We found a good holding sand bottom at 18' to 22' in this cove, but haven't spent the night.

Arroyo Blanco: About 4.5 miles N of Punta Baja, this small crack in the wall is ideal for dinghy-gunking or beaching a trailerable boat. It has a dry cave behind the pebble beach, good snorkeling along both cliff walls and tinier cracks to the S. Our GPS approach waypoint outside Arroyo Blanco is 25°53.39'N, 111°10.67'W.

Bahía La Salina

La Salina Bay is the mile-wide bay under Carmen's E arm. It's surrounded in steep hills and white beaches. La Salina Bay is sheltered in all but S wind, although in a strong NW blow, wind can funnel down the valley behind the middle of the beach. If it gets uncomfortable, boats tuck into either corner of the bay or move SE to Punta Perico.

Our GPS approach waypoint off La Salina is 25°59.00'N, 111°06.45'W. A shallow shelf rims the bay, and we anchor in 15' to 36' over good holding sand and mud.

About 200 people lived in La Salina to work the salt-evaporation pond N of town, until 1982 when the company closed and La Salina became a ghost town overnight. A watchman still guards the privately owned church, school, factory buildings, salt evaporation ponds and historic (unsound) pier. Visitors are welcome if they announce themselves, don't litter and take no souvenirs. Behind the town, the mile-long salt pond was the source of great wealth for 200 years. A trail leads N to Puerto de la Lancha.

The shipwreck off the pier is said to be a Loreto supply boat that for many decades sustained La Salina's workers, having sunk when returning for one last load of the workers' belongings. Another wreck lies SE of the pier in deep water, good for diving.

Yellowtail and barracuda during winter cruising season bring many sportfishers to the back side of Isla Carmen. Cabrilla and grouper are found in the reef off White's Point 2 miles SE of Bahía La Salina and off the S side of Punta Perico. Roosters are taken right in the bay.

Punta Perico

This mountainous arm pointing SE has a good anchorage off its S side near the point. This quarter-mile wide cove has cliffs at its E side, which ends in Punta Perico. Our GPS approach position is 25°58.09'N, 111°04.59'W. Anchor in 15' to 20' over sand in the NW corner, not below the cliffs of the point. Rocks trail off the points on both sides of this cove.

In summer calms, another lunch-hook spot is in the little cove a quarter mile NE of the tip of Punta Perico. Anchor off the beach in the SE end of the cove, in 19' to 25' over shell gravel and sand. But S swell it's likely to invade around Punta Perico and the cove's SE point. The next cove E has too many rocks for us, but the beach is nice.

Punta Lobos the N point has an almost detached lump pointing NE. We find 2 interesting coves in the N-

La Salina ghost town has small chapel and remnants of factory.

Isla Carmen's N end has several caves, one you can dinghy into at low tide in flat weather.

facing cliffs between Lobos and the secondary N point, Punta Tinterero. This area is bad in N wind.

V-Neck Cove

is 1.75 miles SE of Punta Lobos but surrounded in lighter terrain. Our GPS approach position is 26°03.71'N, 111°04.96'W. This tiny caleta is blessed with white sand dunes, a white beach and turquoise anchoring shelf. Another name for this popular anchorage is Carmen's V-spot.

A water cave on the S side is large enough to enter by dinghy, and at low tide a beach uncovers at the back end where sea turtles sometimes haul out. Sadly, this unique cave has suffered from litter bugs.

Puerto de la Lancha

About 1.5 miles SE of Punta Tinterero, this small cove is open to any N quadrant, but it's a pretty getaway for long periods of flat calm or summer gunk-holing. The trail from La Salina brought workers here for a skiff ride back to Loreto, hence its historic name.

Our GPS approach off Puerto de la Lancha is 26°03.56'N, 111°06.09'W. You can anchor in 13' to 20' off the darkish SE beach. From this anchorage, we dinghy to snorkeling reefs of Punta Lobos and Punta Tinterero.

Punta Tinterero (female shark) is the lesser and more rounded of Carmen's 2 N points. Nothing of interest lies between it and the next point SE.

Punta Chollas: Beware the reefs jutting about a quarter mile NW from Isla Chollas, which is already detached from Punta Chollas. Give this whole point a wide berth except by dinghy.

COASTWISE continued

From the Loreto Channel, the N end of Danzante Island looks like a cartoon dragon – show the kids.

Islas Coronados

Spanish explorers saw crowns in most volcano cones. These small islands are 7 miles N of Loreto, and there's deep water E of them.

The 928' cone on the larger Coronado drops to a significant sand spit off its SW corner, which was lowered and almost severed by recent hurricanes. In calm summer weather, we've anchored in several spots the area N and NE of the sand spit in 18' to 30' of water. In N weather, anchorage is possible S of the sand spit and off the island's SE corner.

Panga tourists from Loreto come to snorkel, fish and picnic. Current bathes the reefs off the end of the spit and S of the lesser Coronado Island (lighted). In the middle of the 1-mile wide channel W of the Coronados, depths are 24' to 36' with 1- to 4-knot current.

Mangles Rock is a dangerous rock about 1.5 miles off shore and about 2 miles SSE of Punta Mangles (good radar target). We stay 2 miles off shore between the Coronados and Punta Mangles to avoid this danger, but we watch our depth sounder,

Islas Coronados sand spit.

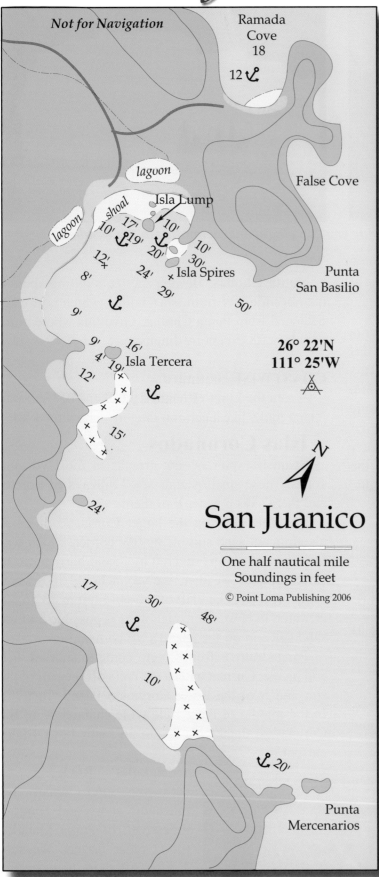

Not for Navigation

Ramada Cove
18
12 ⚓

False Cove

lagoon

lagoon   shoal   Isla Lump
10'   17'   10'
10' 19' 20' 10'
12'   30'
8'   24'   Isla Spires
9'   29'   Punta San Basilio
⚓   50'

9'   16'
4' 19' Isla Tercera
12'
      26° 22'N
15'   111° 25'W

24'   N

                San Juanico

              One half nautical mile
              Soundings in feet

              © Point Loma Publishing 2006

17'
30'
48'
⚓
10'

⚓ 20'

              Punta
              Mercenarios

because Mangles Rock perches on the E edge of a steep shelf that juts 1.5 miles E from shore.

Punta Mangles

Punta Mangles is 10 miles NNW of the Coronados. Our GPS abeam the E tip is 26°17.90'N, 111°22.0'W. Mangles (mangroves) has a small cove that's good in moderate N wind. Mangles Cove is about a mile W of the point, S of the orange cliffs; anchor in 17' to 25' of water. W of this cove is rocky bottom.

Punta Mercenarios, 4 miles up the coast, is the S approach point to San Juanico.

San Juanico

San Juanico (Bahía San Basilio) is a 2-mile long cove with several small spots to anchor amid turquoise shoals, white beaches, tall spires, fantastic geology and fossilized paint pots. A 7-mile gravel road arrived from Highway 1 and the first homes appeared with it, but San Juanico remains a favorite stop on the yatista trail.

Punta San Basilio is the lesser point on the N, and the protruding S point is Punta Mercenarios (layout similar to El Gato). A dangerous pinnacle awash at high tide lies about a quarter mile ENE of the tip of Punta Mercenarios, so give a half-mile berth to this point.

Our GPS approach waypoint half a mile SE of Punta San Basilio is 26°22'N, 111°25'W.

In calm weather, you can anchor almost anywhere in 15' to 30' over sand. Similar to El Gato, the tighter N end is better sheltered in N weather than is the wide open S end. NOTE: When yatistas cart off buckets of fossils and crystalline deposits, we are destroying an ancient natural wonder. Please take photos, not souvenirs.

Juanico S: In this larger basin SE of Isla Tercera, you can anchor almost anywhere off the beaches in good holding sand. A submerged reef runs almost half a mile NW from the hill at the base of Punta Mercenarios. We've anchored outside the reef closer to the Punta in 20' of water, and inside the N tip of the reef in 17' to 30' of water well off the beach.

Juanico N: You can anchor almost anywhere

Juanico N has Spires and a Lump, great snorkeling.

among (and S of) the landmark Spires Rocks and Isla Masa (Lump). Multis enjoy tucking up onto the turquoise outer ledges off the N beach. The first homes overlook the Spires, and RVs reach Ramada Cove.

Isla Tercera lies due S of the Isla Spires, and another rock reef runs SE from Isla Tercera. We've seen smaller boats anchor inside (12') and outside (20') this reef circle in calm weather, but we've done it only in a dinghy.

False Cove: Departing San Juanico to N, this cove on the NE edge of Punta San Basilio is larger than we thought, has a sand bottom at about 24' but no beach.

Ramada Cove

On the N flank of Punta San Basilio peninsula, a quarter-mile wide bay is good for S wind in depths of 13' to 22' over sand. Its pretty beach is connected by dirt road to San Juanico's N end. A goat ramada used to stand on the E end of this beach, hence its local name.

Hiking the canyons is interesting. Rancho San Juanico 2 miles NW across Rio San Juanico has a graded road to Highway 1. Pangas enter the mouth of Rio San Juanico.

COASTWISE continued

Saquicismunde: About 4 miles NW of Punta San Basilio or 2.5 miles SE of Punta Pulpito, kayakers, trailerable and shallow-draft vessels might find this tiny cove useful. This place was first described by Jack Williams in 1988 as 200 yards wide, 6 fathoms deep, possibly a rocky bottom.

Gull Rock Ravine: Whenever you

approach Punta Pulpito from S, stay at least a mile off shore to avoid Gull Rock and other rocks on the extended shelf up to Pulpito. But charter boats anchor off the ravine (no shelter) just N of Gull Rock to tend kayakers ashore.

Punta Pulpito from SE looks most like a pulpit.

Punta Pulpito

(Pulpit) This dark 1,600' promontory 8.5 miles N of Punta San Basilio projects about 0.75 of a mile E from the hilly shore, attached by a 500' sandstone bridge. (From N, Punta Pulpito's 3 crests look like a large dog curled up.)

We have anchored S of the sandstone-backed beach

Ramada Cove N of San Juanico.

Medano Blanco, left, is one of 3 small indents along the outside of the Concepcion peninsula. The flattened pillar shapes among the reefs are seen all along this unprotected stretch of coast.

in 18' to 30' of water at GPS position 26°30.7'N, 111°26.9'W. When rounding Punta Pulpito's S side, avoid the dangerous pinnacle about 200 yards off the SE corner of the point.

The N side of the pulpit has an indent, and its S half may be useful (15' to 20' over sand) for dead calm or light S weather. Punta San Antonio, about 1.5 miles NW of Pulpito is the N horn on this major turning point. Antonio has an open bight W of a detached shoal that runs half a mile N.

Isla San Ildefonso Light on the island's N tip marks a reef that runs almost a quarter mile N of the island. Because the bottom drops off sharply E of this island, fishing for marlin, tuna and dorado is good in warmer months.

Caleta San Sebastian

San Sebastian Cove is 8.5 miles NW of Pulpito, 6 miles W of Isla San Ildefonso, marked by a low green spot in the hills. This pretty 1-boat cove has palms, red-roofs and pink homes behind the private beach (no shore landing) and an improved 13-mile road to Highway 1, which now runs N of San Sebastian.

The S side of the entrance juts farther E than does the N side. Dangerous flat-topped reefs line both sides of the narrow entrance. In a 62' twin-screw motoryacht, we anchored bow-and-stern in the center of the cove in 22' over sand; our GPS at anchor reads 26°30.78'N, 111°26.90'W.

Concepción Afuera: Outside Bahía Concepción's peninsula, the next 60 miles NW have no reliable shelter for ocean-going yachts during cruising season, no roads, no service, just reef-fringed points and rugged mountains. We normally traverse it 3 or 4 miles off to stay in deeper water. However, in absolutely flat calm of summer, we've seen small beachable boats in the following small hopes.

Punta Medano Blanco is about a mile

NW of Punta Santa Teresa, which has no anchorage. Medano means beach berm or sand dune; this pretty point has both. Shelter from S to SSE wind is found in about 24' in the first dune cove W of the point, but it has rocky sides and beach farther in. Our GPS approach is 26°42.93'N, 111°35.63'W.

Side coves toward Punta Santa Teresa are good only for dink exploration.

Punta San Linito, next door to Medano Blanco, is half a mile wide and has anchoring shelter from SE to SW wind.

San Lino Cove: Its E side is marked by the first of many pillar-rock reefs along the outside of Concepcion peninsula, but this sandy cove has a house and road over the berm from San Lino seasonal fishing village. Our GPS approach is 26°44.33'N 111°37.31'W. San Lino Cove has OK shelter from S swell.

Punta Rosa, a delta point almost half

Caleta San Sebastian's green arroyo is visible from air and sea level.

way up the peninsula, has a reef to avoid. Our GPS stand-off waypoint is 26°47.00'N, 111°39.75'W.

Punta Pilares about 2 miles SE of Punta Concepción has an abandoned mining operation below the zigzag road scar. In flat calm weather, small boats might anchor in the mile-wide cove on its W side.

Punta Concepción: 26°54.10'N, 111°49.21'W is our approach waypoint. From this turning point at the top of the Concepción peninsula, you can see 7 miles W to Mulegé. (See below.) First we're entering Bahía Concepción.

Bahía Concepción

Bahía Concepción (Conception) is 21 miles NW to SE, only 2 to 4.5 miles wide - called "the sea within the sea." Yatistas find many anchorages around the tiny islands and sandy beaches of Bahía Coyote, in Concepción's NW shoreline.

After the fabled chocolate clams were "over utilized," nature opened a niche for rough-shelled butter clams, only 1.5" wide but delicious. An hour of easy snorkeling around the rocky islets yields enough for a dandy lunch. Bahía Concepción has the largest cordon cactus forest in Baja, studding the red pumice hillsides.

APPROACH: After rounding Punta Concepción, round the lighted Punta Aguja (Needle) and Punta Santo Domingo at least half a mile off.

Santo Domingo: On the S side of this point, you can anchor on a narrow shelf with 15' of water over sand. Our GPS approach waypoint is 26°52.05'N, 111°50.96'W, so take a look before you commit.

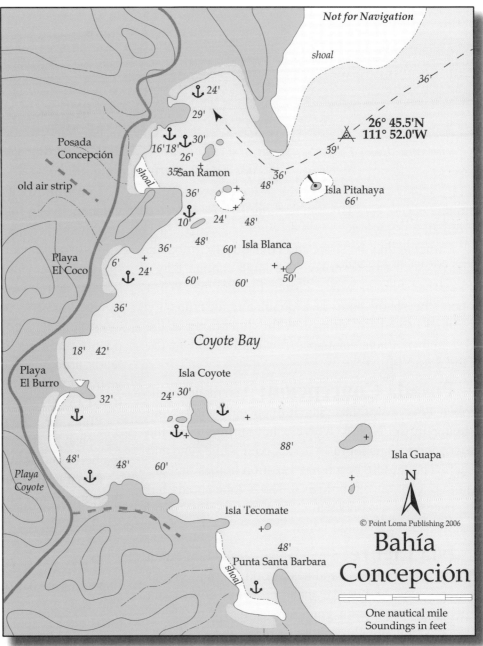

Stay in the center of the 3-mile wide channel into Bahía Concepción to avoid migrating shoals on the W side, until you're 1.5 miles SE of Punta Arena (low, sandy, cactus covered).

Coyote Bay

Our GPS approach waypoint on the N entrance to Coyote Bay is 26°45.5'N, 111°52.0'W. Enter between low Punta Pedrito and tiny Isla Pitahaya, which has a nav light.

Playa Santispac: N of Isla San Ramon, this most popular cove has a turquoise shoal, but shore access is good. Anchor just about anywhere, over sand and shell gravel. Or at our GPS 26°45.7'N,

Panorama shows Playa Santispac and islands in N end of Coyote Bay. Santispac is popular with RVs but not a particularly tranquil anchorage.

111°53.24'W, which is S of the J-shaped beach W of Punta Pedrito, N of Isla San Ramon. This is protected from all but S winds.

Campers line the shore and Highway 1 climbs the arroyo, so it can be noisy. The large cantina Roy's Place has limited water, closes for months. When open, the shady patio is a popular rendezvous for running errands to Mulegé. A tiny hot spring at the SW end of Playa Santispac flows after rain in the Gigantas.

Posada Concepción: This smaller multi lobed cove W of Isla San Ramon has better wind shelter in the N end, where a hot springs is in the rocky ledge. Anchor in 18' to 25' over white sand and shell. The middle beach has vacation homes that are quiet except on big holidays. The S lobe shoals but its beach has a wonderful cafeteria in the big round palapa; see EcoMundo below.

Isla Liebre: S of Isla Ramon and E of Punta Tordillo, this small island has a good snorkeling reef on its E side, and we've anchored N and SW of Isla Liebre's W reef with good shelter in 10' to 12' of water. The nautical meaning of liebre is a dead eye; maybe Salvatierra buried one here as a shore mooring when he discovered this bay in 1702.

EcoMundo: The restaurant is still on Posada Concepción in the round straw-bale palapa, but the sustainable ecology center moved just S of Punta Tordillo on Playa Escondida – very quiet location off the highway. Under new owners, EcoMundo rents kayaks and bikes, leads half-day kayak tours for novice yakkers and 1st time visitors to this delicate environment. EcoMundo festivals have solar- and people-powered boat races, displays of edible landscaping, solar-powered boating and camping gear, recycling, plus nightly BBQs and song fests; (615) 153-0320 or ecomundo@aol.com

Playa El Coco: Rectangular by radar, El Coco Cove has 12' to 15' in the middle, a tidal marsh behind the berm and clamming shallows on both ends.

Playa El Burro: About half a mile SW of El Coco, this picturesque cove has 22' over sand in the middle, 12' in the N end below the road, but the shoal S end is sheltered by a high ridge accessible only by water.

Playa Coyote: Larger than Santispac, Playa Coyote has room for 20 boats almost anywhere. The ends have less road noise. The N end outside the shoal has shelter under the cliffs. The middle has easy shore and road access. NOLS (National Outdoor Leadership & Survival) kayak school is between private homes and RV parks. The S end has better S wind shelter, and it's nearest a hot spring at the S end of the Coyote Beach, but road noise from the hill is possible.

Isla Coyote: A mile E of Coyote Beach, this is one of the most private and beautiful spots in Bahía Coyote, though a ways to shore. We've anchored S and N of the rocks off the island's E side, also in the beach bight on its NE side (GPS

Novice kayaks are for rent at EcoMundo on Posada Concepcion.

Coyote Bay's islands provide day anchorages, good snorkeling and fishing.

26°43.49'N, 111°53.16'W), which has a mushroom rock. Snorkeling is good in the rocks off the S side and E point.

Playa Santa Barbara:
Furthest S of the Coyote Bay coves, this one is farthest from road noise, the best in S wind and some shelter from Tecomate Island in N wind. We've anchored N of the turquoise shoal and W of the ridge in 15' over sand. A small lagoon and palms tuck into the shady corner. However, we've had bees swarm us here.

NOTE: As we go to press, Fonatur announced plans to develop hotels and home sites on the Bahía Concepción beaches of Santispac, Escondida, El Burro, Coyote and Santa Barbara. We wish this could be preserved as a marine park.

Concepción lo de mas

The rest of Bahía Concepción has a few points of interest.

Rocas Frijóles: Bean Rocks is a dangerous set of pinnacles rising abruptly to about 5' depth at low tide, the tips of a

22' deep sea mount almost out in the middle of Bahía Concepción at its narrowest width. We've found one pinnacle with fish traps and buoys at our GPS 26°41'668'N, 111°49.335'W, and another pinnacle is reported at about 26°40.62'N, 111°50.04'W. Pangueros anchor here in calm weather.

Playa Buenaventura
8 miles S of Coyote Bay has a roadstead anchorage, grooved concrete launch ramp, dinghy dock, camping and an air-conditioned restaurant/bar. Our GPS approach position N of Playa Buenaventura is 26°38.80'N, 111°50.64'W.

Isla Requesón:
Ten miles S of Coyote, multis and trailer boaters can anchor

Punta Amolares on Concepcion's E shoreline.

(GPS 26°38.31'N, 111°49.51'W) S of the pretty shoals around Isla Requesón ("ray-kay-SOHN") and its adjacent sand spit, which has camping and beach launching.

Playa Pasajera:
In fair weather, yatistas have careened off Playa Pasajera (Passenger Pigeon) at the extreme S end of Bahía Concepción for quick repairs. It's also known as Kivi Beach for the schooner whose bones remain – wasn't quick enough.

The low land SE of Bahía Concepción gives almost no shelter from S wind. The road behind Playa Pasajera goes to San Sebastian and up the W side of the Concepción peninsula.

Punta Amolares:
On the E shore of Bahía Concepción (3 miles E of Playa Santa Barbara in Coyote Bay), the S side of this low, 2-cornered delta may provide shelter in N wind, in 12' to 17' of

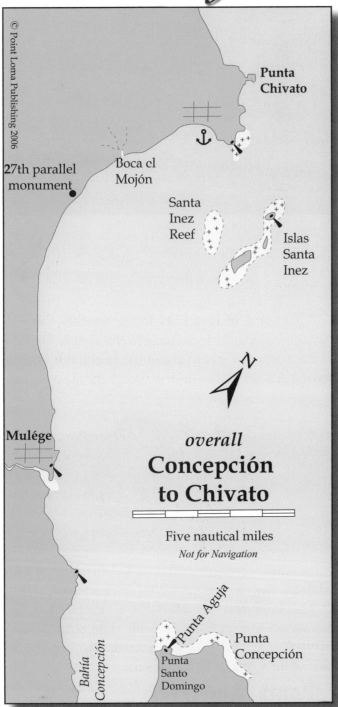

© Point Loma Publishing 2006

Punta Chivato

27th parallel monument

Boca el Mojón

Santa Inez Reef

Islas Santa Inez

N

Mulége

overall
Concepción to Chivato

Five nautical miles
Not for Navigation

Punta Aguja

Punta Concepción

Punta Santo Domingo

Bahía Concepción

water. Our GPS approach waypoint SW of the SW corner is 26°42.88'N, 111°48.70'W.

Amolares are molar teeth, perhaps for the boulders ashore or sharp teeth in the sierra skyline nearby. The delta is low scrub with cordon and narrow beaches. Some charts indicate a Punta San Ignacio on this side, but not at this location.

Mulegé

Pronounced "moo-lay-HAY," this pleasant town lies 5 miles NW of Bahía Concepción, 70 miles

N of Loreto, 33 miles S of Santa Rosalia. Just off Highway 1, Mulegé (pop. 2,610) is a date-palm oasis on the N bank of Rio Santa Rosalia. The town has 2 Pemex stations, good grocery stores, an Internet café, outboard mechanics, fishing and diving shops and lots of restaurants.

Rio Santa Rosalia is said to be Baja's only navigable river, but recent hurricanes have shallowed the N channel and closed the S channel inside that ends before the bridge dam. Yatistas can clear in by VHF with the Capitania on Sombrero Point without entering the river. At high tide, dinghies, pangas, small fishing boats and multis can pick their way over the bar, but ocean-going yachts should stay outside.

Approach: From Punta Concepción on the N tip of the big peninsula, it's 7 miles due W to Mulegé. From Punta Chivato, Mulegé is 10 miles due S, but avoid the reefs SW of Isla Santa Inez.

Punta Prieta is N of Mulege's river mouth. Punta Gallito (Little Rooster) is an attached islet with a nav light and lighted antennas 2.5 miles S of the river mouth. Shoals foul the shore from Gallito N to the river mouth.

Punta Sombrerito (Little Sombrero Hat) is an almost detached hill forming the N side of the river mouth, carrying a reliable nav light. This 119' hill looks like a sombrero with a thick brim, and it's visible from Punta Concepción and Punta Chivato.

Our GSS at the river bar is 26°54.04'N, 111°57.11'W with 4.5' to 6.5' of water over rocks and sand, and local mean tide is 3.5'. Uncharted shoals of mud and rock flank the shore down to Punta Gallito.

Inside the river, hurricane runoff filled in the S channel, leaving some private docks far from the water, until that channel can be reopened.

Anchor & Berth

Punta Prieta: We found only 11' of water but shelter from S wind N of Punta Prieta; GPS 26°54.87'N, 111°57.53'W. The gravel road goes into town.

Sombrerito Cove: There's a small cove off the N side of Sombrerito with 16' to 20' of water over sand and mud, also a beach with El Patron panguero cantina and dirt road to town.

Roadstead: The .25-mile long roadstead outside the river has no shelter, and patches of eel grass sometimes compromise the otherwise good holding sand and mud. We don't leave the boat unattended here. We've anchored in 18' to 22" of water about 75

Sombrerito Light and view into the river from the reef bar.

yards off the beach E of Punta Sombrerito at GPS 26°54.'N, 111°57.26'W.

Rio Docks: If you can ford the bar (hire a panguero piloto) and enter the river, we found 8.4' off the sportfishing and panga docks at the SW foot of the sombrero, where a local 35' sportfisher berths. The Capitanía is behind the fishing docks, and by the road along the N bank of the river town is less than a mile.

Rio Shoals: Trailer boats, mini-cruisers and multis can anchor almost anywhere in the river, but don't block the traffic channel. Mosquitoes emerge at sunset, especially if the wind quits.

Mulegé: the river's S shore has homes with docks.

Local Services

The Capitanía is on the N side of Rio Santa Rosalia, and his office covers Mulegé, Concepción and Chivato. Santa Rosalia has its own port captain.

Fuel is by jerry jugs from either the Pemex in town or a mile S on Highway 1. However, you can try to hire a helper who has a pick up, or you can hire a taxi at the docks near the Capitaníí.

Chandler: El Aleman (The German) has marine parts and electronics, but owner and former cruiser Jens Kolbowski passed away. Store is (615) 153-0235.

Mulegé has 3 grocery stores, Claudia's Laundromat, Don Roberto's hardware, and a propane depot in town. Mulegé Divers rent equipment and guide tours (615) 153-0059. The bakery is on the S bank at Villa Maria RV Park.

La Serenidad Hotel has the first small concrete dinghy dock (max 4' alongside) on the S bank. Get permission from the office inside the walled compound W of the air strip. Hotel Serenidad and 3 RV parks on the S river bank have docks, ramps and campgrounds. Serenidad also has a good restaurant, pool, ramp and reasonable rooms. If the hotel isn't full, we've bought hot showers ($5 for 3) before having dinner here; (615) 153-0530, saralaurajohnson@hotmail.com

Hotel Serenidad has the most reliable Mulegé's 3 airstrips. It's on the S side of the river mouth, graded 4,000' but none has av gas. Use UNICOM 122.8, and this flight destination is now "El Gallito" not Serenidad.

Eats: In town, our favorite restaurant is Los Equipales, upstairs in a brick building on Calle Moctezuma, the 1-way street out of town. Another good one is the patio bar at Hotel Las Casitas on Calle Madero a block E of the plaza.

History & Culture

Mulegé's Mission is a museum.

Mulegé's Tri-Centennial is Nov. 11 to 14, 2005; Mulegé300@yahoo.com.mx

Mulegé is from a Cochime word meaning "large ravine with white mouth." The town streets built in 1705 were wide enough for horse carts; many are

*Santa Inez Reef with light tower,
and Punta Chivato (right) from NE approach.*

one-ways cramped by RVs. The museum building formerly housed a prison famous for its honor system. The 1st time we visited Mulegé, the prison was still in operation, and we bought a sweater from the car thief who knit it. Misión Santa Rosalia is SW of the bridge, strikingly built of dark stones and light mortar, restored and in active use. That dinky road crosses Baja to Punta Pequeña.

Mulegé is famous for campestres or cave paintings and petroglyphs. For boaters, the closest are found up the river canyon inside a grotto behind a fresh-water pool that's perfect for cooling off on a hot day. More campestres are at San Borjita. 2 recommended guides in Mulegé are Ramon Monroy (615) 153-0223 and Salvador Castro D. (615) 153-0232.

Rio Santa Rosalia begins as an underground stream seeping down from another palm oasis at San Ignacio, high above the port town of Santa Rosalia (See next section.), emerging W of the Mulegé's

Cave paintings (campestre): See them from Santa Rosalia or Mulegé.

highway bridge. Some springs are warmed geo-thermally W of the tidal estuary. Technically, it's not a river, but who cares.

Besides the fall Date Festival, the town caters to tourists year round: RVs, sportfishers and sail boaters are drawn to Bahía Concepción and local waters up to Punta Chivato, which are great for fishing and diving. For RVs coming down from the US, Mulegé is the 1st good place to launch a boat into the Sea of Cortez –you see many here.

The rare fresh water creates a unique habitat for kayaking and birding and mosquitoes. Local pangueros fling circular hand nets to catch bait in the river. Snook may be a legend, but dorado, yellowtail and sea bass are regular catches.

NOTE: Fonatur plans to develop the NW shore of Bahía Santa Inez from Playa Santa Inez to Punta Chivato for golf and sportfishing resorts.

COASTWISE continued

Mulegé to Santa Rosalia is about 35 miles by way of Punta Chivato and Isla San Marcos.

Chivato Routing: From Mulegé roadstead to Punta Chivato, stay at least a mile off the shallow NW coast of Bahía Santa Inez (pronounced "ee-NAYZ") where a monument marks the 27th parallel. Lay your course to avoid the rock-sand shoals surrounding Islas Santa Inez.

If you're bypassing Concepción Bay and Mulegé, head N from outside the Concepción peninsula to a deep-water point (GPS 27°03.60'N, 111°53.50'W) about a mile E of the N Isla Santa Inez. The offshore approach to Punta Chivato is safer from around the E and N sides of the Santa Inez Islands and reefs, due to unmarked shoals about 2.5 miles W of the S island. Some rise from 15' of water and rarely break.

Punta Chivato

Punta Chivato village is a vacation-home

Hotel Point is the most SW of Chivato's points.

community 23 about nautical miles SE of Santa Rosalia, 12 miles off Highway 1 by the new road. Chivato village has camping, 2 airstrips (no av gas) and a landmark hotel The Punta Chivato headland has a launch ramp and big anchorage, maybe moorings someday, but presently no marine services.

Lay of the Land

The 3 Santa Inez Islands rise less than 30' above sea level, and their rocks and shoals extend roughly 3 miles N-S, 2 miles E-W. Nav lights are on the smaller N island and larger S island. N Inez Island lies 1.75 miles SE of Punta Santa Inez (also lighted), the SE part of the larger Punta Chivato headland. We round this whole point 3-quarters of a mile off the points to avoid the islands' hazards.

The Punta Chivato headland is 2 miles wide and has 4 significant points. The more rounded Hotel Point facing S has trees and the landmark hotel Posada de las Flores (formerly Hotel Punta Chivato). Then pointing SE, Punta Santa Inez is lower, lined in white beaches including its low T-shaped seaward end, and it has a nav light. Next, Dune Point has a dark rocky projection pointing ENE and is backed by lighter sand dunes with narrow beaches. Finally, the namesake Punta Chivato is the NE corner, a sloping

Chivato's N side is comfy in S wind.

bump and also has a nav light.

Anchorage

Hotel Point: In prevailing N wind, the best anchorage is in the large lee WSW of Hotel Point. We've anchored in 21' to 30' at GPS 27°03.69'N, 111°57.52'W.

Punta Chivato Yacht Club (homeowners group) may install moorings in part of this sheltered area, hopefully leaving room for anchoring. From here, you can dink around to the snorkeling reef off the S tip of Punta Santa Inez or maybe out to the islands.

The deeper E side of the Santa Inez islands offer good fishing and expert snorkeling, but beware of razor-sharp oyster shells.

Chivato N Cove: In S wind or calms, local sportfishers anchor in a cove off the northernmost point of the Punta Chivato headland, in 15' to 24' of water. Our GPS approach N of this N cove is 27°06.19'N, 111°58.99'W.

Local Services

Posada de las Flores (formerly Hotel Punta Chivato) has a rocky landing near the anchorage, with stairs to the restaurant, bar and pool. New owners welcome yatistas who buy food and drink (615) 153-0188. This hotel operates one of the airstrips.

The village has a mini-store, Pilots Club steak house, another restaurant and many homes in construction and the new 12-mile graded road S around Bahía Santa Inez and out to Highway 1.

If the PCYC gets organized, maybe they'll provide diesel and a floating dinghy landing for their moorings guests.

COASTWISE continued

From Punta Chivato to Santa Rosalia is about 25 miles going outside Isla San Marcos, about 22 via the Craig Channel. The Baja coastline NW of Punta Chivato has little of interest to yatistas, and the bottom rising sharply from 2,400' to only 26' to 30' causes radical current. So we prefer traveling E of Isla San Marcos.

Craig Channel is SW of San Marcos Island. Safe passage is limited to a width of about 1.25 miles of what may look like a 2.5-mile wide channel, due to rocks off the Baja side and a dangerous mostly submerged shoal extending at least 1.5 miles S of the S tip of Isla San Marcos – what we call the Craig Channel Reef. Use extreme caution, radar, depth sounder, accurate navigation and plenty of power,

because very strong current in this restricted pass can set you off course very quickly.

Transiting the Craig Channel in 18' of water, our GPS position is 27°08.82'N, 112°04.35'W.

Isla San Marcos

Emergency assistance is available at the commercial port on the SW side of the island. Hail "Isla San Marcos Capitanía" and ask to come alongside (12') the wooden docks on the S side of the giant concrete T-head pier, which has navigation lights at both ends. Our GPS approach waypoint is 27°11.56'N, 112°05.35'W.

Puerto San Marcos: Gypsum dominates the port, which has 24-hour ship traffic, noisy rock-crushing machinery, night lights and far-flung gypsum dust that coats your decks and lungs. We don't recommend the anchorages (12' to 15') NE and SE of the big dock.

Bahía Puerto Viejo: E of the dangerous

Craig Channel reef, we find good N wind shelter in

Sweet Pea Shelf is S of Piedra Blanca.

Bahía Puerto Viejo, the large cove S of the island, in 15' to 20' over sand. A road goes to the port and company village.

Punta Piedra Blanca:

The island's prominent NW corner has a nav light on a detached rock. In NE to SE weather, a long narrow ledge SE of Punta Piedra Blanca allows confined anchorage in 12' to 35' close to the cliffs.

Trinity Coves: NE of Punta Piedra

Blanca, 3 small beach coves spread NE for 2 miles to Punta Lobera, the island's N tip. These have good shelter in S and E wind. Our GPS at anchor in the larger cove adjacent to the N side of Punta Piedra Blanca is 27°14.51'N, 112°06.36'W. The next coves NE are divided by submerged reefs, and they have sea caves and arches.

Arches & caves at Trinity.

Another reef extends a mile N of lighted Punta La Lobera on the island's N tip. Yellowtail and cabrilla are caught here and in a sea mount 4 miles NW of this reef.

COASTWISE continued

From the N end of Isla San Marcos, your view N is the 6,000' peaks of Volcán de las Tres Vírgenes (3 Virgins) in the background, and Punta Agueda in the foreground. Aim for the virgin until you're clear of the Agueda Point (about 17 miles NW of Isla San Marcos), which has a navigation light on a detached rock.

Caleta San Lucas W of Isla San Marcos is too shoal for all but dinghies, multis and trailer boats to enter, and the campground and its channel are both abandoned (not dredged). Anchorage is possible outside the sand spit in 15' over sand

Generally, stay a good 1.5 miles off this shore

Trinity Cove next to Punta Piedra Blanca has nice beaches and reef to snorkel.

until you enter Santa Rosalia.

Santa Rosalia

Santa Rosalia (pop. 17,800) is a small all-weather port 95 miles NW of Puerto Escondido, 125 SE of L.A. Bay, and about 70 miles W of Guaymas on the mainland.

Thanks to tiny Marina Santa Rosalia and fuel trucked to its floating dock, this historic mining town is a nice stop for yatistas exploring the mid and upper Sea of Cortez or crossing to the mainland only 75 miles E of here.

APPROACH: Some of Santa Rosalia's landmark smoke stacks and foundry buildings are being demolished, but red tailing piles N of town are still visible 5 miles out.

Santa Rosalia's breakwater contains slag boulders from the copper smelting operation that began in 1885. It shelters the quarter-mile wide commercial harbor from prevailing N winds, so the lighted entrance opens S.

Our GPS approach waypoint off the entrance to Santa Rosalia is 27°20'N, 112°15.7'W. Small shoals grow SE of the entrance and to starboard just after you enter the breakwaters. The main channel inside the harbor runs N-S along the E breakwater.

Lay of the Land

A beautiful new paseo or pedestrian walkway surrounds the harbor seawalls and the city waterfront. The marina is on the N end of the harbor's W seawall, and beyond it the shallow NW corner is for pangas. The ferry terminal and gypsum boats are in the SW corner. Navy docks are on the N wall, and the E wall has shrimpers.

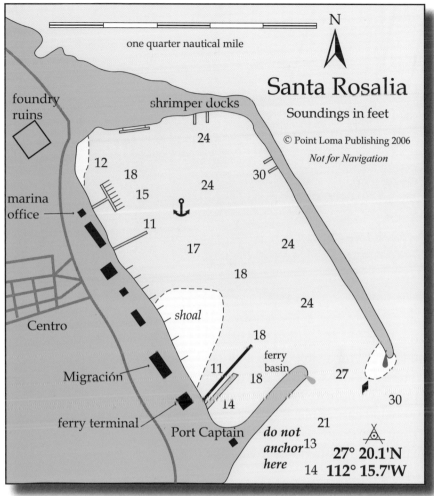

Berth & Anchor

Marina Santa Rosalia has 15 floating slips for boats to 50' and 6' draft, 110-volt power, city water and a 24-hour security guard. We berthed a 62' trawler here, and our bow hanging out 12' was no problema. The gated marina ramp is divided from the marina office by the public paseo, completed in June, 2005.

The marina office occupies a historic wooden

Calm or Norther, the entrance at Santa Rosalia harbor is welcome.

Marina Santa Rosalia with harbor entrance at right.

Port Captain controls everything up from Bahía Concepción and N to L.A. Bay. The Capitanía (615) 152-0935 is on the S side of the Guaymas ferry terminal.

Emergency: General Hospital (615) 152-2180.

Fuel: Marina Santa Rosalia has some diesel on hand, but it can arrange a tank truck with a hose to reach the slips, or they can arrange for larger quantities of fuel to be brought to a pier in the N end. This is the last fuel dock for quite a distance: about 75 miles E to San Carlos, 275 miles NW to San Felipe, 270 miles N to Puerto Peñasco, or 115 miles SE to Puerto Escondido. Gasoline comes from the Pemex on Highway 1 S.

Haul out: N of the harbor is a repair dock for shrimpers – not generally for yachts, but good in emergencies.

Mechanics: This is a good town for diesel and OB repair; ask the marina.

Provisioning is best in winter. Stores restock from the ferry, so shop after it arrives. Summer is hard on refrigerated items. Locally purified water in plastic jugs has been excellent. Santa Rosalia has 3 banks, self-service laundries, a bus station and a swap meet. Downtown is 2 crowded 1-way streets that start at the train monument on Highway 1 and go E and W in the narrow valley.

building but has a fax, cooler, library, shower and coin laundry. The office handles your in-slip fueling and gives you a street map and list of local services. You're 6 blocks NE of downtown. Highway 1 noise reaches the marina; NW wind carries black sand aboard. From April to October, Marina Santa Rosalia often has a wait list. (615) 152-0011.

Just E of the marina is the safest area, where the night watchman can see your boat. We've anchored in 12' to 24' over stinky but good holding gravel and mud, then paid the marina for dinghy landing. Avoid the turning basin in the NE corner, the main channel and the ferry turning basin in the SW corner. The Port Captain warns that abandoned cables foul the wind-sheltered spot S of the SW breakwater.

Local Services

Santa Rosalia is an API Port of Entry, and this

History & Culture

French company El Boleo began mining Santa Rosalia's copper ore in 1885 and built the brick smelting forges and landmark stacks, a vertical

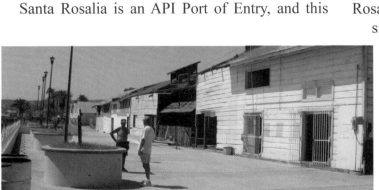

Historic Rosalia: The marina office (left) on the waterfront paseo and Eiffel's unique modular church (above) are among the many historic buildings in town.

El Boleo Bakery makes Baja-style French bread.

scholarships, and the summer Dorado Festival is growing.

Explore Ashore

Marina Santa Rosalia has been a reliable place from which to explore nearby.

San Ignacio, atop the amazingly steep grade, is a date oasis fed by volcanic springs that seep down to Mulegé. Take an early bus up to San Ignacio, have lunch on the square and visit the beautiful mission church before returning to Santa Rosalia by bus before dinner.

Baja's most remarkable cave paintings are around Sierra de San Borjita; La Trinidad also has petroglyphs. Hire a guide and air-conditioned car at the Turismo office S on Highway 1.

funicular for ore cars, a 25-mile rail line to the docks, and wooden homes for the workers. Gypsum and manganese from Isla San Marcos were smelted here too.

El Boleo reportedly mistreated Mexican workers; by 1903 more than 1,400 died of silicosis, and labor strikes continued for 50 years until the ore petered out and the French left. After failed attempts to salvage the smelters, the toxic operation was closed for good in favor of fishing and tourism. The locomotive (photo below) is one of many historic parks around town.

Gustav Eiffel (as in The Eiffel Tower) built Iglesia Santa Barbara in 1884 of modular cast-iron plates and displayed it at the Paris Exposition of 1889. El Boleo's director bought the portable church in

Brussels, had it shipped to Santa Rosalia and reassembled. It's known as Eiffel's Church

The historic wooden homes and buiildings that survived the 2004 downtown fire have been replicated with ornate balconies and porches. The museum in Hotel Francés and the Mahatma Gandhi Library have enlarged photos of tall ships filling the roadstead up to Cabo Vírgenes.

Santa Rosalia's annual Foundation Festival is in mid October. The June Pig Races fund college

Back-packers climb Los Tres Vírgenes (3 Virgins) and El Diablo Rojo (Red Devil) in winter.

Sailing N from Santa Rosalia, the 3 Virgin peaks are beautifully backlighted at sunset.

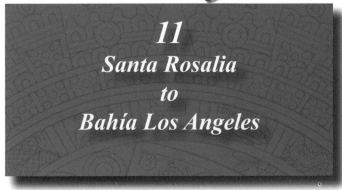

11
Santa Rosalia
to
Bahía Los Angeles

Adventurous yatistas find their way N of Santa Rosalia into the sparsely populated middle Sea of Cortez, including the Midriff Islands and LA Bay. All-weather anchorages and yacht services are almost non-existent up here, and the weather and extreme tides affect you much more, so prepare well.

ROUTE PLANNING: Rosalia to LA Bay

The 125-mile coastal route between Santa Rosalia and Bahía de los Angeles has only 2 reliable overnight

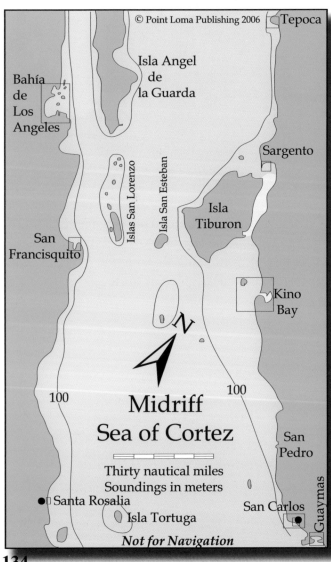

anchorages, almost no permanent residents and zero services en route. The first 75-mile leg to Bahía San Francisquito has fairly boring scenery and less bottom-contour current (good candidate for a night passage 5 miles off shore), then it's 35 miles (more current and traffic) to Bahía de Las Ánimas, and a final 18 into LA Bay – this leg with all eyes wide open. Current in the Canal de Salsipuedes (Leave if You Can) is very strong.

Keep your WX-radio tuned for word of a Norther building, and be watchful for elefantes, this region's unique weather phenomenon. Tubular elefante clouds roll along the bluff tops, signaling strong winds about to blast down the mountain sides and fan 5 miles out to sea. This is a good place to read about elefantes in "MexWX: Mexico Weather for Boaters" by Capt. John E. Rains.

COASTWISE: Rosalia to San Francisquito

Four miles N of the harbor, Highway 1 disappears up Baja's steepest road grade, never to be seen N of here. From 5 miles off shore, the 6,500' peak of Tres Vírgenes is visible 14 miles inland. Stay 2 to 5 miles off shore to avoid off-lying rocks.

Punta Santa Maria: 6 miles N of Santa Rosalia, 4 miles S of Cabo Tres Vírgenes (nav light is on a lesser point a mile N), this tiny point has a riprap groin and T-head gypsum-loading pier. In a N-wind emergency, shelter is possible S of the groin in about 25' over sand. It's possible that elefantes swooping down from Tres Vírgenes might pass over the top of this – or not. Gypsum dust is toxic to breathe and turns to cement on your decks, so we've managed to avoid stopping here so far.

Punta Trinidad: About 12.5 miles NW of Santa Marina, Punta Trinidad is a dark 200' hill projecting NE (good radar target) from a mile-wide beach. Less than a quarter mile NW of Trinidad hill (Cerro el Majón) is the low Islote el Racito, surrounded by shoals. In calm or S weather, the anchorage is W of Punta Trinidad's hill in 15' to 20' over sand. Behind the beach between Majón and Racito the panguero village of Punta Trinidad has a long road to civilization.

From Punta Trinidad to Bahía San Francisquito is 39 miles of alternating blond sand beaches, dark bluffs, dry knolls dotted with cactus, small points and off-lying rocks and islets within 2 miles.

NOTE: Set your ship's clocks back an hour as you

pass Punta San Carlos (28°N, dividing line and time change between BCN and BCS) 11 miles N of Punta Trinidad or 47 miles NW of Santa Rosalia.

Cabo San Miguel is another small hope about 8 miles SE of Bahía San Francisquito. This rocky projection paints a 3-headed picture on radar, and the N-wind anchorage is S of the S point in about 18'. Rancho El Barril about 5 miles up the coast lacks shelter due to shoals. 4 miles farther is good shelter at below Punta Santa Teresa; see below.

Bahía San Francisquito

About 75 miles NW of Santa Rosalia, 53 SE of LA Bay, Bahía San Francisquito or "Little San Francisco" is good place to observe the weather before crossing the Sea of Cortez, or to rendezvous with friends after crossing. Although the main bay is open to the NE, it's a fine stop in settled weather.

The village has a modest fishing resort where John Wayne is reported to have flown in many times with his fishing buddies. Now it's more for RVs, but long-time resident Alberto Lucero (XCE2/KCUEJ on the Chubasco Net) is a friend to yatistas.

Locals poke fun at their remoteness by calling this "San Francis Quito" – where St. Francis quit. For centuries, Cochime tribes harvested oysters in these shallow coves.

Lay of the Land

Playa Santa Teresa is a mile of white beach SW of Punta Santa Teresa (rocky bluff capped by a 571' 3-peak hill) and her companion Punta San Gabriel. The main bay, which locals also call Ensenada las Palomas (Doves), lies W of lighted Punta San Gabriel. The squarish bay has a mile-wide opening on its NE. A sand shoal fronts the W corner's arroyo beach. Our GPS approach waypoint outside the main bay is 28°27'N, 112°52'W.

A smaller rectangular cove opens off its the S corner. The cove's shallow (and narrow entrance is narrowed further by rocks, so enter carefully. The S end is very shoal, so there's not much room. Locals call this Cala San Francisquito;

a cala is larger than a caleta. The fish camp in the cove's S end links to the village behind the berm of the beautiful mile-long Playa Santa Teresa – which faces the open sea.

2 smaller calas within a mile NW of the entrance to Bahía San Francisquito are Cala Mujeres and Cala Niños.

Anchorages

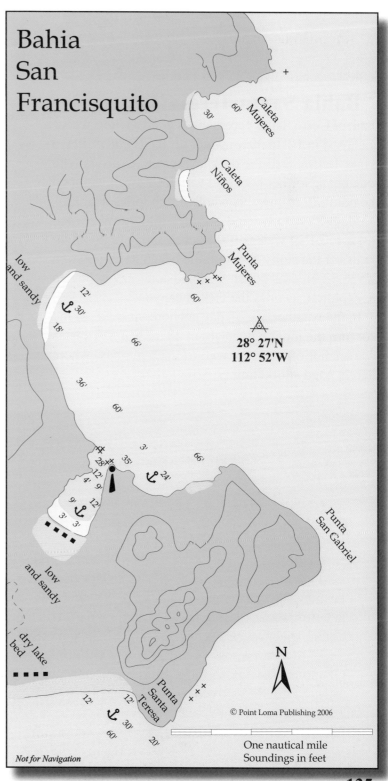

Bahia San Francisquito

28° 27'N
112° 52'W

Punta Mujeres

Caleta Mujeres

Caleta Niños

Punta San Gabriel

Punta Santa Teresa

low and sandy

dry lake bed

N

© Point Loma Publishing 2006

One nautical mile
Soundings in feet

Not for Navigation

Panguerso head out from Cala San Francisquito.

Bahía Santa Teresa:
In N wind, the S flank of Cerro Santa Teresa gives good shelter. We've anchored in 12' to 30' of water off the N end of Playa Santa Teresa, S of the dark lava patch. Cruisers who rode out a Norther here said very little swell wrapped the point. In calms, this whole beach looks doable.

Main Bay: In N wind, we tuck into the W corner, in 12' to 24' of water off the beach shoal, or about 40 yards off the stony N end of the beach. GPS position 28°26.22'N, 112°52.81'W. Sandstone caves beg to be explored, as does the forked canyon.

In flat weather, we've day anchored just NE of the slot into the inner bay, in about 28' of water. Yatistas also anchor off the NW wall of the main bay, where there's good snorkeling.

Cala San Francisquito
San Francisquito Light is on the W bank of the narrow entrance gap (4' min. depth, 8' tides, enter at high tide), which has rocks on both sides, so keep in the middle. The cala's S half is shoal, but yatistas anchor in the middle (8' to 12' on sand) or off the NE wall. In a bad Norther, this tiny refuge gets crowded.

Cala Mujeres:
Watch out for black lava heads along both sides as you enter this pristine, intimate hideout for one boat bow and stern. We found 36' over sand 100 yards off the dainty beach, but only marginal shelter from light NW wind and swell. Cala Niños has surge but good snorkeling scenery.

Punta Ballena is the next point 1.5 miles to the NW, forming the S end of the large open Bahía San Raphael. Just W of the point is another long white beach of a roadstead, for S wind anchoring – but just outside VHF range from boats inside Bahía San Francisquito.

COASTWISE continued
Stay at least 2 miles off the shallow W shore of Bahía San Raphael to avoid inshore hazards.

Crossing the Midriff
Yatistas use the Midriff Islands as stepping-stones across the Sea of Cortez to the mainland. Here are some routes.

1.) In fair weather on a powerful boat, we depart Bahía San Francisquito ENE to Isla Turner (35 miles) where anchorage is possible on the SE side of Isla Tiburón, then into Kino Bay (18 miles) where we anchor S of Isla Pelícano.

2.) During cruising season when N wind is most frequent (or to stay within sight of land), this next route has some shelter off the S sides of the islands: Depart Baja from Bahía San Francisquito heading NE, check navigation after crossing the Canal de Salsipuedes by passing close off the S sides of Isla San Lorenzo (10 miles), then off Isla San Estéban (10 miles) and Isla Turner (14 miles) before anchoring off Kino Bay's Isla Pelícano (18 miles).

3.) Starting across from LA Bay, it's 22 miles E to the anchorage off Isla Estanque (SE side of Guardian Angel Island), 30 miles E to Punta Willard on the W tip of Isla Tiburón (Shark Island), 20 miles SE to the S tip of Isla Turner, and 18 miles NE into Kino Bay. If a Norther threatens, you may want to cross from Punta de las Ánimas to the N side of Isla Salsipuedes, to the S sides of Isla San Estéban and Isla Turner, then into Kino.

San Francisquito Bay in the Midriff area.

Canal de Salsipuedes (Leave If You Can), one of the steepest and deepest (4,200') spots in the Sea of Cortez, has upwellings and very strong current that, when adverse, can shrink your fuel range. Winter NW winds and an ebbing tide can cause rip tides around the points and W sides of the Midriff Islands (See below.).

This 10-mile wide channel runs NW for 30 miles to Punta las Ánimas. Fishing is excellent on both sides, but expert seamanship and vigilance are required.

Canal de Ballenas (Whales) is the N extension of Salsipuedes Channel from Punta de Las Ánimas 30 miles NW to the NW corner of Isla Angel de Guarda. Ballenas Channel is wider and not quite as deep. Upwellings develop where the 2 channels divide at a sea mount SW of Guardian Angle Island, drawing blue whales, Bryde's, fin backs, false killers, grays, humpbacks, real killers, pygmy sperms and non-pygmy sperms, plus playful bottle-nosed and common dolphins. Bryde's are common here, often mistaken for fin backs.

San Lorenzo Islands

The San Lorenzo chain of 6 steep-sided islands, islets and rock piles perch on a narrow ridge running NW. They're also known as the Lesser Midriff Islands. The Canal de Salsipuedes separates them from San Francisquito and Punta las Ánimas.

Isla San Lorenzo is a high, 10-mile knife blade lacking anchorage. Each island moving NW is smaller.

Isla las Ánimas almost links to the N end of San Lorenzo and has a tiny cove on its NW side. Moving up chain, avoid shoals in the middle of the 2-mile pass, which can develop rip currents.

Isla Salsipuedes has peaks and marginal N wind shelter on its S side: in or just outside the narrow isthmus (no pass) of it S half; in the next cove west; or in the larger cove

off the island's NW side. Beaches and snorkeling are beautiful.

Isla Raza (white, flat) lies 4 miles N of Salsipuedes, and Roca Raza (dome) is a mile NW with a reef off its SW side. Most of the world's Hermann's Gulls breed and nest on Isla Raza, so it's one of the most constantly studied and vigilantly protected islands in the Islas del Golfo nature preserve. No protected anchorage is found.

Isla Partida: The underwater ridge runs 5 miles N of Isla Raza and widens around Isla Partida (almost divided by a low isthmus) and Roca Blanca to its N. In S wind, anchor on the N side almost anywhere in the half-mile crescent cove off the low isthmus in 24' over sand. Roca Blanca has a reef jutting half a mile N.

From here, you're only 8.5 miles S of Isla Angel de Guarda (Guardian Angel Island), which we'll explore after LA Bay.

Partida's Ghost: An island similar to Isla Partida shown on some charts to lie about half a mile E of here has been proved not to exist, thanks to satellite photos and personal observation. Cartographic ghosts have long been charted off Isla Angel de Guarda and

Yatistas go fishing with pangueros at Bahía Las Animas.

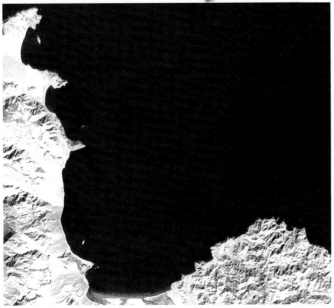

E of Huatulco as well.

Bahía las Ánimas

This 5-mile wide bay has a few ATVs and jet-skiers who arrive by the newly graded 20-mile road from LA Bay. But yatistas find several austerely beautiful anchorages.

The bay takes its name from Sierra las Ánimas, the mountains along the bay's W side; Punta Soldado (Soldier) is the bay's NW arm. The bay's SE mountain is Sierra Agua de Soda, and Punta las Ánimas is its N tip. The term las Ánimas refers to church bells tolled at sunset to summon 'lost souls.'

Approaches

Danger: About 5 miles SE of Punta las Ánimas, avoid off-lying Rocas San Bernabé and their dangerous reefs jutting W and SE. They are reported to lie about 28°47.47'N, 113°11.37'W.

More than one yate has holed here, so stay 5 miles off shore until you're safely oriented. Tides here average 13' and current over San Bernabé shelf is strong. As you approach the N end of this peninsula, another point is labeled Punta San Bernabé.

En Medio Cove (GPS 28°50.33'N, 113°14.50'W) lies 3.5 miles NW of Punta San Bernabé, is about a quarter-mile wide and has decent protection in the SW corner (22' to 30' over sand) from light WNW winds. Islets shelter the NE entrance, but not a great beach.

Satellite photo shows Bahía las Ánimas.

Las Ánimas Slot (GPS 28°50.47'N, 113°14.78'W) is next door, but as you move between these 2 tiny gems, go way out and around, due to submerged rocks a quarter mile N of the dividing peninsula.

Ánimas Slot is very narrow (one boat), runs NE to SW. It gains shelter (18' to 26' over sand) from the barely detached island forming its NW wall, and a rock shoal NW of the island blocks swell. Boaters report comfort here even in a strong Norther. It has a pretty beach and 2 side arroyos for picnics.

Playa las Ánimas: In flat weather you can anchor almost anywhere off the miles of regular sand beach around Bahía las Ánimas. The SW corner (GPS 28°48.46'N, 113°20.87'W) is near the RV camp and sand launch area.

Punta Soldado's S side (GPS 28°52.02'N, 113°21.76'W) has shelter from NW breeze. Soldado is soldier.

Isla Racito: Enter the anchorage on the islands SW side (GPS 28°52.80'N, 113°21.76'W) via the N and W sides, due to a connecting reef S of the island. Isla Racito is the SE end of Bahía Alacrán. Racito means scythed level, like this islet.

COASTWISE continued

Let's creep around the corner toward LA Bay.

Scorpion Bay (Bahía Alacrán) lies between low Punta Soldado and Punta Alacrán. In N wind, the anchorage (GPS 28°52.84'N, 113°22.42'W) is in 14' to 22' of water S of Punta Alacrán's headland. Kayakers haul out on the sheltered N end of this pretty beach.

NOTE: Scorpions are part of the naturaleza ashore; they hide in cactus skeletons and driftwood. Small sting rays are also common, so splash loudly and wear old tennis shoes when disembarking the dink toward these beaches.

Bahía Pescadero: Shelter from NW wind is good (GPS 28°55.35'N, 113°23.30'W) W of the small island in the N end of this bay, in 20' over sand. But approach S of island to avoid rocky shoals N of it (good snorkeling). Abandoned palapas line the beach. S weather anchorage is in the open S end of Bahía Pescadero.

The narrow window at Puerto Don Juan is composed of small flat stones.

Ensenada Quemada: Punta
Quemada (Burned) is the low but N-most tip of this Sierra las Ánimas peninsula; the point's E face is reddish black lava, hence its name. It's sometimes called Punta Don Juan. This 1.5-mile wide bay between Punta Pescadero and Punta Quemada has good shelter from S wind. As you pass Punta Quemada, stay at least a quarter mile off the N tip (GPS 28°56.47'N, 113°22.70'W) to avoid detached rocks.

Bahía de los Angeles (LA Bay)

Bay of the Angels is an excellent place summer over close to the hurricane hole of Puerto Don

Puerto Don Juan

This natural harbor is the best hurricane hole in the upper Sea of Cortez. It lies about a mile SE of Punta Quemada and 6 miles E of the town of LA Bay. Our GPS approach waypoint 28°57.28'N, 113°26.58'W is in middle of the N end of the narrow, bent entrance channel which runs SW.

A small, almost enclosed side lobe called the Bath Tub is a popular place for sailboats to careen for a quick bottom scrub and inspection.

The main bay then opens out on all sides with swinging room, if need be, for 100 boats; 10 to 20 is more normal in summer. Its sheltering W wall is a 100' high volcanic peninsula attached at its S end only by a narrow bridge about 10' above sea level, a window ledge composed of brick-like rocks. Our favorite fair-weather spot is in the SW corner in about 20' with a view out the window. The middle of the bay (GPS 28°56.55'N, 113°27.09'W) is only 30' deep, good holding.

Although it's called Puerto, nothing port-like has been developed here yet – thank heavens. The town of Bahía de los Angeles is within sight, and to the N are many island getaways, dive spots and fishing holes.

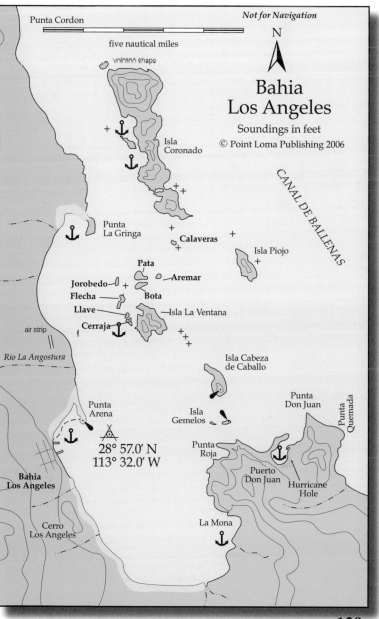

Los Gemelos greet yatistas entering LA Bay.

Juan. The small desert town of LA Bay (pop. about 550) has a new Pemex station in construction, outboard repair service, RV and fishing camps, a few eateries, a comparatively large community of retired gringos, emergency medical care, a paved airstrip and a bus the outside world. All the nearby islands have memorable names.

Approaches

From E, our GPS approach waypoint 28°57.13'N, 113°28.68'W is S of the 2 small islands, Los Gemelos (pronounced "HAY-may-los") or twins. They're not identical, and a reliable nav light is on the larger eastern twin.

Or you can enter close N of the twins. Isla Cabeza de Caballo (horse head) is the next island N, and it has the area's 2nd nav light on its S side; avoid a submerged rock off its SW corner and reefs off the horse head's N end. The 3rd nav light is on Punta Arena on the western shore just N of the town of LA Bay.

Anchorages

NOTE: Plan for a tide range up to 11.5' and sudden elefante wind blasts.

Town Roadstead: At least 300' off the 3 launch

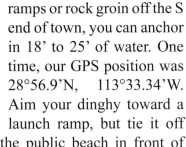

ramps or rock groin off the S end of town, you can anchor in 18' to 25' of water. One time, our GPS position was 28°56.9'N, 113°33.34'W. Aim your dinghy toward a launch ramp, but tie it off out of the way or on the public beach in front of Guillermo's.

La Mona (The Monkey) is a smaller village in the SE corner of the bay, and in long periods of calm weather boats can anchor N of the 2-mile long regular beach in about 24' of water over sand. This spot is sometimes mispronounced as Limona or lemon.

Isla La Ventana (Window) may have been named for the arch on its SE point, which streams E with a good diving reef (beware of a dangerous submerged pinnacle at the SE end of this reef), or for the fact that you can see this island from inside Puerto Don Juan's window.

Anchor in the open bight on the S side (GPS 28°59.99'N, 113°30.84'W), or in the smaller enclosed cove on the NW side, which has rocks off its N arm and a view of Isla Flecha (Arrow), also called Borrego. Both Ventana spots are decent in NE wind.

Lock & Key: Immediately W of Ventana are the tiny Islas Cerraja and Llave (Lock & Key), which fit together like their namesake. Boats anchor off both sides and dinghy between. The lock's E indent is at GPS 28°59.79'N, 113°31.06'W.

NOTE: A dangerous rock pinnacle lies about an eighth of a mile E of Isla Jorobado (Hump-backed), which is the lower island N of the taller Flecha and W of the taller Cerraja & Llave.

Islas Bota & Pata (Water Cask & Paw) create a well

Rada Cove is to the right. Lagoon to the left is shallow.

Punta La Gringa Light.

sheltered anchorage between them (GPS 29°00.74'N, 113°30.78'W) in about 35' of water.

Punta La Gringa: This seemingly detached hill and low S tip (GPS 29°01.74'N, 113°32.31'W) form Ensenada la Gringa, which is shoal in the NE end. Anchor off the NW corner in 18' to 22' over sand. RVs camp and launch over this nice sand beach. The 5-mile road to town has a few cantinas, campgrounds and the Turtle Farm.

Smith Island (Isla Coronado) is 4 miles long with many indentations, culminating at the N end in a mile-wide 1,550' flat-topped volcano cone – the most prominent landmark in Bahía de los Angeles.

South Smith is the more E of 2 indents on the S side of Smith, at GPS 29°02.22'N, 113°29.80'W.

NOTE: Avoid a dangerous submerged rock reported S of the more westerly indent. One report has it within 60' of water (29°02.18'N, 113°30.11'W) just outside the westerly cove. Another has it at 29°02.01'N, 113°29.91'W or half way down to Isla Calavera (Skull). We assume they're both right.

Rada Cove on the SW side of Smith Island is the one E of our GPS 29°02.715'N, 113°30.42'W. The lagoon close N is great for dinghies and kayaks.

Isla Mitlan is off Smith's W side, and you can anchor NW of Isla Mitlan if you come around its N side, because its SE side is foul. Or, SE of the detached

rocks SE of Isla Mitlan, there's 30' over sand at GPS 29°03.61'N, 113°30.71'W.

Pie del Volcán: Foot of the Volcano is about a quarter mile N of Isla Mitlan, SE of the tidal estuary literally at the SW foot of the magical volcano slopes; GPS 29°04.53'N, 113°31.05'W.

The only islands without anchorages are the tiny Isla San Aremar, Isla Calavera (Skull) and larger Isla El Piojo (Louse), which is a pelican rookery.

Local Services

NOTE: Fonatur plans to create a full-service marina with fuel dock and dry storage, a resort hotel with pool and golf course. Fonatur promised to make LA Bay the E terminus of the Land Bridge, trucking yachts (size unknown) from here across Baja to and from the Pacific at Santa Rosalillita. Locals would be happy with the promised paved road, gas station, 24-hour electricity, potable water and schools for their kids. Check for Updates on www.MexicoBoating.com

Fuel: Until a Pemex station is built in town and kept supplied, diesel and gas are sold from PVC drums outside a shed (de-wheeled truck trailer) near the plaza, or drums at a stand near the road inland. When they run out, it's 35 miles inland, and that

Sunrise over Horsehead Island off LA Bay.

anchorages and points of interest. Remember the tidal range is about 12' on average.

Punta Colorado: At 20 miles ENE of the town of LA Bay, Isla Angel de Guarda Light stands on its square S tip. Our GPS approach waypoint is 28°59.04'N, 113°07.13'W.

Ghost Islets: Satellite photos and personal observation prove that 5 islets shown on many charts to lie off this SW shoreline don't exist. Maybe they were pencil shavings left from the 1870s cartographic voyages, copied for safety's sake.

Esta Ton: This tiny bubble of a cove lies 13 miles NW of Punta Colorada, 55 miles SE of Puerto Refugio, N of our GPS approach waypoint 29°09.50'N, 113°19.78'W.

Amid miles of sheer and inhospitable rock, Esta Ton opens S and provides good shelter from N winds in about 30' over sand in the middle. Reefs jut S from both sides of the entrance, a sand spit on the SW side can be awash at higher tides, and an even tinier side beach lies to the SE.

Our dictionary says the word ton is used only in the phrase "Sin ton ni son," meaning without motive or cause. Judging from its inhospitable and unlikely surroundings, this cozy shelter exists sin ton ni son.

Humbug Bay: Deep water close to shore prevents anchoring with any shelter, but some trailer boats and multis might haul out on the sandy beach to hide from N wind. Our GPS approach waypoint is 29°15.13'N, 113°26.04'W.

Pemex often runs dry.

Provisions: The town has 3 small grocery stores with canned goods, some produce in winter, bottled water. The Fruteria is N of Vita Villa. The small medical clinic is open different days depending on the season. Air evacuation is possible from the paved airstrip N of town.

Eats: Guillermo's (S ramp) has easiest land access, a great restaurant and cantina, motel (hot showers) and campground. Casa Diaz and Villa Vita are similar but inland, and Larry & Raquel's is off Ensenada la Gringa.

Guardian Angel Island

Isla Angel de Guarda is the 2nd largest island in the Sea of Cortez, stretching 41 miles beneath 2 peaks (2,625' and 3,300') and a narrow central valley. We'll circle it clockwise from the S end, checking out

Unknown Bay: About 2 miles SE of Roca Vela, the roomy S side of a rocky, curved peninsula might provide decent N-wind shelter, but we haven't had time to explore it. Our GPS position just S of this unknown bay is 29°30.47'N, 113°34.30'W. 2 smaller and less likely indents are N of this one, before you reach Puerto Refugio's W opening.

Roca Vela (Sail Rock) looks like a sloop under full sail, until you notice it's 167' tall. From about a quarter mile N

11 Santa Rosalia to LA Bay

of Roca Vela (GPS 29°32.17' N, 113°35.85'W), you can aim toward the W entrance into Puerto Refugio (GPS 29°32.48'N, 113°34.51'W) without getting too close to either (a.) the dangerous unmarked rocks (GPS 29°32.24'N, 113°34.70'W) a quarter mile W of the S point of this opening or (b.) the mostly visible reef jutting S from Punta Monumento on the S tip of Isla Mejia.

Puerto Refugio:

This natural refuge (ray-FOO-hee-oh) is not a developed port and has no services. It's a remote aerie of 2 pristine bays, 3 islands and lots of rocks strung across Guardian Angel's N end. It has a several anchorages for a variety of wind directions, but it's not a hurricane refuge – as discovered by at least one cruising boat that dragged ashore in recent storms. Ten yatistas scattered around Puerto Refugio is not unusual, but sometimes you can have it all to yourself for a few days.

Guardian Angel Island

Refugio West:

Less than 3 quarters of a mile SW to NE, this bay is framed by the NW side of Guardian Angel, the SE side of Isla Mejia (may-HE-yah) or Cheek Island and the W side of tiny Isla Division, which divides W from E. You can anchor almost anywhere.

NOTE: From Refugio West, the only passage into Refugio E is via the narrow slot (70' of water, strong current) N of Isla Division; the S end is blocked.

Mejia Cove: Off the NE corner of Refugio West, you can anchor in 15' of water S of or outside this turquoise lagoon on Mejia's E side. Rocks rise in the middle of the entrance, a fishing camp lines the SW beach and the NE beach almost goes under at high tide.

Refugio E: This larger bay is E of Isla Division and S of (GPS 29°33.73'N, 113°32.29'W) Isla Granito (Granite), which has a nav light on its E end. The bay's middle is fairly deep except for the jagged Piedra Blanca, which has a reef off its NW side. Anchoring depths are found either side of Arch Rock, also on both sides of Isla de las Cuevas and SW of East Point. The E entrance is clear.

NOTE: Entering Refugio E from N, avoid the reef jutting at least 800 yards N of Isla Mejia to about GPS 29°34.29'N, 113°33.91'W.

Punta Pulpito on Guardian Angel's E side, about 27 miles SE of Puerto Refugio, has only marginal shelter from NW wind, found in about 30' of water

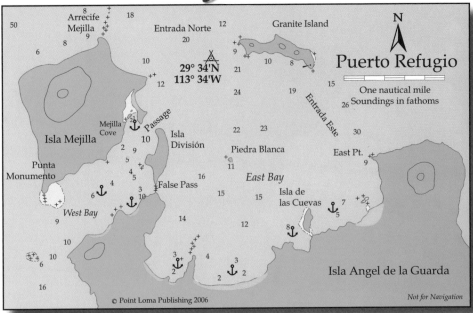

Arrecife Mejilla · 8 · 18 · Entrada Norte · 12 · Granite Island · **Puerto Refugio** · N

50 · 6 · 8 · 9 · 20 · 9 · 10 · 8 · One nautical mile · Soundings in fathoms

10 · 29° 34'N 113° 34'W · 21 · 10 · 8 · 15

12 · 24 · 19 · 26 · 30

Mejilla Cove · Passage · Isla División · 22 · 23 · Entrada Este · East Pt. · 9

Isla Mejilla · 2 · 9 · 10 · Piedra Blanca · 11

Punta Monumento · 5 · 4 · 5 · False Pass · 16 · East Bay

6 · 4 · 3 · 10 · 15 · Isla de las Cuevas · 7 · 5

West Bay · 9 · 14 · 12 · 8

10 · 10 · 4 · 3 · Isla Angel de la Guarda

6 · 2 · 2 · 2

16

© Point Loma Publishing 2006 · *Not for Navigation*

off its SW side; GPS 29°22.71'N, 113°21.31'W. The N side of the point is rocky.

Ensenada Pulpito is the 11-mile wide bay between Punta Pulpito and Punta Rocosa (GPS 29°16.75'N, 113°09.74'W). This bay and side of the island is much less steep than the W side of the island.

Caleta Pulpito: This wedge shaped cove on the S shore of Ensenada Pulpito is 6.5 miles W of Punta Rocosa and just E of landmark red and white banded cliffs. Our GPS position just N of the cove is 29°17.48'N, 113°17.51'W. We've anchored in the middle (20' over sand), but it's open to any N wind. The beach has a tidal lagoon behind it. A smaller cove is 1.25 miles E of here. Both are good for summer's S weather.

Punta Rocosa is the largest headland on Guardian Angel's E side, but give it a 5-mile berth due to off-lying rocks. Fishermen come here for cabrilla and yellowtail. Outside the rocks, the bottom drops off steeply.

Laguna Once Media: 5 miles S of Punta Rocosa, a sandy bulge (GPS 29°11.50'N 113°10.11'W) has a tidal lagoon for a beach hike.

Isla Estanque and Caleta Cubeta on Guardian Angel Island.

Isla Estanque:

5 miles NNE of Punta Colorado, 13 miles SE of Punta Rocosa, this small but interesting island connects on its SW side to the SE corner of Guardian Angle by a no-passage reef with strong tidal current. The word estanque means a tank, reservoir or pond; this island has a pond on its W side that's open to the sea, but you have to approach (GPS 29°03.76'N 113°06.00'W) the pond via the N side of Isla Estanque. Piedra Blanca (and its dangerous reef about 200 yards WSW) is half a mile SW of Isla Estanque.

The island anchorages are (a.) just outside Estanque's pond (See GPS above.) in 15' to 20' over sand, (b.) inside the pond if you keep to starboard and draw less than 6' in the channel (18' inside), and (c.) in 20' to 30' over sand close off the SW side of Isla Estanque (GPS approach waypoint 29°03.26'N, 113°05.54'W) by staying E of Piedra Blanca. Watch the volatile currents all around the island.

Playa Estanque is the inviting mile-long beach W of the island. In fair weather you can anchor in 30' over sand almost anywhere N of the beach, which has a lagoon behind the E end.

Caleta Cubeta:
The tiny cove at the W end of Playa Estanque had no name, so we dubbed it Caleta Cubeta (Bucket), for its relation to Estanque's tank or pond. It's a 1-boat cove for S weather.

This chapter covers the upper Sea of Cortez N of the LA Bay region up to San Felipe, across the shoal upper reaches to Puerto Peñasco, then down the "Lost Coast" to Sargento, Tiburon Island and Kino Bay in the middle latitudes.

Hundreds of yachts summer-over in the middle and upper Sea of Cortez, because hurricanes are less frequent this far north. This chapter illuminates all the getaway places of summer. Winter cruising season can bring a cool N wind off the high desert plateau, and the gusty *elefante* winds off Baja are much less common. Panguero fishing camps move seasonally.

Hundreds of gringos are retired at Gonzaga, Puertecitos, San Felipe, Peñasco and Kino Bay - in order to fish year round. Thanks to improved roads to the US border, trailer boats flock here on holiday weekends. For example, during Cinco de Mayo (May 5th) and spring break, the waters off San Felipe are packed with jet boats and gringos going *coco loco.*

Seamanship skills are required. Coastal depths are shallow here, tides and tidal currents are extreme, safe anchorages and harbors are a good distance apart, marine services are few, and so far only 2 small marinas have slips. Another marina might be built E of Puerto Peñasco by 2007 or 2008, and Fonatur has plans for improving Gonzaga and San Felipe. Check for Updates on www.MexicoBoating.com

ROUTE PLANNING Upper Sea of Cortez

From Puerto Refugio, the first leg is about 150 miles NW to San Felipe. The only reliable anchorages en route are in the Willard-Gonzaga area, about 40 miles up from Refugio. Puertecitos (35 miles further) is not reliable shelter for deep-draft boats. San Felipe (47 miles) has a commercial fuel dock inside a man-made breakwater.

From San Felipe it's a 95-mile passage ENE to Puerto Peñasco, which has a sheltered commercial harbor with a commercial fuel dock, 2 commercial shipyards and a small marina.

From Peñasco it's about 215 miles SE to Kino Bay by way of Isla Tiburon's W side. Avoid the Canal de Infiernillo (Little Hell Channel) E of Tiburon, as rip currents and rocky shoals make it impassable. Small hopes on this side of the Sea of Cortez are at Cabo Tepoca (75 miles), Lobos-Libertad (25 miles), Sargento (45 miles), the N and S end of Tiburon (55 miles), then 16 miles to Kino Bay.

Tide extremes range from 12' at Gonzaga and

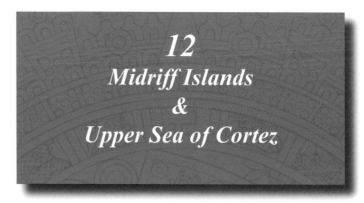

12
Midriff Islands
&
Upper Sea of Cortez

Kino Bay to a whopping 22' at San Felipe and Puerto Peñasco. Currents up to 5 knots at max ebb must be calculated when planning your route.

COASTWISE: L.A. Bay to San Felipe

Punta Remedios on the Baja coast has no reliable shelter. The Baja coastline is a succession of rocky 100' bluffs backed by the high Sierra Columbia.

Bahía Calamahue (32 miles NW of Puerto Refugio) is 8 miles S of Punta Final. Wedged between 2 500' rock peaks, the crescent Bahía Calamahue is wide open to north, provides good shelter in S weather and is OK in flat calm.

Anchor off the center hill or W beach in 20' to 30' over sand and mud. The E side of the bay has a few bottom rocks but may serve. Spring tides are 15' here, so tend your rode if staying long.

Calamahue (accent on last syllable) locals told us their village was founded by Jesuits in 1740, abandoned in 1767, resettled by pangueros in 1970.

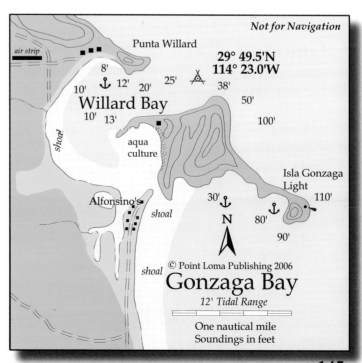

Not for Navigation

Punta Willard
air strip
29° 49.5'N
114° 23.0'W
8'
10' 12' 20' 25' 38'
50'
Willard Bay
10' 13'
100'
aqua culture
Isla Gonzaga Light
Alfonsino's
30' 110'
shoal
80'
N 90'
shoal
© Point Loma Publishing 2006
Gonzaga Bay
12' Tidal Range
One nautical mile
Soundings in feet

Melted adobe blocks behind the E beach are said to be from the 265-year-old mission, but we can't verify that. The road out the W valley was graded in 2005.

Gonzaga - Willard

About 77 miles SSE of San Felipe and 40 miles NW of Puerto Refugio, this 9-mile stretch has 2 adjacent bays, 3 tiny villages with a small market, 2 restaurants, a Pemex station and a few anchorages – depending on tide and wind.

Lay of the Land

The larger and more open Gonzaga Bay (Bahía San Luis Gonzaga) is S of Willard Bay, which is tiny and enclosed. The bays are separated by Isla Gonzaga and a shoaly sandbar on its W side.

Gonzaga Bay: The bay's S end is sheltered W of a broad multi-pointed headland called Punta Final. Our GPS position a quarter mile N of Punta Final's 2 N tips is 29°46.51'N, 114°16.57'W. Radar shows you Snoopy Rock, an attached islet SW of the headland.

Punta Final village on the SW beach has an airstrip, 40 homes and some RV camps. 4 miles E of the village, a graded road N has side roads to Alfonzina's and Willard Bay, but it's faster by dinghy. Gonzaga Bay is fairly shallow a quarter mile out and runs 5 miles NW, ending behind Isla Gonzaga. The beach is divided by Gonzaga's Belly, a 1.5-mile long bulge in the shoreline.

At the NW end of Gonzaga Beach you'll find 2 airstrips (one submerges at high tide), Alfonsina's Motel & Cantina, a Pemex with gas, a small market with ice and beer, and 75 homes old and new. At low tide, the N tip of Alfonsina's sandbar dries, allowing dune buggies out to the SW tip of Isla Gonzaga. At high tide, kayaks and small dinghies can access Willard Bay.

Isla Gonzaga (540') is quite hilly, detached at high tide and carries Isla Gonzaga Light on its protruding 100' high SE arm. Our GPS position off the light is 29°48.44'N, 114°21.90'W. This arm is almost detached from the island – but provides good shelter. (One road map calls this Isla Willard.)

Willard Bay is half a mile wide, nearly enclosed between Isla Gonzaga and the less protruding Punta Willard (185'). Enter in the middle of the bay's quarter-mile wide mouth. Our GPS position in the entrance is 29°49.5'N, 114°23'W. Punta Willard Light is visible from N and east, but is obscured from S by Isla Gonzaga. Papa Fernandez Camp and 20 homes line the steep N side, and a seasonal aquafarm in the bay's S side may obstruct access to the tidal sandbar.

Anchorages: S to N

Most of the indents and fingers around the Punta Final headland make better dinghy explorations or trailer-boating spots than reliable anchorages for ocean-going yatistas … but here are small hopes and tips.

Paraje Chichon (Bump Spot) is marginal for small boats in flat calm with high tide, because it's open to N and has a 5' bar (the bump) across its entrance. On the E side of Punta Final, Chichon Cove is the narrow V-shaped cove W of a spindly protrusion of rocks. It's a quarter mile front to back, and a lagoon lies behind the sand berm on the cove's W side. Our GPS position just outside Chichon Cove is 29°16.08'N, 114°15.72'W. We found 14' over sand in the middle, but didn't stay.

Tijereta Cove on the W side of Punta Final is steep-sided and 2-headed or swallow-tailed as its name implies. A frigate bird is called *tijereta* for its swallow-like tail; scissors are called *tijera*. Pretty as this cove is, we found 50' over slippery rock in the middle, and the side niches too constricted for all but smaller boats to swing. Our GPS outside the entrance to Tijereta Cove is 29°45.26'N, 114°17.41'W.

Bajo Snoopy: We note a yellowish rock shoal between Tijereta and Snoopy Rock, at GPS 29°44.98'N, 114°17.48'W.

Snoopy Rock reclines on the beach a mile SW of Tijereta Cove, so you have to round Punta Final. It looks like Snoopy dreaming atop his

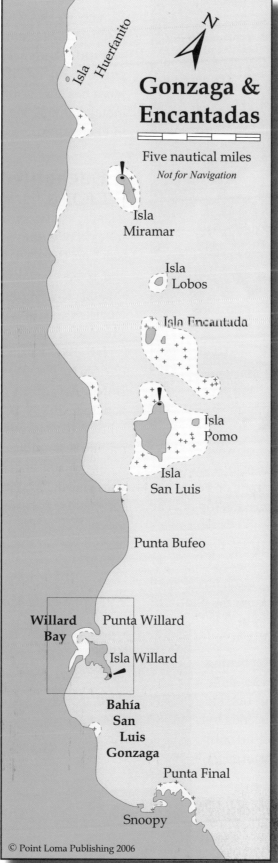

dog house, well, sort of. It's only 0.15 of a mile NE to SW and protrudes about a quarter mile N of the beach. Punta Final village is SW of Snoopy Rock.

Anchorage W of Snoopy Rock has good shelter from S wind and swell, in 12' to 18' over sand around GPS 29°44.56'N, 114°18.41'W.

Gonzaga's Belly: Stand clear of rocks fringing this bulge in the middle of Gonzaga Beach. It's debris from an ancient deluge in the 2400' high mountains W of Gonzaga-Willard.

Gonzaga's Pesos:

Isla Gonzaga's contorted S side provides yatistas with 4 small semicircular coves spread W to E like old-fashioned peso coins: 2 coins, a flat spot, then 2 more coins. This is excellent shelter from N wind and swell. We've anchored in the farthest E coin, or cove, in 30' of water over sand. From here it's easier to get ashore on Isla Gonzaga, and good snorkeling is found off this SE arm. Also in the 2nd from the E at GPS 29°48.60'N, 114°23.29'W, in 20' to 24' over sand. From here it's a quick dinghy trip to the village.

Alfonsina's motel (built in 1961) has a restaurant, and if their 16 rooms are not booked up you can buy a shower before dinner. Alfonsina's son Joaquin will know if the Rancho Grande Market (convenience store, ice) is open, or can help you hire someone to truck gas from the Pemex. Alfonsina's monitors VHF 22.

Willard Bay: The

entrance is open to NE wind. Be aware of the average 12' tidal range here. During low

tides, we've anchored in 10' to 12' of water (MLW) over sand and mud at GPS 29°49.45'N, 114°23.81'W. Dinghies can land at the launch ramps or below the houses on the N side. The S side is shallower. The aqua-farm in the shallow cove behind Isla Gonzaga's NW point has a new dock, but they don't allow visitors.

Papa Fernandez Camp on the beach has a small restaurant popular for lunch. Check out the photos of Papa with John Wayne, who flew in to fish.

COASTWISE continued

Unless you intend to fish or shelter behind or anchor in the Encantadas, you can angle offshore from Isla Gonzaga, going outside this less-than-enchanted chain of islands by staying 6 miles off the Baja shoreline until you're abeam Isla Miramar Light, then angle NW toward Puertecitos or San Felipe.

Fishing from Willard to San Felipe is excellent for corvina (rare S of here), barracuda, grouper, cabrilla, sierra, pargo and late summer yellowtail.

Fresh water is a valuable commodity in the Upper Sea of Cortez.

Arroyo Blanco 1.5 miles NNW of Punta Willard is too rocky for anchoring.

Punta Bufeo 6 miles WNW of Punta Willard points north, and the anchorage (15' to 20') W of the point has shelter in light S breeze. The village has a motel, cantina, airstrip and dirt road along the coast to Puertecitos.

Enchanted Isles

Las Islas Encantadas are a chain of 6 volcanic islands, islets, shoals, reefs and rocks that runs 15 miles NW within 5 miles of shore. They include Isla San Luis (largest), Islote Pomo (Apple), several reefs and rocks, Isla Encantada (Enchanted), Isla Lobos (Seals), Isla Miramar (Look-at-the-Ocean) and Isla Huerfanito (Little Orphan). The only nav aid is Isla Miramar Light.

Isla San Luis: The S end of 729' Isla San Luis (29°58'N, 114°25'W) lies about 2.5 miles N of Punta Bufeo. A visible sand spit runs SW from the island, and the slot N of Punta Bufeo is an underwater bottleneck, but passage in about 65' of water in the middle is possible.

Shrimpers anchor off either side of the island's shoal, but the whipping current makes it uncomfortable for yachts. A better anchorage is found off the SE indent below the peak. Another anchorage is in an open cove on the NW corner just E of the volcano

Enchanted Isla Miramar has a nav light.

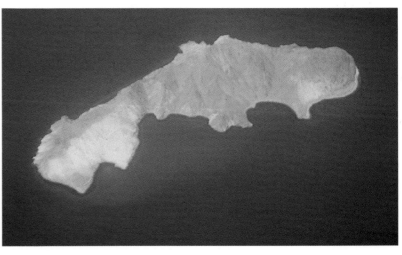

12 *Midriff Islands & Upper Sea of Cortez*

San Felipe's darsena breakwater opening.

cone; avoid a dangerous rock about a mile NNW of the island's N tip.

Islote Pomo lies 1.5 miles off the NE corner of Isla San Luis, connected by a submerged rocky reef. A cove on tiny Pomo's NE side has sheer rock walls, a small beach and a 1-boat anchoring shelf in about 15' of water.

Isla Encantada (tilts south) and its 2 detached white-washed islets to the E have no anchorages. We suggest you avoid the 2.5- to 3-mile triangle between Isla San Luis, Isla Pomo and Isla Encantada, due to numerous uncharted rocks – except perhaps for dinghy exploration in calm weather with high sun.

Isla Lobos (tilts west) is small and has 2 islets off its E side, but we don't know of an anchorage.

Isla Miramar lies 2.5 miles NW of Isla Lobos (white washed, no anchorage), and Isla Miramar Light (30°06'N, 114°36.8'W) stands on its S tip. There's a deep-water anchorage (48' to 50') in an indent about 1/3 of the way down the E side offering good shelter from N wind. Although this island is sometimes also called Isla Muertos, we use the older name Miramar (Look-at-the-Ocean) as a reminder that it's the only island in this chain with a navigation light.

Isla Huerfanito is the farthest N of this chain (5 miles NW of Isla Miramar), is the smallest, and it lies about half a mile off Baja's low arroyo-cut shoreline near a small fishing resort (Campo Nacho's or Campo Huerfanito). As a day mark, Isla Huerfanito is a 76' blazingly white pinnacle. A shoal point off Little Orphan's SW side may provide anchorage in N wind.

COASTWISE continued

Puertecitos is a shallow south-opening bay about 13 miles NW of Isla Miramar, 34 miles NW of Punta Willard. Puertecitos Light (30°26'N, 114°37'W) stands about 5 miles N of the bay. RVs with trailer boats line Puertecitos, but the bay is too shallow and

tidal (20' range) for all but multis or boats that can safely sit on the bottom at mid to low tide.

In light N wind, local sportfishers anchor briefly close SW of a detached islet on the SW side of the bay's mouth. If you dinghy ashore, land at the launch ramp just inside the NE arm. The cantina and Pemex (gas only) keep odd hours, and the hot sulfur spring nearby uncovers at low tide. Note the ham-radio buff's antenna.

On the next 27-mile hop NW to San Felipe, small RV fishing camps dot the low sandy beach. Travel at least 2 miles off to stay in 40' of water. Santa Maria and Percebu drain dry at low tide.

San Felipe

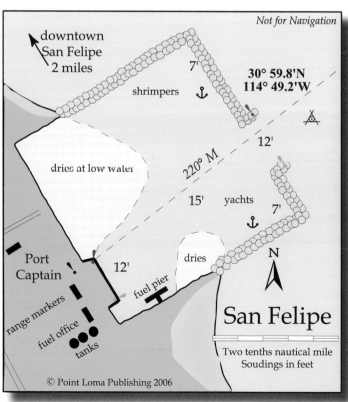

*San Felipe Light
and Cerro el Machorro.*

Lay of the Land

Punta Estrella (Star Point) is a low sandy turning point marking the S end of 9-mile long mostly shallow Bahía San Felipe. Our GPS just off the point is 30°56.29'N, 114°42.97'W, and a nav light is on a small bluff a mile NW. ATVs frequent the dunes.

West of Punta Estrella and San Felipe, the dramatic 10,184' white peaks of San Pedro Martír rise from the sloping coastal plain. *Iicj Icooz* is the Seri name for that peak, but we have no idea how to pronounce it. N of San Felipe is the mud-flat mouth of what used to be the Colorado River – not for yatistas.

At 6.4 miles NW of Punta Estrella you'll see 944' Cerro el Machorro (the Hatchet) jutting up from the beach. Our GPS position 31°02.65'N, 114°48.63'W is just off the hatchet landmark. San Felipe Light tower is on a smaller hill (Punta San Felipe) 1.5 miles SE of el Machorro at GPS 31°01.64'N, 114°49.70'W. The town spreads S from el Machorro toward the municipal harbor, which is 3.3 miles SE of el Machorro.

San Felipe is 47 miles NNW of Puertecitos, 76 miles NNW of Gonzaga Bay and 66 miles WSW of Puerto Peñasco. The small municipal harbor or darsena has a concrete dock where diesel and gas are usually sold. San Felipe has no docks or slips, so yatistas either Med-moor inside the darsena or anchor about a mile off the town at high tide due to 22' extreme ranges.

San Felipe (pop. 22,700) swells to 30,000 during holidays: Hobie races; March spring break; Cinco de Mayo; Baja off-road races in March and November. Since 1988, early November's 4-day Shrimp Festival has Mexico's best chefs competing.

Timing is everything. During an average low tide, mud flats uncover almost 3-quarters of a mile out. Don't ignore the tidal clock, or spend hours sitting on your bottom in thick mud way off shore.

Anchor & Berth

If you anchor off town, use radar to find a spot about a mile off the beach. We recommend leaving someone onboard to tend lines and watch the tides. Many who anchored off San Felipe get stranded ashore when the dinghy gets mired in 2-foot deep ooze.

We prefer the darsena. The squarish

*Sand & mud shoals uncover
well off shore of San Felipe.*

breakwater-enclosed darsena (.3 of a mile per side) is 6.4 miles NW of Punta Estrella, 3.3 miles SSE of Cerro el Machorro. From offshore, the darsena looks black against the white sand N of it. Our GPS position just outside the darsena's lighted entrance is 30°59.78'N, 114°49.21'W.

Upon entering, ignore the range markers (220°M) that lead to a fish-unloading dock, not for yachts. Instead look immediately to port and Med-moor in that NE corner, stern to the E wall, not the N wall. Shrimpers moor in the NW corner. We set the bow hook in about 7' of water (MLW) and, if the Capitanía hasn't already sent someone out to take our stern lines, we use the dinghy to take 2 extra long stern lines ashore. The climb can be slippery. Underwater, the riprap isn't so steep, so give it room.

Town has grown toward the darsena: taxis and scooters are handy for running errands up town.

Local Services

The Capitanía overlooks the harbor. Notify the Port Captain by VHF of (a.) your arrival in the area and (b.) if you want to take fuel. San Felipe Capitanía is (686) 577-1544 and 577-1577.

Fuel: Ask the Port Captain about the state of the tide and harbor conditions before you enter the harbor. Med-moor and go ashore to make your diesel arrangements in the office next to the big tank. The concrete fuel dock is in the SE corner of the darsena. Fuel at half-tide and rising; tend your lines and fenders. For gasoline, San Felipe has 2 Pemex stations.

Provisions: We've rented scooters to run errands. San Felipe has 5 grocery stores but limited refrigerated produce in summer. Watermelons and bottled water are sold on street corners. Outboard motor repair shops and auto parts stores are abundant.

Etc.: The closest swimming pool is at Mar del Sol RV park on the way into town from the darsena. They also have a restaurant and coin laundry, and a convenience store is nearby. Eateries abound.

The historic icehouse on Punta

San Felipe is long gone, replaced by a disco and pedestrian bridge from the new malecon and sea wall. The Virgin of Guadalupe shrine on Punta San Felipe is renovated. The airport S of the darsena has a control tower (118.5 SFE), paved runway and charter flights to the US. San Felipe has regular bus service: 120 miles N on Highway 5 to Mexicali, or W on Highway 3 to Ensenada.

ROUTE PLANNING Felipe to Peñasco

From San Felipe's darsena, we head ENE (067°M to 070°M) for about 67 miles, using Roca Consag as a landmark 19 miles out from San Felipe. We plan landfall either at the main port of Peñasco or Bahía Cholla about 6 miles NW of the port. Wind is usually N in winter, S in summer.

Extreme tides and current are your main concerns. N of this route line is Bahía Altar, which should be avoided. The head of the gulf can have 6-knot currents and 25' to 30' tides exposing extensive mud flats. We don't recommend exploring it by boat.

COASTWISE Felipe to Peñasco

Roca Consag (31°07'N, 114°29'W) 19 miles ENE is a 286' white pyramid with a nav light on its W side. Rip tides form around Roca Consag and rocks half a mile west.

Bahía Altar: Avoid Bahía Altar. If you spot the 11-mile light of Punta Borrascosa (Tempestuous Point), you're being set N and should compensate south. From that angle you would first see Punta Cholla (about 40' high), and you'd need to clear Punta Cholla and go ESE for 5.5 miles.

Punta Peñasco (Cerro Peñasco) is a 60' to 100' high whitish promontory with houses and trees, separating the low landscapes of Bahía Adair to the W from Bahía San Jorge to the east.

Cerro Peñasco Light overlooks approaches. New pier at foot of this headland may change the approaches.

Puerto Peñasco

Also called Rocky Point by its many gringo residents, Puerto Peñasco (pop. approx. 18,000) has a sheltered commercial harbor, a fuel dock, at least 2 large haul-out yards, many repair services, marine hardware and grocery stores, a gringo sportsmen's club, launch ramps, many trailer boats and 2 small marinas. Despite 23' spring tides and shallow water, recreational boating is the main industry.

Puerto Peñasco ("pen-YAH-skoh") lies 105 miles N of Puerto Refugio, 100 miles NNE from Gonzaga Bay, 67 miles ENE of San Felipe and 200 miles NW of Kino Bay via the W side of Isla Tiburon.

Yatistas come to here primarily to get diesel or haul out for repairs. But each year, more ocean-going yachts from the US are launching into the upper Sea of Cortez at Puerto Peñasco or further S at San Carlos. Trailer boaters have long enjoyed easy access S of Gila Bend, Arizona, through Sonoyta, Sonora,

UPPER SEA OF CORTEZ BIOSPHERE RESERVE

All of the sea and coastal planes from San Felipe ENE to Puerto Peñasco, and N to the Rio Colorado River Delta are included in the huge Reserva de la Biosfera de Alto Golfo de California – covering 770,000 hectares. A smaller nucleus zone (164,779 hectares) covers the Colorado River delta up to the Cienega de Santa Clara and almost to the border.

No shrimping or commercial fishing are allowed in the biosphere, in order to protect the habitat of at least 2 highly endangered species: the vaquita and the totoaba.

At no more than 4.5 feet in length, vaquita (or baquita) are one of the world's smallest cetacea (group that includes whales, dolphins and porpoises), and they have the most limited geographic range of any cetacea. They are found only in the biosphere's nucleus zone, yet they once roamed from L.A. Bay and Kino Bay north. According to the latest estimate by NOAA, fewer than 500 individual vaquita (Phocoena sinus) are still alive, so they are critically endangered. Consider yourself fortunate if you spot one.

What's it look like? The vaquita is distinguishable by its small black nose patch that curves – making it look like it's always smiling – and it's small black eye patches. They contrast against the vaquita's light gray body. It has a relatively large dorsal fin, which is black, as are the tail and pectoral fins. A small white patch is sometimes seen at the front base of the dorsal fin, plus a thin white streak along the leading edge of the dorsal fin – areas of maximum sun exposure.

Totoaba (or totuava, or machorro) is a large bottom-dwelling fish, up to 300 pounds and 6' in length. Closely related to the corvina, the totoaba (Totoaba macdonaldi) is so tasty that it was fished to near extinction. Commercial sport fisheries destroyed the totoaba's annual spring (January to June) breeding migration into the shallow brackish waters of the Rio Colorado delta. They once ranged from Mulege and Guaymas N.

An adult totoaba looks a lot like a white sea bass or an orange-mouthed corvina. But the totoaba has 3 sets of chin spores, no raised ridge of scales along its abdomen; the middle rays of its tail fin are longer than those above and below, and the inside of the totoaba's mouth is a dull yellow.

If you think you may have hooked a totoaba, release it immediately. Besides Mexico's restrictions and fines, US Customs and the National Marine Fisheries Service has increased enforcement – and they use forensics to test even frozen fillets. Totoaba tasting can cost you up to $50,000 per person and one year in jail.

Illegal gillnetting continues to decimate the dwindling numbers of vaquita and totoaba in the upper Sea of Cortez. If you see either one offered in a restaurant, please don't order it; you'd be rewarding the extinction of these unique species.

As visiting mariners, we applaud Mexico's efforts to protect this threatened environment – and we should all do everything we can to be good examples and worthy guests of Madre Nature.

Entrance to Puerto Peñasco harbor.

via paved 65 miles of paved Highway 8. The height limit is 14' due to low wires, but commercial boat movers now get permits to have wires raised. See Local Services.

Lay of the Land

The Gran Desierto de Altar surrounds the town, which covers and surrounds the main hill Cerro Peñasco. The narrow harbor entrance channel (running ESE) lies close on the N side of Punta Peñasco, the W tip of Cerro Peñasco. A tall tower stands on Cerro Peñasco. Pass the point to starboard and you will see the harbor entrance.

Our GPS position 31°18.5'N, 113°33.2'W is right outside the well marked entrance channel. Range markers keep you in 12' of water between shoal edges and lead to the small-boat anchorage W of the fuel dock. From there the harbor opens north.

Berth & Anchor

Marina Peñasco: This 19-slip marina in the NW corner of the harbor is often full of excursion boats, but the friendly dockmaster tries to find room for yatistas, especially if you make a reservation; PO Box 37, Lukeville, AZ, 85341. They monitor VHF 16 and 26; call (638) 383-5858.

Safe Marina-Boat Doctors: This smaller marina on the E side of the harbor has been part of a boat yard; offers dry and wet storage, mechanical and maintenance service. (638) 383-1145.

Another marina is planned inside the shallow Estero La Pinta, about 6 miles SE of Cerro Peñasco at the new Mayan Palace hotel. No details were available at press time, but check Updates at www.MexicoBoating.com

The harbor's designated small-boat anchorage is off the S wall W of the fuel dock. We found 10' to 12' (MLS) just past the panga beach.

Playa Miramar anchorage is an open roadstead off the long NW-SE beach below Cerro Peñasco. We've anchored in 15' to 30' a quarter mile off shore for shelter from N and NW winds, and several restaurants are on the beach.

Punta Cholla 5 miles NW of the harbor is the main launch ramp, but shallow-draft yachts can anchor N of the point in 4' to 5' (MLW).

Local Services

The Capitanía is 2 blocks NE of the harbor, and they've been known to treat yatistas as celebrities. Ask them about SEMARNAT permits to visit Isla Tiburon. The Capitanía is (638) 383-3035; Migración is 383-2526.

Fuel: The municipal fuel dock is a stationary

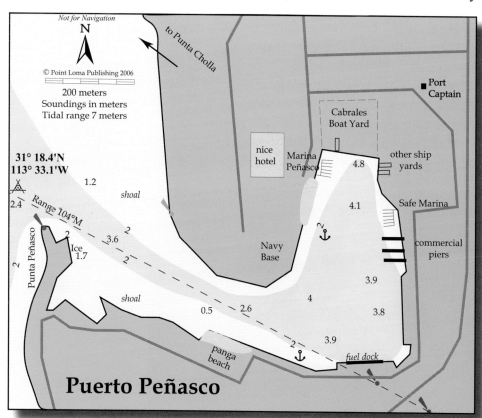

Not for Navigation

N

© Point Loma Publishing 2006

200 meters
Soundings in meters
Tidal range 7 meters

to Punta Cholla

31° 18.4'N
113° 33.1'W

1.2

shoal

2.4

Range 104°M

Punta Peñasco

2

Ice
1.7

3.6

2

2

2

shoal

0.5

2.6

panga beach

2

Port Captain

Cabrales Boat Yard

nice hotel

Marina Peñasco

4.8

other ship yards

4.1

Safe Marina

commercial piers

Navy Base

4

3.9

3.9

3.8

3.9

fuel dock

Puerto Peñasco

Fuel dock & anchorage in Peñasco harbor.

platform on the S wall of the harbor, to starboard as you enter; (638) 6035 and 2105. Look for the round tanks at street level behind the beefy, non-floating dock. Come alongside at high tide. The pump is very fast, and the nozzle has a shutoff. By low tide, the platform may be way overhead, and your boat may be sitting on the mud bottom. Don't leave a boat unattended here, because dock lines need constant tending, and shrimpers are notorious for trying to come alongside and raft outside you – yacht or not.

Cholla Bay Sportsmen's Club (VHF 09) at Bahía Cholla for local trailer-fishermen welcomes visitors, shares local knowledge. They operate a Rescue Service on VHF-16. Cholla Bay has a Pemex (gas) and grocery store amid the new hotels and subdivisions.

Haul-out: 7 boat yards around the harbor handle shrimpers. But the Cabrales Boatyard in the NW corner uses a 150-ton Travelift with padded straps, and we've had good report about their work on delicate yachts. Check out their client book of big gringo yachts. Cabrales is family owned & operated, related to Malvinas yard in Mazatlán. Cabrales yard works with boat movers from the US; (638) 383-2111 and

6174. S & S Boat Transport is (800) 256-5671.

Provisions: Peñasco has many grocery stores, fruterias, ferreterias, farmacias, 2 coin laundries, refrigeration repair, internet shops, many banks, propane, diving & fishing supplies. Cheiky's Pizza delivers to the fuel dock; 383-3627.

Emergency: Clinca Santa Fe emergency hospital is (638) 383-2447. Air med-evac is (800) 321-9522. Red Cross is 383-2266.

History & Culture

In 1826, British Lt. Robert William Hale Hardy who explored the Sea of Cortez and Altar Desert named this Sonora headland Rocky Point, which translates to Punta Peñasco. During Prohibition, a gringo built a casino and started sportfishing. Al Capone had a vacation house in town.

Puerto Peñasco harbor was dredged in 1975 for the emerging shrimping industry, then enlarged in the 1980s for barges used in building the nuclear power plant at Palos Verde, Arizona. With paved roads, tourism replaced shrimping as the town's main business. The ocean-front malecon was built in 2005; the city plans to add 3 fishing piers.

The Lost Coast

The "Lost Coast" is our term for the 200-mile stretch of Sonoran Desert coast S from Puerto Peñasco to Kino Bay. We call it *lost* because it's so sparsely populated, because the indigenous Seri people were almost extinct, and because this stretch is sadly ignored by other guidebooks. Sad, because

Typical cactus fruit develops after blooms are pollinated. Some cactus fruit are edible.

Pangas are more common than trucks & cars in the Upper Sea of Cortez.

it's prettier than much of Baja. If solitude and unspoiled nature are what you sought from cruising, you'll linger along the Lost Coast.

We hope you'll explore the cultural history of the Seri people, the last surviving hunter-gatherers of North America. The complex Seri language was oral, never written, until the 1920s. Now that many Seri place names are recorded, we're including a few you'll see along the Lost Coast.

ROUTE PLANING: Peñasco to Kino

Coasting SE from Puerto Peñasco, standard and deeper draft vessels will plan to point-hop straight between the anchorages of Cabo Tepoca, La Libertad at Cabo Lobos, Isla Patos, Bahía Sargento, Agua Dulce and Punta Willard on the outside of Isla Tiburon. Patos and Agua Dulce have S wind shelter, and the rest have some N wind shelter.

WARNING: All boats should route along the W side of Isla Tiburon. Avoid Canal de Infiernillo (Little Hell Channel) on the east side due to shifting shoals and dangerous rip tides.

COASTWISE: The Lost Coast

Estero La Pinta (6 miles ESE of Cerro Peñasco) is a shallow bay where the new Mayan Palace hotel plans to dredge and build a marina. See www. MexicoBoating.com for updates. Estero Almejas is the next lagoon east.

Isla San Jorge Light (24 miles SE of Peñasco) stands at 31°01'N, 113°15.3'W on a cone-shaped ice-burg. Most of Bahía San Jorge N of this islet is only 40' to 50' deep backed by mud flats and 18' depths out a mile from shore.

La Soledad Light (15 miles SSE of Isla San Jorge) stands on a low sandy point, but stay at least 4 miles off this point to avoid shoals. Rely on your depth sounder, as this light seldom works.

Rio Concepción Light (20 miles SSE of La Soledad Point) marks a 6' deep shoal off the mouth of Rio Concepción. Annual floods change the bottom, so we couldn't chart it.

Seri People of the Upper Sea of Cortez

Seri people camp around Bahía Sargento (Zaaj Cheel) setting fish traps in 2-mile long Estero Cocha and Bahía Bruja, small lagoons at the base of Cerro Tepopa N of the bay's wide berm. Don't take your dinghy in and don't disturb their traps or beach camp.

More than 500 people are now thought to have some Seri blood, but fewer than 100 full-blooded Seri exist, according to 2005 statistics. Most marry Mexicans and leave the reservation for Hermosillo factory jobs.

Traditional Seri families lived off the land and sea, trapped fish in estuaries and paddled tiny balsa boats far off shore. Seri men carved sea and desert animals of ironwood as a religious act, and Seri women stitched dolls and wove intricate baskets. Authentic Seri handcrafts are usually old, somewhat crudely made but very expensive, hard to tell from clever factory copies. See the Seri cultural center in Kino Bay. This region is a good place to read "The Seri Indians of Sonora, Mexico" by Bernice Johnston, University of Arizona Press.

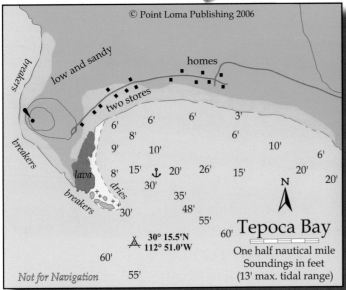

© Point Loma Publishing 2006

breakers

low and sandy

homes

two stores

breakers

lava

dries

breakers

6' 6' 6' 3'
8' 6'
9' 10' 10'
8' 15' 20' 26' 15' 20' 6'
30' 20'
35'
48'
30' 55'
60' **Tepoca Bay**

30° 15.5'N
112° 51.0'W

N

60'

60'

55'

One half nautical mile
Soundings in feet
(13' max. tidal range)

Not for Navigation

In fair weather, we anchored (marginal) in the open roadstead off a 12' shelf below a collection of houses in the arroyo. However, this was not good holding, is not suggested as an overnight stop, and would be untenable in windy weather. The panga village has electricity, phones and paved road 50 miles to Cobarca.

Cabo Tepoca

About 74 miles SE of Puerto Peñasco, Cabo Tepoca is a 300' white hill carrying Cabo Tepoca Light, which can be seen for 20 miles. (Don't confuse this with Cabo Tepopa near Bahía Sargento.) Almost detached, Cabo Tepoca first appears as an island. In Seri, this headland is *Hast Heeque Coopol.*

Monte Plano (1,584') 6 miles NE and Pico Tienda de Compana (2,462') 4 miles ESE are the start of the Sierra Madres that end 1,300 miles SE at the Gulf of Tehuantepec. This is about the end of the shallows of the upper Sea of Cortez.

Breakers line the W side of the lighthouse point, and a black lava reef (Tepoca Reef) fringing the SE side of the point uncovers at low water. Houses line

*Cabo Tepoca Light and Tepoca Reef
as seen from the anchorage.*

156

the mile-long neck. The 5-mile wide indent on the S side of the point is Bahía Tepoca. N of the point was too rocky to anchor.

Good overnight anchorage in N weather is found SE and E of Tepoca Reef. We've anchored at GPS position 30°16.06'N, 112°50.96'W, which is off the middle of the beach neck in about 20' of water. In strong NW winds, you can get closer to the W end of the beach, behind the reef, in 10' to 15' over sand and gravel. In light S wind, boaters anchor off the NW tip of Cabo Tepoca in about 30' of water, but E of there is too rocky.

Tepoca village has 2 grocery stores and about 30 vacation homes. The gravel road S curves along the beach to the next small point 14 miles SE, which has no anchorage. From there it's 9 miles to Cabo Lobos and La Libertad.

La Libertad

Cabo Lobos headland (706') and power station lie 23 miles SE of Cabo Tepoca, 42 miles N of Sargento Bay, and 111 miles N of Kino Bay. Smoke may point you here. Cabo Lobos (*Xpano Hax* in Seri.) shelters La Libertad power station. Supply ships anchor in the large bay SE of the point.

Yatistas can anchor closer off the rocky, undeveloped shoreline NW of the power plant's lighted outer pier. We've anchored at in 36' to 40' of water close to the steep shore. This anchorage is open to the south, fine in fair weather but rolly in N wind.

The S seaward end of this N-S running pier is at GPS position 29°53.72'N, 1123°41.88'W, and Puerto Libertad Light is on this T-head pier. Guards prohibit visitors coming too close to the piers or stepping ashore.

Desemboque

This small river mouth is 29 miles SE of La Libertad, 12 miles NW of Bahía Sargento. Rio San Ignacio Light on the N side of the indent marks a shoal that runs E and ends W of the village.

However, we found a slightly sheltered roadstead in front of the village, which is next to the Rio San Ignacio valley at the foot of

Tepoca village is on the S side of Cabo Tepoca.

steep hills. The Spanish nautical word *desembocar* means to sail out the mouth of a river mouth, but this river isn't navigable. We anchored at GPS 29°30'N, 12°24'W in 30' of water over mud; a shelf prevents getting closer.

A gringo retiree hailed us on VHF to say he and his neighbors maintain unmarked channels for their own trailer boats. Further, he said Desemboque is the best place to hire a Seri guide if we plan to go ashore on Isla Tiburon, because they charge more at Kino Bay. Just hail "Seri guide" on VHF 16; some speak English and can come out in a panga. The Seri name for this river mouth is *Haxol Ihom.*

Seri Reservation Preserve: Desemboque and everything S to Kino Bay is the Seri Indian Reservation, including Islas Tiburon, San Estéban, Turner and Pelícano. Rules prohibit stepping ashore on an island without having hired a Seri guide. Seri people used to roam the waters from La Libertad to Guaymas and W to Isla Angel de Guarda (Zazl Iimt) and San Felipe.

COASTWISE continued

Cabo Tepopa (35 miles SE of La Libertad) is a headland W of the landmark 1,868' Cerro Tepopa. Seri called the mountain *Zpajquema*. Our GPS just half a mile W of Cabo Tepopa is 29°22.54'N, 112°25.87'W. An equilateral triangle formed by Cabo Tepopa, Isla Patos and Punta Sargento has 6 miles to a side.

Bahía Sargento

This shallow bay and picturesque sheltered anchorage lie 1.5 miles NE of low Punta Sargento (pronounced "sahr-HEN-tow), which is entered 7 miles SE of Cabo Tepopa. A 2-mile low neck of blazingly white sand runs S to a hill on Punta Sargento. Our GPS just off this point is 29°17.42'N,

112°20.04'W.

This neck submerges in spring tides, and the half-mile wide shoal along its E side (inside the bay) dries at low water. Bahía Sargento offers good N shelter, and it's useful for timing smaller boats in transit around the W side of Isla Tiburon.

Enter the bay about a quarter mile S of Punta Sargento (cross & anchor marker), and don't turn N until you've passed the shoal E of the peninsula. Then come N until you're about half a mile S of the head of the bay. It has a 2-mile long E-W beach berm shielding Estero Cocha.

We've anchored in 12' over good holding sand at GPS 29°19.15'N, 112°19.06'W. Allow for the 12' tidal fall. If the wind turns south, move to Agua Dulce 7.5 miles SW of Punta Sargento.

The snowy powder sand is spectacular. Beach-strolling, kayaking and hiking are superb. Avoid seasonal stingrays in the shallows.

COASTWISE continued

From Sargento, it's 7.4 miles to the anchorage in Agua Dulce on Tiburon Island. We found shoals

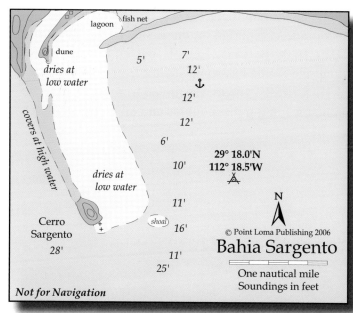

Bahia Sargento
One nautical mile
Soundings in feet
Not for Navigation
© Point Loma Publishing 2006

Sargento Bay in relation to Agua Dulce on Isla Tiburon and tiny Isla Pato. Canal de Infiernillo is lower right.

birds. The Seri name for this island is *Hast Otiipa*. The 1800s wreck the tallship Thayer is reported to be a good dive in 45' of water off the NW point: GPS 29°16.48'N, 112°27.80'W.

Isla Tiburon

Largest island (1,208 square miles) in the Sea of Cortez, Isla Tiburon (*Tahejoc* in Seri) is the jewel of the Seri Reservation lands, believed to be where their spirits roam after death. Don't go ashore without a Seri guide, usually hired in Kino Bay, maybe also in Desemboque. This mountainous mass (peaks to 4,000') has 5 anchorages, but avoid the dangerous Canal de Infiernillo (Little Hell) on its E side.

The NE corner at the top of Little Hell canal is a 2.5-mile long sandbar jutting NE. That dangerous tip is about 29°15'N, 112°16'W, but we didn't get right on it. It's 5 miles SW to Bahía Agua Dulce.

Agua Dulce

5 miles SE of Isla Patos, this 2.5-mile wide indent on the N side of Isla Tiburon gives good anchorage in all S weather and not much current, but is open to all N quarters. A Navy outpost visible near the mouth of the long green valley is occupied seasonally, like the S end of Tiburon. Agua Dulce refers to a seasonal spring up this 5-mile long valley.

and strong current 3 miles S of Punta Sargento. Any farther, and you're too close to the Canal de Infiernillo.

Isla Patos (6.5 miles ESE of Punta Sargento) is a tiny steep-to island peaked by Isla Patos Light (29°16.4'N, 112°27'W). The roughly triangular cinder cone has reefs off all 3 pointy corners. An anchorage is reported on the E side of the SW point at 29°16.00'N, 112°27.60'W, but almost anywhere along the S side has some shelter from N wind.

Historically, guano was mined from Isla Patos, the name meaning gulls, boobies and all web-footed sea

Isla Pato on horizon from inside Sargento Bay. Mid ground is Punta Sargento sand bar.

Powder white beaches of Sargento Bay.

The Navy patrol boats may be moored off the protruding arroyo delta in 15' to 20', which is a good anchorage: GPS 29°11.44'N, 112°25'06'W. We've also anchored NE of the Navy building in 25' to 30' of water, also NW of the arroyo delta in 21' to 25'. You can land a dink SE of the delta.

When you come ashore, Marines may saunter down to see if you need help. They've been friendly to us and other yatistas. They joked that the small pier gets destroyed in winter, patched in summer

Going around the W side of Isla Tiburon shows 2-mile long facades of rock, no anchorages until Willard.

Isla San Estéban (St. Steven) 9 miles S of Tiburon's SW corner may help when crossing the Sea of Cortez, but its E side is plagued with tidal overfalls. In N weather, marginal anchorage (22' over sand) is found off the S side of the sand spit on the island's SW corner. Isla San Estéban Light (28°42.8'N, 112°32.2'W) is on the NW tip of Isla San Esteban. The Seri name is *Coftecol.*

Punta Willard

Willard Point (24 miles SW of Agua Dulce) is the prominent pointy SW tip of Isla Tiburon. 2 anchoring coves are found on the N flank of Willard Point, which carries a nav light, and another anchorage is on the S side.

Caleta las Dunas: This small dune-filled cove is on the E side of a narrow rock point jutting north. The point, Punta Las Dunas (dunes), is 1.5 miles NE of Punta Willard, and the cove is a quarter-mile wide. Anchor SE of the point in 15' to 13' over good-holding sand. Our GPS approach is 28°53.51'N, 112°33.60'W.

Caleta Las Dunas is fine in S weather, but open to north, even NE wind that swoops down Tiburon's slope. It has a small beach, also good snorkeling off Punta Las Dunas and over a rock pile on the NW end of the beach. The other side of Punta Las Dunas looks like an interesting dinghy ride.

Willard North: Half a mile SW of Punta Las Dunas is a stubby point jutting west. The quarter-mile bay S of it has intermittent beach and rocky protrusions. Some yatistas anchor out in the middle in 15' to 20' over sand and gravel. Our GPS approach is 28°53.00'N, 112°34.28'W.

Watch for tidal overfalls as you round Punta Willard a quarter mile off.

Sunset over Isla Tiburon.

Punta Risco Colorado (left) and its reef (right).

Willard South: In N wind, the best anchorage is in a mile-wide indent that lies 1.3 miles SE of the point, around a hilly bulge and below the steep cliffs. Our GPS approach to Willard S is 28°52.02'N, 112°33.78'W. Anchor in 20' to 30' over sand and gravel.

Punta Peña Blanca: At 5.8 miles SE of Punta Willard, avoid this hooked point at the foot of landmark Monte Peña Blanca; it has small reef with severe tidal disturbances, so we don't think it's an anchorage. Our GPS position half a mile off the reef is 28° 49.00'N, 112°29.30'W.

Bahía Risco Colorado

At 16 miles SE of Punta Willard, the big reddish Punta Risco Colorado (Reddish Cliffs) forms the NW arm of Bahía Risco Colorado, which runs 2.5 miles SE to Monument Point. Our GPS off Punta Risco Colorado is 28°45.55'N, 112°21.53'W. The bay's W end has 3 consecutive coves, each about a quarter mile wide, divided by low points. This end of Bahía Risco Colorado is Tiburon's best shelter from NW wind. The westernmost cove below a seasonal Navy base may be the choicest spot. We've anchored here in 25' over sand. The other coves are OK too.

Seri camp: In the E half of Bahía Risco Colorado .75 of a mile NW of Monument Point, a small Y-shaped point with 2 mounds sometimes serves as a Seri camp when they lead kayakers here. Our GPS for this point is 28°45.27'N, 112°19.37'W.

Monument Pass

When moving between Willard Point and Kino Bay, you'll probably transit Monument Pass, which runs E-W between Monument Point and the off-lying 151' high Seal Rock (*Hast Isel* in Seri). A reef connects Seal Rock to Isla Turner, so don't cut through there.

The visible opening between (a.) Monument Point on Tiburon and (b.) Seal Rock measures about .54 of a mile. However, you'll need to avoid both a quarter-mile long reef that juts N from Sea Rock and a submerged reef that juts less than a quarter mile S from Monument Point. Veteran cruisers pass in deep water a little N of the center of this pass. Our GPS position a quarter mile S of Monument Point is 28°44.63'N, 112°18.52'W. Use radar and depth sounder; expect strong current.

Alternative: If you go S of 1.6-mile long Isla Turner (no anchorage), beware of Dead Man Rock, an uncharted pinnacle reported to rise from deep water about half a mile SSE of Seal Rock and .62 of a mile SW of the N end of Isla Turner. This might put it about 28°43.75'N, 112°18.39'W, but we didn't spend much time looking for it.

Satellite shows Isla Tiburon's S end, Isla Esteban (lower left) , Turner, S end of Canal de Infernillo (top center) and Kino Bay (right).

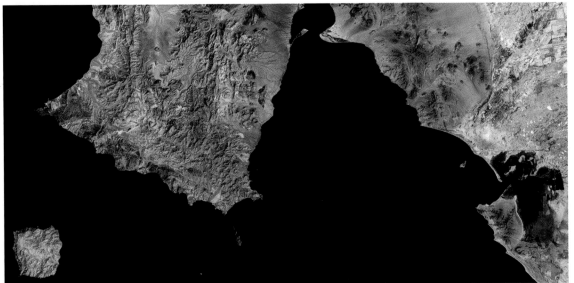

Isla Turner Light (28°43.4'N, 112°19.5'W) on the S tip of Isla Turner (no anchorage) warns of tidal rip current.

Monument Bay immediately NE of Punta

Monument is a 1-mile curve with a fair anchorage off the more sheltered E end (GPS 28°46.00'N, 112°16.44'W) near Punta *Hast Haquim*. Anchor in 18' to 22' over sand and gravel.

Punta Hast Haquim (GPS 28°45.75'N,

112°16.00'W) is the southward point at the E end of Monument Bay, a Seri name that's sometimes extended to so-called Puppy Cove .3 of a mile to its east. Punta *Hast Haquim* is about .75 of a mile WSW of Dog Point.

Dog Point

At the protruding SE tip of Isla Tiburon, Dog Point or Punta Perro (*Mashem* in Seri) looks like 2 hills almost separated a mile from the island. Maybe one hill looks like a dog. From our GPS position a quarter mile E of Dog Point (28°46.04'N, 112°15.47'W), Pelican Island off Kino Bay is 15 miles at 080°T.

Puppy Cove: A tiny cove tucked into the SE side of Dog Point has anchorage in 18' to 22' of water. Our GPS just outside the cove is 28°46.04'N, 112°15.47'W. This is sometimes called *Hast Haquim* for the larger point to its west. At springs, some current may back-eddy into the cove. The rocks off Punta *Mashem* have had too much current for us to snorkel safely.

Dogs Bay

Bahía los Perros (*Taij It* in Seri) is a beautiful 2-cove bay about a mile NW of Dog Point. It has good shelter from NW through S wind, and you can anchor in either lobe, 13' to 20' of water over good holding sand and mud. Our GPS position in the N cove is 28°47.24'N, 112°16.23'W.

2 more small coves N of here might be worthy. But you may feel tidal pull during new and dark moons, because you're almost in a funnel the Seris call *Kun Kaak*, the S entrance to the Canal de Infiernillo. *Kun Kaak* is Isla Tiburon's biggest mountain and it overlooks this funnel. *Kun Kaak* is another term the Seris apply to themselves.

From Dog's Bay, it's 11 miles N to Punta Chueca, the Seri town at the jaws on the Kino side of the funnel. If you want to hire a Seri guide to show you Little Hell, you may start from Punta Chueca and

Tiburon blooms.

go north. An unpaved road connects Kino Bay to Chueca and up to Sargento Bay.

Kino Bay

Kino Bay is about 215 miles SE of Puerto Peñasco, 55 miles NE of Bahía San Fransicquito via the Midriff Islands, 72 miles NW of San Carlos-Guaymas.

Yatistas can anchor off Kino Bay and dinghy ashore on blazingly white beaches loaded with jerry jugs for Pemex gas and diesel, bags for the great provisions and a good appetite for the many eateries. But shelter isn't good enough to leave a boat unattended very long. A marina has been promised to Kino Bay; check Updates on www.MexicoBoating.com

Kino Bay Sportsmen's Club (Club Deportivo)

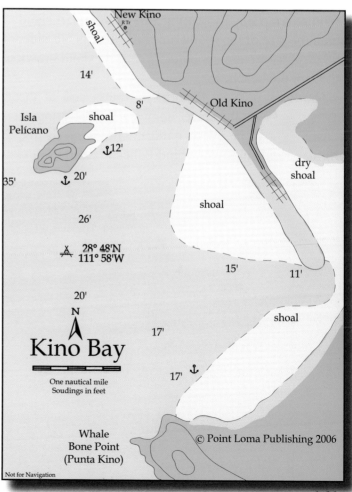

New Kino
R Tr
shoal
14'
8'
Old Kino
Isla Pelícano
shoal
12'
dry shoal
35'
20'
shoal
26'
28° 48'N
111° 58'W
15'
11'
20'
N
shoal
17'
Kino Bay
One nautical mile
Soudings in feet
17'
Whale Bone Point (Punta Kino)
© Point Loma Publishing 2006
Not for Navigation

is a very active fishing and boating group who love to help visiting yatistas; call on VHF 16 for a tide report. Club volunteers operate the region's Rescue One service on VHF 11. This is trailer-boat country.

Lay of the Land

The bay named for Padre Kino (not the wine) is 5 miles wide from Punta San Ignacio SE to Whale Bone Point (GPS 28°45.59'N, 111°57.44'W). Isla Pelícano rises 545' roughly in the middle of Kino Bay.

Enter Kino Bay by coming S of the island. A shoal about the size of the island runs NE from its NE side, and there's a small pass before a shifting shoal grows out from the beach.

The town of New Kino along the N end of the bay is filled with the newer homes of retired gringos, a fishing boat in every garage. Old Kino is the original Mexican town behind Pelican Island. You'll

see a fishing panga pulled up on every beachfront there too. A few homes are S to the tip of Punta Kino peninsula.

The SE corner of Kino Bay is mostly shoal, except for a 12' deep channel (not maintained) to Punta Kino. Estero Santa Cruz behind Punta Kino is shoal except for some channels worked on by locals.

Anchorage

Pelican Island: In NW wind, we anchor S (20' of water over sand) and ESE (12') of this .75 of a mile long, guano spotted rock. The nav light is on its NE side, marking a shoal that runs .75 of a mile NE. Locals said that in S wind, yachts anchor N of the island in 15' to 20' over sand. Pelican Island is *Tassne* in Seri.

Whale Bone Point, backed by a cluster of 1,340' hills, provides shelter in calms and S wind a quarter mile off its N tip in about 17' of water. We've noticed shrimpers anchoring anywhere between the island and Whale Bone Point in any weather.

Local Services

Dinghies land at the paved ramps: 2 are on the N side of right-angled Punta San Ignacio, one on its S corner, another at the N end of Old Kino behind the island. For shallow dinks, at least one ramp is inside Santa Cruz Lagoon on the back side of Old Kino.

Fuel & provisions: Old Kino has a Pemex station (gas, sometimes diesel) on the highway and at least 2 restaurants. New Kino has a Pemex, 5 grocery stores, Club Deportivo, marine hardware & tackle shops, propane, banks, farmacias and half a dozen gringo eateries.

Kino Bay's launch ramps are handy to land a dinghy. Both ramps are at the N end of New Kino.

Licensed Seri fishing guides recommended by local guide Tom Crutchfield are Ernesto Moreno and the Antonio Robles family (8 sons). Hail them by name on VHF 16.

Club Deportivo: Everyone in Kino Bay owns a boat and goes fishing. Club Deportivo (Sports Club) has an air-conditioned clubhouse in New Kino, 600 members, operates the ramps & tractor launcher. Visiting boat owners can check in on VHF, join the Friday fish-fry and other clubhouse activities. Club Deportivo is (624) 242-0321.

Rescue One is their volunteer network of rescue boats and 24-hour VHF monitoring. File a float plan on VHF 11, you'll be missed if you don't call by dark. They've logged 1000s of medical, mechanical, navigational rescues in this end of the Sea of Cortez, some assisted by US Coast Guard and Mexican Navy.

History & Culture

The Seri Cultural Museum in the middle of town is a must, and it's hard for us fellow mariners to resist the Seri ironwood carvings of their religious icons: turtle, seal, shark, gull and pelican. Seri women weave wonderful baskets.

Kino Bay was named for Jesuit Father Eusebio Kino who founded 25 desert missions. He landed here by boat in 1687. The Seri people were "rediscovered" by anthropologist W. J. McGee in 1894 when he explored Kino Bay to Sargento for the US Bureau of American Ethnology. We've used Seri place names from McGee's remarkable book called *The Seri Indians of Kino Bay and Sonora, Mexico*, and from GeoNative.com.

Rescue One: Volunteers and staffers man this Kino Bay public service station on VHF 11, operated by the Club Deportivo.

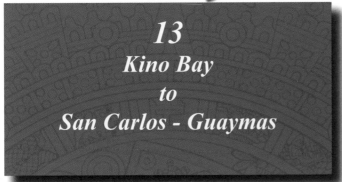

13
Kino Bay
to
San Carlos - Guaymas

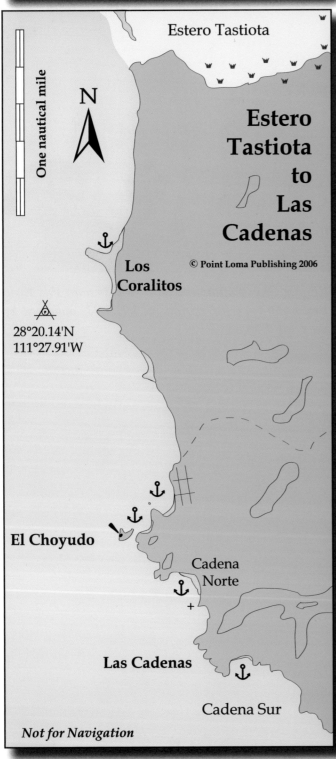

Estero Tastiota

One nautical mile

N

Estero
Tastiota
to
Las
Cadenas

© Point Loma Publishing 2006

Los
Coralitos

28°20.14'N
111°27.91'W

El Choyudo

Cadena
Norte

+

Las Cadenas

Cadena Sur

Not for Navigation

When we researched this 75-mile coast in 1994 - 1995 for a previous guidebook (***Boating Guide to Mexico: West Coast edition***, long out of print), we decided the vast shoals and paucity of reliable shelter between Kino Bay and San Carlos made it impractical for ocean-going yachts, better turf for trailer boats launching at either end. For that reason, we didn't give it much attention in our 1st edition of "***Mexico Boating Guide***." But so many readers asked for details, that we came back in 2005 to update our previous research on this stretch.

ROUTE PLANNING Kino to San Carlos

It's 75 miles from Kino's Whale Bone Point going SE to San Carlos. If you can do it in one fell swoop, that's Plan A.

The northern 40-mile stretch off a low shoaly shore has no hope of a secure anchorage. Stay at least 5 miles off shore (or in deep water) the first 24 miles SE to Punta Baja, which we give a 5-mile berth due to a migrating shoal off the low point. Likewise for the next 16.5 miles ESE to a waypoint off Estero Tastiota.

The southern 35 miles from Tastiota to San Carlos is mountainous, rocky and has a series of 20 "small hopes." Most of the tiny coves are too small to protect larger *yates* anchoring overnight, but OK for smaller *yatitas* in flat conditions. Most have some shelter in moderate N wind, a few maybe in light S wind – but no reliable multi-directional anchorage nor all-weather protection for bigger boats.

Guaíma Environmental Preserve covers from Tastiota to Cabo Haro outside Guaymas harbor. Within its protective boundaries are 11 coastal canyons and 34 islands, the largest being Isla San Pedro Nolasco. When the Guaíma (pronounced "wah-YEE-mah") preserve is fully implemented, commercial fishing and shrimping will be replaced by fishing and diving tourism. Cabrilla, grouper, bass and barracuda are in the rocky points.

If a red tide begins blooming, we suggest you re-route S until you reach clear water. During a red tide, the algae in the water smells like blood, and you can't eat the fish, run a watermaker or swim. A red tide can bloom for 3 days to 2 weeks.

COASTWISE Kino to San Carlos

From Kino's Whale Bone Point, stay at least 5 miles offshore for 24 miles SE to a waypoint (GPS

28°24.50'N, 111°47,44'W) 5 miles SW of shoaly Punta Baja.

Punta Baja Shoals: At 24 miles SE of Kino, Punta Baja Light marks Punta Baja Shoals, which extend as much as 4 miles off the low coast. The coast turns more easterly, and for the next 16.5 miles, stay 3 or 4 miles off. Cerro Bocana abruptly rises 759' from the San Juan Bautista Plains that end at the mouth of Estero Tastiota.

Estero Tastiota: At 15 miles ESE of Punta Baja, shoals extend 2 miles off the shallow mouth of Estero Tastiota at the foot of Cerro Bocana (785'), so we stand at least well off. Estero Tastiota is too shallow except by dinghy, so we turn S at GPS 28°20.88'N, 111°3.00'W, which is 2.5 miles outside the lagoon entrance. Behind the berm, shrimp farms extend 3 miles NW. The Tastiota were a band of Seri people.

Los Coralitos: Less than a mile S of
Tastiota waypoint is a tiny sandbar jutting NW, lighter than a smaller point just S . S shelter is found off the N side of the larger Coralito (GPS 28°20.63'N, 111°27.65'W) if you can tuck into 12' of water over good holding sand.

El Choyudo 1.5 miles S of Coralitos is a
detached rock with a light tower, a minor turning point. Our GPS 28°19.02'N, 111°27.56'W is just W of El Choyudo. Anchorage is possible NE of El Choyudo off a small curving beach in 18' to 22' over sand. Also, in the NE cove off the village beach (15' to 18') you may find some shelter from S swell. Locals said the road goes to the town of Tastiota, and the bare peaks 2 miles E are called Los Japoneses, the Japanese.

Las Cadenas: Within the next 1.5
miles SE are 2 tiny oval coves, like chain links, with good N-wind shelter in both coves. A small reef divides the northern link, but you can anchor in either end. We stopped in its N end GPS 28°18.73'N, 111°27.16'W and found 28' over sand.

Morro Colorado is a prominent 600' furrowed cone on a round point 2.5 miles SE of El Choyudo. Our GPS waypoint a quarter mile SW of Morro Colorado is 28°17.00'N, 111°25.74'W.

Caleta Colorado immediately E of
the cone has N-wind shelter in 25' to 30' over

Overall
Estero Tastiota to San Carlos, Sonora

© Point Loma Publishing 2005

salt pans

Estero Tastiota

Los Coralitos

El Choyudo

Las Cadenas

Caleta Colorado

Bahía San Agustín

Pozo Moreno

Julio Villa

Punta Moreno

Rada Pasito

Bahía Jojoba

Roca el Mollete

Punta Blanca

Caleta Venecia

Caleta Seri Muerto

Caleta Amarga

Bahía San Pedro

Las Barajitas Guaíma Preserve

Punta Agua Escondida

Is. San Pedro Nolasco *is 4 miles WSW of this location*

Bandito Cove

Punta Bandito

Chollado

Punta Mangla

Bahía Algondones

Not for Navigation Punta San Antonio

San Carlos

N

Five nautical miles

Palo Verde trees thrive in seasonal arroyos, such as Caleta Colorado.

sand off the village. A bus stops here from Highway 132. This and Agustín are larger than what you've just passed.

Bahía San Agustín: This 1.5-mile long bay has shelter at both ends. In N conditions,

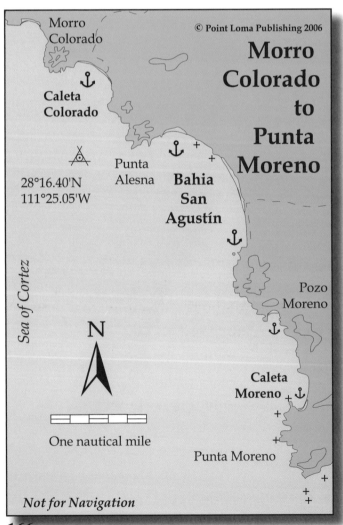

we tucked a third of a mile E of Punta Alesna (awl) and anchored in 15' over sand at GPS 28°16.49'N, 111°23.98'W. The S end is tiny, we couldn't tuck in behind the rock, but it's reported to serve in S and SE conditions.

Pozo Moreno: This cute little horseshoe cove a mile around the corner from the S end of Agustín is only 200 yards wide. Fine in flat calms, it suffers from refractive rollies in N wind. Our peek-in GPS is 28°14.55'N, 111°22.81'W. *Pozo moreno* is a dark-water well.

Caleta Moreno: In S wind, a small N-S cove a mile N of Punta Moreno has good shelter. Our GPS in the middle is 28°13.89'N, 111°22.49'W.

Punta Moreno headland (7.7 miles SE of El Choyudo) has a **dangerous detached reef** off its S side. Our GPS waypoint 28°12.76'N, 111°22.43'N is a quarter mile S of Punta Moreno in deep water. Moreno means dark, like this lifted cliff.

Bahía Jojoba is the open 3-miles long curve from Punta Moreno almost to the Punta el Mollete headland. From shore, the broad Valle de Jojoba runs NE to the N side of Canyon del Diablo Biosphere Reserve, but there's no access from here. Oil from the desert shrub *jojoba* is used in cosmetics. Roca Acero in the middle of the bay (GPS 28°11.50'N, 111°21.48'W) is about 2 miles S of Punta Moreno, 1.1 miles SE of Punta Jojoba. *Acero* is steel, as in a sword blade.

Julio Villa Cove: At the N end of Jojoba Bay, less than a mile NE of Punta Moreno and framed by 2 obvious detached rocks, this undeveloped 2-boat cove has shelter from N and NW wind. Our peek-in GPS is 28°13.08'N, 111°21.59'W.

Rada el Pasito 1.25 miles ESE of the waypoint off Punta Moreno is too shallow to tuck much NE of the detached rock, but 2 hills NE and NW may help. We stopped at GPS 28°12.70'N, 111°20.99'W in 15' over sand, but did not stay. *Rada* means open roadstead.

Roca el Mollete: On the SW side of the 2.5-mile wide bulge S of Jojoba Valley, this rounded rock barely protrudes W from a similarly round-topped point nearby. *Mollete* (mo-YAY-tay) is a muffin; *molletes* are cheeks. A reef juts S from the point. Our GPS waypoint in deep water close W of Roca el Mollete is 28°09.51'N, 111°19.96'W. Small boats anchor in the tiny slot E of the reef in flat calm.

Punta Blanca (GPS 28°08.51'N, 111°19.05'W) is a distinct ridge point 1.3 miles SE of el Mollete. Himalaya, a small slot on the N flank may give S -wind shelter to one small boat, but another cove behind a thumb point to the N is foul.

Caleta Venecia: 1.5 miles SE of Punta Blanca, the second of 2 coves has shelter from N wind in 14' to 18' over sand. A stubby reefs juts SW from the S entrance. Our GPS peek in point is 28°07.73'N, 111°17.80'W. The smaller cove just N has a village and road link.

Caleta Seri Muerto

At 3.8 miles SE of Punta Blanca is rectangular and roomier than its neighbors, 0.3 of a mile per side. The NE corner is foul for anchoring right off the beach, but the SE corner is fine. In the middle of the cove, our GPS is 28°05.32'N, 111°16.55'W. Half a mile up are some islets and rocks for diving, and just down and around the corner from Seri Muerto is a pleasant slot.

The next 2.8 miles SE to Bahía San Pedro is fringed in lava-like finger points.

Caleta Amarga (Bitter) is the S side of a large finger point N of San Pedro Point; it's doable in 20' to 26' over sand. So is the N side of Punta San Pedro.

Punta San Pedro is a landmark

along the Guaíma. Our GPS waypoint a quarter mile SW of the bulbous 528' San Pedro headland is 28°03.02'N, 111°15.51'W. From here Estero Tastiota is 20 miles NW, San Carlos is about 10 miles SE.

Bahía San Pedro

This bay is only 0.6 of a mile wide, but its crescent is almost enclosed E of San Pedro Point, shielded at the S end by a finger point. San Pedro Bay has shelter in its ends from light N and SE winds, but open SW. Our GPS off the sandy beach in the larger N end is

Tide pools and caves at Punta San Pedro are fun for kids.

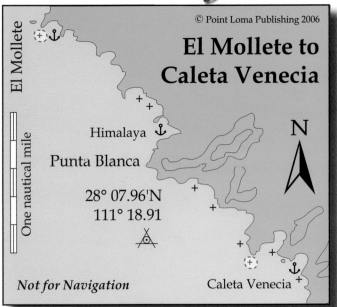

© Point Loma Publishing 2006

El Mollete to Caleta Venecia

El Mollete

One nautical mile

Himalaya

Punta Blanca

28° 07.96'N
111° 18.91

N

Caleta Venecia

Not for Navigation

28°03.38'N, 111°14.65'W in 18' to 24' over sand. In a Norther, some swell can wrap the rocky point. A wreck dive and cave are on the big point.

Excursion boats from San Carlos come here when it's too rough near Isla San Pedro. From here S, you'll see more sportfishers and dive boats.

Las Barajitas:
At 3.6 miles SE of Punta San Pedro, Punta Agua Escondido has only marginal shelter on its S side (GPS 28°01.16' 111°11.56'W). However, 2 shipwrecks (60' depth) are popular dives off the new solar powered eco-retreat Cañon las Barajitas: the 180' tuna boat *Albatun*, which sank here, and the elderly 330' ferry *Presidente Diaz Ordáz*, towed from Mazatlán and sunk here for divers. Las Barajitas underwater canyon is part of the Guaíma preserve. More artificial reefs are planned.

Isla San Pedro Nolasco:
Largest island in the new Guaíma nature preserve, 3-mile long San Pedro Nolasco Island lies 8 miles SW of

Punta San Pedro, 15.4 miles WNW of Punta San Antonio, a few miles further from Punta Doble. Our GPS off the N tip is 27°59.36'N, 111°23.31'W.

In calm weather and with lots of chain, you can anchor in 30' to 40' in the small cove on the NE side near the light tower. This is a favorite spot for dive boats in the mornings, but we've never stayed here overnight. Pedro Nolasco was a 13th century monk.

Bandito Cove:
6.5 miles SE of Punta San Pedro, S -pointing Punta Bandito shelters 2 coves on its E side. Our GPS position 27°59.45'N, 111°10.10'W is just outside the second cove, with shelter in light N wind. Mt. Algodones dominates inland.

Playa Chollado
half a mile SE of Bandito Cove is a tourist beach, but it has a semi-detached finger point with intimate anchorages on both sides in 14' to 20' over sand. Diving is excellent off the islet and a reef off its S tip. Our GPS position S of Chollado Reef is 27°59.04'N, 111°54'W. *Chollado* means infested with crows, but we haven't seen any here. The next point, square Punta Manga has *nada* for *yatistas*.

Islas Venado & San Luis:
a new marina basin is in construction behind the beach NE of these 2 finger islands. Our GPS position just outside the entrance is 27°58.00'N, 111°06.97'W. Check for Updates on www.MexicoBoating.com

Bahía Algodones

This 1.5-mile crescent beach is framed by the finger islands Venado and San Luis (good snorkeling) and bulkier Punta San Antonio with its landmark Tetakawi peaks. Playa Algodones is billed "Catch 22" Beach for Joseph Heller's war satire filmed here in 1969. Anchorage is possible almost anywhere off the pretty Playa Algodones (cotton balls), but weekends bring water skiers and jet boats.

The entrance to Marina Real is at the SE end of this beach, as are several anchoring coves around Punta San Antonio.

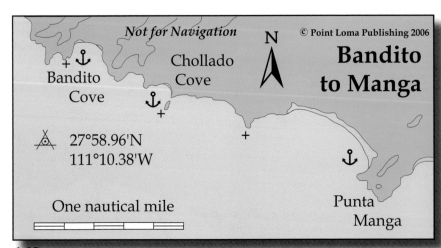

Not for Navigation

N

© Point Loma Publishing 2006

Bandito to Manga

Bandito Cove

Chollado Cove

27°58.96'N
111°10.38'W

One nautical mile

Punta Manga

San Carlos - Guaymas

The light-hearted resort port of San Carlos, Sonora (pop. approx. 15,500) is the most important boating destination on the mainland middle of the Sea of Cortez, thanks its natural hurricane shelter and 2 full-service marinas.

About 10 miles SE, the traditional port of Guaymas (pop. 140,500) has bigger supermarkets plus the shipyards and marine services for the dwindling shrimp fleets, some now shifting to recreational boating.

San Carlos

More than 400 yatistas call the marinas of San Carlos their homeport year round. More than 400 trailerable boats base here year round as well, because it's only 300 paved and divided highway miles S of Tucson, Arizona.

Hurricane Season: Summers are crowded, because nearly landlocked Bahía San Carlos and the tiny side bay in which Marina San Carlos' slips are located serve as a hurricane hole. To a lesser extent, so does Marina Real's yacht basin behind Playa Algodones. Statistically, San Carlos is on the N edge of the hurricane belt.

Truck & Store: Yachts to 45' LOA can be trucked between Marina San Carlos and anywhere in the US, thanks to Ed Grossman's unique service. See Local Services.

Many small- to mid-sized coastal cruisers get hauled out at Marina San Carlos to spend the summer safely parked a mile inland at their huge dry storage yard, Marina Seca, while their owners fly to the US. Boats also are hauled to Marina San Carlos' repair yard next door.

Guaymas

Guaymas is a traditional town of siestas, parades around the cathedral plaza, chaperoned teenagers in the parks – and hospitality to tourists. It's called the Pearl of the Sea of Cortez.

Sheltered in big hills, the picturesque harbor has a commercial port with Pemex, and container docks on the N side of the entrance, and 400 shrimpers

Indian Head Point is to starboard as you enter Bahía San Carlos.

and small fishing boats homeport here – not all in at once. Fishing and tourism are the main activities, but the surrounding ranchos raise premium beef cattle, vegetables and citrus. This is a great place to provision with Sonora beef. Cowboy garb is as typical as ranchero music.

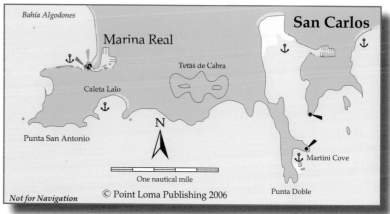

Lay of the Land

Bahía Algodones to the N of Punta San Antonio has the sheltered entrance to Marina Real. Tetas de Cabra or Tetawawi is the twin-peak landmark

resembling a goat's udder upside down, rising 1,115' between Punta San Antonio and Punta Doble, the folded point 3 miles SES.

Bahía San Francisco and its pretty beach spread 6 miles between Punta Doble and Mt. Bacochibampo. San Carlos is behind its NW end.

Bahía San Carlos: At the W end of Bahía San Francisco, the natural steep-walled entrance to tiny Bahía San Carlos is hidden at the NE side of Punta Doble. Our GPS approach waypoint just outside the lighted entrance is 27°56.0'N, 111°03.6'W. Favor the right side and head NNW for half a mile.

Bahía Bacochibampo at the E end of Bahía San Francisco is a larger rectangular bay at the S flank of 235' Mt. Bacochibampo. Older vacation homes line Playa Miramar beach peninsula. Estero Bacochibampo is good for pangas, dinghies and Sunfish racers at Marina Bacochibampo - but it's too shoal for yatistas.

Cabo Haro is a prominent headland and major turning point with a reliable nav light between San Carlos and Guaymas. Our GPS position off the S tip of Cabo Haro is 27°50.20'N, 110°53.10'W.

Punta Baja 4.2 miles NE of Cabo Haro is the turn into Guaymas harbor; GPS 27°54.00'N, 110°51.29'W.

Caleta San Antonio: A reef blocks new basin just outside Marina Real.

Guaymas harbor: Guaymas North means N of the 2 Islas Almagres. This part of the harbor has the commercial port and navy docks, then a small anchoring bay E of Punta Ast, all surrounded by the older downtown. S of the Almagres, the bay shallows and has lots of smaller repair yards, new developments and laid-back anchorages off Las Playitas. Ten years ago, this harbor was cleaned up, and unemployment almost doesn't exist, so it's clean and safe – we don't hesitate to visit Guaymas.

Anchor & Moor
San Carlos to Guaymas

Starting outside Bahía Algodones and moving around the corners to Bahía San Francisco, around Cabo Haro to Guaymas, here are some anchorages we found.

Caleta San Antonio: In strong S wind, we've anchored comfortably overnight on the NW side of Punta San Antonio behind the islet near its S tip. Our GPS position 27°56.32'N, 111°06.27'W is in 24' to 30' over sand and gravel.

A breakwater just N of this anchorage forms a sheltered cove with new homes and guards; the cove's narrow entrance has a rock dead in the middle and was roped off last time we visited.

Lalo Cove: This horseshoe cove 1.75 a mile W of Punta Doble opens south. Lalo Reef is detached 300 yards S of the cove's E arm. There's deep water all around the reef, but it's unmarked and mostly submerged at high tide.

Anchor either in the E side of the cove in 16' to 20' over sand and scattered rock, or in the middle of the cove (GPS 27°56.35'N, 111°05.44'W) in 30' over sand. The W side has a rocky bottom. Campers use the pretty E beach, and a new house lines the road up to the overlook on the W arm. A W side slot and Lalo Reef are good snorkeling.

Lalo Cove is between the marinas.

Martini Cove:
On the E side of Punta Doble, the cramped but popular anchorage is in the N end, N of a barely detached islet, but avoid submerged rocks off the N approach. Our GPS is 27°55.90'N, 111°03.58'W is in 15' over sand.

By day, dive boats hog the S end for good snorkeling behind the island. Dinghy to a cave in the slot at the S end of Punta Doble.

MSC   Moorings:
About 30 moorings belonging to Marina San Carlos are in the N end of Bahía San Carlos, a few also in the side cove. Hail "Marina San Carlos Moorings" on VHF-14, and a staffer will lead you to one that's your size and not rented.

Bahía San Carlos:
The N end of this N-S bay is shoal, and some room is taken by MSC's moorings. But everywhere else is fine. We've anchored in the middle of the bay (12' to 29') and in the SW cove (14' to 20') behind the slanted point of rock; both are good holding sand and mud. Small fee lets you use the marina landing, other services.

For all-around storm shelter, this is next best to being berthed in the land-locked marina. But damage is caused by unattended boats dragging onto others.

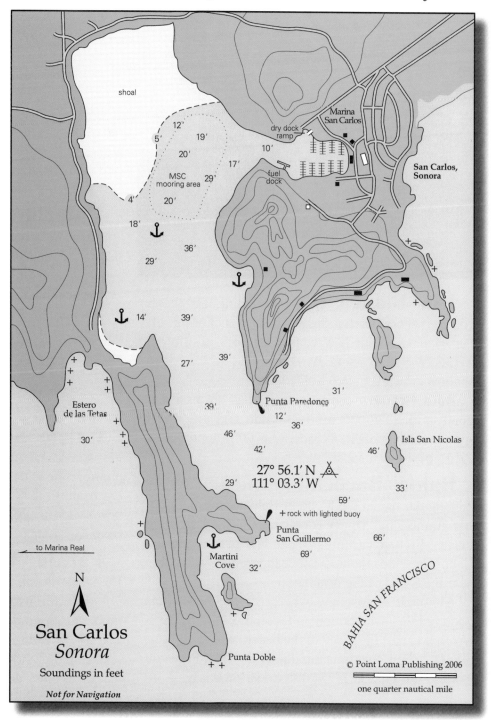

Bahia San Francisco

This large bay between Punta Doble and Cabo Haro has several spots.

Indio Cove is NE of the entrance to Bahía San Carlos, between Indian Point, Isla San Nicolas and the larger semi-detached Islote. Anchor at the N end, W of Islote, but avoid rocks along the cove's W cliff. Our GPS peek-in is 27°56.34'N, 111°03.23'W. Rocks foul between the islets, also off Playa Shangri-La in the smaller cove to the E.

Playa la Posada: This indent at the W end of 4-mile Playa San Francisco is a popular stop for lunch at Hotel la Posada. The next indent E is 2 blocks S of a Pemex. Almost anywhere off Playa San Francisco has good holding sand, but the E end shoals off Estero Soldado.

Isla de la Raza:
You can anchor in 12' to 15' just E of the sand spit off the NW corner. Our GPS approach is 27°57.29'N, 111°01.74'W.

171

Isla Blanca: Good snorkeling off the S end is accessible by dinghy when anchoring off the island's NE or NW ends. Our GPS position is 27°56.18'N, 110°59.42'W. The bay NE of the island shallows toward Estero Soldado.

Roca Ventana: This tiny islet has an arch and good snorkeling reefs off its NE side, and a marginal spot to anchor off its N side. Our GPS approach is 27°55.60'N, 110°59.49'W.

Bahía Bacochibampo is the large

rectangular bay at the E end of Bahía San Francisco. It's framed by Mt. Bacochibampo, the mile-long Playa Miramar vacation village and beach, and the Cabo Haro headland. An oceanographic school is near the S end of the beach.

Although almost any where off the beach has good holding sand bottom, a favored spot in flat or S weather is past the S end of the beach, where you can dinghy ashore for romantic dinner at Hotel Playa de Cortes. Our GPS is 27°54.93'N, 110°56.92'W.

Estero Bacochibampo: Behind Playa Miramar the estuary is being finger-filled for new homes, and although we found 8' in the entrance at the N end of Playa Miramar, the rest is less than 5'. Marina Bacochibampo has Lasers and dinghies.

Chincho & Peruana: Blocking the S

approach to Bahía Bacochibampo, these mark a mine field S of them, so stay half a mile off shore when rounding N from Salinitas or Haystack.

Punta Chincho attached by a sandbar has rocks off its S side. Isla Peruana is 360 yards NW; we don't pass between except by dinghy. Good in S wind, the anchorage off the N side of Punta Chincho's neck has sand and rock at 15' to 20'. Our GPS is 27°54.48'N, 110° 56.92'W. *Chincho* is the nautical term for a plumb line. *Peruana* is a Peruvian woman.

Caleta Salinitas, 1.5 miles SE of Isla

Peruana or 1.2 miles NNW of Haystack Point, is a quarter mile wide and has pretty little Isla las Gringas out front. In flat calms, you can anchor off the N end beach (15' to 20' sand) were the road comes over from Miramar.

Paraje Viejo: Along the E flank of

Haystack Point, the sheltered NW corner of this .75 of a mile wide 2-headed cove is comfortable in moderate N wind. Our GPS at anchor is 27°52.76'N, 110°56.00'W in 23' over sand.

Avoid rocks along the bay's E side. The NE corner has Guaymas' noisy water treatment plant, so we avoid that half of the cove.

Caleta Carrizal is a tiny 2-headed

cove 2.5 miles W of Haystack, 2 miles NW of Cabo Haro. Only 320 yards wide at the entrance, it's a quarter mile deep between steep hills. Carrizal provides good shelter in moderate N

Side cove off Bahia San Carlos has moorings & anchorage.

wind, but 3 boats is a crowd. Our GPS at the entrance is 27°51.78'N, 110°54.47'W. *Carrizal* means a place with reeds. This is the easternmost cove in the Guaíma Nature Preserve.

Proyecto Islas de San Carlos will include all the tiny islands from Punta San Pedro SE to Haystack Rock near Cabo Haro, to be protected from development and preserved for recreational diving and fishing. Ask at Sonoran Sport Center, El Mar Diving Center, Marina San Carlos and Ocean Sports Scuba Center.

Catalina Cove:
2 miles NE of Cabo Haro, this 3-lobe cove has good shelter from NW to SW wind in its SW corner, 18' to 26' over sand; GPS 27°51.76'N, 110°52.66'W. In a strong SW wind, gusts can breach a low canyon, so move to the northern lobes. Guaymas is extending the road here.

Vicente & Pitahaya:
On the approach to Guaymas harbor, anchorage is possible in a chain of 3 small coves to port: SW of Isla Vicente and SE and NW of attached Isla Pitahaya. A Pemex dock in the first cove and commercial docks W of Pitahaya aren't hazards to yatistas. Our GPS N of Pitahaya is 27°53.27'N, 110°52.01'W.

Isla Pajaro:
Since Guaymas built more ship docks, fewer shrimpers anchor off the mile-long Isla Pajaro, but that's never stopped us from anchoring in Pajaro Cove (GPS 27° 53.46'N, 110°50.74'W) on its SW side. Stay 100 yards off the low tip, and anchor in 15' to 18' over good holding mud. Larger yachts anchor SE of the island's S hill.

Guaymas north:
Passing N of Islas Almagre (ocher), we anchor (12' to 16') E of Punta Ast, with its famous fisherman statue. This anchorage (GPS 27°55.25'N, 110°52.84'W) is well sheltered, and the Navy and Port Captain are on this cove's E shore, so it's very safe to leave your boat under their watchful eyes. You can anchor W of Punta Ast, but traffic rounding the corner can be noisy.

Guaymas south:
S of the Almagre Islands, you can anchor almost anywhere off the beach resorts of Las Playitas. One Fonatur plan calls for a 500-slip marina around this third island. Check MexicoBoating.com for Updates.

Guaymas harbor anchorage off the Navy base is safe and close to downtown.

Marina San Carlos has lush landscaping, shops and yatista community.

Marinas

Marina Real: NW of Tetakawi, jetties (GPS 27°56.7'N, 111°05.7'W) breach the S end of Playa Algodones, forming the entrance to a large gated darsena of Marina Real (Royal). It has 356 full-service slips and end ties for boat to 80' LOA, 12' depth. Pass the floating fuel dock on starboard as you enter the curving channel. The marina office is condo #1 N of the slips, monitors VHF 16. Marina Real has a public launch ramp at the W end, where boats are trailered to Marina Real's fenced marina seca across the street.

Marina Real is W of town, surrounded in nice residential developments and condos. They plans a new chandler, restaurant, bar and convenience store. Call Dario or Isabel: (622) 227-0011 or marinareal@prodigy.net.mx

Marina San Carlos: E of Tetakawi and enclosed in a side cove off the NE end of sheltered Bahía San Carlos, Marina San Carlos' land-locked darsena is a good hurricane hole. Past the floating fuel dock to starboard, Marina San Carlos has 350 full service slips to 51' and end ties to 93' LOA, with 7.5' depth in the main fairway. The marina office is the 2-story building behind the 10-ton crane and ramp on the N seawall.

Around the basin are a deli, 2 restaurants, dive shop and hotel. Because this marina is next to San Carlos, nearby are 2 chandlers, supermarket, laundromat, outboard repairs, more restaurants, dive shops, hotels, ice cream shop, church, etc. This is a popular spot to summer over. Marina San Carlos rents 30 moorings in the N end of Bahía San Carlos and monitors VHF 14. Ask for Heidi Grossman: (622) 226-1230 or 226-1202, or email info@marinasancarlos.com or visit www.marinasancarlos.com

Marina Seca is the huge dry storage yard and boat-repair yard operated by Marina San Carlos. Boats to 60 tons are hauled out and stored in a secure fenced facility a mile inland, some under sheds. Almost 400 boats summered over in Marina Seca in 2005. If you intend to do repairs, your boat is stored in the adjacent work yard. Marina Seca (622) 226-1061 or 1062, or marinaseca@marinasancarlos.com

Marina San Carlos yacht transport trucks boats (50' LOA, 16' beam, 30 tons) to Tucson on special hydraulic cradles, then to any US city. This has been a very successful operation since 1995. Ask for Jesus: (622) 226-1061 or transport@marinasancarlos.com

Marina Guaymas is a Fonatur plan for 500 slips, tourist and cruise ship piers in

Marina Real just N of San Carlos has its own dramatic peaks, big boat slips.

*Fuel dock at Marina San Carlos
is just inside the natural harbor.*

the S side of the harbor. Check for Updates on www. MexicoBoating.com

Local Services

Guaymas Capitanía is at the street entrance to the commercial port; (622) 222-0170. Marinas handle domestic clearance.

Fuel: Both marinas have floating fuel docks at the entrance. Marina San Carlos' 93' long dock is open 0600 to dusk; Marina Real's is open 0800 to 1700.

Provisions: Ley supermarket on the way into Guaymas is the region's best source, and the Comercial Mexicana is farther into Guaymas. Several markets and fruterias in San Carlos have a good selection. Produce is a lot better in winter and spring. Sonora beef is some of the world's best, so stock up here.

Boat yards: See Marina San Carlos details, above. The INP yard in N Guaymas handles yachts to 200 tons; manager Enrique Aguilar Ruiz (622) 224-2023. A smaller yard is in the W end of Guaymas harbor. Marina Seca Guaymas, S side of harbor, is in the industrial park just W of the shrimper repair yards; hauls yachts to 30 ton or 40' LOA, also multihulls, stores on stands very reasonably. Liveaboard is fine, showers, power, water; (622) 221-7200, mgrs cell (622) 109-1330.

Chandlery: We found parts and repair for radios and nav electronics in San Carlos, more in Guaymas; shipping US parts through Guadalajara has been a problem. Dive shops abound, fill tanks, rent gear and local guides. Going on one of the touristy charter boats is a quick and safe way to learn a diving area before you take your own boat there.

Transportation: The Sematur car and passenger ferry runs twice weekly between Guaymas and Santa Rosalia. This is a great way to explore the other side of the Sea of Cortez, to decide if you want to move your boat there. The highway to Tucson is a divided 4-lane. Guaymas has flights from Phoenix, and San Carlos has a paved strip.

Eateries: San Carlos has more than 20 eateries, many catering to gringos – even health-food stores and veggie cantinas. Some close for summer. Guaymas has some fancy steak and seafood houses, plus lots of great little taquerias around the harbor.

Culture & History

Multi-colored salt-water pearls are cultured in San Carlos. Visit the Perlas del Mar de Cortez pearl beds and display room in Bacochibampo.

Sonora Saguaro: Saguaro cactus is sacred to Sonora's indigenous people – and protected by law. Some are centuries old, growing to 60' height. With long poles and small baskets made of the saguaro spines, indigenous Sonorans carefully pick the ripe fruits during rainy season. It is unthinkable to toss rocks or sticks at a saguaro, for fear of disfiguring the life-giving trunk. The sweet red fruit, *atun*, is made

*Ed Grossman of Marina San Carlos
transports boats across the border.*

Marina Seca near Marina San Carlos.

into a jam, and its seeds are roasted and ground for high-protein meal cakes. A prayer of thanks is said when the first *atun* is received.

Explore Ashore

Copper Canyon: This and Mazatlán are the best places to leave your boat safely in a marina and visit the fabled Cañon de Cobre. It's a spectacular 13-hour train ride into the Sierra Madres, gaining 8,000' elevation with pine forests, rushing rivers, Mexico's 2 highest waterfalls, rest stop in historic mining towns. Book 1st class tickets on Chihuahua al Pacifico's express train (restaurant, bar & better heads) leaving Los Mochis at 0600 or El Fuerte at 0730, arrive Chihuahua 1930 and spend the night. Pick seats on the S side of the car for best scenery. You can opt to spend a night in the Tarahumara village of Creel, continue the next day. The Tarahumara people have their biggest festival during Easter week; authentic costumes, dances, flute & drum music, native foods, craft displays.

Let a travel agent book your trip, maybe air return. Here are 2 we've heard of.

Native Trails, Copper Canyon Tour Operator: (800) 884-3107, info@nativetrails.com or www.nativetrails.com

Mexico Adventures Ltd. Copper Canyon Tour Operator: (800) 206-8132, jrood@mexmail.com or www.Mexonline.com/mexadv.htm

The Fisherman statue overlooks Guaymas harbor. Cathedral spires (right) are in downtown.

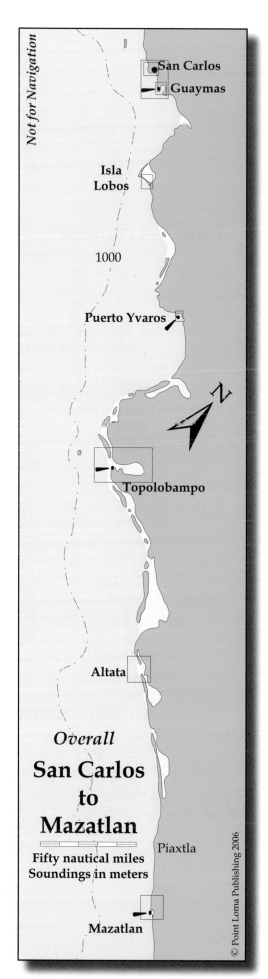

Overall

San Carlos to Mazatlan

Fifty nautical miles
Soundings in meters

Not for Navigation

14
Puerto Yavaros
through
Mazatlán

Yatistas don't have to cross the Sea of Cortez to get from San Carlos-Guaymas to Mazatlán. If you must cross the Sea of Cortez, these small ports and gunk-holes might help you await a safer weather window or gain a better sailing angle.

This Sonora-Sinaloa coastline offers at least 12 sheltered anchorages, some with fuel stops and provisions, all with friendly locals. We've transited this 445-mile stretch many times and find it densely populated with fishing villages, tourist beaches and palm plantations backed by some of Mexico's richest farms – not isolated and rugged like much of Baja. It's decidedly tropical!

We first researched this coastline in the 1990s but left it out of "Mexico Boating Guide" 1st edition for lack of space. We hope this edition will fill that info void and encourage other guidebook authors to expand their research as well.

Despite the lack of data, more yatistas have explored not only Topo, but also the smaller ports like Yavaros and Altata, even tiny Piaxtla, and they report being treated like visiting royalty. Locals are building a full-service marina at Altata, and Fonatur promises moorings or a marina for Yavaros, so you may want to see this area before it's discovered.

NOTE: This stretch does have shallow water 3 or 4 miles off some known points, so watch your depth sounder, stay in 25' to 30' of water. Use the dredged channels. Shrimpers draw about 8' of water, so watch where they go.

Before coming into Yavaros and Altata, you can hail the Port Captain and tell him your draft, then ask for the tide status and the minimum depth in the entrance channel. Both channels usually have some breakers on each side. If you say you're *en dudo* or *nerviosa*, he can send a pilot out in a panga to guide you in safely. It's usually a free service, but we suggest a tip for the *piloto*.

Mexico Boating Guide

Route Planning: Guaymas to Mazatlán

Depending on the weather and your draft, anchorage is possible at these places, some with fuel docks. Distance from previous location, then total from Guaymas:

Punta Lobos anchorage, (50 miles total).
Bahía Santa Barbara, 65 miles (105 total).
Puerto Yavaros, 10 miles (115 total) FUEL.
Bahía San Ignacio, 80 miles (195 total).
Topolobampo, 15 miles (210 miles) FUEL.
Puerto Altata, 115 miles (325 total) FUEL.
Punta Piaxtla, 105 miles (410 total).
Mazatlán, 35 miles (445 total) FUEL.

COASTWISE Guaymas to Topolobampo

Punta Lobos offshore waypoint: Departing the S side of Isla Pajaro,

it's 40 miles SE to the Punta Lobos offshore GPS waypoint 27°16.78'N, 110°41.21'W, which is 5 miles WSW of lighted Punta Lobos (Racon K: *dah-di-dah*). It's the SW corner of low, sandy Isla Lobos, the barrier island outside Estero Lobos. Avoid uncharted shoals extending N and NW of Isla Lobos.

Punta Lobos anchorage: Shelter

from NW wind is found outside the SE barrier of Estero Lobos. This wide roadstead (GPS 27°15.47'N, 110°28.00'W) is about 10 miles ESE of the offshore waypoint, but be sure to clear the S end of the Punta

Lobos shoals before edging NE. Depths of 35' are found within 3 miles of shore. Estero Lobos' entrance has breakers and is reported shoaled up.

At 18 miles SE of the Lobos waypoint, the coast indents toward Estero Huivuilay and the town of Tovari, available for emergency. But we hop straight from Lobos to Arboleda. Behind the coastal marshes lie Sonora's rich agricultural lands where fruits and veggies are grown. The climate changes from desert to tropical overnight.

Punta Arboleda: At 54 miles SE of

the Punta Lobos offshore waypoint, this forested (*arboleda*) and lighted point is on the N side of Rio Mayo, where pangas enter but we pass a mile W at GPS 26°50.44'N, 109°54.16'W.

Bahía Santa Barbara: Ten miles SE of Punta Arboleda Light, Punta Rosa is the south-pointing and lighted point with dunes. Our GPS a mile S of Punta Rosa is 26°39.32'N, 109°40.00'W. Bahía Santa Barbara is a 1.5-mile wide bay in the lee just E of Punta Rosa, and the bay has sheltered anchorage (20' to 30' sand) from N wind. Fonatur plans a port of refuge here. Hautabampito behind the berm has shrimp ponds.

In N wind or calms, anchorage (30' to 40') is possible outside Bahía Yavaros, SE and SW of the shoal points.

Bahía Yavaros Entrance: The quarter-mile wide deep-water entrance (reported 8' at MLW) is between Punta Lobera on the W and Punta Yavaros a half mile NE of Lobera. A narrow but half-mile long shoal juts S from Punta Lobera, where a breakwater no longer exists. From the seaward tip of Punta Yavaros, a 1-mile long shoal juts S then SSE, forming an island between the 2 points.

Yatistas should hail the Port Captain to ask for a guide, because silt from each summer storm alters the channel, and we haven't been here since Hurricane Marty. The town is about 3.5 miles from our GPS outer approach waypoint 26°39.4621'N, 109°29.2531'W. From here, it's 1.5 miles NNW to 26°40.7678'N, 109°29.3876'W, which is between the entrance shoals. Then it's 1.4 miles NW to 26°42.1242'N, 109°30.0200'W, which is half a mile ESE of the town's acute angle point, called Punta Isla de las Viejas at 26°42.27'N, 109°30.46'W.

Punta Lobos, Sonora
Five nautical miles
27° 15.6'N 110° 31.8'W
© Point Loma Publishing 2006
Not for Navigation

Puerto Yavaros

This small but active port town (4,000 pop.) is on convoluted Isla de las Viejas (Old Women), which juts into Bahía Yavaros's SW corner. In 2005, the fishing docks on the town's S side were renovated, and the same is planned for a larger pier off an industrial park NW of the town point. The Navy dock is just past the industrial park. Topolobampo is the nearest Capitanía.

Anchorage (15' to 18' sand, mud) is taken off either side of the town, per wind direction. Diesel and gas are available at the fishing docks on the S side of town, where at least 6' is reported alongside. To reserve fuel or arrange a large quantity, call Pesqueros Yavaros; (622) 259-6100.

Yavaros town has gas, 2 restaurants and a bus 3 miles to Huatabampo.

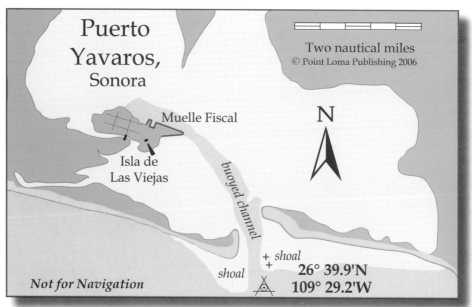

NOTE: If you go ashore here, please visit Huatabampo, the home of 2,000 recipients of micro-credit loans from Grameen de la Frontera and Women's Empowerment. Some of the annual profit from retail sales of this nautical guidebook helps support their good work; see details in the front of this book. Stop by and visit these women's tiendas, buy their bakery goods, cheeses, jams and fresh produce. Nearby is the town of Navajoa and Interstate 15.

The Mayo people thrived for centuries between present day Guaymas and Mazatlán. Huatabampo,

Many women of Huatabampo are self-employed thanks to micro-credit.

12 miles inland, has a Mayo cultural museum and crafts shop of their baskets and weavings. Fonatur plans a marina in Puerto Yavaros.

COASTWISE continued

From Bahía Santa Barbara, we head 65 miles SSE to a waypoint (GPS 25°38.30'N, 109°27.61'W) 3 miles W of shoaly south-pointing Punta San Ignacio, en route passing 2 miles off Punta Ahome ("*ah-HO-may*") and its shoals, which lie 20 miles N of Punta San Ignacio. These landfalls are in Sinaloa.

The lighted, blazingly white Farallón San Ignacio (GPS 25°26.43'N, 109°22.16) (no anchorage) lies 10 miles S of Punta San Ignacio and 14 miles SW of the Topo sea buoy.

Bahía San Ignacio: Give a 3-mile berth all around the shoal SE side of Punta San Ignacio when entering this 11-mile wide bay NE of the point, open to S. In NW wind, sheltered anchorage (25' to 33' sand) is found almost anywhere (GPS 25°38.31'N,

and crowns, brass bands, local cuisine, fireworks and homespun fun.

Approach

Go close to the *boya recalada* or sea buoy (about GPS 25°31'40'N, 109°10.82'W) (Racon XS), which is 3 miles S of Punta Santa Maria. En route, hail the Capitanía to request entrance for anchorage, fuel, etc. The 12-mile channel (32' deep) is half a mile wide between lighted buoys. Breakers form outside the channel and around the 2 entrance points, Punta Santa Maria (GPS 25°33.48'N, 109°09.92'W) and Punta Copas, which is 2.5 miles ESE.

109°17.78'W) along the steep sand beach of 100' high Isla Santa Maria. We've seen yatistas anchor here and, in calm weather, take the dink 12 miles into the port, to check it out before deciding to enter or not. If you do this, stay clear of any ships in the channel.

Topolobampo

Topolobampo's beauty has been compared with the Greek isles, because the pleasant little town (pop 8,500) climbs steep hillsides and is surrounded by islands. Topo is primarily a cargo port with several sheltered anchorages for yachts, numerous piers, 2 boat clubs with sportfishing tournaments, at least 2 fuel docks, excellent provisions, basic marine repair shops, plenty of dinghy waters to explore and an airport at the close end of Los Mochis.

Cruise ships stop at Topo, because nearby Los Mochis is where the Chihuahua al Pacifico tourist train starts its all-day climb into the fabled Copper Canyon. So tourism is taking hold in Topo.

Dia de la Marina is the last weekend in May or first in June; every boat has colors flying for the parade around the harbor, beauty queens with gowns

Lay of the Land

Uninhabited sand islands and mangrove estuaries are N and S of the main channel that runs 12 mile Eward through Topo Bay, making 2 gentle bends. The port facilities recently extended SW on a peninsula and an attached island from the town center (GPS 25°35.82'N, 109°02.99'W), which is on high ground N of the E end of the main channel.

Secondary channels: Yatistas can also use 2 smaller channels: before you get to the town, one channel turns N at Buoy # 14 to get behind Isla Santa Maria; another bears NE opposite Buoy # 31 and leads to more anchorages, the Marina Club and Club Nautico, the shrimper darsena (GPS 25°35.75'N, 109°03.68'W) and the N side of the town. Beyond the town, a secondary channel ESE enters vast Ohuira Bay.

Anchorage

Yachts are allowed to anchor anywhere outside the main channel, as long as they don't block traffic.

Santa Maria Hook: Depart the main channel at Buoy # 11 and go N a mile to the sandy-hook bay (GPS 25°34.54'N, 109°09.67'W) on the NE side of this barrier island, anchor in 15' to 23'over sand. Multis can get farther into the hook.

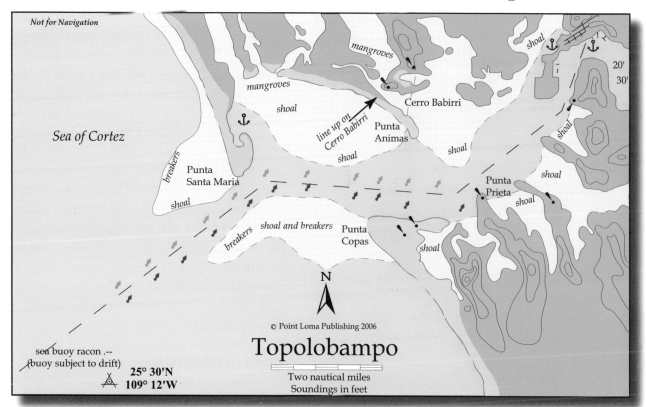

Not for Navigation

Sea of Cortez

mangroves

mangroves

shoal

shoal

line up on Cerro Babirri

Cerro Babirri

Punta Animas

Punta Santa Maria

breakers

shoal

shoal

shoal

shoal

Punta Prieta

shoal

shoal

breakers

shoal and breakers

Punta Copas

shoal

shoal

20'

30'

N

© Point Loma Publishing 2006

Topolobampo

sea buoy racon .--
(buoy subject to drift)

25° 30'N
109° 12'W

Two nautical miles
Soundings in feet

Punta Copas: In mild S weather, you can anchor off the N side of Punta Copas, at the foot of the range markers on the hill, or a bit E between Punta Copas sand spit and Punta Prieta as long as you stay S of the channel.

Punta Animas: Leaving the main channel around Buoy # 17, you can anchor in calm weather off the S tip of a sand and mangrove island, connected to town by a road and low bridges.

Isla Zacate: Taking the 2nd secondary channel toward the N side of Topo town, you can anchor NE of Buoy # 22 and S of Isla Zacate. The road bridge connects Isla Zacate to town.

Club Nautico: You can anchor off this
small private club, which lies off the S side of the secondary channel to the N side of Topo town. Ask permission to leave your dink at their loading dock and to get through their gate into town, usually for a small daily fee.

Marina Club: Next door, you can anchor
off this floating dock and ask permission to use their landing and shore facilities, which include a pool and giant shady palapas.

Bahia Ohuira is 7 miles wide, contains 6
islands, 12 coves and is surrounded in jungle.

Local Services

The Capitanía and Migracion overlook the older basin on the town's S side, where you can anchor (35') temporarily and use the panga landing.

Fuel: The Port Captain can help you arrange for fuel, either at the Marina Club (5' to 6') on the S side of the 2nd secondary channel to the N side of Topo town, or at the large shrimper darsena (10' depth) located (GPS 25°35.75'N, 109°03.68'W) a few hundred yards past Club Nautico. The handiest Pemex for jerry jugs is just past the shrimper darsena.

Provisions: Topo has 2 small grocery stores OK for local produce in winter, but Los Mochis (bus or taxi) has at least 2 supermercados and the region's big farmers' mercados. Topo has a bank, a restaurant and repairs for basic marine electronics and outboards.

La Paz Ferry: Baja Ferries makes the overnight run, docking at the new port extension. Visist website BajaFerries. com for their schedules.

Club Nautico may have room for about a dozen

of its 100 members' boats to Med-moor to floating platforms off its seawall, where we found 6'7" average depth. It has 4 ramps with loading docks, about 30 launchable sportfishing boats, marina seca and a clubhouse with bar and swimming pool. Their sportfishing tournament at the end of May draws more than 100 participating boats, each with a 4-man team; deportes@debate.com.mx

Marina Club Topolobampo next door has six 30' floating slips (min 7' depth), usually filled by members' sportfishing boats, plus a 60' end tie that they try to keep open for guests. If you can't get a slip, you might anchor off the secondary channel and get permission to use their newer landing and shore facilities, which include a pool and giant shady palapas with tables; deportes@debate.com.mx

Explore Ashore

Ohuira Bay: We met cruisers who spent a week exploring Ohuira Bay's coves, islands and river inlets. Similar to Gatun Lake in the middle of the Panama

Canal, yachts cruise around ships at anchor in the lush jungle setting, parrots squawk from flowering trees.

Copper Canyon: See San Carlos for more details. This spectacular all day train ride starts from Los Mochis at 0600, so stay in one of that town's dozen hotels the night before. Plaza Inn is a safe bet; (800) 862-9026 or (668) 818-1042. Or, if you can get to the town of El Fuerte, you can sleep in an extra 90 minutes and stay at Villa del Pescador, a restored colonial mansion that's less expensive than Plaza Inn; www.villadelpescador.com The famous Chihuahua al Pacifico train is called "Chepe." First class train tickets are about $135 per person; train agent (800) 884-3107. Book seats on the S side going up for the best seeing. We got good service from Native Trails www.nativetrails.com

COASTWISE Topo to Mazatlan

Clear the sea buoy and turn SE. It's 93 miles to the entrance to Bahía Altata. This avoids indents and shoals at Boca Macapule, Isla Saliaca and Punta Colorado.

Punta Pico Aguapepa 13 miles NW of the entrance to Bahía Altata gets a 4-mile berth for shoals.

Puerto Altata

Altata is a resort port (pop. approx. 2,000) like the San Carlos-Guaymas area, but condensed. The S end of the town's beachfront is a vacation community filled with very nice, very private beach homes belonging to wealthy Culiacan residents – no hotels yet. The N part of the town has several fishing docks, a fuel dock, a seafood warehouse (shrimp, oysters) and the Capitanía.

The main anchorage off Playa Altata has half dozen seafood palapas, and one Restaurant La Perla gained fame in 2001 when owner Gustavo and his family befriended the first gringo sailboat to enter the port. Next year, 4 gringo yachts arrived. By 2003, more than 20 boatloads of yatistas had signed their names on La Perla's wall. *Latitude 38°* hailed Altata as the cruising discovery of the decade. Altata's nearest newspaper hailed the cruisers as the start of the tourism boom long promised by the government.

Huichol traditional beadwork
and string art is colorful.

In 2004, locals built a new bridge to let the world in, but they quit waiting for Fonatur to bring the mountain. The Soto family who owns all the waterfront property SE of Altata plans to build a full-service Marina Altata and hotel within the new nature preserve. Marina construction began in 2005. Check for Updates on www. MexicoBoating.com

Approach

Isla Lucenilla is the barrier island sheltering Altata Bay, and you enter at Lucenilla's SE end, where the lighted, red & green channel buoys define the approach route from the NW. Shoals off to both sides of the 20' deep entrance can break hugely, especially in S wind. The best time to enter is high slack, when tidal flow is least. Use plenty of power to prevent yawing. At max ebb or flow, the entrance is blocked by standing waves. Once inside, it's calm. Pabellón Bay is SE, but you turn NW and go 15 miles up the bay to reach Puerto Altata.

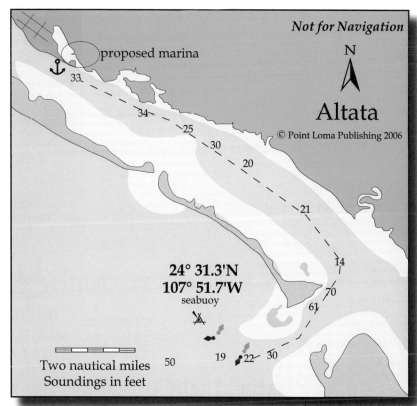

Not for Navigation

N

Altata

© Point Loma Publishing 2006

proposed marina

24° 31.3'N
107° 51.7'W
seabuoy

Two nautical miles
Soundings in feet

Anchorage

La Perla: Almost anywhere along the sandy beach has anchoring depths of 15' to 36' but dinghy wheels are handy for landing on this shallow-angle beach. The main anchorage is off La Perla Restaurant, in 23' to 30' of water over sand & mud at about 24°37.62'N, 107°55.70'W. In SW wind, local boats anchor across the bay off Isla Lucenilla or up the side channel where the new marina will be – except for construction in both locations.

Puerto Altata: Anchorage is possible in the N end of town off the sportfishing docks or Navy dock.

Local Services

Puerto Altata's Capitanía is at the N end of town overlooking the fishing docks and commercial anchorage, about 2 miles up from the yacht anchorage. This Port Captain has been very helpful. If you need to make a crew change, the Migración office is at Culiacan airport 30 miles inland.

Marina: When Marina Altata is completed, it will be in a well sheltered basin SE of town. Before you get to town, turn NW off the main channel at about GPS 24°37.14'N, 107°54.56'W. Marina Altata

plans 100 full-service slips for boats to 65', showers, laundry and dinghy landing in one basin, and the floating fuel dock, restaurant, small chandler and taxis to town in an adjacent basin. Check for Updates at www.MexicoBoating.com

Fuel: Until the marina fuel dock is open, ask the Port Captain or Gustavo to help you arrange diesel at one of the fishing docks. They also assist boaters

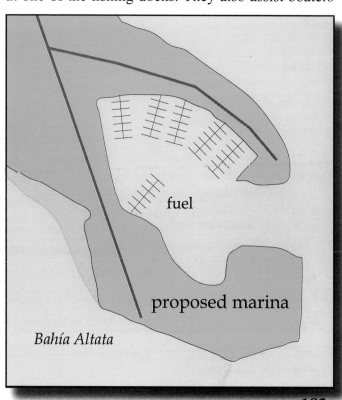

fuel

proposed marina

Bahía Altata

who need mechanical and electrical repairs.

Provisions: Altata has a bakery and convenience stores. But trucks bringing fresh fruits, veggies & meats to Altata's restaurants will take orders and sell to visiting yatistas as well. Ask Gustavo at La Perla or the manager of another restaurant to place your order the day before the next truck is due. Otherwise, bus to Navolato or Culiacan to shop, and get a taxi back.

COASTWISE continued

Depart Altata Bay at high slack tide, and use the marked outer channel leading N until you're well clear of the shoals before turning.

Boca Tavala Light 26 miles SE of Altata Bay marks the entrance to a long estuary.

Rio Elota 34 miles SE of Boca Tavala spreads silt miles seaward after rains, dries in winter, isn't for yates.

Punta Piaxtla Light (23°38.8'N, 106°49.1'W) is 78 miles SE of Altata Bay and about 33 miles NW of Mazatlan. This hill point juts NW to form a small cove with shelter from moderate S wind. We haven't stopped here, but cruisers sent us photos showing a panga village and circular bay E of the lighthouse. However, avoid rocks off the N side of Punta Piaxtla.

Punta Cameron (GPS 23°18.25'N, 106°29.80'W) is 2.5 miles NW of Mazatlán's marina channel. A small bay E of Punta Cameron is rocky.

Punta Piaxtla Light marks reef at entrance (left).

Mazatlán

Mazatlán, Sinaloa, (pop. approx. 500,000) lies about 170 miles NW of Puerto Vallarta, 120 miles NW of San Blas, 165 miles E of Los Frailes on Baja's East Cape. It's almost on the same latitude as Cabo San Lucas – but way more tropical: swaying coconut palms, mangoes, papayas and bananas growing along side the roads.

Mazatlán has a split personality. The newer "marina district" inlet at the N end of town has 2 marinas and a large liveaboard community. More than 200 boaters summer over in the marinas and inland basin. Many berth here to visit the Copper Canyon. Mazatlán's Old Port at the S end of town has been renovated, has a municipal anchorage and commercial harbor. Zona Dorado hotels, restaurants and nightclubs line the beach E of the islands.

Mazatlán offers 3 yatista fuel docks, an informal yacht club, 6 sportfishing charter docks, an API anchorage, 4 big-boat haul-out yards, cruise ship and La Paz ferry terminals, international airport, lots of night life, internet cafes, plus excellent provisioning and eateries around this charming town.

Pulmonias (literally, pneumonias), Mazatlán's unique open-air cabs, hold 3 passengers and groceries, cheaper than car taxis. Older pulmonias are golf carts with tiny VW engines, but the new faster ones are built in Mazatlán. Great unless it's raining.

Lay of the Land

Marina District: The lighted jetty entrance is 2.5 miles SE of Punta Camaron, just a mile NE of Isla Pajaros, the northernmost of the small islands. Inside, Marina El Cid's guest slips and fuel dock are to starboard. (See all marinas below.)

Going E, a circular huge basin contains Marina Mazatlán. N of this basin, shallow Laguna Sábalo is lined in residential development, and S of the basin, a channel leads to private homes and more Marina El Cid guest slips.

Even though 2 of the inland marina basin is well sheltered, hurricanes hit Mazatlán almost every summer – so it's not a hurricane hole. But when a direct hit is imminent, local shrimpers tell us they ground and hunker down in soft mud and mangroves along the estuary SE of the old port. This might also be possible in the marina district's Laguna Sábalo.

Old Port: Traveling south, stay a mile outside the islands (Pajaros, Venado, Lobos, submerged Roca Tortuga) until you can swing SW of attached headland Isla Creston (515'), marked by Isla Creston Light (23°10.6'N, 106° 25.7'W) and racon "C" dah-di-dah-dit. The harbor jetties are slightly offset to baffle waves.

Favor the W side when approaching the jetties, to avoid a submerged pinnacle that lies on a straight line drawn between Piedra Negra Light on its islet then N to the end of the E harbor jetty.

Inside, the municipal anchorage is to port, the cruise ship and ferry terminal next north, and the ship channel leading NNE to Navy docks, ship yards and the 10-mile long estuary.

Anchorages

Municipal anchorage: In the old port, this large basin W of the main ship channel has 12' to 20' over mud and has some shelter from Isla Creston and the skinny isthmus connecting it to Cerro Vigil, but holding is poor. Dinghy landing along the W side is about $3/day. To leave a boat here long, rent a mooring block or berth at one of the sportfishing docks. Getaway day anchorages are in side lobes of the estuary SE of the harbor, and around Islas Pajaros, Venado and Lobos outside the harbor.

Marina district: Get permission from Marina Mazatlán to anchor in their round and very well sheltered basin; dink and shore amenities privileges extra. Marina El Cid also has arranged for large yachts to anchor in their private channel, the 2nd turn SE off the round basin.

Isla Creston rises behind municipal anchorage.

Map labels

Punta Camaron

33'

23° 16.0' N
106° 29.0' W

39'

Marina El Cid

18'

Isla Pajaros

20'

20'

53'

31'

Isla Venado

36'

30'

28'

39' 33'

43' 39'

42'

N

Roca Tortuga

17'

26'

Los Hermanos

88'

Isla Chiva

Isla Creston

69'

Piedra Negra

Mazatlán
Soundings in feet
© Point Loma Publishing 2006

two nautical miles

mangroves

mangroves shoals

palm plantation

Not for Navigation

Marina Mazatlan

office

fuel dock

fuel dock
office

El Cid Marina

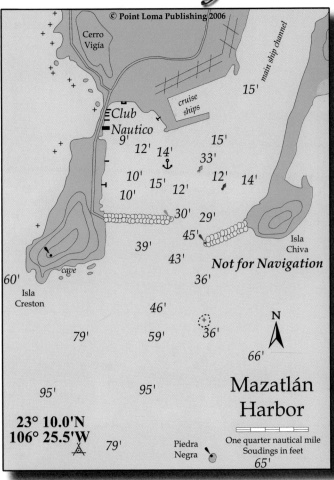

© Point Loma Publishing 2006

Cerro Vigía

Club Nautico

main ship channel

cruise ships

15'

9' 12' 14' 15'
33'
10' 15' 12' 12' 14'
10'
30' 29'
39' 45'
43' 36' Isla Chiva
46'
cave
60' Isla Creston
59' 36'
79' N
66'
95' 95'
Mazatlán Harbor
23° 10.0'N
106° 25.5'W
79' Piedra Negra
65'
One quarter nautical mile
Soundings in feet

Not for Navigation

Berthing

Control depth in the entrance channel to the marina district is 12' at MLW. A seasonal bar at the mouth may cause a few steep waves, but inside the baffled breakwater it's calm. Taxis and pulmonias take you 9 miles S to the Old Port.

Marina El Cid, immediately to starboard in front 5-star El Cid hotel, has 100 full service slips and 3 end ties to 120' LOA. All hotel amenities are available to marina guests, including restaurant service to your boat. The marina's Pemex fuel dock (65') is in front

of the Yacht Club building, which has coin laundry, sundries and chandlery. The marina sponsors a Billfish Classic tourney in November. Marina El Cid may rent single docks at private villas SE of the next basin inland. Marina El Cid (669) 916-3468 or marina@elcid.com.mx

Marina Mazatlán, half a mile inland in this 12' deep channel, has new owners who are upgrading 260 full-service slips to 130'. Dock # 3 on the E seawall is the floating 120' fuel dock. The new marina office (VHF 16 & 18), laundry and boaters' lounge are at the head of Dock #7. Restaurants, a grocery store, dive shop, spa and hotels are in construction on Isla Marina, a man-made island amid the basin (no longer a separate marina). Pickups deliver produce, bottled water and beer dockside. Marina Mazatlán (669) 914-7799 or www.marina-Mazatlán.com.mx

Local Services

Mazatlán is a Port of Entry. The Capitanía and port offices are clustered in the Old Port near the cruise ship terminal. Yatistas are asked not to use VHF 09 and 06. Mazatlán gets hurricanes and mountain-born chubascos with thunder and lightning. The Port Captain closes the port, so you can't leave, but of course you can come in to seek refuge. Radio Costera (VHF 16) gives daily tropical WX reports.

Fuel: In the Old Port, the new 200' fuel dock is just past the ferry dock; good prices. Also Marina El Cid's fuel dock is to starboard at the end of their slip basin below the hotel. Marina Mazatlán renovated its Dock 3 fuel, E side of the basin.

Provisioning is good in the supermercados year round. The Mercado Central Pino Suarez under a huge ornate roof is surrounded by Ocampo, Valle, Juarez and Serdan; open 0600 daily. Some bargaining is acceptable.

Haul-out: We've had good report on 4 yards in the Old Port that haul 200' yachts: Servicios Navales & Industriales SENI (mario_uribe@seni.com.mx); Astilleros Mazatlán

Fuel dock at Marina El Cid.

Dorado for lunch on the docks at El Cid.

(669) 982-5311; Industrial Naval de Mazatlán INM (669) 985-5520. Astilleros Malvinas (669) 981-1242 or mikekowal@hotmail.com

Repairs: Many small chandlers, marine electronics repair, AC and reefer service are on Calle Leyva W of the Old Port channel and in Bonfil industrial park. Boaters Bob Buchanan (669-932-8767) is a mechanic; Rick Cummings does boat work captnrick@pocketmail.com; Bob on Griffin procures lube stuff (669)912-1928; Mike Walden repairs sails svdestinysdream@yahoo.com

Net: The yatista net is on VHF 68 at 0830, M-Sat, with tons of local info and welcome to new arrivals. Marina Mazatlán has a pamphlet of local contacts

La Paz Ferry: Only 12 hours across twice/week; great way to see the other side without taking your boat. We book a *cabina* for a place to lie down and private head.

Misc: Lean Spanish 1:1 at Aprenda Español Ya; mixapixa@hotmail.com Club de Vela's Jose Villalon invites cruisers to join club activities, PHRF, fun cruise to Isla Isabela for southbounders.

IGT's annual Mazatlán Billfish Classic is mid November; US (714) 258-0445. Guide Juan Patron Unger takes visitors fly fishing; fishmaz@yahoo.com

Ever seen a vermillion flycatcher or golden tropical kingbird? Kayak birding tours; Mazatleco@ Mazatlán.com.mx Also see the Aquarium, tequila factory tour, or head up to colonial mountain town Copala. Any travel desk can book you for the Copper Canyon, but board the train at Los Mochis or El Fuerte.

History & Culture

Mazatlán is Nahuatl for place of deer; 16th C. explorers hunted deer on the island they named Venado. Pirates hid behind these islands to ambush Spanish ships, so villagers built a presidio on Cerro Vigía to guard the town from attack. Today Cerro Vigía has a weather station and Café Mirador. Also in midtown, Cerro Nevería (Freezer Peak) is riddled with caves. Before refrigeration, some caves became storehouses for blocks of ice barged from San Francisco.

In 1847, the US Navy occupied Mazatlán for 8 months of the Mexican-American War. In Mexico's Revolution, Mazatlán became the 2nd city in the world to suffer aerial bombardment. A single-engine plane dropped leather pouches of dynamite and nails over the main street; they conked a few surprised citizens on the head, but the dynamite didn't explode.

Pulmonia taxi (left) takes yatistas to the Mercado.

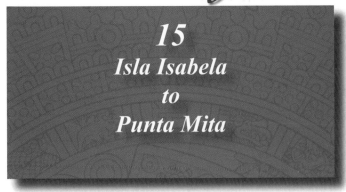

15
Isla Isabela to Punta Mita

Between Mazatlán and Punta Mita (Banderas Bay), we've found 6 stops on this 180-mile voyage: Isla Isabela (frigate and booby preserve), the sheltered port of San Blas, its sidekick Matanchén Bay (summer

Overall
Mazatlán to Cabo Corrientes

Fity nautical miles

Mazatlán

N

Punta Buluarte

© Point Loma Publishing 2006

Teacapán

Isla Isabela National Park

Matanchen Bay

Islas Marias prison islands

San Blas

Chacala

Guayabitos

Punta Mita

Roca Corbateña

Bahía Banderas

Puerto Vallarta

Cabo Corrientes

Not for Navigation

surf city), coco-palm clad Chacala Bay, and in flat weather Guayabitos Cove (Jaltemba). Of these, Isla Isabela and Chacala are more interesting.

NOTE: If you plan to visit Isla Isabela, we suggest you try to pay the $2 fee at SEMARNAT in Mazatlán or PV before you go to Isabela, or promise to pay it as soon as you get back to the mainland, due to reports of snafus at San Blas.

ROUTE PLANNING: Mazatlán to Punta Mita

Between Mazatlán and San Blas we found nada for yatistas. In fair weather, we angle SSE offshore to visit Isla Isabela (86 miles), then ESE to close with the coast at San Blas (39 miles) for fuel and provisions; total 125 miles. Isabela has 2 small marginally sheltered anchorages (S and SE sides), so it's OK for light prevailing N winds of winter and spring, but not sheltered enough in a Norther, and it's wide open to S wind.

San Blas straight to Punta Mita is about 47 miles SSW. If you stay coastal, this leg is about 55 miles. The Nayarit coast is fragrant jungle, hillier as you move S. Chacala is an interesting overnight anchorage; Guayabitos Cove (Jaltemba) is marginal. Pacific SW swell unsheltered by the Baja peninsula is possible in shore.

Crossing: To cross the Sea of Cortez to San Blas from Las Frailes on East Cape (200 miles), a stop at Isla Isabela (at mile 160) may allow a daylight entrance at San Blas, and you'll need to avoid coming within 20 miles of all the prison colony islands, Las Islas Marias.

In hurricane season, this stretch gets tropical storms from the S and evening chubascos rolling down from the Sierra Madres. Avoid it in late summer or transit quickly nonstop.

Isla Isabela

Isla Isabela lured Jacques Cousteau here 30 years ago to film the rare frigate nests and a pristine underwater habitat. Today, tiny Isabela (281' volcanic peak, not a mile long) is a National Wildlife Preserve managed by the University of Guadalajara. Volunteers built an unmanned observation shelter SW of the panguero village on the S end. Grad students spend their vacations studying and protecting 500 frigate and booby nests all over the island. Children of all ages are moved by this rare interaction.

Visitors are welcome ashore, but don't touch the nesting trees (10' to 15' tall) nor any birds or nests. Don't approach birds mating, nesting or feeding their fuzzy nestlings. Male frigates puff their huge red neck sacks. Blue-footed boobies have amazingly blue legs and feet. Brown boobies have lime green *patos*.

Dogs and cats aren't allowed ashore, but if Fido needs to go, visit the E beach with a poop bag to remove hard evidence.

Approach: Coming from Mazatlán's Isla Creston, angle SSE (about 149°M) for 86 miles to approach Isla Isabela's SE side. We avoid the NW, N, NE and E sides, due to dangerous submerged reefs and buoys among and just outside the off-lying Isla Pelón (bald) (GPS 21°51.42'N, 105°53.57'W) close NW of the island and Las Moñas (mannequins) off the E side. A breaking rock field spreads a third of a mile square just S of Isla Pelón.

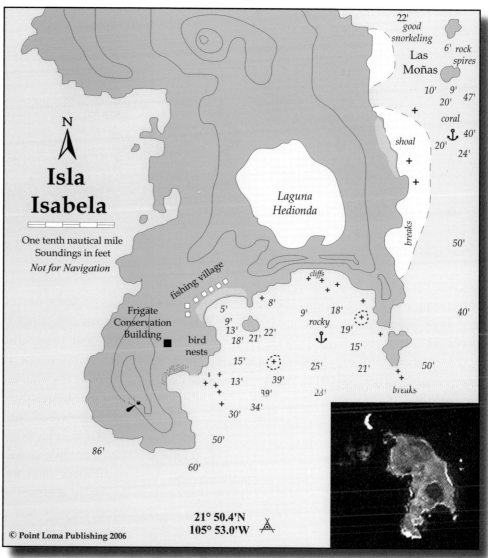

The mild current generally sets you W; spring tides are 4' or less.

Our GPS approach waypoint 21°50.4'N, 105°53'W is .75 of mile SE of the nav light, just S of the cove on the island's S side. Isla Isabela Light tops a hill on the island's SW corner.

Caleta Isabela (South Cove)

The cove on Isabela's S side is less than a quarter mile wide. Its E interior reveals the collapsed S flank of the island's primary caldera, and a lava-flow reef shields a tiny W lobe.

Impinged by rocks on both sides, South Cove's main lobe for anchoring is only 240 yards wide. For one or 2 boats, it's open to swell from any S quarter, but heavy N or NW wind makes it too rolly. A steep cliff at the head of the cove shows distinct red and black folded bands and provides the shelter, but avoid rock-fall at the cliff base. We anchor just outside the middle of the cove in 20' to 25' over sand between rock patches.

NOTE: Avoid a dangerous submerged (depth 5') rock pinnacle a few hundred yards SSE of the rocky arm that separates the 2 lobes. Several boats report hitting it.

Village Beach: South Cove's tiny W lobe is

Frigate chicks are fed by both parents. Nests are just above head high.

Las Moñas at Isla Isabela is the preferred spot.

framed by a lava flow (great tide pools) that limits the entrance to all but pangas and dinghies. The coral and lava beach fronts seasonal Isabela Village and gives access to the frigate observatory and Crater Lake. Isabela Village gets propane and medical care monthly from San Blas. Navy patrol boats stop frequently.

Observatory: Land on the SW end of Village Beach. A path zigs up through the main frigate rookery (dozens of low trees bearing frigate nests at head level) then up to the shelter roof and observatory hill. Iguanas sunbathe on the steps, hoping to be fed.

Each frigate and booby nest is numbered, so volunteers with binoculars can record how many eggs, when they were laid and hatched, how many times a day the fuzzy white nestlings are fed, when they become fledglings, first flight, etc. If student volunteers are here, they welcome food and water donations.

Crater Lake: The path N from the village leads past the open latrine to Crater Lake (not potable).

Las Moñas (East Side)

NOTE: When moving around the island's SW tip, give a wide berth due to an off-lying rock that breaks only occasionally.

Las Moñas: Isabel's E side is dominated by 2 twisting rock spires (150' tall) called Las Moñas (the Mannequins, meaning women's dress-making forms) that lie 200 yards E of a sandy beach ("dog beach"). Seasonal aquaculture buoys float within a mile E of the Moñas, and a research shack is on a cliff W of the Moñas.

The statuesque Moñas are fairly deep close to; we sounded 22' on the N side, 10' on the W side, 9' on the S side, 40' on the E side, and 6' in the pass between. We usually anchor S of the Moñas in 20' to 30' over shallow sand, coral rubble and then rock. If you're well set, this is good shelter in N and NW wind, usually less rolly and constricting than Caleta Isabela. However, a *yate* was lost recently when it dragged into Las Moñas.

In calm weather, boats anchor a bit farther SE in 40' and deeper sand. Some anchor on the 10' sand shelf between the Moñas and dog beach for quick access to the middle of the island.

All around the Moñas is good snorkeling, colorful corals and reef critters. A rocky shoal immediately S of the beach juts 50' offshore for more snorkeling, but the S end of this shoal breaks. By dinghy, it's half a mile between Isla Isabela's 2 anchoring spots.

Each time we've been here, the reported anchorage on the island's W side has been a mass of

Panga village on S side of Isla Isabela below frigate nests.

anchorage
newer fuel dock
for yachts
SAN BLAS
landlocked estuary San Cristobal
Piedra
Blanca
del
Tierra
harbor entrance
call for pilot
VHF-22
Punta San Cristobal
Punta Camarones
Matanchén
Bay
breakers
breakers

surge and backwash. We love this remote island, but if the WX is not right for a stop, it's safer to push on.

San Blas & Matanchén

San Blas, Nayarit (pop. 8,500) is a small shrimp port a mile up the Rio Pozo estuary, rebuilt since hurricanes of 2003 and 2004. Offshore catches are marlin, sailfish, dorado and corbina. Snook fishing in the estuaries is picking up, but most yatistas enjoy the nice Pemex pier and good local produce.

However, San Blas estuary, San Cristobal estuary and Matanchén Bay have bighting *jejenes* for 2 hours around sunset if the wind quits. Locals taught us to burn dried coconut husks like incense as a natural insect repellant.

Huichol women sell fantastic beadwork in the plaza; it's very collectable. Just outside town, ruins of Iglesia de Nuestra Senora del Rosario and its bell tower atop Cerro San Basilio are immortalized by H. W. Longfellow's final poem, *The Bells of San Blas*. La Tovara is a fresh-water spring to have lunch.

Matanchén Bay is 4.8 miles around 2 corners E from San Blas harbor, NE of breaker fringed Punta Camarónes. Radar paints 3.3 miles across shallow Matanchén Bay, which runs a straight line NW to SE with a small curve in the NW end. Only the middle is anchorable and only in winter and spring; it closes out June to October. Ramada cantinas line the beach for the summer surf crowd.

Lay of the Land

Piedra Blanca del Tierra (52') is less than a mile WNW of the entrance to San Blas harbor. Punta San Cristobal (GPS 21°30.69'N, 105°16.01'W) guards the harbor's SE approach. A striped light tower stands on the NW side of the jetty entrance, and two lighted riprap jetties and lighted buoys lead you up the channel, N then NW. Seasonal shoals inside are buoyed. Follow a shrimper or ask the Port Captain for a panga guide.

In the channel, to starboard you pass the Navy dock, panga & dinghy landing, Aduana building and the old shrimper basin (rectangular) with the new

Big new fuel pier in San Blas harbor is N of shrimper basin.

Capitanía on its W seawall, then the new Pemex fuel pier. Another man-made basin to starboard up the channel is in flux, then around a channel bend is a newly dredged lobe of the estuary.

Anchorage

San Blas harbor: Anywhere W of the channel and N of the dinghy landing is good holding mud in 10' to 15', but plan for max 3-knot tidal current. The lobe 100 yards NE of the town has been dredged for anchoring and may have fewer bugs. Set screens before sunset.

Matanchén Bay: When moving between the harbor and the bay, don't mistake Punta San Cristobal (estuary behind it) for Punta Camarónes (GPS 21°30.65'N, 105°14.87'W), which lies a mile farther east. Both points have breakers. See satellite photo. Anchor (15' soft mud) about 1.5 miles E of Punta Camarónes. Dinghy to Matanchén village in

the NW corner and bus to town. Dinghy vandals have been reported. Santa Cruz village in the E end is usually too rolly.

Local Services

San Blas is a port of entry, and its jurisdiction covers Matanchén Bay. The Capitanía is in the shrimper darsena; Aduana is a block N of the dinghy landing; Migración is 2 blocks farther N, or 2 blocks S of the plaza.

If you want a ship's agent, call Irma on VHF 22. Sportfishing skipper Norm Goldie on VHF 16 and 22 helps yatistas, but some call him the Enforcer.

Fuel: San Blas's new easy in, easy out Pemex pier is a stationary concrete platform, 200' long on the channel side, 100' on both ends. Storm relief gave San Blas Mexico's cheapest diesel

Bells of San Blas are silent at Longfellow's church in ruins.

in 2005, but we can't tell how long it will last.

Provisions: Several grocery stores and mercados uptown have excellent local fruits & veggies in winter and spring. Off the plaza is Botica, a good pharmacy.

The ice house behind the shrimper darsena uses purified water, has block & cube.

Misc.: We found a few hardware stores, outboard motor parts & repair shops, and commercial fisheries gear for shrimpers. As San Blas' sportfishing tournament grows, we expect to see more boat supplies.

Huichol women sell their beadwork at the plaze in downtown San BLas.

Culture & History

The pretty plaza on Calle Mercado is the center of town life. May 13 starts a 2-week Virgin of Fatima festivities with special foods, dancing and arts.

Nayarit's natives are the Huichol people, and their bead-covered animals and geometric objects are trendy in US and European art galleries (like *molas* from Panama), so if you like it, think of it as an investment and souvenir in one. Huichol women come from distant villages to San Blas' zocalo or plaza.

Founded in 1535, San Blas wasn't developed as a port until 1768. Father Junipero Serra and Padre Kino landed at San Blas to begin their missionary work in N Mexico.

The pirate John Clipperton was captured in Matanchén Bay and hanged, thankfully after he'd discovered Clipperton Island 700 miles off Acapulco.

COASTWISE San Blas to Punta Mita

Punta Custodias is at GPS 21°20.84'N, 105°15.00'W, 6 miles SSW of Punta Santa Cruz. From San Blas, lay a course 11 miles S to stay a mile off this low rocky point and to pass inside the 30' high pinnacle reported to lie 3 miles W of the point.

Nine Mile Beach: The next 9-mile beach (Playa Chila) ends at a hilly 5-mile long protrusion containing Volcan Cerobuco and its smaller twin. In the middle of this green protrusion is Chacala Bay.

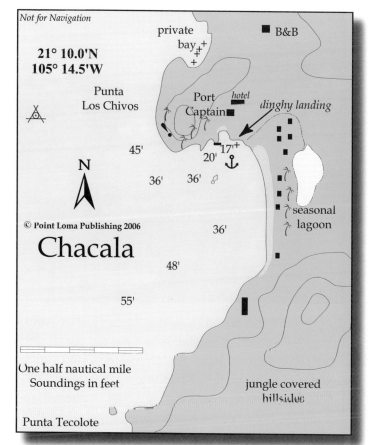

Not for Navigation

21° 10.0'N
105° 14.5'W

private bay

B&B

Punta Los Chivos

Port Captain

hotel

dinghy landing

N

45'

20' 17'

36' 36'

seasonal lagoon

© Point Loma Publishing 2006

36'

Chacala

48'

55'

One half nautical mile
Soundings in feet

jungle covered hillsides

Punta Tecolote

21°09.77'N, 105°13.93'W. Isla Tecolote (Owl) at the SW end of Chacala Bay is at GPS 21°08.72'N, 105°14.22'W. The tiny cove N of Chacala is rocky and not anchorable.

Chacala indents only half a mile, runs .75 of a mile NE-SW. The N end's pretty beach is less than half a mile long, full of mature coco palms (former plantation) with a dozen palapa cantinas below, and

Chacala Bay

Chacala Bay lies 21 miles S of San Blas, 30 miles NE of Punta Mita, immediately SE of Punta Chacala. Its nav light is buried in palms, but our GPS position close off the S side of Punta Chacala is

Palms surround Chacala Bay.

2 hotels dot the S end. Semana Santa (Easter week) brings thousands of inlanders to Chacala beach with tents, RVs and jet skis. It's almost deserted unless yatistas stop in winter and spring.

No fuel and few supplies are had in the village behind the N end of the bay, as provisions come from Las Varas 6 miles inland. Locals say the English pirate Thomas Cavendish was here in 1587. Chacala has some very pricey homes.

Anchorage

In moderate N wind, we tuck up into the NE corner (25' to 36' sand, mud) just S of the big panga landing. There's good holding anywhere NE of the Navy mooring buoy. In flat periods, you can anchor off the beach, outside the shore break. The dinghy & panga landing is inside a tiny separate bight NW of the beach. The bay's SW end is rocky.

Local Services

The Capitanía overlooks the landing, but it's often closed.

For excellent breakfast and lunch, climb the street beside the Capitanía; just over the crest there's a B & B; ask for service 30 minutes ahead. At the S end of Chacala, a holistic retreat and women's clinic is open by appointment.

Take a taxi 6 miles to Las Varas (nice drive) for 2 good grocery stores, coin laundry, huge fruteria, bus to Puerto Vallarta.

COASTWISE continued

Caleta el Naranjo: 1.7 miles SSW of Punta Chacala, we haven't sounded this tiny, jungle-clad but seemingly sheltered cove with private homes. A smaller N lobe has a private pier.

Punta Guayabitos: 2.5 miles S of Punta Chacala, this forested bluff is the N end of the 6-mile long beach that ends at Guayabitos Cove.

Guayabitos Cove

This cove with indifferent anchorage is 23 miles NE of Punta Mita, 28 miles S of San Blas. Three resort villages, Jaltemba (pronounced *hahl-TAYM-bah*), Rincon de Guayabitos (guavas corner) and Los Ayala, crowded the S end of this 6-mile long beach that starts at Punta Guayabitos (GPS 21°07.27'N, 105°14.33'W) and curves SW along Playa Jaltemba to end at Guayabitos Cove, which lies 1.2 miles SE of the prominent Punta Raza headland (GPS 21°02.34'N, 105°18.66'W). Playa Jaltemba is N of Guayabitos Cove; Los Ayala is private homes that climb the hillside in the Navy base cove between La Puntilla and Punta Raza.

Isla la Peña (GPS 21°03.16'N, 105°16.38'W) is rounded, palm-and-guano clad, and has 2 docks and a restaurant. It lies a mile NE of Punta Raza and 5 miles SW of

Provisioning at Las Varas yields tropical fruits galore.

Guayabitos Cove is pretty, best in flat calms or S wind.

Punta Guayabitos, so it somewhat shelters Guayabitos Cove from N wind. *Peña* is the nautical term for the top of a mizzen mast. A smaller islet half a mile SSW of Isla la Peña is wreathed in rocky shoals where crabs pots are set.

In light S wind, we've anchored off Los Ayala in 14' to 23' over sand; it's tight beside the Navy mooring, and Ayala an get refraction around Punta Raza. In moderate S wind, anchor among the panga buoys in Guayabitos Cove, 12' to 17' over sand. Weekend nights can be disco noisy, but the hotels' beach cantinas have early morning espresso.

In N weather, the only shelter is S of Isla la Peña. Anchor in about 30' outside the coral heads, but it's not very sheltered. The delicate corals are protected by law. Guayabitos Cove is a fair-weather stop, and even then we don't leave a boat unattended. Fonatur has plans to build a marina off the island.

North Head (GPS 20°47.63'N, 105°31.14'W) is the bold N tip of the Punta Mita headland, which runs almost 2.5 miles NE to SW. North Head has 545' cone-shaped hills and radio antennas.

Punta Mita: Round all sides of Punta Mita at least a mile off to avoid dangerous pinnacles. We use the name Punta Mita, because that's what the locals call it. See next chapter.

COASTWISE to Punta Mita

Half a mile SW of Punta Raza, a shallow boat channel leads E to homes on three S channels. The next 23 miles SW to the Punta Mita headland are sculpted by small beaches backed by Highway 200. We stay 2 or 3 miles off.

Punta Sayulita: Ten miles NE of Punta Mita's N flank, this forested point juts NE forming a 2-mile wide bay, crescent beach and artsy town of Sayulita. Waves wrap the corner in any amount of wind and the bottom is rocky.

Ensenada Litibu, the 5-mile wide bay SE of North Head, is backed by low land only half a mile wide, so development spills over from Punta Mita.

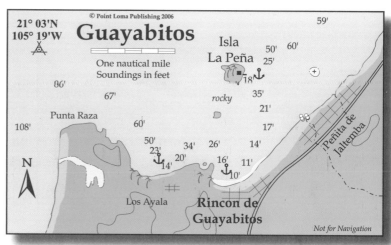

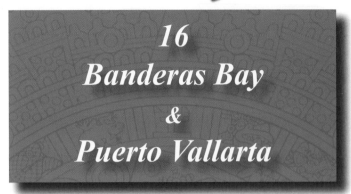

16
Banderas Bay
&
Puerto Vallarta

Bahía Banderas (Flags) is Mexico's largest sheltered bay, part in Nayarit, mostly in Jalisco. The bay is 20 miles N to S, about 15 miles E to W. It's N side is formed by hilly Punta Mita and the Islas Marietas, and its larger S shoreline is sheltered by the 9,000' Cerros Moronades ending at Cabo Corrientes.

Puerto Vallarta is on the ENE shore, backed by Sierra Madre foothills. PV and Nuevo Vallarta Inlet have 3 marinas, at least one floating fuel dock, a boat yard and dry storage, good marine service and repair, fair parts supply. PV as it's affectionately known, is Mexico's primary boating destination.

We'll look at each location as they appear circling Banderas Bay: Punta Mita, La Cruz, Bucerias, Nuevo Vallarta Inlet, Rio Ameca shoals, Puerto Vallarta's municipal harbor, PV's downtown at Rio Cuale, Los Arcos Marine Park, Mismaloya, Tomatlán, Las Animas, Quimixto, Yelapa and Cabo Corrientes.

Hurricane Hole: Both marina basins in Banderas Bay have good reputations as hurricane holes. Cabo Corrientes and its mountainous spine the Cerros Moronades have effectively blocked major hurricanes from striking Puerto Vallarta for the past 156 years. No hurricane has ever entered Banderas Bay straight from the W, between Cabo Corrientes and Punta Mita, because a cyclonic storm's spin and curving path can't normally make such a radical right-hand turn. If one does, take cover.

Summer brings 20-knot squalls, torrential rain, lightning and flash flooding to PV, so prepare for it. About 400 yates summer over in PV-NV marinas, half of them while their owners leave for all or part of the summer.

Approaches to Banderas Bay

> ### Mita Pass Rocks
> Between Punta Mita and the Tres Marietas, 3 separate pinnacles rise from deep water and have about 3' of water over them. We found and photographed 2 of them at our GPS positions
> (a.) 20°45.61'N, 105°32.89'W and
> (b.) 20°45.64'N, 105°33.16'W. We haven't found the third pinnacle, reported to be 2.25 miles at 230°M from Punta Mita, but that doesn't mean it's not there.

Crossing: From Cabo San Lucas to Punta Mita is about 276 miles. A course of about 108°M should keep you SW of the 20-mile security perimeter around all the Tres Marias Islands, a prison colony. The lighted Roca Corbeteña (20°43.9'N, 105°51'W) and her smaller sister should lie about 4 miles to starboard.

NOTE: NIMA, DMA and SM issued paper charts of Banderas Bay contain an error offset of up to 1.5 miles, and so do electronic charts based on their data. Trust your eyes, radar and depth sounder before your chart or electronic plotter.

Punta Mita: Between Punta Mita and the Tres Marietas, we recommend favoring the island side of this 3.6-mile wide pass.

Tres Marietas: If you enter Banderas Bay by swinging S of the 2 larger, lighted Tres Marietas, avoid (a.) La Onda, a large isolated rock patch 1.7

Punta Mita headland is gateway to Banderas Bay.

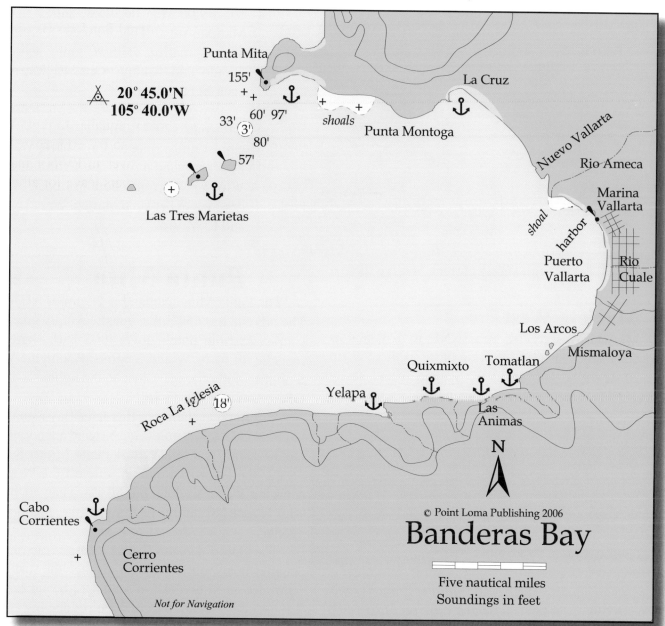

20° 45.0'N
105° 40.0'W

Punta Mita

155'

33'   60' 97'
(3')
80'
57'

shoals

Las Tres Marietas

Punta Montoga

La Cruz

Nuevo Vallarta

Rio Ameca

Marina Vallarta

shoal

harbor

Puerto Vallarta

Rio Cuale

Los Arcos

Mismaloya

Roca La Iglesia

18'

Yelapa

Quixmixto

Tomatlan

Las Animas

Cabo Corrientes

Cerro Corrientes

N

© Point Loma Publishing 2006

Banderas Bay

Five nautical miles
Soundings in feet

Not for Navigation

miles SW of Marieta West, and (b.) El Morro, a dry pinnacle and rock patch (GPS 20°40.06'N, 105°39.00'W) at 2.1 miles SW of La Onda, and (c.) a smaller rock patch 0.3 of a mile W of El Morro. We find deep water between Marieta West and La Onda and El Morro.

Cabo Corrientes: We try to round this major headland with an overnight or early morning in order to avoid amplified afternoon Cape Effect wind. Corrientes means currents.

Tres Marietas

The Three Marietas is a 5.6-mile long chain, all protected as a National Wildlife Preserve. The Marietas consist of 2 small but primary islands

(Marieta East, Marieta West) plus the fishermen's favorite rock patch we call La Onda at 1.7 miles SW of Marieta West, plus El Morro, an isolated pinnacle 2 miles SW of La Onda. We often see whales entering Banderas Bay close to the Marietas. They have no overnight anchorages, just popular lunch stops and day-ventures.

Marieta East

This lighted, flat-top (180') island runs NE to SW. Our GPS off the NE tip is 20°42.31'N, 105°33.75'W, about 3.6 miles SW of Punta Mita's S tip. Marieta East is almost inaccessible, so it's thick with seabird nests and pristine flora. Larger yachts can anchor in about 55' over sand within a quarter mile S of the island. Scuba excursion boats anchor below the cliffs on the island's S corner, hooking precariously in 50'

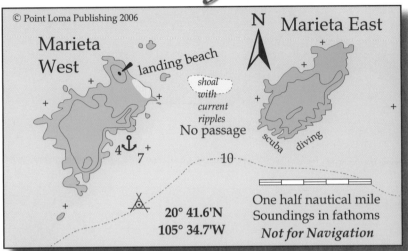

© Point Loma Publishing 2006

Marieta West

N Marieta East

landing beach

shoal with current ripples
No passage

scuba diving

4 ⚓ 7

10

One half nautical mile
Soundings in fathoms
Not for Navigation

20° 41.6'N
105° 34.7'W

105°39.00'W) lies 3.8 miles SW of Marieta West. This isolated 13' pinnacle attracts marlin, sailfish, tuna, yellowtail, dorado and fishing boats. El Morro has been lighted, then not.

Two other rock piles in the Marieta chain: La Onda (20°41.00'N, 105°37.00'W) is almost midway between Marieta West and El Morro; and a rock reef a third of a mile W of El Morro is a bottom ripper. We find deep water between Marieta West, La Onda and El Morro.

over rock debris with strong current, so give them a safe berth.

Marieta West

Marieta West (120') runs NNE to SW and is also lighted. Our GPS position close to the SW tip is 20°41.49'N, 105°35.32'W. Slanted E and easily accessible, Marieta West draws tour boats by noon,

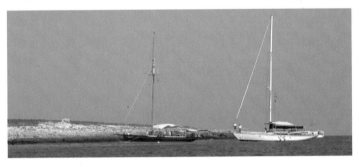

Above: Marieta E anchorage.
Below: Cave on Marieta W.

so come early. Snorkeling and fishing are excellent all around this island.

Approach from S, anchor off the cliffs and caves along the SE side, in 30' to 40' over sand and rock. From there dinghy around the rocky E point to land below the nav light on the sloping E beach, which is sheltered by 2 islets to the N. One amphitheater-like cave you can enter by dinghy. The Marietas are a national park; take only photos, leave no litter.

Marieta El Morro

Third in the group is El Morro (GPS 20°40'06'N,

Punta Mita

The Punta Mita headland is 2.5 miles NE to SW. The NE end has 454' hills, but shockingly green golf courses and big hotels cover its S half. Dangerous reefs lie off its N, W and S points. Round the W and S points a full mile off. Close to the lighted S tip, our GPS position is 20°45.36'N, 105°32.02'W.

First real shelter in Banderas Bay is in the lee of Punta Mita. The mile wide N-wind anchorage (22' to 30' sand) is a mile NE of Punta Mita's S point. A 12' shelf almost a quarter mile off the W side of curving Playa Anclote, but 50 yates can anchor off the N and NE shore. In S swell, the anchorage is gone.

The riprap darsena (being enlarged) is only for charter boats, but if you can manage the surf-prone entrance in your dink, it's an OK beach landing. Time-share sharks ask if you're staying at the Four Seasons. The beach has a sundry store and 3 restaurants (Rocio's, El Dorado, El Acuario). Uphill are cafes, some town services and bus to La Cruz, Bucerias and PV.

Punta Pontoque is a rocky shoal point 2 miles E of this anchorage. Punta El Burro and Distiladeras are tourist beaches E of Punta Montoga.

La Cruz de Huanacaxtle

This Nayarit town's name refers to a cross carved of wood of the huanacaxtle tree, pronounced wah-nah-KAHSH-lay. But everyone calls it La Cruz.

La Cruz is a pleasant older fishing village with brightly painted gringo restaurants for folks getting

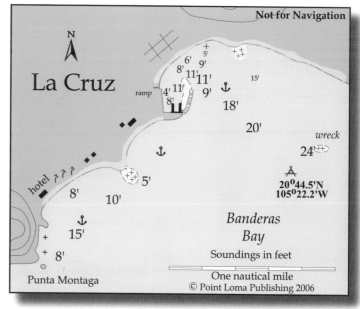

away from PV; locals moved across the highway. La Cruz is even more popular than Punta Mita as a long-term yatista hangout, because it's more sheltered, has more services and is closer to PV.

At 7.5 miles E of Punta Mita, Punta Montoga and its Piedra Blanca is a minor headland sheltering La Cruz Bay, the 8-mile indent and beach to its E. Anchorage half a mile NE of Montoga (10' to 15') below the arched seawall is OK in flat weather, rolly in afternoon swell.

La Cruz harbor is fairly sheltered 1.5 miles NE of Punta Montoga, half a mile E of a seasonal arroyo. The harbor is a small L-shaped jetty opening E that protects panga moorings, 2 concrete fishing piers (one silted in) and a launch ramp. Behind the jetty is mostly shoal, but it's a good dink beach. A visible wreck (good snorkeling) lies 0.8 of a mile SE of the tip of the jetty.

It's normal to find 30 yates anchored outside the breakwater or E of the seaward tip (20°44.93'N, 105°22.8'W) in 15' to 22' over good holding mud. La Cruz is barely within VHF range of NV and PV, so boats here with strong signals relay the morning VHF net for those at Punta Mita.

La Cruz has a Port Captain (VHF 10) and Navy yard overlooking the harbor. The town has laundry, groceries, bakery, propane, boat repairs, a clinic and lots of eateries. Philo's has BBQ, burgers and karaoke catering to cruisers, but there's also Hikuri Gallery Café for good food and Huichol art, Tapas del Mundo, Caledonia, Mango and Black Forest Café (Papasitas).

A marina might be built here; check Updates on www.MexicoBoating.com Bucerias is the next village ESE toward PV, but it has no anchorage.

Nuevo Vallarta Inlet

Nuevo Vallarta Inlet's lighted and jetty-lined entrance lies 3.5 miles NW of PV's municipal harbor. Nuevo Vallarta is in the state of Nayarit, but PV is in Jalisco. You may see planes landing a mile SE of Nuevo Vallarta Inlet at Puerto Vallarta's international airport.

Our GPS position at the seaward end of Nuevo Vallarta Inlet's S jetty is 20°41.26'N, 105°17.77'W. The entrance channel is usually dredged to 10' or 12'. But after heavy rain, a bar (5' to 8' MLW) may form, so hail Marina Paradise Village or fellow yatistas for the status.

Once inside the baffle, bear to port to avoid shoals off the little beach and seawall starboard. Nuevo Vallarta's estuary is huge, contains 2 marinas and is being dredged to make room for more slips.

Dingy beach at La Cruz is NE of the harbor.

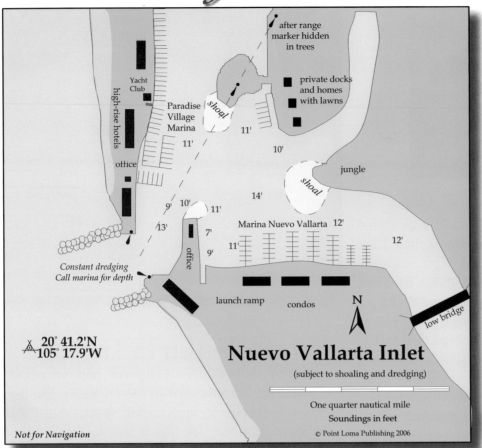

after range
marker hidden
in trees

private docks
and homes
with lawns

Yacht
Club

high-rise hotels

Paradise
Village
Marina

shoal

11'

11'

office

jungle

shoal

9' 10' 11'

14'

13'

7'

Marina Nuevo Vallarta 12'

office

9'

11'

12'

Constant dredging
Call marina for depth

launch ramp

condos

N

20° 41.2'N
105° 17.9'W

Nuevo Vallarta Inlet

(subject to shoaling and dredging)

One quarter nautical mile
Soundings in feet

Not for Navigation

© Point Loma Publishing 2006

Overlooking the entrance, the Nuevo Vallarta Capitanía (VHF 10) is different from PV, so you contact must notify both. Beside the Capitanía is a high concrete seawall where diesel can be ordered and pumped from a truck.

Marina Paradise Village is N or to port after you clear the entrance. Marina Paradise Village has at least 204 full-service slips to 160' and 210' end ties, within the gated Paradise Village Resort. Dockmaster Dick Markie delivers 5-star service, 22-page cruiser directory. Guests have access to the resort's many amenities; air-conditioned Paradise Plaza mall and zoo are walking distance; it's a 1.5-mile shuttle ride out to Highway 200, about 15 minutes to the airport, 30 minutes to PV. Slip reservations are a very good idea; (322) 226-6728, or from the US (800) 995-5714 to ask for the marina. Visit www.paradisevillage.com or email marina@paradisevillage.com

Vallarta Yacht Club's clubhouse overlooks MPV. This real yacht club puts on the annual Banderas Bay Regatta in March (www.banderasbayregatta.com), hosts the Northbounders, Southbounder and Puddle Jumper seminars, provides the 22-page cruisers directory full of maps & lists of local stuff updated each fall, working toward a PV to Mazatlán Regatta. It's a nice group, we're members; (322) 297-2222.

Both marinas plan a fuel dock and dry storage.

Marina Nuevo Vallarta is to port after you pass the Capitanía. New owners plan 200 new full-service slips (30' to 200' end ties) by fall 2006, plus a fuel dock, chandlery, boat yard, dry storage and restaurants. Dockmaster Juan Estrada speaks English; (322) 297-7000. Check Updates on www.MexicoBoating.com

Rio Ameca Shoal

A quarter mile SE of NV Inlet or 2 miles NW of Puerto Vallarta's municipal harbor entrance, this broad 3' silt shelf doesn't always reveal itself in breakers, and it reaches almost a mile offshore, depending on runoff from the Sierras. Deep-draft vessels can anchor half a mile SE of Rio Ameca Shoal.

Time change: Passing Rio Ameca and into Jalisco, you enter Central Time (an hour earlier than Mountain Time, 2 hours earlier than Pacific).

Marina Paradise Village in Nuevo Vallarta Inlet.

Puerto Vallarta

The city of Puerto Vallarta (pop. approx. 250,500) covers 10 miles of the NE shore of Banderas Bay. Red tile roofs and white sun-splashed walls of the Spanish colonial architecture climb the jungle-clad foothills of the Sierra Madres. Rio Cuale divides to form a pedestrian-only island amid the historic El Centro. Fun sculptures dot the restored beaches S to Mismaloya. Cruise ships dock in the entrance or turning basin of the municipal harbor, and the international airport lies between PV and NV – together bringing 1.5 million visitors annually.

Thanks to PV and NV's 3 marinas, fuel, haul-out, chandler and repair service, this area is the largest long-range boating destination in Pacific Mexico. Banderas Bay offers year round fishing, sailing (Banderas Bay Regatta in March), snorkel and scuba diving, getaway anchorages and inland excursions.

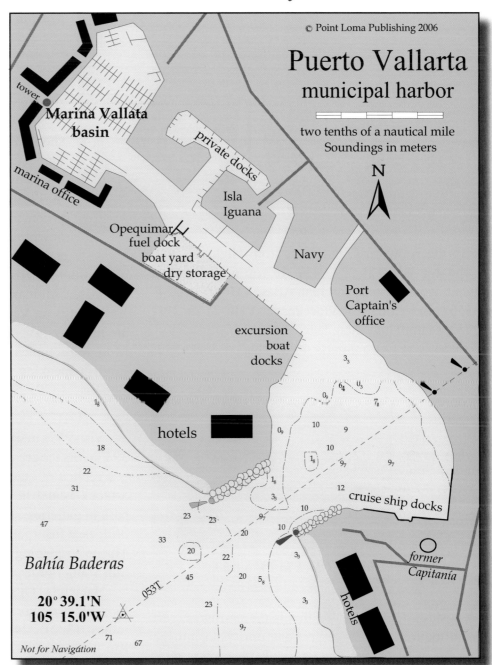

© Point Loma Publishing 2006

Puerto Vallarta
municipal harbor

two tenths of a nautical mile
Soundings in meters

N

20° 39.1'N
105 15.0'W

Bahía Baderas

Not for Navigation

Municipal Harbor

PV's large municipal harbor on the N side of town (3 miles SE of Nuevo Vallarta Inlet) contains a large marina, fuel dock, boat yard – all NW of the cruise ship dock. Lighted jetties (Racon K dah-di-dah) mark the half-mile wide entrance. Our GPS waypoint just outside PV's entrance is 20°39.1'N, 105°15'W.

The entry basin contains the cruise ship docks, Navy base, Capitanía and Med-moorings for excursion boats. Anchoring is no longer permitted in the harbor. Go NW up the main channel (8' MLW) lined with excursion docks, and you find Opequimar fuel dock & boat yard to port. (See Local Services.)

Two side channels go NE to Isla Iguana villas and excursion docks.

Marina Vallarta: In the large basin at the N end of the channel, Marina Vallarta's decorative lighthouse greets you. Marina Vallarta has 470 full-service slips to 140' and end ties to 200'. They provide the 22-page cruisers directory too. This original marina in PV is for sale; we hope dredging (10' min.) and dock maintenance won't lag. Until the marina across from Paradise Village is rebuilt, slip reservations here are a good idea; dock-mistress Adriana (322) 221-0275.

Local Services

PV is a port of Entry. The new Capitanía (VHF 13) is on the NE side of the harbor turning basin

Mexico Boating Guide

Marina Vallarta in PV municipal harbor.

with the Navy base, but enter from Highway 200. Capitanía is (322) 224-0427. If you need a ship's agent, we use Paperman Juan Arias; VHF 22 or 224-3555; also Vilma Habelloecker on VHF 22 or 221-2752, seatur97@yahoo.com

Fuel is at Opequimar's 40' U-shaped docks (12'

Opequimar fuel dock in PV harbor.

alongside). Unfortunately, this is the narrowest part of the main channel, so larger boats must poke into the fairway or lay across 2 fingers, and afternoon wind is on the beam. This region is overdue for another fuel dock; check Updates at www.MexicoBoating.com

Haul out: Opequimar's 50-ton Travelift hauls max 17' beam, fenced storage, watermaker parts & service, chandlery; (322) 221-1800. PV has several Zaragoza Marine Hardware

PV's downtown has lots to see & do in plaza and Rio Cuale.

stores for paints, pumps parts, OB, nav stuff, chain, VHF; ask any taxi.

Provisions: The big grocery in NV shopping center is handy for that basin. Sam's Club and WalMart across from PV's Capitanía are handy to MV. The ComMex in Plaza Marina next to MV has good produce, also at Mercado Emiliano Zapata downtown. Mercado Municipal on the N end of Isla Cuale is a cultural experience; check out the herbalist booth.

Misc.: All marinas provide lists of local services. VHF Net is on VHF-22 weekdays 0830. Most boats are in PV & NV; side group relays La Cruz & Punta Mita. Main topics are WX and which is the cheapest English-speaking dentist (Dr. Cecelia Gamboa in Bucerias; (329) 298-1866).

Culture & History

Visit PV's main zócalo for mimes, art displays and 39 Flavors ice cream. Our Lady of Guadalupe's dome is a replica of Queen Carlotta's crown. Isla Cuale, a 5-block island in Rio Cuale, is a shady pedestrian park of galleries, shops and eats; enter at stairs off the bridges at Insurgentes or Ignacio Vallarta. We like the Museo Arqueologia de Rio Cuale; T-Sat 1000-1500, Sun 1000-1400.

Hacienda Ojo de Agua in the Sierra Madre foothills does horse-back tours to missions & silver mines; (322) 224-0607. Jungle canopy tours over Rio Tomatlán get good reports; www.canopytours-vallarta.com

December 12 is Guadalupe Day in Quimixto; decorated fishing boats promenade down the shoreline, and panguero women sing hymns to the Virgen de Guadalupe – Mexico's patron saint. New Years all boats dress up and get blessed for Mariners' Day. June through October the Turtle Preservation Program peaks; children & adults help "liberate" baby turtles on hotel beaches.

Natives carrying banners greeted Francisco Cortez (nephew of Hernán) in 1524, so he called it Banderas Bay. Pirates & trading schooners took on

Las Animas is South Banderas getaway.

water and waited out storms around the bay. In 1880 the village at Rio Cuale was named Puerto Vallarta for Jalisco governor Ignacio Vallarta. By 1954, director John Huston had a fishing getaway at Las Animas, and in he brought down Night of the Iguana Richard Burton & Ava Gardner; Elizabeth Taylor was in the background as it was filmed in Mismaloya, but she and Burton soon had their own adjoining homes just E of Isla Cuale – now called Gringo Gulch. Casa de Kimberly (Elizabeth) is a B&B; tours Sunday mornings.

Explore Ashore

Guadalajara is 126 miles E of PV by modern bus. High in the cooler mountains, Guadalajara is Mexico's San Francisco, sophisticated & hip. Mimes, street theater, folklorico dance in the pedestrian Plaza Central. Visit the university's oceanography department, tequila tasting tour at Sauza Distillery, and shop Tlaquepaque near Guadalajara. Anchor at San Francisco Plaza Hotel or Guadalajara Plaza Hotel, both clean, reasonably priced and well located.

South Banderas

The beaches S of PV have no anchorages. Los Arcos Marina Park 6.5 miles S of downtown PV has underwater caves and arches in coastal boulders. Anchoring is prohibited, so come with a dive boat.

Mismaloya

This high-rise beach cove is a mile SW of Los Arcos. Like all anchorages on S Banderas, it's deep close in to the narrow shelf, open to NW winds. Our GPS position 20°32'N, 105°17.61'W has some shelter from NW swell. John Huston filmed Night of the Iguana on the SE point; tours daily. A bus goes to Eden, a waterfall & swimming hole favorite with yatistas.

Boca de Tomatlán

Wedged between high green hills with a split hill at the back, this pretty little bay 2.5 miles W of Mismaloya is fed by Rio Tomatlán – a good fishing spot. A split-level hotel on the bay's E flank has a bus up to the 2 Chico's freshwater hangouts, also to the jungle canopy tours. Anchor in 70' of water about

50 yards off the middle of the back beach. Our GPS position is 20°30.8'N, 105°19.04'W. Highway 200 turns E, not to be seen again until Careyes.

Las Animas

John Huston's fishing-hunting lodge is on the E beach at this next little indent W of Tomatlán. Panga taxis shuttle from here and Yelapa. Deep water close in makes Las Animas excellent fishing, but an indifferent roadstead. The small piers sometimes rent a mooring or side tie for the afternoon. Otherwise, we've anchored in 50' at GPS 20°30.55'N, 105°20.68'W.

Quimixto

Pronounced key-MEEKS-toh, this slightly wider anchoring shelf 2.25 miles W of Las Animas has fewer boats, a pretty white beach, steep jungle hills split by

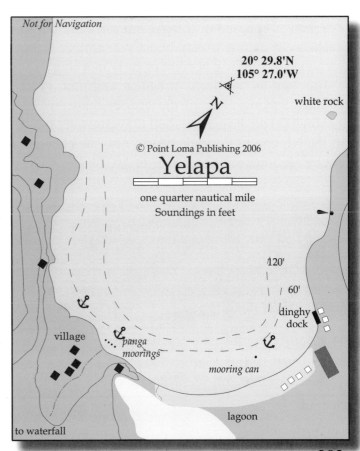

Not for Navigation

20° 29.8'N
105° 27.0'W

white rock

© Point Loma Publishing 2006

Yelapa

one quarter nautical mile
Soundings in feet

120'

60'

dinghy dock

village

panga moorings

mooring can

lagoon

to waterfall

Yelapa is prettiest cove on S Banderas, but not a great anchorage.

a stream with a seasonal lagoon and waterfall behind the beach. Majahuitas resort is just S of the village. Too bad Las Animas is open to NW wind. In calms, we've anchored in 25' to 30' at GPS 20°30.36'N, 105°22.19'W.

Yelapa

"A palapa in Yelapa beats a condo in Redondo." This 1960s mantra of California ex-pats is printed on T-shirts sold on the beach! Hippies, yuppies and cruise-ship escapees throng to Yelapa's beach palapas. But for yatistas, Yelapa is just a marginal fair-weather stop 14.5 miles SW of PV. Our GPS approach waypoint just outside the entrance is 20°30'N, 105°27'W. Yelapa Light is on the bay's steep E point.

Yelapa is exposed to N wind and can close out in breakers. In calms, it may boost you around Cabo Corrientes 16 miles E at night or early morning.

The bottom is deep, irregular and not great holding. Staying clear of the charter buoy, we've anchored (a) on the narrow shelf (25' sand over rock) off the NE end of the main beach, near the concrete dinghy landing; and (b) in 35' to 50' on the wider shelf off the village in the SW corner of the bay; you may need bow & stern hooks to avoid the panga moorings.

Yelapa's coarse-sand beach requires shoes. From the NE beach, horses take you up to a large waterfall and swim pool. From the S end, a path meanders up and over the rocky wedge separating the beach from the real village. We have fun diving with local kids off this platform into the deep turquoise pool below. On the bay's SW side, village houses cling to the steep jungle walls like hanging gardens, and you can walk to the smaller waterfall in the steep cut.

Cabo Corrientes

The best time to round Cabo Corrientes is during the late night or early morning; worse time is mid afternoon.

Going toward Cabo Corrientes, stay at least 1.25 miles off shore. At 8.5 miles WSW of Yelapa you pass breaking shoals a mile off Punta Chima and Roca la Iglesia (Church Rock), both hot fishing spots. Our GPS position just outside them is 20°29.81'N, 105°36.16'W.

Caleta Corrientes: A narrow slit on the NE flank of Cabo Corrientes' lighthouse point extends almost a quarter mile SE, is open to N swell, has sheer rock walls and a steep boulder beach at the back. We haven't anchored here, because it looks too narrow to turn around inside. But it may serve in an emergency. Our GPS just outside Caleta Corrientes is 20°25'N, 105°40.65'W.

Cabo Corrientes (508') is a major headland on the SW approach to Banderas Bay, 28 miles SW of Puerto Vallarta. The point is backed by 2,000' crests, and low Punta. Corrientes means currents; here's where winds and currents mix and amplify. In stormy weather, this cape is a washing machine. 2 miles off we find less current and wave action.

Punta Ysatan and Las Cucarachas reefs jut about 0.3 of a mile off shore, within about 6 miles S of Cabo Corrientes.

Yelapa dinghy landing.

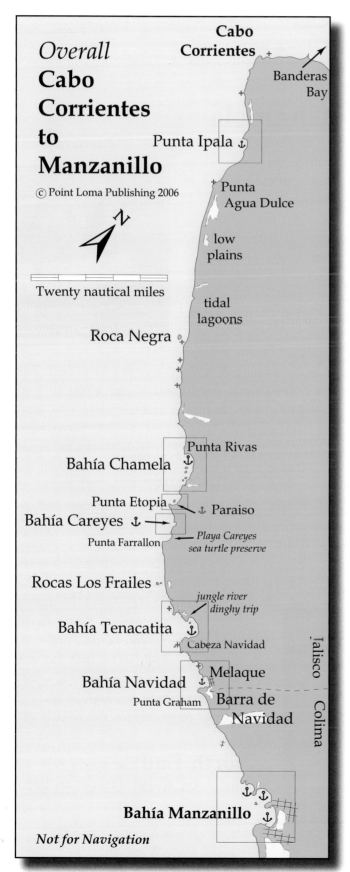

Overall
Cabo Corrientes to Manzanillo

© Point Loma Publishing 2006

Twenty nautical miles

Cabo Corrientes

Banderas Bay

Punta Ipala ⚓

Punta Agua Dulce

low plains

tidal lagoons

Roca Negra

Punta Rivas ⚓

Bahía Chamela

Punta Etopia — ⚓ Paraiso

Bahía Careyes ⚓

Punta Farrallon

Playa Careyes sea turtle preserve

Rocas Los Frailes

jungle river dinghy trip

Bahía Tenacatita ⚓

Cabeza Navidad

Melaque

Bahía Navidad ⚓

Punta Graham

Barra de Navidad

Jalisco

Colima

Bahía Manzanillo ⚓ ⚓ ⚓

Not for Navigation

17
Gold Coast

The 115-mile "Gold Coast" from Cabo Corrientes to Manzanillo doesn't get golden until 60 miles S when you reach pleasant bays with multiple overnight anchorages, good spots to dive, fish and explore by dinghy or ashore. After Ipala, the golden spots are Chamela, Etiopia, Careyes, Tenacatita, Melaque, Barra Navidad and Manzanillo.

West Coast yatistas often cruise the Gold Coast and Zihuatanejo, then turn N for the Sea of Cortez. East Coasters often find the Gold Coast similar to cruising grounds in Panama and Costa Rica — but less rain and bugs, less sheltered.

ROUTE PLANNING: Cabo Corrientes to Manzanillo

This 115-mile coast runs NW to SE, may get NW wind in winter and spring, and has marinas and fuel at Barra Navidad and Manzanillo. Ipala is 13.5 miles SE of Cabo Corrientes, then 47 miles to Chamela, and from there S you can enjoy beautiful day-hops between overnight anchorages.

N-bounders use Ipala (except in S wind) to await favorable conditions for rounding Corrientes.

Crossing: To depart to Baja, we use Los Frailes Rocks between Tenacatita and Careyes, because it's a straight shot to Cabo, and we have to stay outside Los Frailes anyway.

COASTWISE: Cabo Corrientes to Ipala

After rounding Cabo Corrientes, stay half to 2 miles off. At 3 miles S you see low Punta Ysatan, and at 6 miles S of Corrientes you see breakers around Las Cucharitas Reef that juts about 0.3 of a mile out. 7 miles farther S is Ipala.

Punta Ipala

Ipala isn't golden; it's tiny and humble, but it's functional and welcomes yatistas.

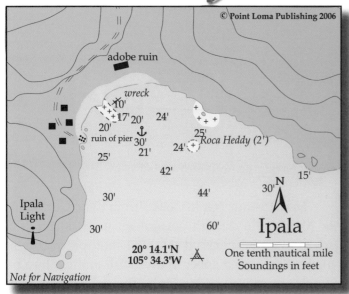

© Point Loma Publishing 2006

adobe ruin

wreck

10'
17' 20'   24'
20'
ruin of pier   30'   Roca Heddy (2')
21'   24'
25'
42'
15'
30'   44'   30' N
Ipala
Light
30'   60'   Ipala

20° 14.1'N
105° 34.3'W   One tenth nautical mile
Soundings in feet

Not for Navigation

Lighted Punta Ipala (315') points SSE and is a good radar target 13 miles S of Corrientes. In NW wind, cozy anchorage is on the E side of the point, tucked up as far NW in the cove as possible. Round the rocky point a few hundred yards off. If you're coming up from the S, the saddle and road cut in the back of the cove is a good marker.

Avoid a submerged pinnacle Roca Heddy (20°14.23'N, 105°34.31'W) in the NE side of the cove, covered by only 2' of water. Near the beach are an old wreck, old pier and small reef. We anchor (20' to 30') off the end of the reef, or elsewhere between rocky patches.

Ipala sprouted 3 cantinas to lure yatistas; good seafood. The 17 families living in Ipala village drive 8 hours on a dirt track from Yelapa, so we try to drop off school supplies for Kinder through 8th grade.

COASTWISE Ipala to Chamela

We stay 1.5 to 2.5 miles off shore on the 48-mile Ipala to Chamela leg. Along here, the Sierra Madres are visible.

Roca Negra (46') is 30 miles S of Ipala and a mile offshore. We pass within a quarter mile of Roca Negra.

Roca Blanca is 7 miles S of Roca Negra and similar except in color.

Chamela

Bahía Chamela (48 miles SE of Ipala, 56 miles NW of Manzanillo) is a 2 x 4-mile cruising ground with one large anchorage and lots of tiny ones around the bay and 8 small islands, weather dependent. But 20 yates is not uncommon in winter.

Pasavera Island.

Chamela (chah-MAY-lah) Bay has 2 villages (Pérula and Rebalsito), small hotels and vacation homes dot the whole shoreline, but the town of Chamela is 2 miles inland on Highway 200. From here to Guatemala, Highway 200 loosely flanks the coast.

Chamela Bay was such a relaxed hangout that a few dinghies were reported stolen off the beaches after dark, then ransomed back, one sans OB. Now we cable dinks and motors together and keep an eye on them.

Punta Rivas is an obvious radar target, easy visual ID. This mile-wide S-pointing headland shelters the N half of Chamela Bay. Our GPS approach waypoint 1.25 miles S of Punta Rivas is 19°33'N, 105°08.5'W. Punta Pérula is the SE corner of Punta Rivas, and the visible Pérula Reef runs a quarter mile E from the S tip of Punta Pérula, so clear the reef (good snorkeling) as you enter the N half of the bay.

North End: In strong NW wind, we find snug shelter tucked up into the

Ipala village anchorage is good in NW wind, friendly ashore.

206

bay's NW corner (24' to 30') where the curving beach meets the rugged Rivas hills. A stream from a mangrove estuary cuts the berm at the W end of Pérula beach. In moderate N wind, anywhere off this long curving beach and Pérula village is fine. Pérula village has 10 seafood cafes, the El Super and El 4 groceries inland and weekend tourists.

South End is less sheltered in N wind, wide open to S weather. Isla Pasavera (True Pass; you enter N of it) and Isla Colorado (Colored, reddish) are the larger islands. In the triangle formed by these plus smaller Isla Novilla, we find 3 tiny beaches, each with an intimate anchorage for one or 2 boats, great swimming, diving and fishing. It's a popular rendezvous given the nickname Pasavera Cove.

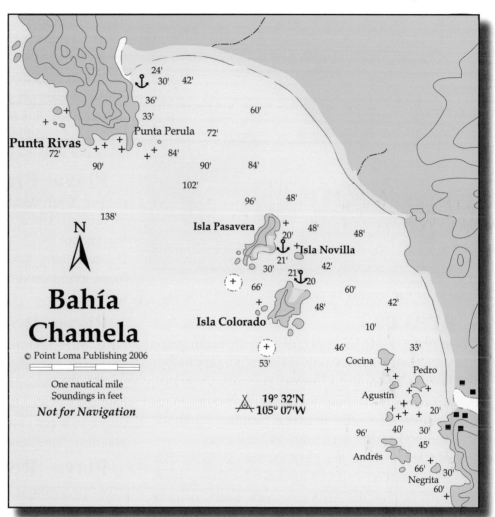

The 5 tiny islets in the SE end of Chamela subject to NW swell, but we've anchored between them and the beach. Clustered in the SE end of Chamela Bay are 5 smaller islands. They're open to any W swell, but anchorage can be had between the inner islands and Rebalsito. One of 4 tiny coves S of Rebalsito is La Virgencita Shrine.

Rebalsito has a restaurant, groceries, gasoline and phone office. It's the beach road down from Chamela, which has a clinic and bus to PV or Manzanillo. The new Chamela-Cuixmala Biosphere Reserve E of town contains 700 plant species, 180 of them deciduous trees, and has been undisturbed for several hundred years.

Rancho Paraiso

About 9 miles S of Punta Rivas, Punta Etiopia juts 1.75 miles W. In the rincon on its N side, 2 small islands hide this tiny cove and coconut plantation. Just outside the cove, our GPS is 19°28.6'N, 105°04.0'W. In S weather, we anchor off the S beach in 15' to 18' over sand.

Rancho Paraiso is a private estate patrolled by armed guards, including the cove and beaches. Anchoring is tolerated, but landing is prohibited. LOBO, the name of a sportfisher sometimes moored here, is spelled in white rocks near the helicopter pad.

Chamela: North End has cantinas.

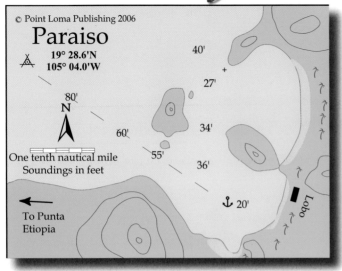

© Point Loma Publishing 2006
Paraiso
19° 28.6'N
105° 04.0'W

80'
N
60'
55'
One tenth nautical mile
Soundings in feet

40'
27'
34'
36'
20'

⚓ 20'
Lobo

To Punta Etiopia

3.5 miles N of Punta Farallon Light, 10 miles SE of Chamela and about 44 miles NW of Manzanillo. Our GPS waypoint 19°26.4'N, 105°02.5'W is close W of the submerged pinnacle just outside the entrance.

Bahía Careyes is 3 pocket bays and several islets that provide fair shelter from N and NW wind, but Play Rosa and Playa Recife suffer in swell from the W, and it's all open SW.

Playa Blanca,
the N cove is the best shelter. Club Med was torn down; this is a posh private residence, so don't go ashore or use the dock. We anchor in 15' to 20' over sand and coral gravel. If you dinghy through the shallow slot SE to Playa Rosa, avoid snorkelers, private dock and prop-eating rocks.

Playa Rosa
is the less sheltered middle cove, often cramped by excursion boats. We anchor anywhere between the beach and the island SW of it, 18' to 27' over not good holding sand. The beach belongs to Georgio's Playa Rosa restaurant (dinner only), so leave your dink below the coco palms while you dine. Stairways leads S to Playa Recife.

Playa Recife:
This beach is sheltered between 2 snorkeling reefs, and its S end is roped off for swimmers by El Careyes Hotel (former Bel Aire). We anchor outside the buoyed rope and SW of the range markers, or from the rope SW toward the outer island, all in 20' to 29' over sand.

Except at Christmas and New Years, beautiful El Careyes Hotel welcomes yatistas as day guests; the $40 fee is credited toward your meals, drinks, pool towels, deli, spa, etc. www.elcareyeshotel.com or (800) 508-7923. Parts of the movie Kill Bill were filmed here. The hotel's private helicopter has whisked injured tourists to Manzanillo airport's ambulance.

We enjoy snorkeling Playa Recife's reefs, below the range tower and around all the islets. The outer island has a sea-level cave.

Careyes

Careyes (kah-RAY-yayz) refers to the endangered carey sea turtles that nest only in this region; see below. We love to poke into Careyes, because it's pretty: bright cottages climbing the cliffs, flowering vines shading the stairwells between beaches, dramatic little reef to snorkel, nice hotel and restaurants.

But Careyes cove is a tight anchorage, especially for larger boats. If you find the safer anchoring spots roped off or crowded with excursion boats, or if W swell is coming in – pass on this one.

Careyes is 3 miles SE of the tip of Punta Etiopia,

Not for Navigation

private home
private dock
Playa Blanca
15'
15'   20'   16'   7'+9'   18'
30'   26'   25'
40'   27'   15'
private dock
Playa Rosa
■restaurant

20'
N   60'   40'   29'   ⚓ 29'   +⊕   hotel
60'   40'   25'
65'   40'   22'
73'   40'
30'   ⚓   30'
30'   40'
cave   50'
56'
⊗ helicopter pad

Range Markers 053°M

19° 26.4'N
105° 02.3'W

Careyes
60'
Two tenths nautical mile
Soundings in feet
© Point Loma Publishing 2006

COASTWISE continued
Careyes Turtle Preserve covers both the tiny Playa Careyes half a mile S of

Bahia Careyes from Playa Rosa.

Playa Recife and the larger Playa Teopa NE of Punta Farallon. The Careyes hawksbill sea turtle is almost extinct, and these 2 beaches are its only nesting sites. There's no anchorage, and landing ashore is prohibited. An adult tortuga carey is 2' to 3' long, weighs 30 to 100 pounds. When nestlings emerge from the sand in December, visitors who have been trained by park guides (ask at El Careyes Hotel) can help the babies reach the water by shooing away predators. This is an educational gold star for kids.

Punta Farallon Light (19°24'N, 105°03'W) marks this low rocky headland about 6 miles S of Punta Etiopia.

Los Frailes Rocks are 6 miles SE of Farallon, about 1.5 miles offshore, so run this stretch about 2 miles off. A dangerous flat-topped rock lies just

recently made a Federal Ecological Zone.

In winter, 50 yatistas anchor for weeks of potlucks on the wide low-sloping beaches, where inflatable dinghy wheels rule. Maria delivers fresh produce and French bread from Barra. The old McHale's Navy movie set Paris Tropicale restaurant is torn down, but the campground cantina at Boca de Iguana makes a good rendezvous. Ten Bay cruisers elect an annual King & Queen who, among other courtly duties, oversee trash collection.

Tenacatita village in the N end and La Manzanilla in the SE corner have groceries, gas, cheap eats, internet, bus, etc. Small hotels send guests on panga tours of the Jungle River.

Playa Recife is reef-bound, has friendly hotel.

below the surface about 4 miles SE of Los Frailes and a mile offshore. Los Frailes is our traditional jumping off or landfall point for crossing between Baja and the mainland.

Punta Hermanas (Sisters): 2 estuary mouths are visible within 4.2 and 2.5 miles N of the S-pointing reef shrouded entrance to Ten Bay.

Tenacatita

Bahía Tenacatita (aka Ten Bay) is one of our favorite anchorages on the Gold Coast. In NW wind Tenacatita's main bay is better shelter than anything N. We love to guide folks through the tidal-estuary channel we dubbed the Jungle River Dinghy Trip,

Lay of the Land

Two estuary mouths are visible within 4.2 and 2.5 miles N of the S-pointing Punta Hermanas (Sisters), which is the NW arm of 2-lobed Tenacatita Bay. Punta Hermanas is wreathed in several offshore rocks, islets and reefs, so give a half-mile berth. Our GPS a quarter mile SSE of the Punta Hermanas rocks reads 19°16.17'N, 104°52.40'W.

Ten Bay's smaller outer beach (1.3 miles long) is NE of Punta Hermanas and its half-mile long La Escollera Reef. That cantina beach curves E to Punta Chubasco, a 2.5-mile wide, hilly headland.

Las Escolleras Reef is a stairs of black rocks jutting half a mile SE from Punta Hermanas, and in calm conditions its E side is ideal for novice

Boca
Las Iguanas

hotel

Tenacatita

jungle river
trip

Punta
Chubasco

palapa
restaurants

Roca Centro

La
Manzanilla village

Punta
Hermanos

Isla
Pajaros

Tamarindo

hotel

hotel

19° 16'N
104° 50'W

N

Bahía Tenacatita

One nautical mile
Soundings in fathoms

© Point Loma Publishing 2006

Cabeza de Navidad

Piedra Blanca

Not for Navigation

snorkelers off the beach. Combined with 4 islets outside, this area is called El Acuario, the aquarium, but in W to S weather, it's closed out.

Tenacatita Bay is 3 miles wide, sheltered NE of Punta Chubasco. Roca Centro (GPS 19°17.41'N, 104°49.69'W) is a 12' tall radar target half a mile E of Punta Chubasco; it rises from 60' of water. A submerged rock is reported W of Roca Centro.

Ten Bay's S arm is rocky Cabeza Navidad (400') about 4 miles SE of Punta Hermanas; give the S end of this point a 2-mile berth due to off-lying rocks.

Anchorages

Boca de Iguana: N of Chubasco headland, the infamous short reef or bar breaks just S or outside the mouth of Rio Iguana (Jungle River entrance). In N weather, the calmest anchorage is N of Chubasco head and outside the bar in 12' to 30' over sand, mud and small rock. Rio Iguana curves around the sand-spit mouth. In the palm grove on the sand spit, the campground's palapa cantina is a rendezvous hangout.

Jungle John Rains charts the Iguana.

Tenacatita village:
Anywhere NE of the Boca anchorage and along the N hills and beach is good in 25' to 35' over sand. Hotels, condos and seafood palapas are no problema. Tenacatita's downtown is a mile inland, so this is its N beachfront. But off the E beach gets refraction from shore break.

La Manzanilla:
In calms or light S wind, the roadstead (30' sand) off this pleasant village is popular. El Girasol has great breakfast, organic coffee, fresh pastries. Tamarindo resort has a small cove with water-ski pier. But in winter, this end of Ten Bay is usually untenable.

Playa Escolleras: The W end of the cantina beach NE of the snorkeling reef has been a day anchorage in calm weather, but the bottom is shallow sand on bedrock, poor holding. It's better as a dinghy destination to meet Jungle River escapees.

COASTWISE continued

After clearing Cabeza Navidad at the S end of Tenacatita Bay, the larger headland Cabeza Navidad (402') lies 2 miles due S. When you're 2 miles S of Cabeza Navidad, the entrance to Bahía Navidad is visible 8 miles due E.

Jungle River Dinghy Trip

This fun self-guided dinghy excursion takes 3 hours round trip, or you can spend all day. Start in the morning with the tide half and rising, so you can cut your OB, listen to the jungle, drift with the incoming tide, and paddle a bit to steer. We try to be back out by half tide on the ebb. As long as you're out before dark, you can't get too lost, because all the side channels are dead ends or loops – great for naps, photos or ambushing your buddies.

To get over the rocky bar, raise your motor and paddle in, or if possible, get out and walk or swim the dink in until you're past the bar. Back in the dinghy, you curve around the palm-covered sand spit with rendezvous cantina and campgrounds (pet crocodile). The main channel depths are 4' to 15' and the general course is W.

Mangroves and flowering vines canopy parts of the channel in cool twilight; elsewhere it's full sun. Tendrils of aerial roots dangle 15' to touch the mirror clear water. Colorful birds (egrets, heron, kingfishers, ibis, anhingas) and butterflies dart through lush foliage. Wild crocodiles hunt iguanas, so don't let your dog swim.

We charted the main channel with recording GPS in 1995, and in 2005 satellite images reveal more detail. About 2 miles upstream, the main channel Ts. If you turn right (N), it widens into a lagoon that shallows out in reeds.

We suggest turning left (S) at the T. It's a short ride to the beach berm and palapa cantinas at Playa Escolleras – ideal for seafood lunch and siesta. Retrace your route and get out before sunset when no-see-ums arrive.

Take sun protection, camera, binocs, bird book, bug repellant, drinking water, oars, anchor – and either a cooler picnic or pesos to buy lunch and cold cerveza at the palapas. We complained to Turismo about pangas ferrying hotel guests at 10 knots around blind bends, and they slowed down to 5 knots! We urge fellow yatistas to set good examples: go slow & listen, don't stir up the bottom or disturb the wildlife, carry out your litter.

Barra Navidad marina and back lagoon with sailboats anchored.

Bahía Navidad

Bahía Navidad contains Melaque village anchorage, the town of Barra de Navidad, and the entrance channel to Laguna Navidad. Inside Laguna Navidad, you'll enjoy a posh marina, fuel dock, several anchorages and another lagoon. A private club up canals on the N side of town has small boat docks for its members, no guest services.

Bahía Navidad (Christmas) has a rich nautical history. Melaque is the site of major St. Patrick's Day celebrations, yatistas welcome. We enjoy the friendly low-key atmosphere in the quaint sandbar town known simply as Barra. But more trinkets arrived with the cruise-ship cattle boats. The marina across the bay is one of the plushest in Mexico, and another is planned.

Lay of the Land

Navidad (Christmas) Bay is 20 miles NW of Manzanillo, 92 miles SE of Cabo Corrientes. The 1.5-mile wide entrance to Bahía Navidad (opening 2 miles NW to SE) is formed between rocky Punta Bahía (200') on the NW and the jungle massif Punta Graham (705') on the SE. Give the SW tip of Roca Cono (W side of Punta Graham) a mile berth due to submerged rocks. Punta Graham shelters the lagoons and marina basin.

Our GPS approach waypoint in Bahía Navidad's entrance is 19°12'N, 104°42'W.

The Jalisco-Colima state line is the channel into Laguna Navidad; Melaque (2 miles N) and Barra are in Jalisco, but the marina is in Colima. The lagoon side of Barra's peninsula is lined in panga docks, dinghy landings and open restaurants.

Melaque plaza is Irish?

See chart. The outer lagoon is mostly shoal, so stick with the channels until you've seen it at low tide. The inner lagoon (entrance NE of the marina) is also shoal, but channels goes SE to an anchorage or SSE to the fuel dock.

Volcan Fuego (12, 533') 60 miles inland on the Jalisco-Colima border erupted in Sept. 2005, spewing gas and ash 3 miles high. It's visible from Barra on clear days.

Anchorage

Melaque: The beach fronting this town on the NE shore is sheltered by Punta Bahía, but it can get swell in stronger NW wind. Anchor in 15' to 20' over sand and gravel, tucked up behind Punta Bahía. We find comfort anchoring bow-and-stern to keep pointed into any swell. In fair weather, the N and NE curve of beach is OK. The

Laguna Navidad's large back bay, with Colimilla village.

Not for Navigation

Cabo Blanco
Marina

19° 12.0'N
104° 41.4'W
30'
26'

town of
Barra de Navidad

26'
20' 16'
13'

10'

hotel

5'
6'
6'

10' 3'

+
+ 19° 12.0'N
104° 41.0'W
shoals

5' 10'
14'

14'

Pig
Island

6'

5'

Low Jungle

channel dredged to 20'

private paired buoys

3'

hotel

3'

hotel

Bahia
Grande
Hotel

20'

13'

fuel dock

20'

16'

16'

13'

20'

20'

13'
16'

3'
3' 10'
13'

shoals

unmarked channel

shoal

13' 3'

16
9 6 5 4
16 8 5
16 5
5 11
16
8
15
14
3

shoal

10
12

15

9 17 9 4

14
14
13
11 12

10
12
12

Colimilla

Isla
McHale

N

Inner Lagoon
dinghies only

Laguna Navidad

One half nautical mile
Sounding in feet

ⓒ Point Loma Publishing 2006

cobble beach gets sandy as you move S, but the mid and S end of Navidad Bay are surf zone.

Melaque's patron saint is San Patricio, unique in all Mexico. Yatistas help Melaqueños celebrate St. Patrick's birthday March 17, but it's grown so big that the religious processions, festival foods, drinks and dances start one or 2 weeks earlier. Come to the main plaza in front of the church.

Laguna Navidad: In the back lagoon, a marked 10' channel leads to an anchorage (10' to 12'

Barra's fuel dock with big boat (left) and trimaran cruiser below.

good holding mud) in the middle of the lagoon, but mosquitoes are thirsty all night. You can dinghy S to Colimilla's cantinas or the basin of a future marina.

Local Services

Barra de Navidad's Port Captain regulates the Jalisco bergs of Melaque and Barra de Navidad. But the Manzanillo Port Captain covers the big marina, big hotel and lagoon village of Colimilla.

Marina: In a sheltered basin off the SE side of the outer Laguna Navidad, Marina Puerto de la Navidad has 207 full-service slips to 150' and jungle landscape in front of the Grand Bay Hotel. Marina guests can use the hotel's pool, restaurants, golf course, concierge desk, airport shuttle, etc. Water taxis cross the bay to Barra's waterfront or the back lagoon. Call "marina dockmaster" on VHF 16, and uniformed guards will guide you to your slip and take your lines. Marina Puerto de la Navidad (315) 355-5950 or visit www.islanavidad.com

Another marina is in construction in a basin on the S side of the back lagoon. We're told the channel will be dredged to 20' before it opens in 2007.

Marina Cabo Blanco is a private club for members' ski boats, not open to yatistas. Fuel dock: The marina's

103' fuel dock is 300 yards inside the back lagoon following the starboard channel, but call the marina for fuel reservations.

Provisions: Melaque's mercado is W of the plaza, Banamex with ATM. Barra has good grocery stores, fruterias and a real French Bakery (VHF 16) that delivers fresh buttery croissants to yates from their panga.

Misc.: Barra has fishing and general boating supplies at Z-Pesca on Legaspi (315) 355-6099.

Ask Cab #14 Eddy about OB repairs, propane, laundromats, Beer Bob's Book Exchange, 4 internet cafes, bike rentals. Spanish lessons by Bonnie Gibson; info@easyspanish.net

Explore Ashore

Patzcuaro is our favorite self-guided retreat, a remnant of Spanish empire in the pine Sierras above the volcano-lake home

Barra's waterfront is cantinas with docks, stairs and water taxi landing.

of the Purépecha people unconquered by Aztecs or Spanish. Patzcuaro is SW of Morelia, capital of Michoacan; it's artsy but less touristy than San Miguel de Allende. We stay in Patzcuaro's old hotels on the plaza for economy & richest cultural experience.

Monarch butterflies (mariposa monarcha) migrate 2,500 miles from Canada to remote Michoacan peaks. All 400 million born en route navigate by generational memory. Feb-March is best viewing, living cloak shimmers on trees & hills. Newborns depart in April. Logging seriously threatens this sole Monarch habitat, so we hope eco-tourism proves more profitable. Naturalist guided tour from Morelia & Zitacuaro.

COASTWISE Barra to Manzanillo

With 2 exceptions, the next 15 miles SE are regular beach backed by lagoons and foothills. 6 miles SE of Punta Graham, a lagoon's silt delta forms half a mile out, so run this stretch at least a mile off. At 13 miles SE of Punta Graham, Piedra Blanca (261') stands about a mile off shore in deep water all sides. Above the high rocky coast are buildings and lights of Manzanillo international airport. 2 miles ESE of Piedra Blanca is Punta Carrizal, the NW entrance point to Bahía Manzanillo.

Manzanillo

Yatistas know Manzanillo for the marina at Brisas Las Hadas, a resort whose architecture was inspired by a famous Moorish fairytale called The Fairies (Las Hadas). Fantastic spires and arches adorn a nearly vertical maze of white adobe walls and red tile roofs. Marina Las Hadas is renovated and has a fuel panga service.

The town of Manzanillo, Colima (pop. 103,000) has good provisioning, marine shops and transportation. Manzanillo Bay has 8 anchorages, sportfishing and diving.

In Feb-March, a biennial race from San Diego to Manzanillo feeds into the MexORC races between

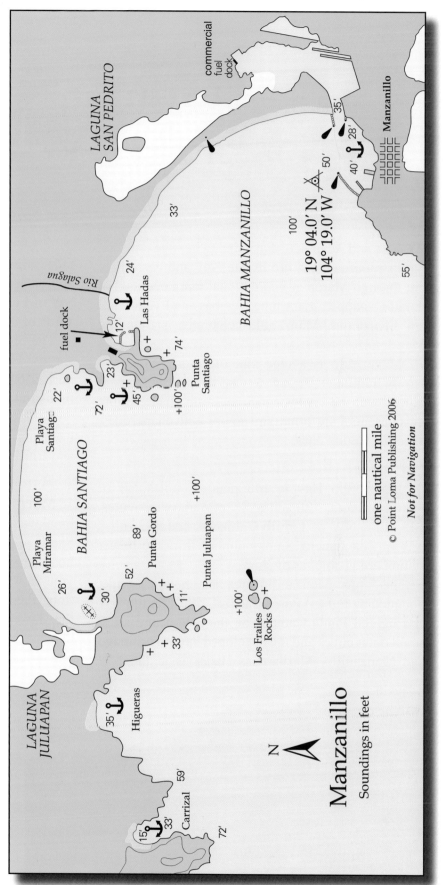

Marina Las Hadas entrance through breakwaters. Hotel overlooks the darsena.

PV, here and Acapulco; expanded to include cruisers. Sailfish tournaments are in late Nov and early Feb, but through March at international tournaments, but dorado, snapper, giant tuna, sea bass and yellowtail are also draws. Manzanillo celebrates is founding May 1 – 10.

Manzanillo is a nice mix of resort living and family traditions. Be sure to visit the pleasant zocaló downtown; ice cream cones in siesta shade, polite kids in school uniforms, shy novios with chaperones, abuelos playing chess.

Lay of the Land

Manzanillo Bay is 148 nautical miles SE of Puerto Vallarta, 120 miles SE of Cabo Corrientes, 145 miles NW of Lázaro Cárdenas, and 182 miles NW of Zihuatanejo. Smoke plumes from the power station are visible far offshore.

The larger Manzanillo area is 7.5 miles wide, bounded by lighted Punta Carrizal (500') on the NW and lighted Punta Campos on the SW. There are 2 small outer coves and the developed bays of Santiago and Manzanillo. Marina Las Hadas is in the NW

corner of Manzanillo Bay. Our GPS position at the marina's entrance is 19°05.97'N, 104°20.68'W.

Los Frailes Rocks are a good radar target half a mile S of Punta Juluapan. Our GPS approach waypoint 19°04'N, 104°24'W is half a mile SW of Los Frailes. 3 submerged rocks are within 25 yards of the N and W sides of Los Frailes.

The old port and Manzanillo cover the E and SE shores. The newer San Pedrito Lagoon commercial port is NE of the old port. Las Brisas is a marine industrial area around San Pedrito.

Roca Vela is a quarter mile S of the Punta Campos headland. SE of Punta Campos, Laguna Cuyutlán and fruit plantations run 10 miles SE.

Anchor & Berth

Marina Las Hadas: This renovated marina in the breakwater-enclosed darsena on the NE side of Punta Santiago peninsula has 70 full-service Med-slots for boats to 80' plus a 120' seawall. Staffers may secure your bow line to a central mooring in the darsena floor, then you stern tie to the floating dock circling the darsena. Las Hadas Resort wraps around the darsena. Marina guests enjoy the resort's many 5-star amenities. Built in the 1960s, this marina and hotel recently got new owners who renovated it and built a new fuel dock. Dockmaster Rubén Zamayoa is very helpful; (314) 331-1010 x 3707 and 3706.

In heavy NW wind, forget the outer coves and expect surge throughout the bay. Don't cruise here in summer; the whole N

Manzanillo's Capitania and all port offices are in this pyramidal building off San Pedrito Lagoon channel.

side gets pounded.

Carrizal Cove on the NW approach is a narrow, steep-sided cove with anchoring shelter (15' to 33') in moderate N wind. Carrizal is the most private anchorage, but it's a 6.5-mile voyage to Las Hadas, 8.5 miles into the old port waterfront.

Higueras Cove (next door) is wider, less protected, more developed. Anchor on the 35' sand shelf off the beach; snorkel the bight below hilly Punta Juluapan.

Elefante Cove is a day anchorage (15' to 36') on the E tip of Punta Juluapan, for diving nearby rock walls.

Boca de Juluapan: Laguna Juluapan's mouth is closed except in rainy season. We've anchored (30' sand) just N of Punta Gorda and E of the lagoon mouth off Playa Miramar.

Playa Santiago: Santiago Bay's crescent beach is 3.75 miles long between Punta Juluapan's Playa Miramar and the sleepy village of Playa Santiago on the W side of Punta Santiago. We anchor off Playa Santiago (22' to 30') away from the swimming rock. Kids play on dinks left at the beach stairway. Ashore are eateries and small hotels.

La Audiencia is the small cove in the rocky SW side of Punta Santiago. We've anchored off the hotel beach, 23' sand, but it's noisy. Another tiny spot amid the pinnacles half a mile S is possible in flat weather, bow-stern, 45' over sand and gravel. Punta Santiago's S end is great scuba diving.

Las Hadas anchorage (12' to 30') is most sheltered and most popular, NE of the marina's breakwaters and E toward Rio Salagua. A small day-fee gets you a secure dink landing in the marina and access to the resort's pools, showers, laundry, restaurants, shuttle 6 miles to town, etc. Some cafés and mini-supers are within 2 miles uphill.

Downtown: Security may limit yatistas in Manzanillo's old port SE of the lighted breakwater and SW of the entrance to San Pedrito Lagoon. Get the Capitanía's radio permission to enter and anchor (20' good holding mud). We spent a week riding out a hurricane here, while the bay's N shore was blasted. This has good access to many dinghy landings behind waterfront cantinas, then walk downtown.

Local Services

Manzanillo is a Port of Entry. The pyramidal Federal Building (Capitanía, Migra, Aduana) overlooks the S side of the channel into San Pedrito Lagoon, service window on 1st floor (314) 322-3470. El Centro bus. WX broadcasts daily 0800 and 1200. Don't use VHF 16 or 12 near Manzanillo Bay.

Ship's Agent: Servi-Port is the ship's

Marina as Hadas again has a fuel dock.

agency that helps yatistas in Manzanillo & other ports. Ask for English-speaking Ing. Alfredo Ibarra Obando (314) 332-3000 ext 104. www.servi-port. com.mx

Fuel: Marina Las Hadas runs a 60' floating fuel dock (diesel & gas) outside and N of its entrance jetties. Larger yachts Med moor off this low white dock. Otherwise, the commercial pier in the N end of San Pedrito Lagoon has a 300' concrete pier with 2 fuel stations; make arrangements through the Port Captain (314) 332-0004. When this pier has been closed, diesel has been available from the Navy docks on the port side as you enter San Pedrito Lagoon.

Haul-out: Manzanillo has small marine ways, 200-ton cranes and lots of repair shops to handle yacht emergencies; contact ship's agent Servi-port (314) 332-3000 x 104. Several ferreterias marinos in Las Brisas, well stocked, and Zaragosa orders US stuff.

Provisions: Soriana's is good, has everything; N of downtown. CoMex between Las Hadas and downtown is good too. The Mercado Municipal is downtown at Cuauhotémoc and Independencia. A specialty shop outside Las Hadas has primo meats, produce, wine & cheese, delivers to the marina, not cheap.

Eats: Restaurant Lychee (Chinese) in the old port has a dink landing handy to walk downtown, but pay them to watch your dinghy. Juanito's Cybercafe on the highway has good burgers and internet.

Misc.: Pacifico dive shop in Las Hadas fills tanks. Manzanillo has coin laundry, internet, cheap colectivo bus, propane. The international airport is 20 miles NW of town, half way to Barra. New bus station is at the entrance to Valle de las Garzas and Auditorium. Locals say Hospital Manzanillo is best in town, N of old port; (314) 336-7273.

History & Culture

Two centuries before Columbus, King Ix of Colima recorded entertaining Chinese traders at the mouth of Rio Salagua. In 1522 Hernán Cortez heard this legend and dispatched Lt. Gonzalo de Sandoval to check out Manzanillo's multi-lobed bay for safe anchoring and ship-building sites. Gonzalo called all the chieftains for an audience on a beautiful beach on the W side of Punta Santiago, hence La Audiencia. After hulls were laid in Laguna de la Navidad, floated over the bar and towed S, many ships & Manila galleons were completed and rigged in Bahía Manzanillo.

Trees with small apple-like fruits used to grow around this bay, so the Spanish called them manzanillos. But the fruit was poisonous, so by 1950 all the trees were destroyed – only the name stayed. True apples don't grow here. The movie 10 with Bo Derek was filmed at Las Hadas, putting Manzanillo on the jet-set map and spurring tourism.

Manzanillo

Not for Navigation

Punta Campos

Overall
Manzanillo to Zihuatanejo

© Point Loma Publishing 2006

Río Ameria

Colima / Michoacan

Cabeza Negra

Río Coahuayana

Cerro San Telmo

Punta San Telmo

Fifty nautical miles

Punta Piedras Blancas

Muruata

Punta Lizardo

N

Bufadero Bluff Caleta de Campos

Michoacan / Guerrero

Rio Balsas

Lázaro Cárdenas

Bahía de Petacalco

Punta Tracones

Isla Grande

Ixtapa
Zihuatanejo
Punta Garroba

Morro de Petatlán Puerto Papanoa

We say Michoacan is marginal because it has no reliable anchorages. The Sierra Madre steps right into the steep, rugged 180-mile shore with deep water close in. The toll road to Manzanillo and Lázaro Cárdenas further isolate the Michoacan coast in between. It has spectacular sea life and scenery, no shrimping, but few marginal rest stops.

If NW wind or S swell have been light for days, some of these tiny coves might be calm enough to let us anchor and get ashore. Otherwise, it can be all breakers. In rainy season, intense afternoon chubascos with lightning roll down from the Sierras and 20 miles out to sea. Install good radar reflectors and lightning protection.

Michoacan's few fishing villages have been courteous and friendly, but drug smugglers also ply these waters, so some yatistas opt to buddy boat between Manzanillo and Ixtapa.

Route Planning: Manzanillo to Ixtapa

Manzanillo to Ixtapa (about 177 miles)
Cabeza Negra is 44 miles SE of Manzanillo.
Bucerias is 19 miles SE of Cabeza Negra (total 63).
Maruata is 9 miles SE of Bucerias (total 72).
Pichilinguillo is 14 miles SE of Maruata (total 86).
Caleta de Campos is 24 miles SE of Pichi (total 110).
Lázaro Cárdenas is 33 miles SE of Caleta (total 143).
Ixtapa is 34 miles SE of Laz Card (total 177).

219

Pelican Rock (right) from Cabeza Negra N.

SE of Manzanillo has big shorebreak, backed by lagoons and palm plantations.

Stay at least 2 miles off shore SE of Manzanillo to avoid 3 hazards. (1.) Roca Vela and the dangerous Ola Verde, an occasionally breaking shoal 1.5 miles off shore, 8-10 miles SE of Punta Campos off the village of Cuyutlán. (2.) A rock half a mile off shore about 26.5 miles SE of Manzanillo. (3.) The shoaly Boca de Rio Coahuayana 12 miles farther SE. Michoacan begins on the SE side of this river.

In moderate NW weather, Caleta de Campos is more likely to provide calm overnight anchorage, and the pleasant town has some supplies and services.

Staying at least 2 miles off shore, you can point-hop from Manzanillo to Cabeza Negra to Bucerias (San Telmo), then coast to Caleta. Stay 5 miles off when passing Lázaro Cárdenas to avoid ships maneuvering, then point-hop to Ixtapa.

COASTWISE: Manzanillo to Ixtapa

Departing Manzanillo: The 43-mile beach

Cabeza Negra

At 44 miles SE of Manzanillo, Cabeza Negra (571') is lighted and makes a good radar target, like an island attached by a low sandy neck. It's a private gated community of nice homes, uniformed guards, and landing ashore is prohibited. However, in an emergency, there's a gated road linked to Highway 200. Cerro San Telmo (2,948') rises 3.5 miles E of this point. We've anchored on both sides; it's usually rolly.

Cabeza Negra N: Pelican Rock is close off the N side, and SE of it a buoyed shark net ropes off the SW end of the half-mile dark sand beach. In flat weather we've anchored 35 yards off the middle of the beach in 30' over good sand. Our GPS position is 18°36.5'N, 103° 41.9'N.

Cabeza Negra S: A reef juts a quarter mile S of the headland's S tip. In N wind, you might carefully come around that reef and anchor (30') in its lee, off the N end of this 3-mile beach. Even in flat weather, the S side has been less comfortable than the N.

An underwater shelf S of Cabeza Negra causes the surf to stack up. Breakers form off Boca de

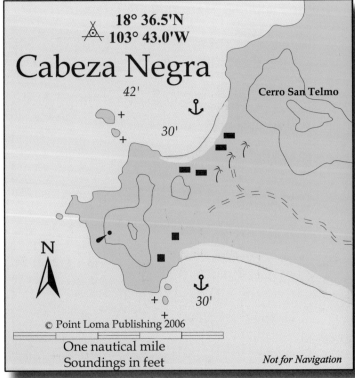

18° 36.5'N
103° 43.0'W

Cabeza Negra

42'

Cerro San Telmo

30'

30'

N

© Point Loma Publishing 2006

One nautical mile
Soundings in feet

Not for Navigation

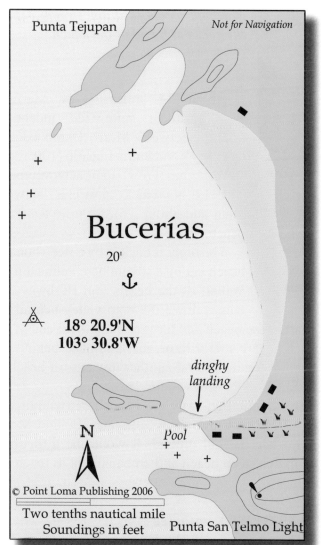

Punta Tejupan

Not for Navigation

Bucerías

20'

⚓

18° 20.9'N
103° 30.8'W

dinghy landing

N

Pool

© Point Loma Publishing 2006

Two tenths nautical mile
Soundings in feet

Punta San Telmo Light

Apisa 12.5 miles SE of Cabeza Negra, and they continue as the coast tends more S.

Bucerias

This tiny, marginal spot is 19 miles SE of Cabeza Negra. If you don't need to stop, we suggest passing 2 miles off shore. Bucerias is tucked into the half-mile gap between Punta Tejupan and San Telmo Light. We'd never anchor here overnight or leave a boat unattended, as the bottom is iffy and the current changeable.

Punta Tejupan (tay-hoo-PAHN) is a half-mile chain of rocks jutting W from where the shore turns more E. Our GPS position 18°21'N, 103°31.5'W is close to the seaward tip of these rocks. Another submerged reef extends a quarter mile S of the above rocks. San Telmo Light stands on a 230' rocky bluff a mile SE of Punta Tejupan. Playa Bucerias (boo-say-REE-ahz) is steep curve of fine white beach on the N flank of San Telmo Light, and the tiny village behind

the beach is Bucerias or Dive Spots.

Boats must approach from the SSE, due to submerged rocks S of Punta Tejupan. Avoid floats marking dive spots and a wreck. There's 15' to 20' of water over not-good holding sand, off the main beach SE of Tejupan's reef.

The sand bottom shallows quickly off the N end of the main beach, preventing landing or swimming. But you might land inside a tiny slot S of a tilted boulder (Morro Elefante, 40') attached by a sand spit and tide pools to the S end of the main beach. From there a path goes to the village or climbs to the lighthouse Faro San Telmo. Cantinas cater to weekend tent campers and scuba tours that dive Punta Tejupan reef and a wreck off Morro Elefante.

Maruata Cove

At 72 mile from Manzanillo and 9 miles SE of Bucerias, this half-mile wide cove is a mile NE of Punta Piedras Blancas, which is a light cliff area (109') with, guess what, a white rock at its base. Our GPS next to what we think is Piedras Blancas is 18°15.72'N, 103°21.64'W.

About .75 of a mile NE of our Piedras Blancas is another set of rocky pinnacles; Maruata Cove lies behind them. From our GPS 18°15.25'N, 103°20'W out in the bay, you can see road cuts higher up the hills, the 1.1-mile beach and the sheltered quarter-mile wide anchoring cove off the W corner beach. Directly above the corner is a landmark municipal

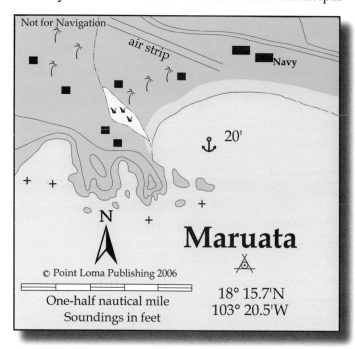

Not for Navigation

air strip

Navy

⚓ 20'

N

Maruata

© Point Loma Publishing 2006

One-half nautical mile
Soundings in feet

18° 15.7'N
103° 20.5'W

Maruata locals ford this stream behind the rocks at S end of the beach.

building (7 ventilators) and Navy base (air strip gone).

We tuck into the W corner of the beach (palms) in about 20' of water over sand and mud. N of the sheltering pinnacles, pangueros launch through the mouth of a lagoon that runs through the indigenous Purépecha village. If this cove is habitable at all, the least shorebreak will be close to the boca. We found a tiny store in the village (no fridge or phone), and some villagers don't speak Spanish.

Lizardo Bay

Lizardo Bay (aka Pichilinguillo) is another tiny, marginal spot we normally pass a mile off shore. If it helps someone in an emergency, great. Don't count on help from the highway; this stretch is notorious for banditos. Pichilinguillo refers to the 17th century Dutch pirate ships that hid here to spring out and attack passing vessels. Caleta de Campos is the nearest medical and mechanical help.

About 14 miles S of Maruata, Pichilinguillo's mile-wide indent is wedged between Morro Chino Islet (2 peaks 99') and Punta Lizardo (100' rocky bluff). Our GPS approach waypoint (18°11.5'N, 103°07.5'W) is between them and about .75 of a mile S off the beach.

The bight is backed by a steep boulder beach cut by a stream bed. Palms top the W half of the beach, and Highway 200 comes down the high valley behind the E half of the beach and turns S along the E end of the beach. There's no village, just a ramada behind the E end of the beach and another tiny cut-off beach to the SE.

In flat conditions only, we've anchored temporarily NE of Morro Chino in 30' of water. Behind Morro Chino Islet is foul ground. It would be difficult to climb this steep beach and embankment to reach the highway.

COASTWISE Continued

The next 24 miles SE are mountainous, fronted by a series of bluffs and surf beaches, no indents.

Rio Nexpa: Stay 2 miles off to avoid breakers that may form a mile offshore, 2 miles N of Bufadero Bluff. This is a popular surf hangout year round.

Caleta de Campos

The town of Caleta de Campos (pop. 2,200) is visible atop and E of Bufadero Bluff. There's no permanent dock, the anchorage is usually rolly, and the new Pemex up on Highway 200 doesn't always have diesel. But "Caleta" has friendly folks, some marine repair services and Michoacan Technical School of Navigation & Fishing. The students (boys & girls) assist the panguero fleet and are fascinated by yates and yatistas.

Lay of the Land

Caleta de Campos (Bufadero Bluff) is about 110 miles down from Manzanillo, 67 up from Ixtapa.

Bufadero Bluff (18°04.32'N, 102°45.42'W) is a

rocky half-mile wide headland at the S end of Rio Nexpa surf beach, but the headland doesn't protrude much. Bufadero Bluff has a red & white lighthouse atop a reddish headland (church steeple, radio towers) above a craggy black volcanic islet – the blowhole.

The half-mile wide cove is NE of Bufadero Bluff, but the entrance is only a third of a mile wide. A low breakwater of dark concrete juts E from the reef-strewn NE flank of Bufadero Bluff. The curved main beach (Huerta de la Luna) is divided by a large rock at the waterline, and a wedge cliff cuts into the beach in the W half.

Punta Corolón (GPS 18°03.96'N, 102°44.63'W), forms the bay's SE side, juts a quarter mile farther S than does Bufadero Bluff. A small cove in Corolón's W side is not anchorable. Punta Corolón has small blowholes all around. E of Punta Corolón is a 1.25-mile wide bay rectangular bay spreading E, but it's foul.

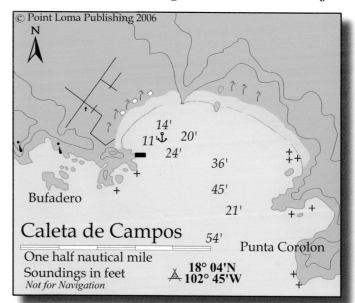

© Point Loma Publishing 2006

N

14'
11' 20'
24'
36'
45'
21'
Bufadero
54'
Caleta de Campos
One half nautical mile
Soundings in feet   18° 04'N
Not for Navigation   102° 45'W
Punta Corolon

Anchorage

The stepped breakwater is difficult to spot from offshore but can easily be seen from our GPS approach waypoint 18°04'N, 102°45'W, which is a quarter mile W of the seaward tip of Punta Corolón.

In cruising season, the best anchorage is NE of the breakwater in 12' to 24' over good sand. Shorebreak is less at the W end of the beach. Palms shade dozens of palapa fishing shacks and cantinas behind the panga beach. A stairs and road go up to the village.

In flat WX, you may anchor off Huerta de la Luna beach along the N side of the bay in 20' to 25' over sand. Locals say that behind this beach there used to be an orchard owned by the La Luna family, hence it's picturesque name.

Local Services

Caleta (area code 753) has fresh groceries, a marine hardware store, farmacia, health clinic and bus terminal. The new Pemex out on Highway 200 sometimes has diesel, but not always, as this is a

very remote region of Michoacan.

The navigation & fishing school is E of the lighthouse on the street atop the stairs. The Surf y Espuma shop has a coin laundry, the Pisacano Mendez family; (753) 531-5010. The Bahía Café is yatista friendly; burgers, salads. For a small fee, Hotel Yuritzi has showers & pool. Pot was a problem here, so you may see federales and a new Navy base. Green Angels patrolling Highway 200 stop overnight in Caleta.

Cara de Nixon: In the W side of the bufadero, a detached islet with a 10' high knob of rock appears to sculpt the head of former US President Nixon looking seaward and upward; a crowning patch of windswept grass even replicates his receding hairline. Local fishermen love to show this islet to yatistas.

COASTWISE continued

Caleta de Campos anchorage off Huerta de la Luna.

Michoacan's rugged cliffs end just S of Caleta de Campos.

Three river mouths breach the rockbound 5-mile shore ESE of Caleta, then a coastal plain widens and broad beaches appear.

Playa Azul: This 10-mile swimming beach has Hobies and windsurfers. Rio Balsas Delta is a 9-mile bulge with a large commercial port.

Lázaro Cárdenas

Mexico's largest commercial port on the Pacific is Lázaro Cárdenas (Laz Card, as we call it). It contains a dirty steel mill, Pemex tanker docks, container cranes, rail sidings, fertilizer yards, grain silos and a hydro-electric plant – so it's not a nice destination. But we include Laz Card because (1.) yacht-shippers deposit their clients here, many miles from a marina or yacht services, and (2.) in an emergency, yatistas can enter the port for help.

If you ship your boat, prepare it for serious Mexico travel before it's loaded on the ship, because no yacht-quality assistance is available in Laz Card (pop. 100,400). Passing yatistas must get permission from the Port Captain (VHF 16 and 12) to enter the breakwaters (explain the nature of the emergency). This isn't a cruising stop, and yatistas shouldn't be gunk-holing here in hurricane season.

Lay of the Land

Laz Card is 33 miles SE of Caleta de Campos, 143 SE of Manzanillo, 41 NW of Zihuatanejo. The breakwaters are 1.25 miles NE of Punta Mangles groin. Our GPS position of the Laz Card sea buoy (17°53.20'N, 102°09.09'W) leads you on heading 337°M into the 660' wide jetty entrance.

Pesquero Basin, a side lobe 200 yards inside and N of the entrance, is restricted to pilot vessels and hazardous cargo, off limit to yatistas. Please don't try to sneak in here, because port security is much tighter than it was 20 years ago.

The turning basin is a mile in. From there, channels run NE, NW and SW.

Anchorage

The Capitanía tells you where to go. Usually, yachts cross the turning basin and go half a mile up the NW Channel to anchor (13' to 24') half an hour or so off Capitanía and Navy base. There's a floating landing, stairs and gates with very polite and helpful uniformed guards to point you to the Capitanía. They

Cara de Nixon: Local landmark resembles former US President.

provide a list of local services.

After paperwork inspection, yachts are directed elsewhere. We've always been sent to anchor in the ENE end of the Secondary Canal, a sheltered spot with 50' of water over good holding mud.

Stepping ashore anywhere within the port is prohibited, and the port is gated and guarded. Dinghy back to the Capitanía's gate and get a pass before exiting by foot or taxi into the town.

Local Services

Lázaro Cárdenas is a Port of Entry and an API port. You can email the Capitanía at jresendes@sct.gob.mx or the API information guy at jvasquez@apilac.com.mx

Industrial cranes can pick up distressed yachts. Diesel and repair are ordered through a ship's agent. Servi-port in Manzanillo (314-322-4370) has agents here, or ask at the Capitanía. Dockwise makes their own arrangements. Laz Card's area code is 753.

Outside the gate N of the Capitanía are chandlers, nav electronics, reefer repair, machine shops, etc. We

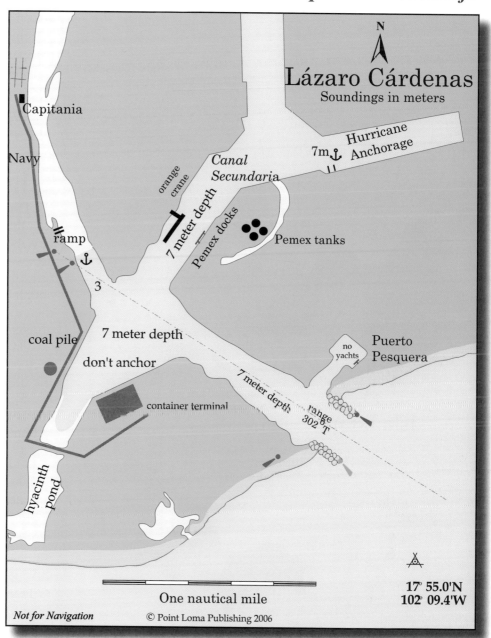

Lázaro Cárdenas
Soundings in meters

17° 55.0'N
102° 09.4'W

One nautical mile

Not for Navigation   © Point Loma Publishing 2006

provisioned well and cheaply from the CoMex half a mile N of the port.

COASTWISE to Ixtapa-Zihuatanejo

Rio Balsas: 1.5 miles NE of the port breakwaters are shoals outside the half-mile wide mouth of the diverted river; avoid this area. The state of Guerrero begins E of Rio Balsas.

Bahía Petacalco indents the next 24 miles SE (no anchorage) with views of mountain peaks 13 miles inland.

Punta Troncones: At about 17°47.61'N, 101°45.09'W) has a 545' hill behind the point. We have not explored the quarter-mile long bay on its N side, open W. Playa Troncones from here 10 miles S has palms and small resorts. Troncones are driftwood tree trunks, an example of why not to cruise here in rainy season.

Isla Ixtapa (aka Isla Grande) is 10 miles SE of Punta Troncones.

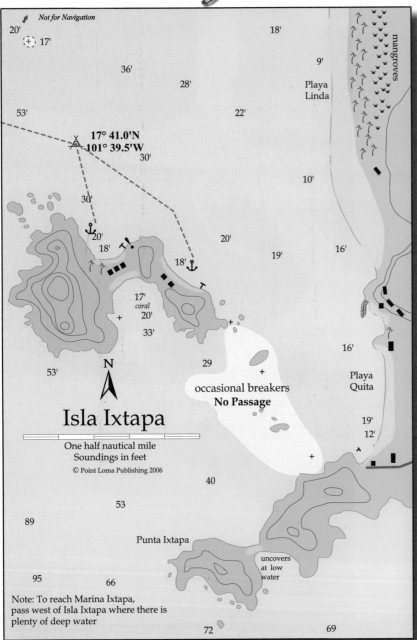

Not for Navigation

20'
17'

18'

36'
28'
9'

Playa
Linda

53'
22'

17° 41.0'N
101° 39.5'W
30'

30'
10'

20'
20'
19'
16'

18'
18'

17'
coral
20'

33'
16'

N
29
Playa
Quita

53'
occasional breakers
No Passage

Isla Ixtapa
19'
12'

One half nautical mile
Soundings in feet
© Point Loma Publishing 2006

40

53
89

Punta Ixtapa
uncovers
at low
water

95
66

Note: To reach Marina Ixtapa,
pass west of Isla Ixtapa where there is
plenty of deep water

72
69

mangroves

also marlin, yellowfin tuna, rooster fish, delicious snook, red snapper, dorado, pampano, striped pargo, cabrilla, rainbow runners and barracuda.

If you're not heading to Huatulco and Central America, we think Zihuatanejo is a better turn-around port than Acapulco.

Isla Ixtapa

Tiny Isla Ixtapa (aka Isla Grande) is less than a mile wide, peaks to 168'. By day its beaches, coral coves and palapas are swarmed by pangas with hotel tourists. Cantinas serve fish, shrimp, octopus and conch for breakfast, lunch and dinner, then close up at 1800. By 2000, only the ghosts of Isla Ixtapa's pirate past remain.

On NW approach, avoid a dangerous rock pinnacle half a mile N of Isla Ixtapa. It's often has a red buoy, and we marked its 5' depth at our GPS 17°41.38'N, 101°39.64'W. The island's SE side connects to Punta Ixtapa by reefs, so no go.

Anchorage

Isla Ixtapa's 2 beach coves on its N side are divided by a hill with Isla Ixtapa Light. The NW cove (anchor 20' over sand) has fine snorkeling and sidewalk to the island's S side. In NW wind, the NE cove is better (18').

Don't anchor in the cove on Isla Ixtapa's S side, because its corals are protected. Visit it by dink or on foot.

Ixtapa - Zihuatanejo

The 10-mile long Ixtapa-Zihuatanejo cruising area in the state of Guerrero includes Isla Ixtapa, Marina Ixtapa, Bahía Zihuatanejo and lesser islands, reefs and fishing holes – rich variety.

Life in Zihuatanejo Bay's anchorages moves at a slower pace, but Puerto Mio there usually has diesel and gas, and the new owners of Marina Ixtapa are working to get their fuel dock back in operation.

Zihuatanejo Sail Fest (end Jan. – Feb.) is fun and games for all boaters, raising funds for the indigenous school. Include Z-fest in your Mexico itinerary.

Snorkeling and scuba, sportfishing and poking around are the prime activities. Dive gear rentals and local guides abound. Sailfish are the largest draw, but

Isla Ixtapa.

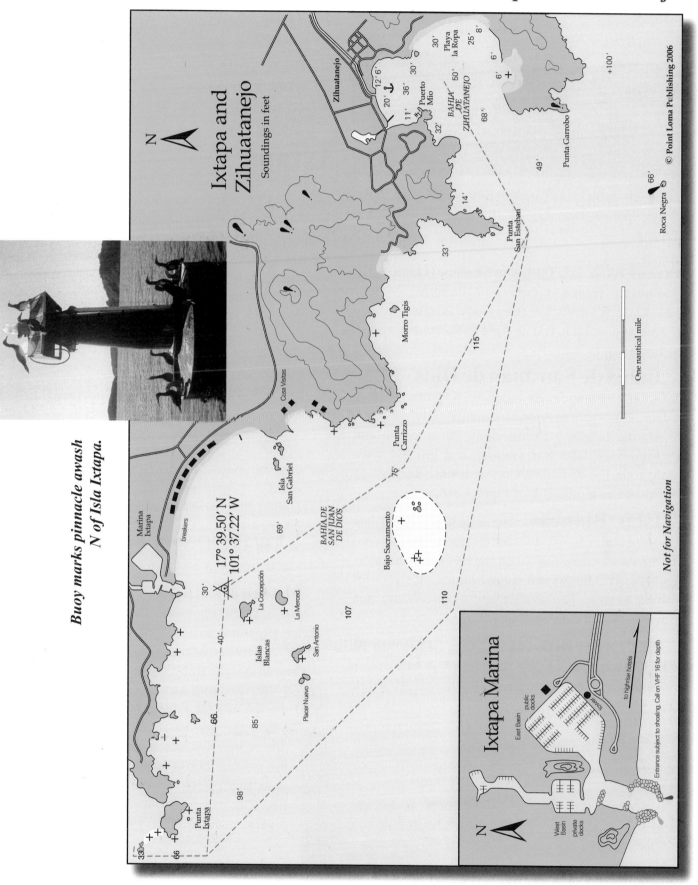

*Buoy marks pinnacle awash
N of Isla Ixtapa.*

Ixtapa and Zihuatanejo
Soundings in feet

N

Zihuatanejo

Playa
la Ropa

30'

25'   8'

12' 6'

20'   36'   Puerto
              Mio

11'   41'

BAHIA
DE
ZIHUATANEJO

50'   6'   6'

6'   6'

68'

32'

49'   Punta Garrobo

Punta
San Esteban

14'

Roca Negra   66'

+100'

33'

Morro Tigis

115'

Casa Visitas

Punta
Carrizzo

75'

Marina
Ixtapa

breakers

**17° 39.50' N
101° 37.22' W**

30'

La Concepción

40'

69'

BAHIA DE
SAN JUAN
DE DIOS

Bajo Sacramento

110

La Merced

107

Islas
Blancas

San Antonio

Placer Nuevo

66'

85'

98'

Punta
Ixtapa

33'

66'

One nautical mile

© Point Loma Publishing 2006

Not for Navigation

Ixtapa Marina

N

East Basin
public docks

West
Basin
private
docks

tower

to highrise hotels

Entrance subject to shoaling. Call on VHF 16 for depth

In flat calm, you can lunch-hook off tiny Playa Quita (panga landing) or the long Playa Linda roadstead.

COASTWISE Isla Ixtapa to Marina Ixtapa

Punta Ixtapa (GPS 17°39.70'N, 101°39.27'W) trails SW from Cerro Ixtapa (720'), and its tip is Isla de Apié connected by a sand spit.

Bahía de San Juan de Dios

is the 3.5-mile wide bay (open W, S) with 4 Islas Blancas, the lighted entrance jetty to Marina Ixtapa, 1.25-mile long Playa Ixtapa and its high-rises, Islas San Gabriel, and last but most dangerous, the .75-mile wide Sacramento Reef which begins .75 of a mile SW of Punta Carrizo.

Islas Blancas: The largest is domed Isla
Concepción, closest to shore; good fishing and diving on all sides, but watch the reef off its SE side. La Merced (Mercy) is a jagged jumble of rocks for fishing, diving. The smaller and more SW are San Antonio (scuba cave) and tiny Placer Nuevo.

Sacramento Reef: Our GPS 17°38'N,
101°37'W is just N of the submerged W half of this .75-mile wide reef. Dive pangas anchor all around it.

Isla Ixtapa's N side anchorage.

To bypass Marina Ixtapa, stay S of Punta Ixtapa and outside the Islas Blancas and Sacramento Reef.

Ixtapa

Similar to Cancun, this string of tall hotels was built in 1975 on mile-long Playas Ixtapa and Palmar by Fonatur. West of the hotels, a 2-lobed marina basin was dredged from a tidal estuary sheltered by Cerro Ixtapa. Golf courses are behind the marina, and what remains of the estuary (crocodiles) runs into the

Sacramento Reef provides good scuba diving.

backs of the marina basins, which share an opening to the sea.

To enter the marina's lighted riprap jetties, come N of domed Isla Concepción to the W end of Playa Ixtapa. Our GPS 17°39.66'N, 101°37.25'W is just outside the jetties, which have an inside baffle.

Marina Ixtapa

New owners upgraded the marina's 621 full-service slips in 2 basins. This is the only marina in 290 miles between Manzanillo and Acapulco.

The marina entrance channel is closed a few hours weekly for dredging (5' to 15'); hail the marina (VHF 16, 14, 18) for status. Enter the larger E basin where the marina office is in the far corner. Shops, eateries, hotels and golf courses circle the marina, but keep Fido aboard; crocodiles grab small dogs on the dock. Dockmistress Elsa Zuniga has managed this marina through several owners; (755) 553-2180 or info@marinaixtapa.com

The fuel dock in Marina Ixtapa's E basin is in construction to reopen. Meanwhile, Zihuatanejo's Puerto Mio has the only other

Marina Ixtapa has landmark lighthouse.

fuel dock. From the marina, it's a 7-mile boat ride going between Punta Carrizo and the visible rocks on the E edge of Sacramento Reef.

Zihuatanejo Bay

Legendary "Z-what." Avid sportfishers come here for sailfish on split tails year round. The International Tag & Release tourney is mid November. Cruisers find their way to Zihua Bay and spend decades anchored off its beaches. Bus drivers yell Zihua and old gringos say Z-town. Aztecs named it Cihuatlán or Place of the Goddess Women. We know single-handers who came here and found love.

Brushy hills with hotels surround Bahía Zihuatanejo, and its half-mile wide entrance blocks N swell in winter-spring cruising season, but strong S weather gets in.

Lay of the Land

Zihuatanejo is about 184 miles SE of Manzanillo, 110 miles NW of Acapulco.

Roca Negra lighthouse (63') is in deep water a mile SW of Punta Garroba Lighthouse. Our GPS 17°37'N, 101°34'W is between Punta Garrobo and Punta San Esteban, the entrance points into Zihua Bay. Heading 015°, the entrance narrows to half a mile, then the mile-square Zihua Bay opens with beaches all around – most for anchoring.

Clockwise: Caleta La Cala; Punta El Morro with breakwater, Puerto Mio fuel dock on the E side of Cero Almacen; a shallow canal goes NW under a concrete footbridge to an estuary; the 1,000' long concrete Muelle Municipal (B/W stripe) for passenger skiffs, not yates; Playa Municipal backed by Fishermen's Walk; dry creek; Playa Madera; Cerro Madera; Playa La Ropa; Cerro Las Gatas; Playa Las Gatas; N end of Punta Garrobo.

Anchorages

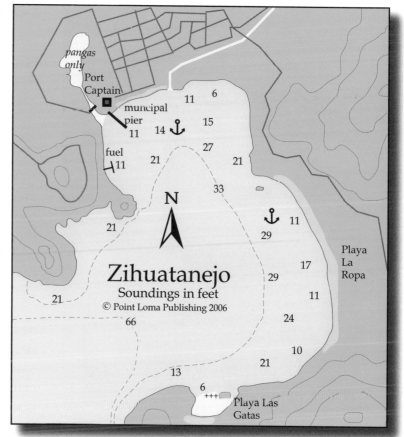

Caleta La Cala: In flat calms, this tiny indent outside Punta El Morro breakwater may have marginal room (32' over sand, gravel) for one yatista between the rocks, but it suffers from wakes.

Playa Municipal: You can anchor outside the panga moorings, but the best protected is NE of the municipal pier. This main anchorage (20' to 30') has good holding sand and mud. Land dinks below Paseo del Pescador, which is full of cantinas, shops, close to el centro. Panga moorings are S of the pier and around Puerto Mio.

Playa Madera: N of the dry stream, this area W of Cerro Madero is generally quieter than el

Zihua municipal pier.

Capitanía is at head of municipal pier.

centro, except for trucks on the hill road. A smaller paseo lines the shore to the footbridge over the dry stream. Avoid a small reef at the base of Cerro Madera. We anchor in 20' to 28' sand or mud.

Playa La Ropa wide swim beach lines the SE shore with cantinas, hotels. We avoid a reef off the N end but anchor (20' to 30') S of it, sand and mud. In calm weather, you can anchor off the S end of Playa La Ropa in 12' to 25', but it has shorebreak.

Clothes from a pirate-scuttled galleon washed up on this beach, hence its name. A more recent shipwreck Fandango lies in 90' off the S end of this beach.

Playa Las Gatas to the S is too rocky for anchoring but makes a good dinghy getaway, as the road doesn't go there. It has an eco resort and restaurant. In 1400, it was a walled-in bathing pool for royal Tarascans, but the beach is named for whiskered nurse sharks.

Local Services

The Capitanía and Navy are at the head of Muelle Municipal. Radio Costera WX is broadcast in Spanish daily; WX-fax charts are posted on the door.

Fuel: Puerto Mio is hard to port as you enter the bay. Beyond their excursion docks (former marina) is a 65' floating fuel dock, diesel & gas, 13' depth alongside. Larger yates hang off the end. Puerto Mio (hotel, dive shop, restaurant, sport docks, diesel dock, real estate) is in transition. VHF 11 or (755) 554-7222; email osn@puertomio.com

Marina Ixtapa says they're reopening their fuel dock in the E basin.

Zihua has 3 Pemex stations; Ixtapa has one.

Provisions: The Super CoMex store has everything; Paseo la Boquita near Plaza Kioto. The traditional municipal market has great produce; Benito Juarez downtown.

Mechanical: We've had luck asking the Navy's Lieutenant to recommend a diesel mechanic and electrician; Navy is VHF 16, 81, 83.

Misc.: The yatista net (VHF 22, 0830) tells newcomers what's where, has a list of local services, street maps, etc. Zihua has 7 banks, Ixtapa 3. Propane (Gas de Guerrero) is a block N of the municipal market. The international airport is SE of Zihuatanejo. Zoe Kayaks tours Laguna de Potosi; (755) 533-0496. Dr. Rogelio Greyeb speaks English (755) 554-5041.

Culture & History

El Museo Arqueologico de Costa Grande is a nice archeological museum displaying Olmec, Chichimec, Cuitlateca, Panteca, Tarascan, Purepécha and Aztec cultures who lived between Puerto Vallarta and Acapulco; E end of Paseo del Pescador.

In 1522, Capitán Juan Alvarez Chico built ships in Tehuantepec to explore this region. Bahía Zihuatanejo became the launching site for many explorers of the Pacific, China and Philippines. When Spain moved its base to larger Bahía Acapulco, the Place of Goddesses slumbered for centuries. In 1960, Highway 200 pushed through the Sierra Madres from Acapulco to find 5,000 people at Zihuatanejo. Ixtapa was built in 1975. Today the region's population is over 100,000, and cruise ships call regularly.

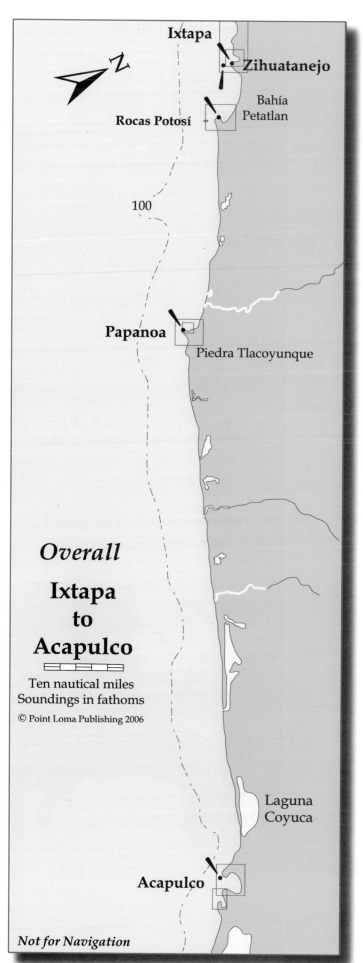

Ixtapa

Zihuatanejo

Rocas Potosí

Bahía
Petatlan

100

Papanoa

Piedra Tlacoyunque

Overall

Ixtapa
to
Acapulco

Ten nautical miles
Soundings in fathoms
© Point Loma Publishing 2006

Laguna
Coyuca

Acapulco

Not for Navigation

19
Acapulco
through
Huatulco

Coasting S from Zihuatanejo, this chapter's destinations are Papanoa, Acapulco, Puerto Angel and the Bays of Huatulco.

Before the marina was built in Huatulco, Acapulco was our last major place to prepare to cross the Gulf of Tehuantepec and step into Central America. Acapulco's slip shortage hasn't improved, nor has the slippery-bottomed anchorage. We haven't found many yatista services here that you can't get in Huatulco, but Acapulco has more of it.

Route Planning: Zihuatanejo to Acapulco

Acapulco is about 110 miles SE of Zihuatanejo. Mild and benign as this stretch is during cruising season, it has only 2 places to stop – Potosi (6 miles), Papanoa (37 miles) – and no fuel or other services for yatistas. However, emergency fuel might be arranged in Papanoa.

We run this tranquil coast 2 to 5 miles off with no surprises. Except at Potosi and Papanoa, it's a regular bottom and a series of straight beaches fronting estuaries and foothills to the Sierra Madre del Sur. At night, cruise ships ply this coast 6 to 10 miles off shore, ablaze with lights and music. The loom of Acapulco can be seen for 20 miles on clear nights.

COASTWISE: Zihuatanejo to Acapulco

Bahía de Petatlan is a 6-mile long indent SE of Zihuatanejo, ending at Morro de Petatlan, an attached and lighted headland (647' high), and its W tip is Punta Gorda.

Rocas Potosí: Detached 1.5 miles W of Punta Gorda, 10 white rocks spread a mile W. Potosí were white-robed friars, but this more resembles a herd of 500' tall white elephants sauntering out for a bath, even a few babies. We sounded 60' to 100' of water on all sides, so we pass inside unless it's full

231

of dive boats. These bold radar targets mark a large anchorage N of the headland.

Potosí Anchorage

Our GPS approach waypoint between Rocas Potosí and Punta Gorda is 17°32.5'N, 101°28'W. In calms or light S wind, the anchorage is E of Morro

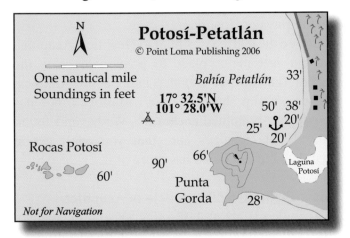

de Petatlan at the S end of Playa Petatlan's palm plantations. We anchor N or NW of the bar in about 20' over good holding sand. In SW wind, you have to tuck S of where you can still see the elephants.

Laguna de Potosí behind this berm is a 6-mile tropical-bird sanctuary, great for kayaking from Barra de Potosi village. To rent kayaks here or get a guided naturalist tour of this lagoon, contact Zoe Kayaks in Ixtapa; (755) 553-0496.

COASTWISE continued

El Calvario Light is 18 miles SE of Rocas Potosí.

Japutica Cove: Less than a mile S of Calvary Light is the more prominent Punta Japutica with a small cove on its N side. Our peek-in GPS 17°23.62'N, 101°10.94'W is half a mile NW of the cove, which we haven't sounded.

Bahía Tequepa is a 9-mile long indent between Punta Japutica and Morro de Papanoa, where the foothills reach the sea.

Isla de las Animas (17°18.50'N, 101°04.32W) is a big white rock close to the beach 6 miles SE of

Japutica, 2 miles N of Papanoa. We haven't sounded inside this rock and shore, but locals say it's a popular snorkeling spot.

Papanoa

This small breakwater-enclosed harbor is a pleasant overnight anchorage for yatistas, built in the 1980s to aid the small shrimper fleet around Papanoa (pop. 3,000); 37 miles SE of Zihautanejo, 74 miles NW of Acapulco.

Papanoa has a 300' long concrete pier, 12' of water alongside, where a fuel truck can be arranged.

Approach

Morro de Papanoa (528') at first appears detached, carries Morro Papanoa Light on its W bluff and is linked to shore by a lower neck. The harbor is on its NE side below a quarry scar in the brush, and 2 overlapping breakwaters form the outer and inner basins. Lamp posts around the basins look like sailboat masts.

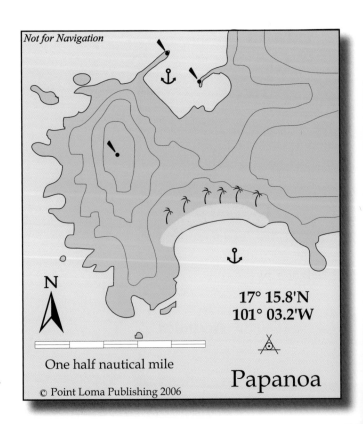

Our GPS 17°16.8'N, 101°03.5'W is just N of Papanoa's NW jetty, where you can see the lighted seaward ends of both overlapping breakwaters and into the outer basin.

Anchorage

In NW wind, the best shelter is in the larger outer basin's W side or S end. We've anchored here (22' to 24' good holding mud and gravel) and found 39' in the center of this basin, which has room for 50 yachts to swing. The ramp in the S end has giant bollards used during storms. Dinks can land on this ramp, along big pier or in the inner basin.

The inner basin is cramped by reefs S of the central rock and off the NE beach. The only spot to anchor (11') is close E of the bend in the smaller E jetty, but don't block the narrow access N of the central rock to or from the smaller work piers. 2 concrete piers at the N end (12' and 9' of water) are for coop fishermen to load and unload. Dinks are fine to land here or on the beach between reefs.

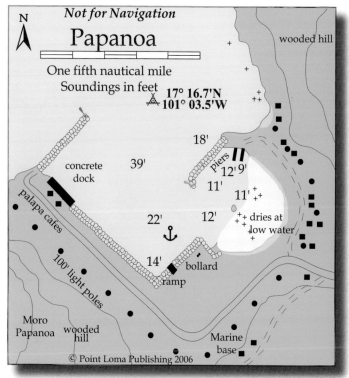

SE of Morro Papanoa, submerged rocks prevent approach to Carabales beach cove.

Local Services

Marines from the base overlooking the harbor may call on VHF 16 to ask if you need assistance. If no answer, they come out to check papers. They've been courteous and helpful.

Papanoa pier in the outer basin is 300' long with 12' alongside its tire fenders and some surge. Here 100' fishing boats take diesel off a tanker truck

Papanoa Pier has room for drying sails, unballing your chain or a game of soccer with the pangueros.

ordered yesterday from the manager of the Pemex 4 miles inland at Highway 200. In an emergency, the Marines might help you order fuel, but it may be 300 gallons, fast delivery, large nozzle.

For mechanical help, ask the Marines or visit with the old salts at the fishing coop building on SE beach in the inner harbor. A coop bus goes to Zihuatanejo.

Papanoa pier has 6 seafood cantinas and a big concrete yard for drying nets or sails. The paved road runs NE into town (no grocery) and E to Highway 200; a gravel road goes SW up to the Marines and stops at the beach SE of Morro Papanoa.

COASTWISE continued

Carabales Cove (GPS 17°15.69'N, 101°03.19'W) close SE of Morro de Papanoa is rock foul. We run the next 68 miles SE at 2 miles

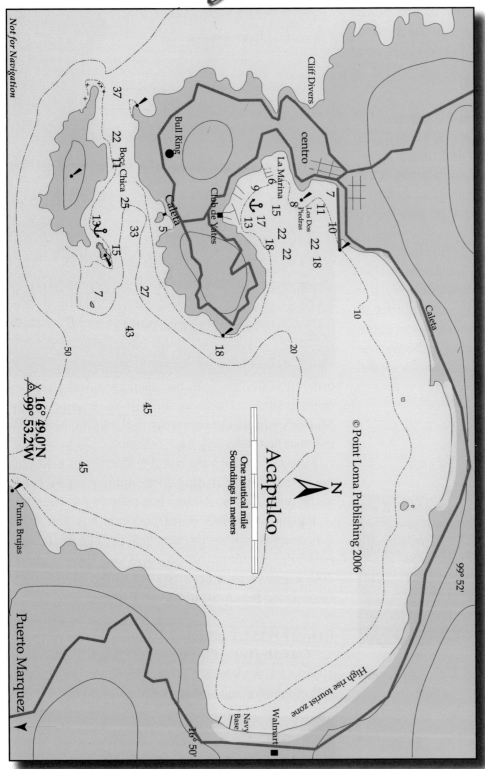

Not for Navigation

37
22
11
Boca Chica 25
25
13
15
7
33
5
Bull Ring
Caleta
Cliff Divers
centro
La Marina
6
9
8
Los Dos Piedras
11
15
17
13
22
18
22
18
7
10
18
22
Club de Yates
27
43
18
20
50
45
45

16° 49.0'N
99° 53.2'W

Acapulco
One nautical mile
Soundings in meters

N

© Point Loma Publishing 2006

Caleta

99° 52'

Punta Brujas

Puerto Marquez

High rise tourist zone

Navy Base

Walmart

16° 50'

Acapulco

This fine natural harbor is surrounded in steep hills and a bustling city (pop. 1 million). Entering the harbor at night for the first time, Pat exclaimed, "It's a bowl of diamonds!" By day, it's lush and colorful.

Acapulco has a fuel dock, 2 real marinas, moorings, an anchorage, a large commercial pier, a Navy shipyard, many marine repair services and an international airport. In cruising season, it's a good stepping stone up and down the coast.

Acapulco, Guerrero, is well within the hurricane belt, so slow cruising boats should not be here in summer. Acapulco is no longer a major yatismo destination, because Acapulco Yacht Club seldom has space for visitors, the other marina is in disrepair, causing a slip shortage, and the yacht anchorage has poor holding among the junkers.

Lay of the Land

Acapulco is 450 miles SE of Puerto Vallarta, 465 miles NW of Puerto Madero on the Guatemala border. Bahía Acapulco is 3.5 miles wide, and Puerto Marques is a separate half-mile wide bay off the E side of the mile-long entrance to Acapulco Bay. Puerto Marques has anchoring room for many yates, but lots of surge and shorebreak.

Enter Acapulco Bay on either side of lighted Isla Roqueta. Boca Chica is deep and 1,000' wide between dramatic cliffs. La Caleta is the tiny bay off the N side of Boca Chica.

Boca Grande is 1.5 miles wide, and our GPS approach waypoint a mile SSE of Isla Roqueta in Boca Grande is 16°48'N, 99°54'W. Cliffs line the E

off except for Piedra**a Tlacoyunque** 3 miles SE of Papanoa which has breakers about a mile off a distinct sandstone cliff.

Boca de Laguna Coyuca 12 miles NW of Acapulco's rocky headlands is where pirates attacked hundreds of Spanish ships. Golden treasures were hidden in and around this lagoon and river mouth – none officially recovered.

side of Boca Grande.

The marinas and anchorage are in the sheltered SW corner of the bay below and S of La Ventana, the dip in the W hills that ventilates the harbor. N of Dos Piedras, the old city and commercial cruise-ship docks are along sea walls in the bay's W corner. San Lorenzo Rocks and Farallon de Obispo jut S from the N end of the bay. Hotels line the N and NE beaches. The E corner has commercial fishing docks and the Navy base and shipyard.

Anchor & Moor

SW End: This is the best shelter and handiest shore access, but sometimes is crowded with cocktail boats moored SE of Dos Piedras Light. We anchor (18' to 30') off La Marina and El Club on slippery mud with an occasional abandoned cable. NW wind blows in the ventana and across the anchorage.

We recommend hailing "La Marina" to rent a mooring S of their main dock, or call "El Club" about a mooring N of their docks. We count less than 20 of these moorings, but they come with dink landing and nice shore privileges.

Navy boats patrol the bay scooping litter and issuing stiff fines for discharging heads or spilling fuel anywhere in the bay.

Isla Roqueta: For a getaway, anchor off the beach (27' sand) on the NE side of Isla Roqueta. This park isle has pretty beaches, dinghy docks and restaurants. Snorkel around the rocks El Morro and Yerba Buena to find the Sunken Virgin (Vírgen Ahogada). Trails go to the lighthouse, past resident burros. Across Boca Chica is Isla La Caleta children's park, surrounded by Playa Caleta, one of Acapulco's finest beaches. You can walk here from the club.

Puerto Marques is 4.5 miles from the yacht club, lined in hills, hotels and a panga dock in the SE corner. Enter 1.5 miles SE of Punta Brujas, the E point of Boca Grande. About a mile SE of Brujas, notice the bronze mermaid atop rocky Playa Pechilingue cove.

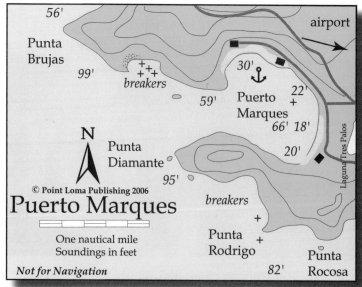

Marques is surgey and open to SW swell. The best shelter (26' to 30' over sand) is usually outside the rocks off the N beach. Our GPS position for this anchorage is 16°48.53'N, 99°50.85'W.

Local Services

Acapulco is a Port of Entry. The Capitanía is on the cruise ship dock 1.25 mile around the malecon (Costera Miguel Alemán) from the marinas. Radio Costera on VHF 16 has WX at 1200 slowly in Spanish. After the broadcast, you can ask for WX in Manzanillo or Huatulco. The VHF 68 net at 0830 follows the ham net.

Both marinas may be full, but each has good shore facilities, pool and security.

Club de Yates de Acapulco (Acapulco Yacht Club) members get first dibs on 200 full service slots or slips: Med-moor at the older concrete docks in the middle, or berth at the newer floating dock to the W. The AYC is Mexico's first yacht club, somewhat formal, host of the MexORC, nice restaurant. We call ahead in hope of a reservation; dockmaster Jose

Yacht anchorage off Acapulco Yacht Club & La Marina.

Marquez at telephone (744) 482-3859.

La Marina de Acapulco's remaining docks are below the fake lighthouse at La Ventana. La Marina has 30 full-service slips to about 45', but they're often full of local boats and haven't repaired their outer guest slips. La Marina has a coin laundry and is a bit closer to downtown, but the stairs to street level (noisy) are a workout. The staff is very helpful; (744) 482-8556.

Fuel: The club's 120' concrete Pemex dock is inside its N dock, around the E end, and there's not much turn around room. We got a 100' boat in here sans bow thruster, but it was tight. Order diesel or bulk oil 24 hours prior to fueling. Slow pump, plastic OK; hail Angel en Club de Yates on VHF 68.

Larger vessels (600 gallons or more) can order it through the club or marina, brought alongside the municipal pier downtown.

Haul-out: The club has a Travelift and dry dock for boats to 55' behind its E seawall. For larger boats, ask the Capitanía about the Navy shipyard in the E

end of the bay, presumably for semi emergency bottom work.

Provisions: Playa la Caleta has a good grocery for basics. Or grab a taxi to WalMart, Sam's Club, several CoMex stores, plus the municipal mercado 2 blocks in from Hornos Beach on Mendoza.

Water: Acapulco may have bad water (ice) after heavy rain. Buy 6-gallon cases of bottled water. If you must fill tanks, treat it heavily. No watermaking in this harbor.

Eateries: Las Cabañas on Playa la Caleta is our favorite, but Acapulco has 100s.

Misc.: VW bug taxis are slightly cheaper than air-conditioned cars. Take the bus marked Zocalo or Centro going E; La Caleta to return. We've rented cars, but traffic is nuts. The international airport is 15 miles SE of town, but count on at least an hour to get there due to traffic. Banks, ATMs, internet cafes, dive shops abound.

History & Culture

Dive on the Rio de la Plata (Silver River), a 300' cruise ship that sank in the E bay in 1944, or on the freighter Corsana off Punta Grifo Light.

El Fuerte de San Diego was built in 1616 to protect Acapulco's Nao de China galleons bound for the Philippines from English and Dutch pirates. The star-shaped stone fort is a museum with seaward cannon.

Acapulco is Nahuatl for Place of Reeds, inhabited since 2500 B.C. by Tlahuican and Aztec, since 1530 by Spanish. Pirate Francis Drake held Puerto Marques many times.

After independence in the Philippines, trade stopped and Acapulco slumbered for 100 years, until President Miguel Alemán fell in love with the port and built the road from Mexico City.

Explore Ashore

Taxco (TAHS-ko) is legendary for Baroque architecture, Spanish silver-smithing and ancient Tlatchtli ball court. Visit the zocalo, St. Prisca church, Casa Borda and the Museo Platería (history of silver treasures).

Day-use fee is ideal for provisioning.

Isla Roqueta Light guards Acapulco harbor.

Costa del Sur

The Costa del Sur or southern coast runs 205 miles SE with Puerto Escondido, Puerto Angel and all the Bays of Huatulco. Puerto Escondido is a small indent, a 1960s hippy surfer hangout, but not a good anchorage. Puerto Angel is a nicer bay and town, a refuge before turning NE into toward the W side of the Gulf of Tehuantepec. Then 11 small coves, most within the national park, make up the Bays of Huatulco. In one of them, Marina Chahué is where yatistas wait to cross the gulf (next chapter).

Route Planning: Acapulco to Huatulco

Staying 3 miles off keeps you clear of the hazards: Tartar Shoals, Rio Verde shoals, rocks off Punta Galera, breakers off Punta de Rocas SE of Puerto Escondido and Roca Blanca W of Puerto Angel. At night, shrimpers work the Agua Dulce shelf, so we head from Acapulco to a point 3 miles off Tartar Shoals and Punta Maldonado. In good weather, we bypass Punta Galera. Puerto Angel is a more

> The only fuel dock is at Huatulco's Marina Chahué, 205 miles from Acapulco.
> Punta Galera, 83 miles.
> Puerto Escondido, 57 miles (140 total).
> Puerto Angel, 40 miles (180 total).
> Huatulco, 25 miles (205 total)

comfortable anchorage than Puerto Escondido. The tiny Bays of Huatulco on either side of the marina are day stops for calm weather only.

COASTWISE: Acapulco to Huatulco

Punta Diamonte SE of Acapulco Bay is reported to have a submerged rock 1/6 of a mile S. The airport is 6 miles SE of Punta Diamonte. The next 60 miles are low beaches backed by shallow lagoons. Avoid runoff debris in the tide lines.

Punta Maldonado Light (16°19.8'N, 98°35'W) is on the NW end (130') of this 2-mile long headland marks the Tartar Shoals hazard, also the Guerrero-Oaxaca border.

Tartar Shoals are dangerous rocky patches (reported 9' to 26' depths) parallel to Punta Maldonado up to a mile off, centered 2 miles SE of Punta Maldonado Light. We stay 3 miles off Punta Maldonado and Tartar Shoals due to 2-knot alternating current and rip tides.

Rio Verde 50 miles SE of Tartar Shoals has a small shoal and debris; 8 miles ESE is Punta Galera.

Punta Galera

Punta Galera Light (15°57.85'N, 97°40.74'W) stands atop this isolated 3-crested headland (105'). It marks submerged Rocas Ahogadas (Drowned Rocks) a quarter mile SSE of the point. Visible rock pinnacles rise half a mile E of the point's rocky E side.

Old charts incorrectly show an opening here

Overall **Acapulco to Puerto Angel**

© Point Loma Publishing 2006

Twenty nautical miles

Not for Navigation

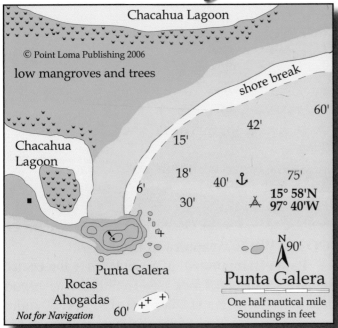

GPS atop Punta Galera required a hike.

into Laguna Chacahua which connects to Laguna La Pastoria to form Lagunas de Chacahua National Park, a preserve for crocodiles, iguanas and turtles. Villagers told us some of them are descendants of African slaves shipwrecked in the 1800s on Punta Galera.

In light NW wind, marginal anchorage may be had off the beach NE of Punta Galera headland. To enter, stay half a mile S of the point and a mile E of the visible pinnacles off its E tip. Don't turn W until you're N of the visible pinnacles. Anchor about a quarter mile N of the pinnacles, not quite half a mile off the SW end of the beach. Our GPS position is 15°58'N, 97°40'W.

Shorebreak lines most of the beach, but pangas land in the sheltered corner behind the point; the village 2 miles W has no supplies.

In heavy weather, small coastal freighters anchor off the beach between Punta Galera and Morro Hermosa. In an emergency, Galera's lighthouse keeper has SSB contact with the Navy at Puerto Escondido 35 miles SE.

COASTWISE continued

Morro Hermosa (842') is 7 miles SE of Punta Galera.

Alcatraz Rocks (17 miles from Galera) jut half a mile off; here the coast turns more S.

Acantilados (Barriers) are steep gray cliffs 16.5 miles SE of Alcatraz and half a mile W of Puerto Escondido Light at the bay's NW arm.

Puerto Escondido

In the 1940s, surfers discovered this small, rather open bay and its village of 400 fishermen. Today it has cruise ships, tour buses, Euro youth hostels, sail-fishing and surfing tournaments and 36,000 residents. As an anchorage Puerto Escondido rates from crowded and indifferent (calm) to rolly (NW wind) to untenable (W to S wind). A Pemex is inland, but no nautical supplies.

Zapotecas sell finely woven wristbands and cotton clothing. Surf tournaments flock to Playa Zicatela SE of the bay. The blend of surfer and hippy lingers in the air.

Lay of the Land

Acantilados to **Punta Zicatela** is 2.25 miles. Between them, the bay of Puerto Escondido is only a quarter mile wide between the Punta Escondido (large white lighthouse) at the W side and Los Marineros Rocks off the E beach.

Puerto Escondido anchorage is far left - or far out, man.
Photo by Dennis Miller

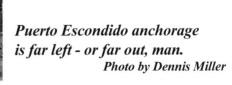

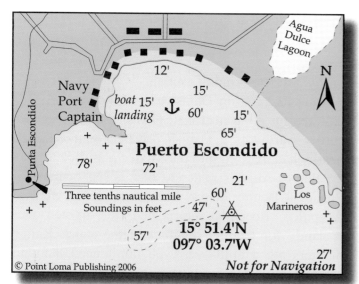

The cove W of Acantilados is rock foul; a paseo runs along the cliffs half a mile from Acantilados to the lighthouse. The first cove N of the lighthouse is not anchorable. Agua Dulce lagoon is neither navigable nor sweet. Shorebreak prohibit close approach to Zicatela Beach year round.

Punta Andador (sidewalk) shelters tiny Playa Andador swim beach where dinks can land at the W end of Playa Principal. Behind the beach seafood cantinas (here called mariscos), the malecon street Perez Gasga is chained off at noon - pedestrians only. All the touristy stuff is S of Highway 200; townies live N of the highway.

Anchorage

Quarter of a mile S of the head of the bay, our GPS is 15°51.4'N, 97°06.7'W. N of a line between Punta Andador and Los Marineros is a small but relatively calm pocket, but the bottom is irregular. We sounded 60' close to the 15' shelf at the head of the bay. Private moorings take most of the room, so yatistas have to squeeze in between.

Just outside that sheltered area, we found an anchorable seamount (47' to 57') a bit more than a quarter mile S of the head of the beach. Larger yachts anchor here.

Dinks can land on Playa Andador, the tiny beach at the SW end of the main beach. Or in calms, land N of Los Marineros; these are a natural shrine to lost seafarers.

Local Services

The Capitanía and Navy overlook Playa Andador. They broadcast Radio Costera WX reports daily. Marijuana grows around here; the Navy sometimes checks boat papers.

Provision: El Jardin has natural foods, and Lupita's has poco de todo; both on Perez Gasga. Ahorrara and the mercado municipal are N of Highway 200; try 11 kinds of bananas that grow here. Oaxaca has giant corn tortillas.

Misc.: A coin laundry is on the W Gasga loop. Farmacia Cortes on Gasga is open late. Graficom internet café, 302 Perez Gasga. 2 hardware stores are on Av. Oaxaca. Propane (Gas de Oaxaca), the Pemex and the small airport are 3 miles W on Highway 200.

Explore Ashore

Your boat attended or on a mooring? Ancient Mixteca ceremonial ball court & 4 pyramids recently discovered 15 minutes W of Puerto Escondido. Anthropologist Gina leads the walking tours; (954) 582-0276.

COASTWISE Escondido to Angel

Punta Zicatela (stay half a mile off) and Barra de Rio Colotepcc (stay 2 miles off) lie 2 and 4 miles SE, each with surf shoals.

Punta de Rocas (11 miles SE of Punta Zicatela) is a slight bulge with breakers on its NW side, stay half a mile off the beach in moderate W weather.

Rocas Negra y Blanca: (3 miles W of Puerto Angel) are half a mile offshore, at about 15°39'N, 96°33'W. Blanca is larger; antennae and Highway 200 are visible.

Playa Zipolite, not to be mistaken for Puerto Angel, is a mile NW of the narrow but lighted

Puerto Angel pier is handy for dinks.

entrace to pretty Bahía Puerto Angel.

Puerto Angel Light is a large white lighthouse on the S side of Punta Izuca (500'), half a mile WSW of the entrance to Puerto Angel. This is the southernmost point on the Costa del Sur.

Puerto Angel

Puerto Angel's narrow, picturesque bay and 2 beach anchorages have more shelter than Puerto Escondido, and this picturesque town and bay

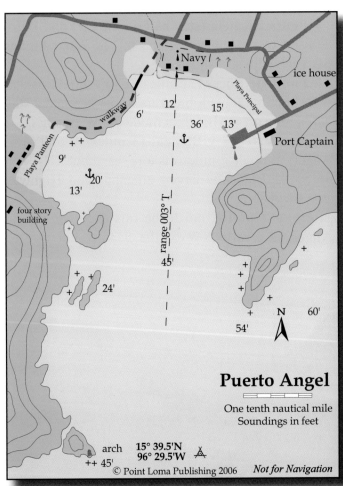

Playa Panteon at Puerto Angel is lovely.

enjoy a quieter kind of tourism.

In 1840, a visiting Danish botanist noticed Mixteca children speaking an archaic Danish dialect. Decades earlier, survivors a Danish privateer that wrecked nearby had married into the Mixtec populace.

Puerto Angel's concrete pier is the bequest of President Benito Juarez, but coastal cargo went to Acapulco. Recently refurbished, the lighted pier is handy for landing dinghies at the stairs. Range markers are a hold-over; you don't need them to enter Puerto Angel, and they may be removed.

Lay of the Land

Puerto Angel (southernmost yatista anchorage on the Costa del Sur) is 40 miles SE of Puerto Escondido, 25 miles NW of Huatulco. Don't mistake Playa Zipolite (surfer village) half a mile W of lighted Punta Izuca for Puerto Angel's navigable opening, which faces SE between cliffs. The outer half of Puerto Angel rocky and deep.

Ranges (003°T) lead you through the narrowest part of the entrance and up to Playa Principal NW of the pier. Our GPS at the outer entrance is 15°39.5'N, 96°29.5'W.

Anchorages

Playa Panteon is the intimate cove on the bay's NW side, prettiest spot in miles. Restaurants, homes and palms cover the hill behind the beach, blocking your view of an old cemetery NW of the beach. We anchor N of the large islet in 15' to 25' over good sand. The best dink landing is N of the islet. We found 0600 coffee at one palapa. A stone paseo connects foot traffic to town.

Playa Principal: Anywhere off this half-mile long beach has 15' to 40' over good sand; don't block the Navy mooring. If a T-pecker is blowing, this gets a bit less swell. Yatistas can land at the stairs on the pier's NE corner, streaming your dink off the NW corner so it doesn't block the stairs. The Marine guard on the pier provides directions and dinghy security.

Local Services

Puerto Angel lacks street signs, so ask!

The Capitanía is SE of the pier; when closed, the Navy responds.

Provisions: To reach the municipal market, turn

A walkway connects Panteon to Principal in Puerto Angel.

left from the pier onto the malecon (Blvd. Vigillio Uribe), turn right up the first side street across from the Navy fence.

Misc.: Pemex is 5 miles N at Pochutla. Uribe has a fruteria, laundry, farmacia, grocery, bus stop and many eateries. Locally grown pluma coffee is great.

COASTWISE Angel to Huatulco

The next 15 miles of rocky coast indent slightly N with a dozen surf beaches, none accessible.

Playa Blanca starts 1.5 miles NW of Punta Sacraficios and ends at its 80' almost detached headland. Stay half a mile off Playa Blanca to avoid rocks.

Punta Sacrificios is 8 miles SW of Huatulco Bay.

Bahías de Huatulco

The next 15 miles NE is known as the Bays of Huatulco, covering 12 bays and tiny coves. In geo order SW to NE: Puerto Sacrificios, Jicaral & Rescalillo, Manglillo, Isla Chachacual, Cacaluta, Maguey & Organo, Huatulco Bay, Chahué Bay, Tangolunda, Conejo. Except for the darsena off Huatulco Bay and the marina off Chahué Bay, these are fair-weather day stops open to Tehuantepec wind and S swell.

Bahías de Huatulco Parque Nacional, like all Mexico's new eco-parks, requires a small fee (approx. $2 US/person/day) to anchor and go ashore within the park – Sacrificios to Huatulco. Yatistas can pay (1.) Marina Chahué or (2.) park office near the Capitanía in Huatulco or (3.) to the park ranger or Navy patrol when they knock on your hull in one of these anchorages.

Puerto Sacrificios

Puerto Sacrificios is the small, cramped fair-weather bay on the E side of Punta Sacrificios, open to S and E. A few homes dot Sacrificios Bay, and covered pangas from Huatulco

bring vacationers to snorkel and fish (snook, dorado, snapper, pampano) Sacrificio's many islets and coral reefs, then to its W beach lined with mariscos, the local name for seafood palapa cantinas.

On approach, avoid sunken rocks S of Isla Sacrificios, blocking the E side of the bay. The best anchoring shelter from small swell is W and N of Isla Sacrificios. The area directly off the NW beach is has a mis-matched pair of rocks (tall W, short E), so cruising boats anchor either NE of the short one, or in the narrow channel S of the reef jutting S from the W rock.

Jicaral & Rescalillo

About 1.75 miles NE of Isla Sacrificios, a white cone-shaped rock marks the SW side of a Jicaral Cove. It's divided from Rescalillo Cove by a blade-like cliff. The seaward end of the cliff between these tiny coves lies at GPS 15°41.76'N, 96°13.48'W.

Both coves have pristine beaches ringed in jungle hills, no road, and in both you anchor in about 24' over sand. Jicaral has a slightly wider entrance than Rescalillo, but the latter has slightly better protection from E swell due to rocks on its SE side.

Manglillo

Within a quarter mile NE of Rescalillo, you'll

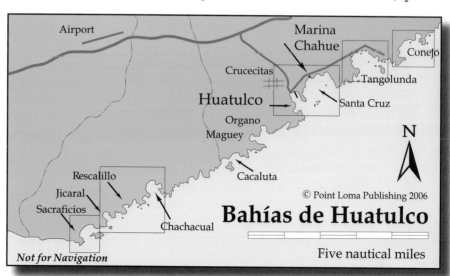

4
5
5
4
3.5
5
7
8 11
3
3.5
4
6
4.5
5
4
5.5
4
5
4
5
8
7
4
3
4
7
7
7
Sunken Rock
Sunken Rock
7
Sunken Rock
'11' at lw
7
7
6
7
7
N
7.5
10
© Point Loma Publishing 2006
15° 40.65'N
96° 14.05'W
Range 001°M
Puerto Sacraficios
One half nautical mile
Soundings in fathoms
Not for Navigation

see Manglillo Cove, but give the rocky headland dividing them a wide berth due to 2 submerged rocks 100 yards SE and NE of the visible detached rock S of the point. Manglillo (mahn-GLEE-oh) is a 2-lobed bight: rocks fill the E cove, but the W cove has a nice beach with a small house. Deep water (50') comes close to the narrow anchoring shelf, but we anchored in about 17' over sand, then dinghied over to the E cove to snorkel among the rocks.

Chachacual & La India

Chachacual
La India
Jicaral to La India
36'
34'
20'
One nautical mile
Soundings in feet
52'
jungle covered hills
Punta
La India
17'Manglillo
15° 42'N
096° 12'W
24'
24'
Rescalillo
Jicaral
white cone-shaped
N
© Point Loma Publishing 2005
Not for Navigation

About half a mile NE of Manglillo is the entrance to 2 adjacent coves, Chachacual (like the dance, plus KWAHL) and the smaller La India. From the E side of Isla Sacrificios, the reef outside the SW approach to Chachacual bears 240°M and lies about 3.75 miles NE. One of its visible rocks looks like a box car or small house painted white, and its submerged reef extends about 100 yards farther SE. Slightly E of the seaward end of this reef, our GPS is 15°42.04'W, 96°12.17'W.

Both these anchoring coves have sandy beaches, again divided by a narrow cliff and off-lying rocks. Chachacual on the W receives decent shelter from Punta La India, which is the fairly large headland just SE of Isla Cacaluta. Anchor off the beach in about 36' over good sand.

La India to the E is smaller and receives additional shelter from SE swell thanks to a stubby reef jutting W from the NW flank of Punta La India. Waves ripple over the reef, but inside is tranquil. Anchor in 34' between the cliff and reef, or in 20' farther behind the reef. In calms, you can also anchor outside the reef in about 36' over good sand.

Locals told us an elderly Zapotec woman, a revered healer, lived alone here for many years, subsisting on fruit and seafood from her patients plus water from the spring. Part of a documentary about her was filmed here.

Isla Cacaluta

About 2.5 miles SW of Bufadero Light, this island's rocky S tip lies at our GPS position 15°43.05'N, 96°09.73'W. The island's lower W side has red, yellow and black geology and is almost bisected, but its higher E side is wooded with cactus. Ashore N of the island is a steep, quarter-mile delta-shaped beach backed by a deep ravine of mostly dry Rio Cacaluta (Black Eagle). A few goat ramadas are spruced up to shade tourists.

We anchor off either (a.) the NW side of Isla Cacaluta (36') or (b.) the NE end of the beach (42') tucked in toward the next point E. We sound 14' in the

Playa Maguey.

passage N of the island, but it's too rocky for anchoring. A cove and rock beach on the island's S side are good snorkeling.

Maguey & Organo

About 1.25 miles NE of Isla Cacaluta is the shared quarter-mile wide entrance to the twin beach coves of Maguey and Organo. The entrance is open to the SE, so the W cove of Maguey is usually less sheltered, and the 4WD road enters it. Still it's a pleasant day anchorage (17' to 21') in calm weather and not far from Huatulco.

Organo has good shelter from E behind a large headland. It's still pristine, with only a shade ramada on the E beach. Anchor anywhere S of the beach in 12' to 20' over good sand. It's easy to switch coves as the weather changes or someone else arrives.

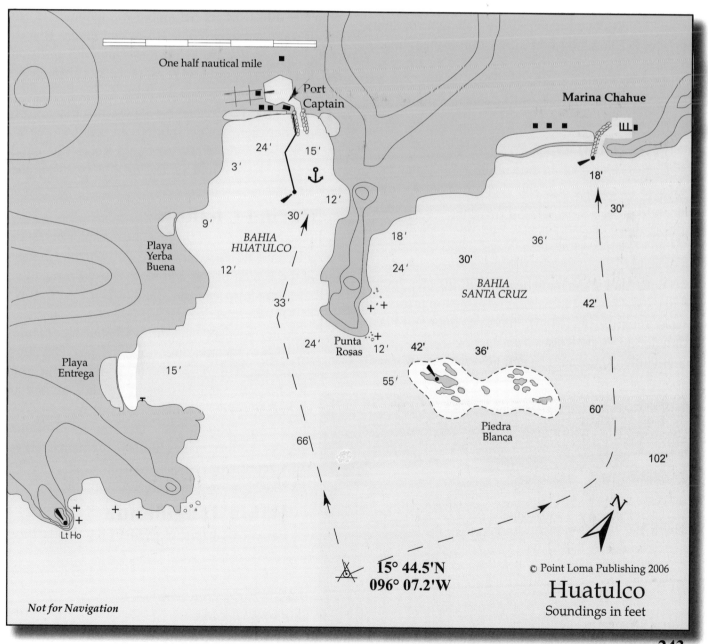

One half nautical mile

Port Captain

Marina Chahue

24'
15'
3'
18'
12'
30'
9'
30'
Playa Yerba Buena
BAHIA HUATULCO
12'
18'
36'
30'
24'
33'
BAHIA SANTA CRUZ
42'
Punta Rosas
24'
12'
42'
36'
Playa Entrega
15'
55'
60'
Piedra Blanca
66'
102'
Lt Ho

15° 44.5'N
096° 07.2'W

© Point Loma Publishing 2006

Huatulco
Soundings in feet

Not for Navigation

Huatulco Darsena: entrance is left.

Playa La Violín

The Violin Beach is a dinghy anchorage and snorkeling gem. Less than a mile NE of Organo is a tiny beach cove hidden at the SW foot of Punta Bufadero (Huatulco Light). La Violin is the pinnacle inside the cove. From here you can dive the coral reef or hike up and over to Playa Entrega inside Bahía Huatulco. The blowhole spouts on the SE side of Punta Bufadero.

Huatulco Bay

Cruise ships dock in the middle of Huatulco Bay, which is about the size and shape of Puerto Angel. Anchoring is prohibited in Huatulco (wah-TOOL-koh), but if you can squeeze into the cove at Playa Entrega (Delivery) at the SW end, we've found 15' over sand.

Dinks land at the main beach W of the pier, handy to taxis and a string of palapas (cruise-ship prices), at Playa Yerba Buena (Mint), Playa de Amor and Playa Matador on Punta Rosas.

Huatulco Darsena: The entrance channel (8' deep)

to the region's older darsena is NE of the cruise-ship dock, but it's not really for yatistas. Between excursion docks and hotels lining the darsena, we find the Capitanía, a stubby pier for taking fuel by pickup barrels and 5 impound slots. A public paseo circles the darsena.

Behind the darsena, Huatulco is just hotels; the real town is La Crucecita (Little Cross) a mile N of Huatulco.

Bahía Chahué

Next door, first timers-should approach Bahía Chahué (chah-WAY) well S of the breaking Piedra Blanca reef, which has one detached submerged pinnacle close off its SE side. (We sounded 12' to 55' of water between Punta Rosas and Piedra Blanca reef, but current can be strong.) Our GPS position in Chahué Bay's mile-wide entrance is 15°45.25'N, 96°07.25W.

Chahué Bay has 3 beaches (Santa Cruz, Esperanza, Tejon) between rocky bluffs. In calms, we've anchored in the cove NW of Punta Rosas (20') and in the cove NE of Punta Santa Cruz (23' to 28') at the bay's E end.

Marina Chahué

In the NW corner of the bay, the marina's entrance has a lighted W jetty, but a 500' hill Morro Chahué forms the E side of the entrance. Our GPS position at the entrance to Marina Chahué is 15°45.620'N, 96°07.209'W.

Inside its own darsena, Marina Chahué has 90 full-service slips to 85' and three 150' end ties, 160 slips when built out. This darsena can get slight surge, but it's far better shelter than any anchorage in 200 miles. We always wait here for our WX window to cross Tehuantepec. Dockmaster Enrique speaks English, makes fuel arrangements, relays WX reports on T-peck. Marina Chahué (958) 587-2652 or marinaChahué@hotmail.com

Bahía Tangolunda

Between Chahué Bay and Tangolunda Bay,

Playa Entrega has coral reefs and white bottom.

the S face of the mile-wide Punta Tangolunda headland has 3 tiny beach coves. Stay 400 yards S of Roca Arrocito off Punta Tangolunda's SE corner due to reefs. We recharted this bay with GPS and satellite images.

Tangolunda means place of beautiful women, apropos to Club Med. Its warrens and cylindrical water towers cover Punta Tangolunda. In the bay's NW corner, a jetty entrance to a panga channel cuts the large Playa Tangolunda, and a visible rock lies close SE of the entrance. Hotels line the main beach and the road behind it.

Turtle-backed Isla Tongola (Isla Montuosa) frames the E side of Bahía Tangolunda, and 2 islets range NW of it. Our GPS approach waypoint in the half-mile wide entrance is 15°45.5'N, 96°05.0'W is about a quarter mile S of Isla Tongola.

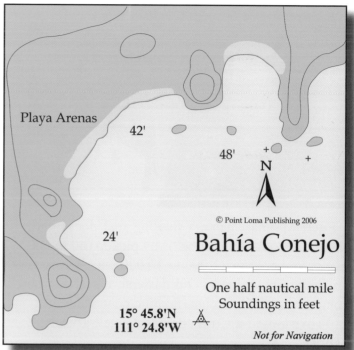

Playa Arenas

42'

48'

N

© Point Loma Publishing 2006

24'

Bahía Conejo

One half nautical mile
Soundings in feet

15° 45.8'N
111° 24.8'W

Not for Navigation

In fair weather, tuck up N of Club Med point, S of the boat channel. Yatistas anchor in 15' to 20' over sand off Playa Ventura (Club Med), Playa Manzanillo and Playa Tornillo. The hotels' BBQ cantinas welcome yate visitors on a cash basis. Another possible anchorage is NE of Isla Tangola in 36' over sand and gravel.

Bahía Conejo

Last of Huatulco's chain of bays, Conejo (Rabbit) is only half a mile NE of Tangolunda. Our GPS in the half-mile wide entrance to Bahía Conejo is 15°46.31'N, 96°04.09'W.

Caleta Conejo: We're told Conejo Bay was named for this rabbit-hole of a dinghy cove off the bay's NE end, reached by a narrow shallow channel; inside is a pristine and seldom-visited beach.

Playa Tejoncito: The SW corner has a tiny cove (24' sand) guarded by 2 rocks, and you can hike over this beach to one in Tangolunda Bay.

Playa Arenas: The main beach splits in 2; we've anchored for lunch in calm weather off the NE half of it in 42' over sand. The SW half is rocky.

Local Services
Huatulco & Chahué

The Capitanía (958-587-0726) in Huatulco overlooks the older darsena entrance; don't let your dink block the passenger landing in front of the Capitanía. Huatulco is a Port of Entry, so you can get your International Zarpe to depart for Guatemala.

La Crucecita has a pretty downtown, lots of eateries.

Marina Chahue entrance is left of cliffs.

Fuel: Marina Chahué's floating fuel dock; until pumps are hooked up, diesel is by pickup (60 to 600 gal.) or tanker truck (1,000 to 10,000 gal.). Cruisers can share pickup loads. Old darsena: diesel can be brought by pickup to a non-floating concrete finger.

Provisions: La Crucecita has 2 small grocers, 2 bakeries.

Misc.: La Crucecita (pop. 10,000) is the modern service town for hotel employees. It has banks, coin laundry, marine hardware, farmacias, hospitals, doctors, ice cream, pleasant plaza, etc. The marina lists repair services. Huatulco international airport is 10 miles NW of La Crucecita.

History & Culture

Olmec, Aztec and Zapotec lived here before Cortez and Drake vied for control of Puerto Huatulco. Drake's crew recorded trading with natives for souvenir huipiles, colorful woven & embroidered garments still being made by hand.

Archeological sites abound. One of the best, Monte Alban near the capital Oaxaca is about 100 miles from Huatulco, a 1-day bus tour arranged at any big hotel (less expensive than renting a car).

Departing Huatulco area:

Rio Copalita 1.25 miles NE of Bahía Conejo discharges silt and dead-heads, so if you're staying close to shore, keep your eyes peeled.

What does *Huatulc*o means?

Huatulco is Nahuatl for Place Where the Wood is Adored. Legend says 2,000 years ago, the apostle St. Thomas floated ashore atop a gnarled tree shaped like a cross, set it into the main beach sand and taught the locals to worship it – which they did for 15 centuries.

In 1587, the pirate Cavendish decided it was the devil's work, so, failing to chop and burn down the Cruz de Huatulco, he tied lines from his ship and tried repeatedly to pull it down. Cross 1, Cavendish 0.

In 1611, Oaxaca's Spanish bishop examined the cross and found its base buried in less than 20 inches of sand; a miracle. Renaming the bay Bahía Santa Cruz, he removed the original cross, fragmented it into smaller ones and distributed them around Mexico and Rome. Sans cross and abandoned as a port, the little bay slumbered for 372 years.

When Fonatur built the darsena in 1983, they resurrected the bay's native name Huatulco.

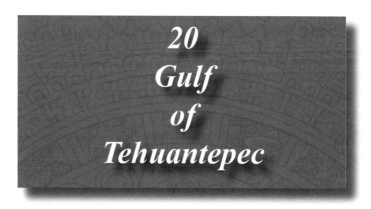

The Gulf of Tehuantepec is infamous for Force 8 gales of N wind called Tehuantepeckers or T-peckers. They occur during cruising season, but they're usually predictable and manageable. Every year, hundreds of well-founded yates safely transit around the Gulf of Tehuantepec, but it requires that we (1.) monitor the WX that produces these gales, (2.) wait for a WX window that fits your speed, and (3.) have the navigation skills to travel in the narrow lee of the land with "one foot on the beach," not straight across.

Even coastal freighters caught off shore when a T-peck gale starts have been blown 200 miles farther out by 60-knots sustained winds into seas 25' and higher. Some break windows, hatches and rigging. Many have capsized and sunk.

Tehuantepec WX Radio

Wind and sea conditions for the Gulf of Tehuantepec are broadcast 3 times daily (0930, 1530 and 2130) over SSB frequencies 2182 Khz and 8792.8 Khz, in Spanish. This is a very valuable service. Radio Costera (VHF 16) at Huatulco, Salina Cruz and Puerto Madero broadcasts conditions 24/7 on the hour.

Lay of the Land

The Gulf of Tehuantepec spreads 260 miles from Sacrificios on the SW (includes Huatulco) to Salina Cruz at its N head, down to Puerto Madero on the SE. The 125-mile wide Isthmus of Tehuantepec and a 75-mile wide gap in the Sierra Madres converge N of the head of the Gulf of Tehuantepec at Salina Cruz and Bahía Ventosa. That's where the wind funnels through.

The W shore of the gulf is slightly irregular and has a few rocks 1.5 to 2 miles off. The E shore is a 190-mile beach curving smoothly between Bahía Ventosa and Puerto Madero, and its sandy bottom slopes very gradually and is mostly regular – except for 2 shoals off lagoon mouths. See those

GPS positions below.

When a Tehuantepec gale (T-pecker) blows, it fans SW, S and SE from Salina Cruz and its tiny Bahía Ventosa.

Route Planning: Tehuantepec

The best time to transit is generally May; early November is second best. Tehuantepec winds are usually lighter May to September, but hurricane risk runs June through October. Gale season (Force 8 or above) is October through April, and wind strengths peak in January.

Huatulco to Salina Cruz: This 60-mile irregular coast is not huggable. If the wind is blowing moderately, parallel the coast only close enough to stay W of the visible wind line but outside the off-lying rocks at Morro Ayutla and Punta Chipehua. If the wind isn't blowing, we travel about a mile off the points.

NOTE: To avoid turning beam on to the wind E of Salina Cruz at Bahía Ventosa, change course SW of Salina Cruz anchorage, put the wind as far forward on your port quarter as is comfortable and aim for anywhere on the beach E of Bahía Ventosa. As you close with the beach, your wind drops.

Salina Cruz: If you're going into Salina Cruz, call the Capitanía on VHF 16 to get permission.

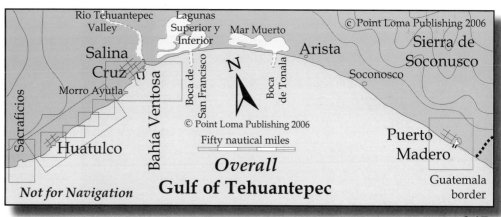

Overall **Gulf of Tehuantepec**

Not for Navigation

When nearing the ship anchorage SW of the port breakwaters, determine which vessels are anchored, which are underway. If it's hooting, you can cut in close and zig through the anchorage in daylight, but use caution. If you're not going in, don't enter the anchorage.

Salina Cruz to Puerto Madero: The rule "one foot on the beach" is fairly easy to follow when transiting the 190-mile E half of this gulf, even in a blow – but it's draining. By constantly minding depth sounder and radar and by constantly adjusting the helm, we travel in about 30' of water about a quarter mile off the beach. Because there's no fetch, the sea surface around us is nearly flat, merely whipped with miniature waves and white streaks. Even diminished, the wind across the decks may carry sand off the nearby beach. Yet travel in the margin remains blessedly smooth. If it's not blowing, we travel in 45' of water. The exceptions are the 2 lagoon entrances:

Boca de San Francisco into Laguna Inferior, GPS position 15°58.23'N, 93°57.28'W.

Wind blows off the beach, but waves are small in close to shore.

Boca de Tonala into Laguna Mar Muerto, GPS position 16°09.63'N, 94°44.96'W.

In a T-peck gale, these shoals break dramatically. To get around them, we run out to the 10-fathom line, pass them abeam (ugh), then head back toward the lee of the beach. Secure everything before beginning this maneuver.

Seldom does a T-pecker reach E of Solo Dios 110 miles ESE of Salina Cruz, but if it's blowing, you'll feel the swell off Puerto Madero.

Cutting across: Don't do it. Cutting straight across from Huatulco to Puerto Arista is 135 miles, saving 55 miles overall. If you're driving a 20-knot powerboat, and if SSB broadcasts confirm that your WX window will stay open for at least 7 hours, count your lucky stars. T-peck windows can slam shut in an instant. If you're too far off to beat upwind to safety, you might have to run off with it. Cutting outside the area of influence is impractical, because T-peck gales can reach 200 to 300 miles off shore.

How to Predict a T-peck Gale

We predict the start of a Tehuantepec gale by studying Gulf of Mexico weather in voice reports from NMN and WX-fax charts from NMG, both broadcast from the E coast of the US.

Beware a cold front moving SE into the Gulf of Mexico. In advance of that front, prevailing E winds shift to the SE and S in the Gulf of Mexico. As the cold front passes, high pressure builds behind it. When that high moves in over Texas, the wind in the Gulf of Mexico clocks around to the N, lines up with the Isthmus of Mexico and funnels strongly into the Pacific. That's a T-pecker.

Cerro Morro (left) and Bahía Ventosa dead ahead, E side of Tehuantepec is to right.

How to Find a Weather Window

Monitor NMN's forecast for the Gulf of Mexico.

Powerboat window: In advance of a cold front, if the wind is out of the S up there, fast powerboats have a chance to scoot across the Tehuantepec down here. Be ready to scoot, because this kind of window may stay open for only a few hours.

Sailboat window: When a cold front stalls out in the Gulf of Mexico and then begins moving NE as a warm front, that usually extends the period of S wind. That's a wider sailboat window. However, that won't cause S wind in the Gulf of Tehuantepec during cruising season; the best we can hope for is that the N wind here will diminish.

COASTWISE: Huatulco to Salina Cruz

From the Huatulco area, stay at least a mile off all the small points to avoid rocks in shore.

Morro Ayutla Light is 22 miles NE on the 271' cliffs, then Punta Bamba is 19 miles ENE. The quarry mined to build the outer breakwater at Salina Cruz is closed, and the channel and breakwater are abandoned, so don't enter Bahía de Bamba.

Punta Chipehua's huge white dune is visible 10 miles. A rock lies half a mile NE of the tip, and ships may anchor N of that rock, but it's not sheltered.

Salina Marquez Anchorage: Ships and tugs move between Chipehua and Salina Cruz breakwater 13 miles NE.

Cerro Morro: To continue across the Gulf of Tehuantepec, we begin angling ENE toward Cerro Morro (459'), the landmark hill E of the port of Salina Cruz. Punta Ventosa is its seaward tip.

Salina Cruz

This commercial port (307 miles SE of Acapulco, 195 miles NW of Puerto Madero) has dock facings and fueling for shrimpers and container ships, but more yatistas stop each year for fuel or emergency

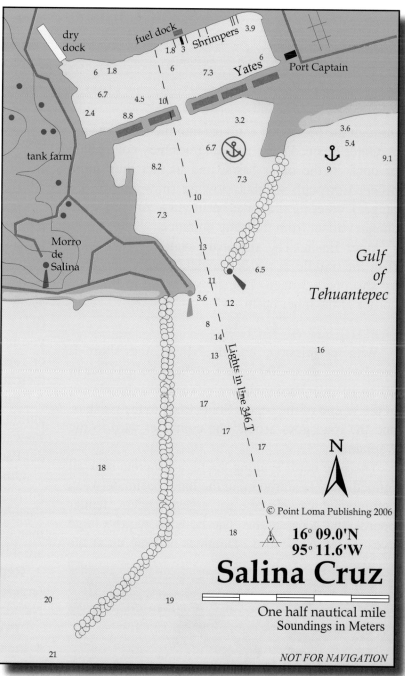

needs. Salina Cruz is not an easy in and out, but it has a shipyard, nav electronics, etc.

If you need to anchor outside or come to a dock inside the port, you must call "Salina Cruz Vessel Traffic Service" in English or Spanish on VHF 06 within 15 miles; announce your intentions and get permission to enter the area. Hiring a ship's agent isn't required, but if your Spanish is minimal, we suggest it to arrange fuel or repairs.

Lay of the Land

2 smaller breakwaters are W of the port's 2-mile long entrance breakwaters. Ships anchor SW of the ports W breakwater. Range lights (346°T) get ships

*Slot into Salina Cruz' inner harbor
is plenty wide.*

through the 635' wide entrance into the outer basin.

Outer Basin: Yachts and dinghies may not anchor or dock in the outer basin, and in fact they must proceed through without slowing (now ignore the ranges), entering the inner basin via a 50-yard wide channel offset from the outer entrance.

Inner Basin: The stationary concrete fuel dock is in the middle of the N seawall, usually obscured by shrimpers 3 deep. The shipyards are in the NW corner of the inner basin.

Anchor & Berth

With permission, anchor NE of the short E breakwater, about 200 yards S of Playa Salina Cruz in 20' to 30' over hard sand. We've seen less shorebreak at the W end of the beach. Stairs to up to the palapas, and the road goes around the container yard to the Capitanía.

The yate berth is along the high concrete seawall immediately to starboard in the inner basin, between commercial vessels. We us largest fenders, fender boards and a passarelle. The bollards require large eyes. Tides are 4' to 6'. Dinghies may tie up at the beach in the NE corner or at a ladder in the SE corner if they don't block ship access.

Local Services

Salina Cruz is a Port of Entry. If you need fuel or repairs but speak no Spanish, the Port Captain may insist you hire a ship's agent. The Capitanía is (971) 714-1335; API is 714-1325.

If you opt to hire an English-speaking ship's agent, we recommend Operistmo Navemar agency: (971) 714-0233 or VHF 16 and 67. The agent guides you in on VHF, takes your dock lines, arranges fuel or repairs. They get such discounts that even with their fee, it's usually cheaper.

Fuel: If a gale isn't blowing, you can arrange 55-gallon drums or a diesel tanker pumped from the SE seawall, a safer location than the fuel dock; Bunkers del Pacifico (555) 545-0902.

Otherwise, with the Capitanía's written permission, go to the big fuel dock in the middle of the inner basin's N seawall. We'd rather raft outside shrimpers than have them raft outside us. Pemex diesel and gas are 4 blocks inland.

Repairs: Salina Cruz has one of the world's largest dry docks, lots of repair services; Talleres Navales del Istmo; (971) 714-3005.

Provisions: Salina Cruz is a pleasant city with 4 supermercados and good fruterias, 4 or 5 blocks inland.

COASTWISE: Salina Cruz to Puerto Madero

Bahía Ventosa, where all the wind seems to come from, has an opening 3.5 miles wide just E of Salina Cruz and Cerro Morro. Rio Tehuantepec empties into the N end of this narrow bay, which is foul with breakers and rocky shoals.

The next 100 miles ESE is beach berm with trees, cut only by 2 lagoons (Superior, Inferior). San

*Alongside in Salina Cruz.
Capitanía is 2-story building at corner of basin.*

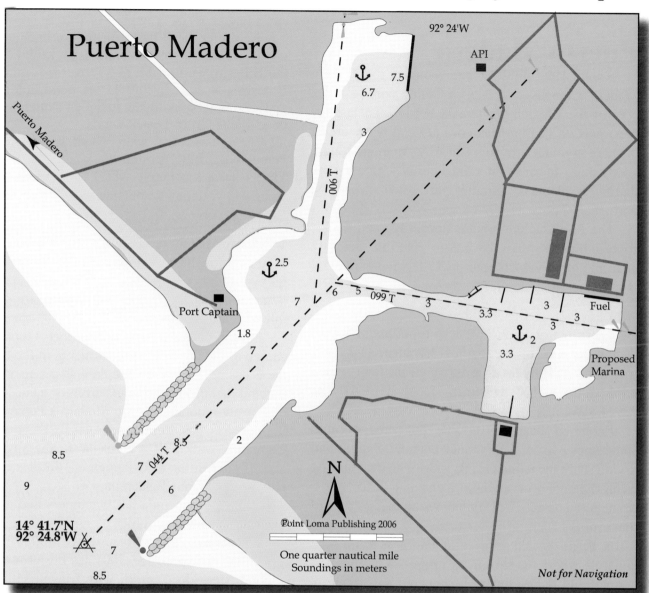

Puerto Madero

92° 24'W

API

7.5

6.7

3

900 T

2.5

6   5   099 T   3

7

3.3   3

3

Fuel

3.3   2

3.3

Proposed Marina

Port Captain

1.8

7

7

2

8.5

044 T   8.5

9

6

14° 41.7'N
92° 24.8'W

7

8.5

N

Point Loma Publishing 2006

One quarter nautical mile
Soundings in meters

Not for Navigation

Francisco Light on a beach pole is about 4 miles W of the shoaly lagoon entrance that it marks.

Boca de San Francisco, 23 miles E of Bahía Ventosa, is the mouth of Laguna Inferior, and a breaking shoal extends half a mile S. The seaward end of the shoal is 15°58.23'N, 93°57.28'W.

Low beach berm with trees, backed by Laguna Inferior and Laguna Mar Muerto extends for 48 miles. La Chichi Light is about 7 miles E of Boca de San Francisco, and La Soledad Light is another 20 miles ESE.

Boca de Tonala, 73 miles ESE of Bahía Ventosa, is the mouth of Laguna Mar Muerto, and a breaking shoal extends half a mile S. The seaward end of the shoal is 16°09.63'N, 94°44.96'W. The state of Chiapas begins E of this boca.

Puerto Arista Light is a round tower on the beach 7 miles SE of Boca de Tonala. Shrimpers may anchor along this open roadstead (15' to 45') in calm weather to visit cantinas on the beach, but there's no inlet and we've never had reason to stop in flat weather. The village is on the other side of the sea berm, and a 9-mile paved road connects to Highway 200.

Paredones de Soconusco are landmark bluffs 12 miles SE of Puerto Arista Light. From here to Puerto Madero foothills rise inland.

Santa Cruz Light 39 miles SE of Puerto Arista Light has often been dark.

Barra de San Juan is 76 miles SE of Puerto Arista Light and 36 miles from Puerto Madero. This lagoon bar is configured like the previous ones; seldom does a gale blow this far S, but if it does, treat this shoal like the others.

As you get closer to Puerto Madero, haze may obscure the entrance; the concrete tower of Puerto Madero Light is 400 yards NW of the breakwaters.

Puerto Madero

About 190 miles SE of Salina Cruz, Puerto Madero, Chiapas, is a 2-basin fishing port 16 miles NW of the Mexico-Guatemala border, the last (or first) port on Pacific Mexico. Fuel and water are in the harbor, minor provisions nearby. An international sportfishing tournament is in February, and a new marina is planned. Summer surf often closes the port.

The Port Captain assigns anchorage and docks, so call him on VHF 16 before entering. Security boarding of all vessels entering or leaving the port is in effect as we go to press.

Lay of the Land

The town of Puerto Madero (pop. about 1,600) is a mile NW of the harbor entrance. Our GPS waypoint a few hundred yards outside the twin lighted breakwaters (1,122' wide, 25' deep) is 14°41.7'N, 92°24.8'W.

Enter on heading 039°M, but dredge pipes sometimes narrow the entrance channel. Pangas and drying shark meat line the NW side of an oval turning basin (no anchoring), where 2 channels lead N or E to sheltered basin. The Capitanía is on the SW side of the turning basin.

N Basin is seldom used anymore, it has a high concrete wharf for shrimpers in the NE corner and a small and buggy but well sheltered anchorage in the NW corner. The sewage outflow creek at the NW corner is fenced off to dinghy navigation.

E Basin is dredged, enlarged and has the new fuel dock in the NE corner. The middle is for anchoring. The Navy occupies the A marina is planned in a third basin E of this one.

Anchor & Berth

We prefer the E basin for fuel or anchorage, but we go where the Port Captain says. In the N end of the N basin, we find 24' to 30' over soft mud. In the E basin's N end we find 12' of good holding mud and sand, not blocking the fuel pier. Both basins have good shelter from T-peck winds.

The E basin has a 65' concrete fuel pier with Pemex sign, and 2 similar work piers can be rented. The N basin's concrete wharf is too high for most yates, but you may tie outside a rusty shrimper.

Local Services

Puerto Madero is a Port of Entry. The Capitanía is off the turning basin, at the head of the W breakwater; go by dinghy or water taxi. But international arrival is not easy, as Migracion and Aduana are 16 miles inland at Tapachula airport.

Fuel: Unless the Port Captain says otherwise, you can go to the 65' concrete fuel pier is in the N end of the E basin. If this is closed, hire ship's agent Rufino (behind fuel pier) to arrange barrels or a tank truck.

For jug amounts, Puerto Madero's Pemex station if open has gas, sometimes diesel. Dinghy to the Capitanía, walk half a block W to the street for a taxi. If closed, the next Pemex is 16 miles inland at Highway 200 into Tapachula.

Repairs: Tapachula has machinery and electrical stuff, no marine electronics.

Provisions: Puerto Madero has limited supplies, but Tapachula (pop. 135,500) has big groceries and a good Mercado Central, with Mayan villagers in huipiles. Tapachula's central Plaza Hidalgo has outdoor cafes.

Departing Puerto Madero: A Mexican Navy ship sails picket a few miles off shore near the Guatemalan border, so every vessel must stop for identification. They are courteous but serious.

Puerto Madero's fuel pier in E Basin.

Buen Viaje, yatista.
Que le vaya bien!

MARINAS

Baja Naval, Ensenada (646) 174-0020 or www.bajanaval.com

Club de Yates de Acapulco (Acapulco Yacht Club), dockmaster, Jose Marquez (744) 482-3859

Club Náutico, Topolobampo deportes@debate.com.mx

Cruiseport Village Marina, Ensenada (646) 173-4157 or www.ecpumarina.com

La Marina de Acapulco (744) 482-8556

Marina Altata, Puerto Altata, future to include fuel dock, check updates at www.MexicoBoating.com

Marina Cabo San Lucas (624) 143-1251 or www.cabomarina.com.mx

Marina Chahué, Huatulco (958) 587-2652 or marinaChahué@hotmail.com

Marina Club Topolobampo deportes@debate.com.mx

Marina Coral, Ensenada US (866) 302-0066

Marina CostaBaja, La Paz (BellPort Group) (612) 121-6225 or www.marinacostabaja.com

Marina de La Paz, La Paz (612) 125-2121 or www.marinadelapaz.com

Marina Don Jose, La Paz (612) 122-0848

Marina El Cid, Mazatlan (669) 916-3468 or marina@elcid.com.mx

Marina Guaymas, Guaymas, future, check for updates on www.MexicoBoating.com

Marina Ixtapa, Ixtapa (755) 553-2180 or info@marinaixtapa.com

Marina Las Hadas, Manzanillo, (314) 331-1010 x 3707 and 3706

Marina Mazatlán, Mazatlan, (669) 914-7799 or www.marina-Mazatlán.com.mx

Marina Nuevo Vallarta (322) 297-7000

Marina Palmira Yacht Club, La Paz (612) 125-3959

Marina Paradise Village, Nuevo Vallarta, (322) 226-6728, or from the US (800) 995-5714 www.paradisevillage.com or email marina@paradisevillage.com

Marina Peñasco, Puerto Peñasco (638) 383-1145 or VHF 16, PO Box 37, Lukeville, AZ 85341

Marina Puerto de la Navidad, Barra de Navidad (315) 355-5950 or www.islanavidad.com

Marina Puerto Los Cabos, San Jose del Cabo (624) 105-6028 or www.puertoloscabos.com

Marina Real, San Carlos (622) 227-0011 or marinareal@prodigy.net.mx

Marina San Carlos, San Carlos VHF 72, Heidi Grossman (622) 226-1230 or 226-1202, email info@marinasancarlos.com or www.marinasancarlos.com

Marina Santa Rosalia, Santa Rosalia (615) 152-0011

Marina Vallarta, Puerto Vallarta (322) 221-0275

Marinas de Baja (624), Cabo San Lucas 143-6523 or www.marinadebaja.com

Mayan Palace Hotel, Puerto Peñasco future, check www.MexicoBoating.com

Safe Marina-Boat Doctors, Puerto Peñasco (638) 383-1145

FUEL DOCKS

Club de Yates de Acapulco VHF 68

Marina Cabo San Lucas (624) 143-1252.

Marina Coral, Ensenada US (866) 302-0066

Marina CostaBaja, La Paz (612) 121-6225 or www.marinacostabaja.com

Marina de La Paz, La Paz (612) 125-2121 or www.marinadelapaz.com

Marina El Cid, Mazatlan (669) 916-3468 or marina@elcid.com.mx

Marina Ixtapa, in repair

Marina Las Hadas, Manzanillo, (314) 331-1010 x 3707 and 3706

Marina Palmira, La Paz (612) 125-3959

Marina Puerto de la Navidad, Barra de Navidad (315) 355-5950 or www.islanavidad.com

Marina Puerto Mio, Zihuatanejo Bay (755)554-7222 or VHF 11, email osn@puertomio.com

Marina Real, San Carlos (622) 277-0011 or marinareal@prodigy.net.mx

Marina San Carlos, San Carlos VHF 72 (622) 226-1230 or 226-1202 or email: info@marinasancarlos.com or visit www.marinasancarlos.com

Marina Santa Rosalia, Santa Rosalia (615) 152-0011

Opequimar, Puerto Vallarta(322) 221-1800

Puerto Peñasco municipal fuel dock (638) 6035 and 2105

HAUL-OUT YARDS

Abaroa's Boat Yard (Big Abaroa's) next to Marina Don Jose, La Paz (612) 122-8915

Astilleros Malvinas, Mazatlan (669) 981-1242 or mikekowal@hotmail.com

Astilleros Mazatlán (669) 982-5311;

Baja Naval, Ensenada (646)174-0020 or www.bajanaval.com

Berkovich Boat Yard, La Paz (612) 121-6363

Cabo Yacht Services, Cabo San Lucas (624) 143-3020

Club de Yates de Acapulco (744) 482-3859

Coast Marine at Marina Palmira, La Paz (612) 121-6738

Industrial Naval de Mazatlán INM (669) 985-5520.

INP yard, Guaymas, Enrique Aguilar Ruiz, mgr (622) 222-6860

Little Abaroa's Boat Yard (5 blocks south of Big Abaroa's), La Paz

Marina at Puerto Los Cabos, (624) 105-6028.

Marina San Carlos (Marina Seca) dry storage and repair yard (622) 226-1061 or 1062, or marinaseca@marinasancarlos.com.

Marina San Carlos yacht transport, ask for Jesus (622) 226-1061 or transport@marinasancarlos.com

Marina Seca Guaymas repair yard and dry storage(622) 221-7200, mgrs cell (622) 109-1330

Opequimar, Puerto Vallarta (322) 221-1800

Servicios Navales & Industriales SENI, Mazatlan (mario_uribe@seni.com.mx);

SHIP'S AGENTS

Agencia Ojeda, Ensenada (646) 178-3615 or agojeda@telnor.net

Beach Comber, Dick Fifield, La Paz (612) 222-2291 or VHF-16

Juan Arias; VHF 22 or (322) 224-3555

Operistmo Navemar agency, Huatulco, Salina Cruz, Puerto Chiapas (971) 714-0233 or VHF 16 and 67

Servi-Port, Manzanillo, Ing. Alfredo Ibarra Obando (314) 332-3000 ext 104. www.servi-port.com.mx

Victor Barreda, Cabo San Lucas (624) 143-0007, or fax 143-0002 or call Sea Preme Agency on VHF 8

USEFUL CONTACTS

Maritime Documentation Services, contact Dona Jenkins in San Diego, (619) 223-2279

Maritime Institute (training & licensing) San Diego (888) 262-8020 or www.maritimeinstitute.com

Port Captains of Mexico are listed by port in geographic order at www.sct.gob.mx

API ports information, www.API.com.mx

Seabreeze Nautical Charts & Books in San Diego (619) 223-8989, order online www.seabreezebooks.com

Baja California Language School in Ensenada www.bajacal.com

Fish-N-Maps of Baja & Sea of Cortez, ask for Curtiss at info@fishnmap.com

Satellite photography WorldView, Inc., www.SatPrints.com

News from all over Mexico distilled for US interests, MexData.com

Restored antique train through colonial cities and hacienda routes of the Maya: www.ExpresoMaya.com

CHARTS & PUBLICATIONS

The following charts cover the areas of this book. Chart numbers area constantly being changed, so refer to the latest NIMA catalogue for Region 2, and check with your chart dealer before ordering. NIMA (National Imagery & Mapping) replaced DMA (Defense Mapping Agency). Future NIMA/DMA charts may come from FAA.

Overall Planning Charts
NIMA 145   N & Central America
NIMA 502*   Pacific Mexico N
NIMA 503   Pacific Mexico S
* out of print, enlarged copies sold by Seabreeze Charts, San Diego.

Coastal Charts
Brit Ad 2324   Baja California
NIMA 21140   Loma to Colnett
NIMA 21160   Colnett to Jose
NIMA 21180   Jose to Eugenia
NIMA 21200   Eugenia to Abreojos
NIMA 21100   Abreojos to Lázaro
NIMA 21120   Mag Bay to La Paz
NIMA 21008   N Gulf of California
NIMA 21014   S Gulf of California
NIMA 21017   Cabo SL to Manzanillo
NIMA 21020   Manzanillo to Acapulco
NIMA 21023   Acapulco to Pto. Madero

Harbor Charts
NIMA 21021   Ensenada
NIMA 21121   Magdalena Bay
NIMA 21122   Pto. San Carlos, Mag
NIMA 21126   Cabo San Lucas
NIMA 21125   La Paz
NIMA 21141   Agua Verde, Escondido
NIMA 21161   Concepción, Chivato
NIMA 21182   Guaymas
NIMA 21301   Mazatlán
NIMA 21338   Puerto Vallarta
NIMA 21342   Manzanillo
NIMA 21384   Lázaro Cárdenas
NIMA 21401   Acapulco
NIMA 21441   Salina Cruz
NIMA 21478   Pto. Madero

Reed's Nautical Almanac, North American West Coast (to Puerto Vallarta)
Sailing Directions for the West Coasts of Mexico & Central America
Pilot Charts for North Pacific Ocean, Gulf of Mexico, NW Caribbean

Yachtsman's Chart Book: Mexico to Panama

Mariner's Ink Corp. (707) 827-5400. This large-format spiral-bound chart book covers the Pacific side of Mexico and continues to the Panama Canal. However, this kit omits NIMA chart 21122 of Mag Bay's Puerto San Carlos.

MexWX: Mexico Weather for Boaters

Capt. John E. Rains. This concise text covers Pacific Mexico's marine weather (seasonal patterns, local phenomena, hurricanes, summering over, Gulf of Tehuantepec & Papagallo) plus how to use shipboard radios (VHF, ham, SSB, WX-fax) to gather immediate weather data. $19.95 plus shipping & tax if applicable. Point Loma Publishing, P.O. Box 60190, San Diego, CA 92166. Toll-free credit-card ordering service: (888) 302-BOAT (2628).

GPS WAYPOINTS

The prudent mariner will not rely solely on any one method to verify his or her position.

Global Positioning Satellites (GPS) systems have demonstrated the inaccuracies in many older charts, but we shouldn't attempt to navigate solely with electronics. GPS interfaced to the autopilot will steer you directly to any waypoint (latitude, longitude) you have installed, constantly correcting for wind and current. Wonderful. But if that waypoint lies on the other side of a rock or peninsula, the autopilot will faithfully steer you straight into it. So we strongly recommend using extreme caution when navigating in the vicinity of these waypoints.

If a waypoint position below is given without a decimal point in minutes, it has been rounded off to the nearest mile. If it contains a decimal, it has been measured to within 0.1 of a mile.

Mexico Boating Guide

PACIFIC BAJA CALIFORNIA
San Diego "SD" (32°37.3'N, 117°14.'W)
S Coronado Island (32°24'N, 117°15'W)
Marina Coral (31°51.5'N, 116° 39.7'W)
Ensenada (31°50.5'N, 116°37.4'W)
Todos Santos Island (31° 48'N, 116°48'W)
San Martín Island (30°29'N, 116°07'W)
Cabo San Quintín (30°21'N, 115°52'W)
Fondeadero San Carlos (29°37'N, 115°29'W)
Isla Cedros, N End (28°23'N, 115°13'W)
Punta Eugenia (27°51'N, 115°05'W)
Turtle Bay (27°38.5'N, 114°54.0'W)
Asunción (27°07'N, 114°13'W)
Abreojos (26° 42'N, 113°34'W)
Cabo San Lázaro (24°48'N, 112° 19'W)
Mag Bay, Punta Entrada (24°32'N, 112°04'W)
Punta Tosca (24°18'N, 111°43'W)
Cabo Falso (22°52'N, 109°58'W)
Cabo San Lucas (22°52.9'N, 109°53.0'W)

SEA OF CORTEZ
Los Frailes (23°23'N, 109°24'W)
Muertos (23°59'N, 109°49'W)
Punta Ventana (24°08'N, 109°50'W)
Bajo Scout (24°22.1'N, 110°18.5'W)
La Paz harbor (24°13'N, 110°20'W)
Isla Espiritu Santo (24°33'N, 110°25'W)
Evaristo (24°54.5'N, 110°42'W)
Agua Verde (25°32'N, 111°03.5'W)
Puerto Escondido (25°48.4'N, 111°17'W)
San Juanico (26°22'N, 115°24.5'W)
Concepción-Mulegé (26°55'N, 111°50'W)
Santa Rosalia (27°20'N, 112°15'W)
Bahía Los Angeles (28°57'N, 113°31.5'W)
Puerto Refugio (29°34'N, 113°34'W)
Bahía Gonzaga (29°48'N, 114°22.5'W)
San Felipe (30°60'N, 114°49'W)
Puerto Peñasco (31°18.'N, 113°33.5'W)
Tepoca (30°15.5'N, 112°51'W)
Isla Tiburon, SW (28°53'N, 112°57'W)
San Carlos (27°56'N, 111°03.6'W)
Topolobampo (25°30'N, 109°13'W)
Mazatlán (23°13'N, 106°29'W)
San Blas (21°31.5'N, 105°17.5'W)
Isla Isabela S (21°50'N, 105°53'W)

PACIFIC MAINLAND
Punta Mita (20°46'N, 105° 33'W)
Puerto Vallarta (20°39.1'N, 105°15.0'W)
Yelapa (20°30'N, 105°27'W)
Cabo Corrientes (20°24'N, 105° 43'W)
Ipala (20°14'N, 105°36'W)
Los Frailes (19°18'N, 104°57'W)
Chamela (19°33'N, 105°07'W)
Careyes (19°25'N, 105°02'W)
Tenacatita (19°15'N, 104° 15'W)
Barra Navidad (19°12.0'N, 104°41.4'W)
Punta San Telmo (18° 20'N, 103°31'W)
Isla Grande (17°40'N, 101°40'W)
Zihuatanejo (17°37'N, 101°33'W)
Acapulco (16° 49.0'N, 99° 53.2'W)
Rio Papagallo (16°35'N, 99°29'W)
Punta Maldonado (16°20'N, 98°35'W)
Punta Galera (15°53'N, 97° 50'W)
Puerto Escondido (15°50'N, 97°04'W)
Puerto Angel (15°39'N, 96°31'W)
Huatulco (15°44.5'N, 96°07.0'W)
Salina Cruz (16°09.0'N, 95°11.6'W)
Boca de San Francisco (16°13'N, 94°45'W)
Puerto Arista (15°56'N, 93°50'W)
Puerto Madero (14°41.7'N, 92°24.8'W)

SPANISH LEXICON

General Boating Terms
Anchor (to): fondear
Anchor: ancla
Anchorage: anclaje
Arrive (to): llegar
Beam: manga
Boom: botavara
Bow: proa
Cabin: cabina
Captain: capitan
Cook: cocinero(a)
Copies: copias
Customs: Aduana
Deck: cubierta
Deckhand: marinero(a)
Draft: calado
First Mate: Segundo a Bordo
Halyard: driza
Helm: timón

Appendices & Resource Guide

Helmsman: timonel
Hull: casca
Immigration: Migración
Jib: foque
Jibe (to): virar
Launch (to): botar
Launch, skiff: lancha
Leave port (to): embarcarse
Line: linea
Mast: mastíl, palo
Oar: remo
Oarlock: chumacero
Papers: papeles, despachos
Pleasure craft: yate de placer
Port Captain: Capitan del Puerto
Port Captain's office: Capitanía
Port hole: tromera
Port: babor, puerto
Power yacht: crucero
Propellor: helice
Sailboat: velero
Sailor: marinero(n)
Screwdriver: tornillador
Sea sick: maréo
Starter: arranque
Tool: herramiento
Winch: molinete, winche
Wrench: llave

Mechanical Terms

Battery: batería, pila
Bearing: cojinete
Bolt: tornillo
Breakdown: parada
Cable: cable
Diesel: diesel
Engine: maquina
Exhaust: escape
Fuel: combustible
Gasket: empaquedura
Gasoline: gasolina
Grease: grasa
Head: cabeza
Hose: manguera
Injector: inyector
Mechanic: mecanico
Nut: tuerca
Oil: aceite, lubricante
Piston: piston

Pump: bomba
Row: (to): remar
Rudder: timón
Screw: tornillo
Sea level: nivel de mar
Seamanship: marineria
Sheet: escota
Ship: barco, buque
Speed: velocidad
Starboard: estribor
Stern: popa
Tank: tanque
Tiller: caña del timón
Tow (to): remolcar
Tugboat: remolcador
Wharf: muelle, embarcadero

Marine Meteorology

Barometer: barometro
Breakers: rompientes
Breeze: brisa
Calm: calma
Clear up (to): aclarar
Clouds: nubes
Degrees: grados
Ebb tide: marea menguantes
Fog: niebla, neblina
Forecast: predición
Front: frente
Gale: viento duro
Gentle breeze: brisa debil
GMT: hora media de Greenwich
Gust: rafaga, racha
Haze: calima
High pressure: alta presión
Horizon: horizonte
Hurricane: huracán
Light air: ventorina
Mist: neblina
Moderate: brisa moderada
Norther: nortada
Rain: lluvia
Shower: chubasco
Squall: turbonada
Surf: oleadez
Surge: resaca
Thunder: trueño
Tide: marea
Trade winds: vientos alisos

Navigation Terms

Altitude: altitud
Barometer: barometro
Bearing: orientación
Breakwater: rompeola
Buoy: boya
Chart: carta
Chronometer: cronometro
Compass: brujula
Course: rumbo
Depth: profundidad
Deviation: desviación
Dividers: compas
East: este, oriente
Fathom: braza
Knot: nudo
Lighthouse: faro
Magnetic: magnetico
Meridian: meridiano
Observation: observación
Parallel: paralelo
Position: posición
Radar: radar
Reckoning: estima
Reef: arrecife
Sextant: sextante
South: sur
Star: estrella
Track: trayectoria
West: oeste, poniente
Waves: olas

Mexico Boating Guide

Index

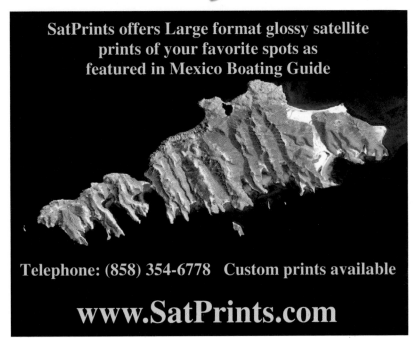

Mexico Boating Guide

Mexico Boating Guide

268

Mexico Boating Guide

Mexico Boating Guide

Point Loma Publishing
P.O. Box 60190
San Diego, CA 92166
www.MexicoBoating.com